Soul on CD

Lloyd Bradley is a classically trained chef, one time DBC Radio and club deejay, owned and operated the Dark Star soul sound system during the 1970s; was part of Parliament-Funkadelic on the *Uncle Jam Wants You* tour; sings lead and background vocals on Bootsy's *Sweatband* album; used to write Delbert Wilkins monologues for Lenny Henry; was a former contributor to *Blues & Soul*, *Black Music & Jazz Review*, *NME*, *Q Magazine*, *The Independent* and *The Independent on Sunday*. He currently writes for *The Guardian* and *The Voice*, compiles *Classic Funk* albums for Mastercuts and, with Ian Dewhirst, occasionally rocks the house at The Jazz Café in Camden Town.

Soul on CD

THE ESSENTIAL GUIDE

Lloyd Bradley

KYLE CATHIE LIMITED

First published in Great Britain in 1994 by
Kyle Cathie Limited
7/8 Hatherley Street, London SW1P 2QT

ISBN 1 85626 162 X

A Cataloguing in Publication record for this title is
available from the British Library.

Typeset by Heronwood Press
Printed by Cox and Wyman Limited, Reading

Soul is a 'musical, cultural expression based on reality'
Guru, Jazzmatazz

'Funk is its own reward'
George Clinton

CONTENTS

ACKNOWLEDGEMENTS

Soul's been good to me, I hope I've done it justice. The mistakes are mine, but the credit belongs to the players of instruments, the singers, the producers, the writers and the deejays.

Inspiration: Parnells, The JBs FC, Greg Edwards, Robbie Vincent, Bob Kilbourn, everybody who used to lounge outside Sunshine Records in Turnpike Lane, Wayne Campbell, Pat 'who shouldn't have sold his records' Clarke, Steve Edwards, Nelson George, Upstairs at Ronnie's, The Birds Nests West Hampstead, Paddington and Waterloo, Columbos, Contempo and anywhere Ian Dewhirst is deejaying.

Big thanks to Andrea, Jody, Nick, Shane, John Crossby, Bob Fisher, Jane Wilkes, Tom Terrell and John Fordham.

Bigger thanks to Beverley, Kyle and Emma.

And of course Tony Riley, researcher extraordinaire.

Five on the black hand side to Stanley and Kester, Kevin, Overton, Ronald, Jazzi and Peter Green. Which isn't really enough for Diana, George and Elissa.

IN MEMORY OF RALPH ELLISON, ROBIN HARRIS
AND CHESTER HIMES

INTRODUCTION
WHAT IS SOUL?

It's easy to see the thread running from Solomon Burke through Al Green to Al B. Sure. Or to see how Gil Scott-Heron, Chuck D. and Reg E. Gaines might be hewn from the same block. But what, other than inventive use of harmony vocals, would be the link between The Orioles and The Horny Horns? How do The Four Tops, Sly Stone and Queen Latifah hang together? What is it that separates the honey-tonsilled crooners Terence Trent D'Arby and Johnny Gill? And why couldn't you file Whitney Houston and Aretha Franklin in the same draw marked 'Soul Diva'?

It's all to do with 'soul'. The first names listed have got it, D'Arby and Houston haven't.

But what *is* soul?

More than anything else, it's a state of awareness. Awareness of what and who you are, how this fits into the world and the responsibilities it carries with it. To be confident in these matters allows a freedom of communication from within. From the soul. A genuine expression of type that will be received on a unique level by its own audience.

This could be applied to any group of people possessed of a certain birthright: Irish, Samoan, Yorkshire . . . But for the purposes of this definition of soul music, it's a black thing. Why? Because the development of that music cannot be separated from the socio/economic changes within black America. Indeed through the entire history of black culture in the western world, as soon as it stops relating to what's going on in the community – starts blathering about being 'beyond colour' – it loses its soul. See Whitney Houston.

It's also a matter of self-definition. The true soul warriors,

1

those discussed in this book, lay down the lines of who they are *for themselves*. What they have won't be dictated by some third party's idea of what it ought to be. Or, worse still, what they anticipate that third party's idea of it will be. Which is why an unrepentant hippie like Sly Stone, a New Jack glamourpuss such as Queen Latifah or a quartet of old men in frilly shirts, as in The Four Tops, can all be covered by the same term. Soul. A series of pre-programmed gestures simply won't work. See Terence Trent D'Arby.

Also, to write your own rulebook is to be in charge, and so be able to evolve the style constantly. To your own satisfaction too. A vital part of the function of soul music (and the similar black expressions that preceded it) is as a saviour of self-esteem within its own community – by creating a private world as an escape from the one that's giving you grief. Thus it has to remain exclusive and will perpetually refashion itself in order to do so. All of which, more so than in the mainstream, finds artists dictating the potential audience as much as the other way around, further contributing to the state of ongoing change.

Perversely, this desire to appease the home crowd by keeping the appeal deliberately focused, isn't the commercial suicide it might be: some of soul music's biggest crossover records have been its blackest, and many of the most sought after stars the most militant. As anybody would expect, tourists will only spend their money if they think they're getting a *genuine* ticket to another world, and therefore specialist market approval is so often the key to widespread success. Your shrewder soul artists are well aware of how this works. They have been since long before Ray Charles.

It's not only soul music either. There are soul books – Ralph Ellison's *Invisible Man*; Chester Himes's *Pinktoes* or the Harlem novels; Nelson George's *The Death Of Rhythm & Blues*. Soul films would include *Boyz 'N The Hood*, Sweet Sweetback's *Badass Song*, *House Party* and *Hollywood Shuffle*. And soul TV runs to HBO's *Def Jam Comedy Hour*, Sinbad's stand up, the first couple of series of Arsenio Hall and Roc.

They've all got that certain quality, like the music of James Brown or Earth, Wind and Fire or Jodeci. A quality that knows who and what it is, how it works in relation to life on both sides of the tracks and the responsibilities that come with it. But most

2

importantly, it's confident to be able to celebrate itself – for no other reason than it exists – at every opportunity. Even soul's frequent cynicism is a party in disguise – it's the old 'knowing you know what time of day it is, but the rest of the world thinks it's putting one over on you' gag.

But all this is theory. Important theory, as until this music is recognised as having far more meaning and substance than its enormous entertainment value it and its exponents won't be taken seriously. This means the music will be allowed to die as record company executives see even less reason to give it any priority – there's far less soul on CD in the UK than there is jazz and blues, simply because in this country there are no lofty books on the subject. Therefore record companies can't see too much credibility to be gained from supporting it.

What is happening in the context of this book is that we begin at Rhythm & Blues in the 1950s and journey through to Gangsta Rap and New Jack Swing in the 1990s, using the criteria we've just talked about as a compass. The rules of inclusion are that an act has records on CD and in the shops – hence the book's title. These titles will then be used as touchstones to tell tales of the people who made them, more from an anecdotal point of view than strictly biographical. There were some enormous characters involved here, and it's how they lived, thought and carried on in general that shapes the story of the music itself. Thus the main thread of the music's development will be carried within the artist entries and importance will be judged more on what their work meant than simply how many records they sold. We'll review how their primary audience reacted to them too, to build up the idea of a vibrant, almost interactive soul scene. Also, to define soul music through what's actually on offer keeps it real and *live*: there's really no point in reading about how wonderful The Temptations' *Solid Rock* might be if you haven't got the chance to buy it. Such an approach also perpetuates the notion of this music as a living, breathing entity, not some dead art form to be examined under glass.

When taken like this it becomes apparent that these seemingly disparate styles are all tributaries of the same river, so it's entirely possible to swim from Ray Charles to Ice-T and back again. Which is why the book has not been subsected into Rap, Funk, R&B and so on, as to do so does Soul Music as a genre a great disservice by putting somebody else's guidelines in place and allowing the – how shall we say this? – less palatable elements to be trivialised. It is ludicrous to decide that Bell, Biv DeVoe fulfil a different function to that of Sam Cooke thirty years previously, or that Gangstarr's cultural expression is less valid than that of The O'Jays. The only divisions here are by decade. And that because such natural watersheds as 'Sex Machine', 'Rappers' Delight' and *AmeriKKKa's Most Wanted* came up as each decade rolled around. As it's impossible to separate this music from its environment, each section will be prefaced with a run down of what went on around that time: cultural, social, technological and political happenings, putting them into context with the music's progression.

That's about the rules. As for the authenticity-of-CD argument, all that guff about the 'warmth' of vinyl or the need to 'feel' the needle in the groove . . . I've never heard such twaddle. I've even had one person tell me a CD isn't the actual music, just a digital approximation. A damn good digital approximation though. And it's curious I've never met an artist who's made a point of telling me how they want their music to include an increasing amount of unscheduled clicks, pops and scraping noises. They never say, 'I laboured long and hard on the LP, spent millions of dollars in a state of the art studio, but my musical vision will only be fully realised when it sounds like somebody's frying chips in the background.'

Also, there's the availability factor. I can buy a copy of The Dramatics' *Watcha See Is Whatcha Get* or Isaac Hayes's *Joy* on CD for eleven quid. Tomorrow. Or I can take the rest of my life off to scour second-hand shops in the hope of being lucky enough to be able to pay three times as much for a knackered second-hand record. I'll opt for the former, every time. It's only this availability that will keep the music going too – once you break contact with the past you lose control of the future. It would be awful if – as almost became the case a few years ago with the so-called Rare Groove scene – an artist's position in soul music history becomes a matter of how much some people will pay for their records. And believe me, it's not without reason that so many of those records became rare so quickly.

Thus we can ignore the cost-of-CDs debate. Anybody who's ever been to a record fair looking to replace their copy of *All The*

Woo In The World, several years after it was stolen, will appreciate the VFM factor of a £24.99 Japanese import CD. However, while it's now becoming possible to fill more and more gaps in a record collection, it's a shame that so many original albums are becoming deleted in favour of the Anthology or the Boxed Set. There ought to be room for them all to co-exist in the racks. Though soul music has to a large extent been a one-song-at-a-time rather than an album-orientated art form, there have been many valuable (from the cultural and purely entertainment points of view) LP tracks that never made it as singles. Thus, they have been lost. Plus, the compilations will too often use the three-minute radio edit of a track that began life as a fifteen-minute epic. For instance, the only way you're going to get 'Papa Don't Take No Mess' by James Brown is on the *Star Time* four-CD set, where it'll last less than four and a half minutes. On the original double album (found as a pricey US/Japanese import) it takes up all of one side and doesn't make sense as the slowly swelling groove-a-thon it was intended until it's run for at least a quarter of an hour.

It's further to the perception of soul music as largely a singles medium – most people know tunes from the radio or in clubs, therefore take them as one-offs – that *Soul on CD* includes Various Artist compilations. This is a rapidly expanding area. Far from being a tacky, cheap cash-in, small record companies are licensing old tunes to have experts compile and package albums with love and sensitivity. It's proving a useful and intelligent way to represent lost grooves. For instance, any soul fan would be poorer for not owning The Undisputed Truth's 'Smiling Faces Sometimes', but even the group's mothers would be going beyond the call of duty to want the whole album. Likewise it enables this book to cover records that made a far greater impact on the soul scene than the group that made them. Creative Source being a case in point: to paint the desired picture of what was going on at the time 'Who Is He And What Is He To You' has to be discussed, but the group itself remains entirely secondary to the tune's impact. And besides, if a compilation is the only place Charles Wright & The Watts 103rd Street Rhythm Band's 'Express Yourself' can be found, then they've got my vote.

And finally, quality control. Although there's still a long way to go before all the soul music that should be out on CD, *is* out on CD, there is no need to include *all* that is available. This is The Essential Guide, i.e. it's highly selective. After all, what would've been· the point of including Curtis Mayfield's *Heartbeat* just to s̩lag it off, when the same space could be given over to *Otis Blue*?

As to deciding what was duff and what wasn't, it's not easy to put it into words. But there's a line in Spike Lee's *Do The Right Thing* when Buggin' Out, a particularly militant character, states of another, 'Either you down, or you ain't down . . .' It speaks volumes, yet at the same time defies translation into anything approaching 'proper' English. The entry qualifications for this book: 'Either it got soul or it ain't got soul . . .'

NOTE: Although the major developments in soul music fall neatly into decades, some artists achieved success over more than one decade. The motif ➨ at the end of an entry denotes that there is more on this artist in later chapters. An arrow at the beginning of an entry reminds you that the artist has an earlier entry.

1950s TO 1960s

The term Rhythm & Blues first came about in America in the 1940s, as a polite way of saying 'black'. In 1949, the music industry magazine *Billboard* changed the title of its black music charts from 'Race Music' to 'Rhythm & Blues'. Such consideration had much to do with the justified grumblings of black GIs returning from the war, who having fought for their country felt it ought to be treating them with a bit more respect. But as important was the economic boom in black America that took place during the 1940s as its population – originally excluded from joining many fighting outfits – took up jobs in the munitions industry or filled manual work vacated by white men who had signed up. By the early 1950s, 30 per cent of black Americans owned the property they lived in, practically double the amount they'd owned when the USA had become involved in the Second World War. With money in his pocket, the black man was being seen as a potential customer, and therefore one to be treated with a little more consideration.

The music itself grew up around the same time as big band jazz and jump began to mutate for both fiscal and artistic reasons. The economics was simple: wages had risen, petrol prices had rocketed and keeping an orchestra on the road no longer made sense, unless it was one of the very biggest draws. The two coincided to create smaller, guitar-driven groups, with gospel and doo-wop influences being ushered in to throw the emphasis on to singing and so compensate for the incredible shrinking bands.

But what firmly established this new style was the growth of black radio at exactly the same time. Commerce in general was quick to catch on to this new relative prosperity in black

America, it meant a whole new set of customers for anything from soap to cars to restaurant dining to refrigerators. And the way to reach them was by radio – radio specifically tailored for them. Although the massive proportion of radio stations were white-owned (the country's first black-owned station was WERD in Atlanta in 1949), executives with an eye on this new source of revenue were becoming keen to incorporate a genuine black perspective and give it the traditionally less popular nighttime broadcasts, instead of the previous, supremely patronising 'Negro Hours'. During the five years from 1947, the number of black radio deejays working in the USA multiplied from less than twenty (one of which was Rufus Thomas) to over 500.

What made the difference, though, was *how* these announcers were black. They no longer had to 'pass' and sound as bland as possible, this new breed were encouraged to be down-home, biscuit-eating, talk-it-like-you-walk-it, butt-kicking BLACK. Rapping was born in the early 1950s as the sharper deejays, popular airwave madmen like Jockey Jack, Mr Mojo and The Ace From Space, spiced up their patter with ad hoc, street slang rhyming.

So desirable was this newly opened up advertising territory that segregated stations – those that still refused to let black people through the front door, let alone on the air – began to employ black guys to coach their white deejays in convincing-sounding ghettospeak. With no notion of irony whatsoever.

Naturally, large amounts of appropriately authentic records were needed for the gaps in which these loose-lipped lunatics weren't actually talking. Hand in hand with the growth of black radio was the mushrooming of independent record labels, founded by enthusiasts, very local in approach – the Chicago 'Sound', the Memphis 'Sound', etc – and small enough to respond to change or accommodate an artist with a unique approach. Atlantic in New York, Chess and VeeJay in Chicago, Specialty in Los Angeles and later Stax in Memphis were the most influential of the early R&B-producing record companies. All operated outside the mainstream US record industry (Columbia, RCA, MGM, etc), frequently using small privately owned studios. The most famous in this field was Rick Hall's Fame Studios in Muscle Schoals, Alabama, which was so integral a part of soul's development that the name of the town became synonymous with funky southern soul. Like the radio stations they serviced each company was white-owned – the Jewish connection of Leonard and Phil Chess, Herb Abramson (Atlantic) and Syd Nathan (King) came about because Jews were only on the fringes of mainstream America and therefore still did business in black neighbourhoods (many of which, like Harlem, had previously been Jewish enclaves). They appreciated black America from a cultural and commercial point of view. Also, as at the radio stations, the creative forces were black. Although a great deal has been made of the white producers and A&R men at these companies it should never be forgotten that much of the trademark sounds were created by black arrangers: Jesse Stone (Atlantic), Willie Mitchell (Hi), Willie Dixon (Chess) and Henry Glover (King).

R&B had initially taken its cue from existing styles, but one single musical occurrence was to change its whole course. By the mid-1950s Leo Fender's electric bass – which was introduced by jazz bass player Monk Montgomery in 1953 – had become widely available. Suddenly the music was totally different: the rhythm section was right up in your face, not gently bubbling under the melody. The black R&B world embraced this stone-rocking funky new sound immediately and material was written to exploit its pumping energy. It turned the small combos into explosions of raucous dance music as the lead instruments turned up the juice to follow suit and were pushed into a far more percussive approach.

But by the same time, rock 'n' roll was making headway. As more and more white kids started seeking out these exciting sounds from uptown, so the record companies and a good deal of the artists saw the sense in catering for it. Many, after a few R&B big sellers softened their rhythms and simplified the multi-layered, frequently scat-based doo-wop attitude to vocals in anticipation of a crossover career. But just as many got tougher, kept the hard-edged beats and used gospel arrangements as a vocal foundation. In other words, like Ray Charles, they stayed black and created what became known as soul music – sanctified singing over the big beat.

Then somewhere in the middle was Motown. As the Detroit motor industry boomed, Berry Gordy picked up on the postwar black prosperity and the wave of optimism that went with it. His master plan was to provide a soundtrack for black social aspiration by taking street-corner musical logic and polishing it up until it was shiny enough to book a table in the most up-market supper club. Damned if it didn't work too. But then it's no coincidence that it took a black record company owner to see this, as he was well aware of a whole spectrum of black social order apart from ghetto roots.

In Kennedy-era black America, Motown's upward mobility represented hope and its creation of an 'acceptable' black face offered opportunity. It was a liberating state of affairs, simply because it was further than anybody else had taken it, and there was a black man very visibly in control. But by the second half of the 1960s it began to look dated: Malcolm X had been assassinated; Civil Rights was moving much too slowly; the Black Panther Party gained ground; the war in somewhere called Viet Nam escalated; inner cities rioted; best-selling black books had titles like *Burn Baby Burn, Soul On Ice* and *Look Out Whitey, Black Power Gonna Get Yo' Momma* . . . Suddenly there was a whole new agenda to go with this growing black confidence. It required a whole 'nother soundtrack. And Old Mr Gordy and well-behaved negroes in evening dress didn't make sense any more.

Neither did making records for 'The Man'. But any ideologically motivated swing away from white-owned record companies was hastened after events at a National Association of Television and Radio Announcers conference in Miami in 1968, intended as a networking bunfight for black radio personnel and record company executives. Stax, Atlantic, Hi and so on were all heavily represented, as was an organisation called The Fairplay Committee. 'Heavily represented' in every sense of the word. On the surface a black equal rights outfit looking after its brothers' interests within the music industry, its methods were questionable to say the least: Marshall Sehorn was badly beaten up in his hotel suite; Jerry Wexler had to leave a dinner given in his honour following threats on his life; Al Bell had to be hidden on a boat for his own safety; Booker T Jones was 'advised' that he shouldn't be playing in a mixed band. Then when they explained motives that involved collecting a share of what they perceived to be plantation-style profits made from the talent and hard work of modern-day slaves, it became clear that The Fairplay Committee was little more than a racially aware payola collection agency.

Although the record companies rode out this wave of violence – and the degree of unpleasantness that came in its wake – with the help of various 'Italian-American associates', The Fairplay Committee lingered around the industry long enough to put a lot of them off working with black acts in the future. A state of affairs that was on the rise anyhow, as so many of these once specialist labels were being bought up by and absorbed into the mainstream. By 1970, Atlantic's founder Ahmet Ertegun was far more interested in wooing The Rolling Stones to the company than in producing the next Aretha Franklin album.

As a natural reaction to this shift in industry attention, a new wave of independent record labels and production companies sprang up. Just like their predecessors of nearly twenty years before, these companies had the ears of the inner city, the inside track to know a change had got to come and the flexibility to react quickly. But unlike those R&B pioneers, these outfits were black-run, if not black-owned. In the cultural climate of the end of the 1960s, making an issue of how black you were was a major selling point. In fact, things had turned full circle, when the day-to-day situation that had precipitated the more militant music was taking its lead from the records that were being played on the radio. 'Keep On Pushin" (The Impressions), 'Don't Call Me Nigger Whitey' (Sly And The Family Stone) and, more than any other, 'Say It Loud I'm Black And I'm Proud' (James Brown) became, quite literally, rallying cries. The effect such stirring sentiments were having on the nation was real and obvious. And they took on a slightly different slant when James Brown went on national TV, for most of the night, appealing for calm, after Martin Luther King was assassinated in 1968.

What made the music so interesting round about now was how this new wave of black nationalism combined with black America's take on a mainstream culture dominated by hippies and the acceptance of rock music as an art form in its own right. Put together with the advancements in recording technology, it had an astonishing reverberation across the tracks. By the end of the decade, Sly Stone had stolen the show at Woodstock, Norman Whitfield was doing some very un-Motown things with The Temptations and James Brown had fired The Famous Flames . . .

LaVern Baker

(Born Chicago, Illinois, November 11, 1929)
In the early 1960s, LaVern Baker wrote to her congressman to protest about the appropriation of R&B music by the rock 'n' roll fraternity: white artists were covering her records, having more success and somehow laying claim to them. A valiant try by the woman whose record company, Okeh, used to bill her as 'Little Miss Sharecropper'. But the singles that were covered were always very rock 'n' roll-ish anyway (a direct line drawn from jump-jive). Where Baker excelled as an early soul singer was on the more considered, subtle album tracks as produced by Jerry Wexler on Atlantic. In spite of her being at the forefront of the company's move towards more mainstream music, it's not difficult to imagine the likes of ARETHA FRANKLIN and Esther Phillips sitting up and paying attention to LaVern Baker's hard-rocking pipes.

*Soul On Fire: The Best Of LaVern Baker; Atlantic 82311; 1990

The cast of characters on this set includes King Curtis, Ben E. King and Doc Severinson. All twenty tracks were cut between 1953 and 1962: on the one hand Ms Baker will rock out with her hits and then take it right down to torch level for numbers like 'I Cried A Tear' and the title track (written by Atlantic Records owner Ahmet Ertegun). It's a vivid illustration of how R&B evolved into both soul and rock 'n' roll at the same time and for a while injected the same passion and fire into each.

SEE ALSO: *Atlantic R&B Volume 3*; Atlantic 781295

Hank Ballard

(Born Detroit, Michigan, November 18, 1956)
Probably more important at this time for his influence on the soul scene, and his work as part of the JAMES BROWN Revue during the 1960s, than for what he actually did on his own, Hank Ballard should not be overlooked. As lead singer with a local doo-wop group The Royals (alumni include JACKIE WILSON and

Levi Stubbs), Ballard worked the old jump-jive sensibilities into intricate vocal arrangements and served them up to an R&B audience. The group's name changed to The Midnighters, then Hank Ballard and the Midnighters in the mid-fifties, about the time they were producing such records as 'Work With Me Annie' and 'Sexy Ways', banned from the radio because of lewdness of lyric. It was at the end of the 1950s that the group did well with a string of dance craze records (Ballard wrote 'The Twist', although Chubby Checker had the hit with it), but much earlier in his career his earthy R&B arrangements and sweet harmony vocals can be seen as the bridge between Louis Jordan and THE TEMPTATIONS, contributing to a facet of vocal R&B that developed the harmonising out of the instrumentation rather than put it on top, fully formed. For ten years, starting in 1962, Ballard toured as part of The James Brown Revue and signed as a solo artist to King, where many of his recordings were James Brown Productions.

Their Greatest Jukebox Hits; King 541; 1988

Reproduced in exact replica of the original 1958 album, including sleeve notes, these are the earlier, earthier hits and far more relevant to this exercise than the end-of-the-decade blind alley of novelty-ish dance records. For curiosity value too, it's mildly interesting to find out what got radio producers so hot under the collar back in 1954, with songs like 'Work With Me Annie', 'Annie Had A Baby' and 'Sexy Ways'.

The Bar-Kays

(Mark I: Jimmy King, guitar; Ronnie Caldwell, organ; Phalon Jones, sax; Carl Cummingham, drums; James Alexander, bass; Ben Cauley, trumpet)
Essentially the second-string Stax house band, The Bar-Kays were always rawer than BOOKER T & THE MGS, being horn- as opposed to organ-led, and slightly younger. They were just beginning to get some credit for themselves with two pumping dance hits, 'Soul Finger' and 'Knucklehead', and an acclaimed album when, in December 1967, all except Cauley and Alexander were killed in

the same plane crash that claimed the life of OTIS REDDING. All were twenty years old or younger. Drummer Carl Cunningham was the father of Blair Cunningham, drummer with Haircut 100 and more recently Chrissie Hynde's backing band.➵

SEE ALSO: Stax Various Artist compilations

William Bell

(Born William Yarborough, Memphis, Tennessee, July 16, 1939) In many ways William Bell and the strong taste of countryfied blues he brought to his recording embodied the rural soul that Stax stood for in the very beginning. Hardly surprising really, he was a local boy. His first hit, 'You Don't Miss Your Water ('Til The Well Runs Dry)', in 1961, looked like setting him up as the company's top male star, but he was called up and by the time he returned from the Army in 1965 OTIS REDDING was in place.

William Bell stayed at Stax until it closed in 1976, in a writing partnership with BOOKER T (Bell wrote 'You Don't Miss Your Water'), providing songs for himself and other artists. His best-known cuts formed during that period are the duet with Judy Clay 'Private Number' and the Otis Redding memorial hit 'Tribute To A King'. He was, you feel, never fully appreciated by either the record company or the public.

The Best Of William Bell; Stax 8541; 1991

Later Stax stuff, this compilation starts in 1968, is produced by Booker T and is undeniably funky. It runs to his two duets with Judy Clay, the sublime ''Til My Back Ain't Got No Bone', 'I Forgot To Be Your Lover' and a thoroughly rocking remake of 'Born Under A Bad Sign'.

ALSO RECOMMENDED:

A Little Something Extra; Stax CDSXD037; 1990

If further proof were needed that Stax didn't know what to do with William Bell, these twenty supremely soulful sides were unreleased until this British-made compilation in 1990.

Bound To Happen/Wow; Stax CDSXD970; 1991

His second and third albums on the one CD.

SEE ALSO: Stax/Atlantic Various Artist compilations

Booker T & The MGs

(Booker T. Jones, keyboards, born Memphis, Tennessee, December 11, 1944; Steve Cropper, guitar; Donald 'Duck' Dunn, bass; Al Jackson, drums)

When 'Green Onions' was cut in 1962 – a record that would make over a million dollars for Stax – The MGs didn't exist as a formal unit and Booker T wasn't considering a career in music. At the time he was earning $15 per session playing the organ and simply thought it was more fun than a paper round. In addition, 'Green Onions' was just a B-side to go with the blues tune 'Behave Yourself', itself somewhat throwaway as it was recorded in spare time by Mar-Keys leaders Dunn and Cropper. Jones and Jackson had merely been playing on that session and stayed on to assist them. Jim Stewart liked the proposed A-side enough to release it, calling the band Booker T & The Memphis Group (immediately abbreviated). Deejays, however, found the flip side made for far more interesting airtime and suddenly the band that did so much to shape Stax Records was up and running. As a purely coincidental by-product, label owner Jim Stewart was always immensely proud of the group's racial make-up – Cropper and Dunn were white, Jones and Johnson black – believing it to characterise the Stax philosophy: in Memphis, that most segregated of cities (Martin Luther King was shot there in 1968), the races could operate in perfect harmony. Quite literally.

Although Booker T & The MGs had their own hits during the next nine years (with Lew Steinberg on bass, who was then fired for poor time-keeping, and Dunn was brought in permanently), their real contribution was as the dictionary definition of soul when, often with ISAAC HAYES supplementing their sound on the piano, they became the Stax/Atlantic house band. They gave it plenty behind WILSON PICKETT, SAM & DAVE, EDDIE FLOYD, RUFUS THOMAS, OTIS REDDING and Albert King, while between them they had a hand in writing 'Dock Of The Bay', 'Soul Man', 'Born Under A Bad Sign', 'Midnight Hour', 'Everybody Loves A Winner' and 'Knock On Wood'. But, and this was probably what stopped them advancing beyond this era, they weren't so hot when it came to branching out: there exists a very odd album of theirs called *McLemore Avenue*, consisting entirely of Beatles' cover versions.

In 1971, Booker T left to work as a producer and solo artist and Steve Cropper set up his own studios in Memphis. Jackson and Dunn carried on as The MGs until Jackson was murdered by a burglar at his home in 1975. Since then, Dunn and Cropper have appeared in the movie *The Blues Brothers* and toured as The Blues Brothers Band.

The Best Of Booker T & The MGs; Atlantic 81281; 1968

A brilliant backing band they might have been, but Booker and the boys were always far too inconsistent with their own material to make their albums sound commercial. Thus the Best Of compilations will weed out most of the dross for you. This one takes them up to 1968, and so includes 'Green Onions', 'Mo' Onions', 'Hip Hug Her', 'Groovin' (a funked-up instrumental take on The Young Rascals' song) and 'Slim Jenkins' Place' (originally titled 'Slim Jenkins' Joint' but they wanted it played on the radio).

Booker T & The MGs Greatest Hits; Stax 046; 1970

A couple of years on, but not much has changed. Thank goodness. The band are still cooking up a mess of onion-style phat Memphis funk and included in the seventeen gems are the BBC cricket tune 'Soul Limbo', 'Time Is Tight', 'Mrs Robinson', 'Eleanor Rigby', 'Hang 'Em High' and Booker T singing (quite well as it happens) on 'Johnny I Love You'.

ALSO RECOMMENDED:

Soul Limbo; Stax CDSXE 009; 1968

Their first album after Atlantic left Stax, and built round the killer groove of their cover of the theme from *Hang 'Em High*.

The Booker T Set; Stax CDSXE 026; 1969

Low-down funky covers of a dozen Motown and pop hits – 'Mrs Robinson', 'This Guy's In Love With You' and 'The Horse' among them.

James Brown

(Born Barnwell, South Carolina, May 3, 1933)
When James Brown was establishing his career, the accepted way forward in the world of R&B was to put out records at market-saturation levels – one every six or seven weeks was considered usual. The problem was, James Brown was almost constantly touring. He got round this by sending somebody ahead to book studio time for after the show in whatever town he was playing. He'd then take his band straight from the theatre to the studio and tell them to 'Play it like you played it on stage.' There was no time to faff about, and because they hadn't yet come down from the show they were 'into it' immediately, pumping out a track with all the adrenaline-surging power of a live performance. Which was all James Brown needed to spur him on to similar heights of self-expression. It was, according to one long-time James Brown sideman, 'Like we were still on stage. James would dance, scream, grunt, spin, do the splits, just like there was an audience. We'd have to keep up with him, with all the same discipline of a live show – get it right, first time. The way he'd see it, there was no point in going for a retake unless you absolutely had to. Didn't matter that it was three o'clock in the morning and we'd done three shows that evening. Everybody put so much commitment into those records.' If anything, James Brown's self-appointed title 'The Hardest Working Man In Showbusiness' was a piece of bashful understatement.

It was determination and self-discipline that had taken Brown from dirt-poor beginnings – being sent home from school for not having any shoes, petty theft, reformatory – to earnings of $12,000 per night in the 1950s. But the increased confidence that came with success blossomed into a blinkered, dictatorial agenda in which James Brown was king of his own castle and what lay beyond the moat didn't really matter. The musical vision was Brown's alone as he assumed writing, producing and arranging duties and band members were routinely bawled out during rehearsals or recording. There was also a system of fines for such onstage misdemeanours as being out of time on a dance step, playing a bum note or wearing scuffed shoes – if Brown noticed an infringement, he'd shimmy over to the offending player during the song and, in perfect time to the music, flash his right hand with fingers spread to indicate a five-dollar fine, twice for ten and so on. The audience, of course, never caught on. And, apparently something that didn't change for years, he had enormous difficulty listening to any music other than his own.

Under normal circumstances, such a stifling, introverted atmosphere would be destructive, but in the control of an individual as far from 'normal' as James Brown it changed the course of American black music both artistically and as a cultural force. Brown had no truck with the opportunities for rock/pop success the second half of the 1950s presented to R&B acts – in fact he didn't even appear to notice what was going on with the advancing strings and the repeating rhythm sections. So while many were broadening their bases by incorporating softer mainstream-friendly affectations, he looked inward and with only what he'd done before for inspiration, began a process of perpetual distillation of the original. Or, more specifically, the rhythm side of his rhythm and blues. Naturally, this was a spiral that became more pronounced as the decade wore on. It also dovetailed perfectly with Brown's unique approach to discipline, as the well-drilled squad that were The Famous Flames had no choice other than to be tight.

As a role model for the self-contained unit (playing, writing, producing, recording), which was practically unheard of among R&B/soul acts, Brown's music evolved from none-too-special R&B into a hard-driving, sweaty force that matched the street-tuff rhythms with ghetto slang lyrics and found enormous favour in black America. Success which he consolidated by the constant touring: he figured the shows, which were minor spectacles of music, costume and dance, made his music and himself seem much more special than just hearing a record; and guest spots on local black radio stations were never too much trouble

– apparently Brown was a master of the 'ten dollar handshake' in which money was palmed to deejays with high listening figures. By the end of the 1950s, James Brown had several million-sellers behind him, could fill the biggest concert venues by himself (not as part of a big-name package) and would routinely be mobbed in the street, yet few white Americans outside the record business had any idea who he was.

This success was so secure that even after the mainstream became interested he continued to develop along his singular path – because he needed nothing from the outside world, they had to take him on his own terms. 'I come from the ghetto,' he'd tell mainstream press interviewers. 'I still have my shoeshine box in my hand.' It was a heartfelt sentiment, the key to James Brown's relationship with black America – he was theirs and they were his. Very obviously. He used such an influence wisely too. Records like 'Don't Be A Drop Out', 'I Don't Want Nobody To Give Me Nothin' (Open Up The Door I'll Get It Myself)' and 'Say It Loud I'm Black And I'm Proud' were essays in black self-awareness and optimism at a time when America's inner cities were burning. To James Brown, these songs were just natural extensions of the time he spent in ghetto schools and youth centres talking to kids. On April 4 1968, when Martin Luther King was assassinated and riots erupted in some two dozen US cities, James Brown stayed on network television far into the night, appealing for calm. Afterwards, Vice-President Hubert Humphrey maintained situations would have been considerably worse had James Brown not volunteered his time.

He didn't neglect his music during all this either. By the end of the 1960s, as his record sales were peaking, he was pushing it towards a style that was like nothing else. Post-'Popcorn' singles 'Ain't It Funky Now', 'Brother Rapp' and 'Funky Drummer' at the turn of the decade were just a taste of what was to come. In 1970 James Brown was about to drop a bomb and soul music could never be the same again.➡

Curiously, James Brown is enormously underrepresented on CD in the UK – ten discs largely reducing his career to half a dozen repackaged, rearranged, remarketed compilations, which repeat themselves frequently yet tend not to dwell too long on the early end of things.

Live At The Apollo; Polydor 843479-2; 1963

If you only buy one live LP in your whole life, it ought to be this. It's the one by which others set their standards – or don't, which is probably what's wrong with so many live albums. Record company heads had for a while rejected the idea of a James Brown live LP, on the grounds that too many people had seen the show, radio wouldn't touch it, it had little singles potential and the R&B LP market was negligible. So on October 24, 1962, on the last night of a six-day stint at the theatre that was the centre of black America's cultural universe, James Brown booked his own recording facilities and taped the final show. When the record company chief heard the results he was convinced. He put it out as soon as possible and it had sold over a million by the end of 1963.

Listening to it now, it's easy to see why. Just over half an hour of the densest, most intense hot sweating funk as is possible without the disc spontaneously combusting. James Brown and The Famous Flames put everything they've got, and then some, into a dozen hits that run through 'Please, Please, Please', 'Night Train', 'Think', 'Try Me' and 'You've Got The Power', and even the primitive recording technique can't get in the way of what is going on between James Brown and his audience. If you've ever wondered what all the fuss was about with James Brown, here's all your questions answered on one easy-to-operate CD.

Roots Of A Revolution; Polydor 8173042; 1989

Forty-two tracks on two CDs that provide a wonderful assessment of James Brown from 1956 to 1964. Not all the hits are here, instead – and very often this can tell you more about an artist as individual as James Brown – it concentrates on his most interesting recordings. Then, as a bonus, the running order is fleshed out with studio banter, alternative takes and various unreleased items. It's in this chronological listing that the discs go way beyond the Roots of a Revolution and plot its entire development.

Please, Please, Please; Polydor 1847; 1988

A readily available Japanese import (Japan has by far the most James Brown CD releases on offer) that represents the best early

James Brown singles compilation. 'Just Won't Do Right', 'Try Me', 'I Want You So Bad', 'I Feel That Feeling Coming On', 'That's When I Lost My Heart', the rocking 'Chonnie The Chon' and, of course, the title track. Although Japanese imports vary in price from £17 to £25, to get all these tracks on the one disc actually makes it the best-value early James Brown singles compilation too.

Star Time; Polydor 8491082; 1991

A four-CD box set that goes from 'Please, Please, Please' to 1984's 'Unity', but the first two discs – subtitled 'Mr Dynamite' and 'The Hardest Working Man In Showbusiness' stop at the end of 1969, to give the best chronology of high-profile James Brown tracks from the 1950s and 1960s. All the hits are here, and as such it's probably far more accessible than, if the truth be told, the rather trainspottery *Roots Of A Revolution*.

Ruth Brown

(Born Ruth Weston – Brown was her married name – Portsmouth, Virginia, 1928)
Ruth Brown had a remarkable voice: big and powerful, with all the emotion of the blues and inventive close control of jazz. It was these credentials that, on the recommendation of Cab Calloway's sister Blanche, got her signed to the embryonic Atlantic Records in 1949, where their R&B gameplan was just a short step away from what she'd been doing as a post-Billie Holiday club singer. In fact the union was so successful that as she began a seven-year run of genre hits, she earned the nickname 'Miss Rhythm', while Atlantic Records became known as, both disparagingly and otherwise, 'The House That Ruth Built'. By the late 1950s, corporate logic dictated the best place for Ruth Brown was the crossover, and she was teamed up with Leiber, Stoller and other pop writers who never managed to do her justice. Maybe such a move was just as well, as the next wave of singers was the Aretha school of gospel-based soul and Miss Rhythm may not have been able to cut it among this new crowd. Or perhaps it was her moving over – she'd dominated the decade – that let them through.

After 1962, Ruth Brown got out of music to devote her attentions to her family. At one time driving a bus for a living, she pursued Atlantic for back royalties and became instrumental in aiding other victims of the 1950s' record business accounting procedures when she set up The Rhythm & Blues Foundation to chase up money owed. She returned to performing and recording bluesey material in the late-1970s – winning a Grammy in 1990 – and ventured into acting with Broadway parts and cameos in films.

Rhythm: The Greatest Hits And More; Atlantic 7567820612; 1993

A double CD set, providing forty songs from her twelve years at Atlantic, and in tracks like 'Teardrops From My Eyes', 'So Long', 'Mama He Treats Your Daughter Mean', '5-10-15 Hours' and 'Love Contest' some of the best original R&B ever made. So fresh it's practically still swimming. Indeed, in these marvellous surroundings, even the later 'Lucky Lips' and 'This Little Girl's Gone Rockin'' are more than simply bearable.

SEE ALSO: *Atlantic R&B Volumes 1, 2 & 3*; Atlantic 781293/4/5

Solomon Burke

(Born Philadelphia, Pennsylvania, 1936)
Even thirty years ago in the annals of black music, where an interesting private life was more or less regulation, the off-stage Solomon Burke must have been a conversation stopper. When not recording, Burke would run an undertaker's parlour, building the business into a chain of such establishments; he'd preach to enormous congregations at his House Of God For All People church; and he'd be doing his wild thing somewhere – the good-looking and charismatic Burke admits to twenty-one children and fourteen grandchildren. As a performer, Solomon Burke would take the stage decked out in fur-trimmed robes, a crown and a sceptre, and had been larger than life since childhood. Known as 'The Boy Wonder Preacher', at the age of twelve he'd be addressing the congregations at his dad's

church, while at thirteen he was a soloist in the choir and had a religious radio show called Solomon's Temple. By age fifteen he was recording for the gospel label Apollo.

Curiously though, considering this man would soon be held up as The Greatest Soul Singer Ever, these records made in the late-1950s weren't very good. Although Burke's style was gospel-based, it wasn't pure gospel and these had him trying to bend it to accommodate gospel songs. In 1960 he signed to Atlantic, where, thanks to his background, they dubbed him 'The Bishop Of Soul', but as he turns his uninhibited, testifyin'-type passion loose within the more liberal framework of their country-meets-R&B philosophy, he pushes the style to a whole new level – one where it makes absolute sense. The beginnings of Atlantic's singular style – and possibly the genesis of soul music as we know it – can clearly be heard in Burke's first hits, particularly 'Just Out Of Reach (Of My Two Empty Arms)' and 'He'll Have To Go', which hijacked straight C&W songs and dragged them 'cross the tracks. Ironically, once this way was established, other singers adopted it as an approach, which led to Burke being overshadowed at the label. He never really found any degree of success after leaving Atlantic in 1968.

Home In Your Heart; Rhino 70284; 1990

Two CDs, covering not just the hits but everything of note from his Atlantic period of 1961 to 1968 – a time that, oddly, only produced one album. This adds up to a staggering forty tracks and proves the argument that Solomon Burke was not only the greatest soul singer of the early-1960s, but possessor of possibly the best deep soul voice ever to grace a recording studio. Down among the stirrers are 'Just Out Of Reach', 'The Price' (a document of his own crumbling marriage), 'Down In The Valley', 'If You Need Me', 'You're Good For Me', 'Everybody Needs Somebody To Love', 'Got To get You Off My Mind' and 'Cry To Me'.

ALSO RECOMMENDED:

The Best Of Solomon Burke; Atlantic 8109; 1965

This was Solomon Burke's only Atlantic album! It takes twenty tracks from the above with no loss of quality, it just ends a bit too soon.

SEE ALSO: Atlantic Various Artist compilations

Bob & Earl

(Bobby Garrett, born Los Angeles, California; Earl Nelson, born Lake Charles, Louisiana)
Bob & Earl came about more or less by accident, after the group they were in just sort of wandered off and left them.

Native of Louisiana, Earl Nelson arrived in Los Angeles in 1956 to join The Hollywood Flames, who had one hit the following year. When fellow group member Bobby Byrd left for a solo career, Bobby Garrett, aka Bobby Relf, replaced him, but a follow-up hit hadn't materialised by 1959 and two more band members took off, leaving Bob & Earl as a duo to concentrate on live work in the LA area.

In 1963 they cut 'Harlem Shuffle', a record arranged by a nineteen-year-old BARRY WHITE. A straight up soul classic it may be, but then it barely scraped the US top fifty and wasn't to make enormous impact until its re-release in 1969 – four years after the pair had split up.

Earl had a hit in 1965, when he called himself Jackie Lee and cut a tune entitled 'The Duck' – he toured just after that, with Barry White as his drummer and road manager – but other than that Bob & Earl have vanished. It seems remarkable, given how enduringly brilliant 'Harlem Shuffle' is that they never did anything again.

SEE: Various Artists; *This Is Soul*; Object FPFCD01; 1989

Clarence Carter

(Born Alabama, 1936)
Blind since childhood, the multi-instrumentalist started recording as half of Calvin & Clarence (C&C), but arrived at Fame Studios in 1967 under contract to Atlantic as a solo act, after

Calvin (Thomas) was injured in a car accident. Essentially a rural blues man – Rick Hall always refused to let him cut a straight country album – Carter was one of the first successful Fame Studios alumni, in many ways setting the guidelines for their countrified soul with his rich narrative-friendly baritone and warm guitar work. As well as writing songs for other artists, he cut a series of minor hits for himself – 'Patches', 'Slip Away', 'Too Weak To Fight', 'Sixty Minute Man' and 'Part Time Love' among them. Twenty years on from this, Carter had something of a second wind, relaunching himself as a multi-instrumentalist bluesman with a series of completely solo albums in the late-1980s.

Snatching It Back: The Best Of Clarence Carter; WEA 8122702862; 1992

One of the best examples of what Southern soul was meant to mean, these two dozen sides are the very cream of Carter's Atlantic years (1965–1971). Country blues telling stories that detail love and life as it is lived in the Delta, with all the back door men, cheatin' hearts, lyin' eyes, undying devotion and unreturned affection that involves. It's a soul music soap opera, built around all his ten hits, but moving through some very interesting misses. 'I Stayed Away Too Long' and 'Making Love (At The Dark End Of The Street)' to name but two.

SEE ALSO: (1) Various Artists; *Soul Hits: Dance Party*; Charly QSCD6005; (2) Atlantic Various Artist compilations

Chairmen of the Board

(Norman 'General' Johnson, lead vocals, born Norfolk, Virginia, May 23, 1944; Danny Woods, background vocals; Eddie Custis, background vocals; Harrison Kennedy, background vocals.)
General Johnson will always be remembered for having possibly the most preposterously enormous afro known to man – rumours that it was a wig devastated large sections of North London womanhood during early 1970s – but also as a gravel-throated Levi Stubbs-soundalike, with a compelling line in vocal urgency, who put together this quartet to drag old school

R&B raucousness into the increasingly modern 1970s. The energetic hits '(You've Got Me) Dangling On A String', 'Give Me Just A Little More Time', 'Chairman Of The Board' and 'Everything Is Tuesday' made the group as Invictus's flagship act, and when performed on *Top Of The Pops* the records became a tribute to Afro Sheen Hairspray's holding power.

*Soul Agenda; HDH HDHCD007; 1989

All the big, obvious hits, but also the subtler – can that word really be applied to Chairmen Of The Board? – 'Elmo James', 'Pay To The Piper', 'Working On A Building Of Love' and 'Finders Keepers'. Perpetually exuberant, this group was about as lively as it ever got in London clubs at the time without straying into that wilderness we called 'Northern Soul'.

SEE ALSO: Various Artists; *Holland-Dozier-Holland Present The Hits Of Invictus & Hot Wax*; HDH HDHCD501; 1986

Ray Charles

(Born Raymond Robinson, Albany, Georgia, September 23, 1930) In 1954 and 1955 rock 'n' roll, as it had been officially dubbed by deejay Alan Freed, was just breaking big. So too was Ray Charles. His 'It Should Have Been Me', 'I've Got A Woman' and 'This Little Girl Of Mine' were huge R&B hits, and hugely R&B in as much as they put a secular spin on the emotionally driven gospel way of doing things, worked off a strong central groove and used melodies as percussion, big band or jump-jazz style, yet still carried a tune. It was at this point in his career – white folks were starting to buy his records and mainstream artists were taking an interest in what he was doing – that no one would have batted an eyelid if he'd gone the way of, say, labelmates LAVERN BAKER or Big Joe Turner or THE DRIFTERS and smoothed out his style to accommodate a pop marketplace that was now looking uptown to fill its release schedule. Or, as 'whitebread' covers of R&B hits were traditionally far bigger sellers, he might well have simplified his rhythms patterns and lyrics and throttled back on the exhuberance to become more crossover friendly – Elvis Presley covered 'I Got A Woman', resulting in, as you'd imagine, a particularly attractive royalty cheque for Charles and his co-writer Renald Richard.

But he did neither of these things. In fact, Ray Charles's records during the mid-1950s were rawer and rootsier – more black? – than the jazz-based material he was producing previously. At the time, Charles appreciated the freedom: 'Atlantic, yeah,' he said in an interview, 'I give them some skin. One of the things Jerry Wexler did when I was over there was that he never ever told me what to do. They would send me material, but if I didn't like it I would sit down and write whatever I wanted to write. I'd have to record, so I'd go in the studio and show them what I had written and they'd say fine, go ahead and record it. And that was that.' It was the support and security of a big company such as Atlantic that allowed Charles to develop his unique visions of gospel/jazz placed within the easier-accessed parameters of dance hall boogie or blues ballad emotion. His music was little affected by parallel trends and came, virtually undiluted, from within its composer. It was soul. And it stayed deep as much out of Charles's sheer cussidness as it did out of his determined sense of black pride.

It wasn't so remarkable that Atlantic allowed him to carry on in such an apparently non-commercial manner either (in spite of R&B listing domination, Ray Charles only had a handful of pop hits during the 1950s). As mainstream record companies increasingly pushed their black artists towards rock 'n' roll crossover, so the small independents began to blossom as, spurred on by Charles's specialist market success, they exploited a post-rhythm and blues gap opening up in their own communities. Other producers were listening keenly to what he was doing, and built on what they perceived as music that stayed true – this was before Civil Rights so keeping as their own as much as possible was even more important to black America, and this deliberately un-rock 'n' roll idiom was very much a cultural backlash. During the second half of the 1950s it turned over big money. Big enough to justify indulging Ray Charles on a strictly fiscal basis, although what was still important to Atlantic (least ways to Jerry Wexler) at that time was to make music that meant something, that stayed in touch with its roots. Thus even if having him on the roster wasn't quite worth it for the prestige alone, he would always act as a magnet for new young talent. Leaving all this aside though, there was enough people with ears in the company to know that Ray Charles had something special.

Atlantic had known that in 1952 when the fledgling company paid $2,500 to secure his contract. A tidy sum, but by then Ray Charles (Charles was his middle name, but he dropped his surname in 1949 to avoid confusion with boxer Sugar Ray Robinson) had been building a reputation as a jazz/blues pianist for five years, both on the road and in the studio. He'd been playing since very early childhood and had studied classical piano and clarinet at a school for the blind in Florida (his blindness was a result of glaucoma at the age of seven), which is where he mastered the music theory that would allow his natural gift for composition and arrangement to fly. As a teenager he was touring as Lowell Fulson's musical director.

By 1954, because he was spending so much time on the road, Ray Charles would be presenting his material to the Atlantic bosses as fully formed: his own orchestra would be rehearsed note perfect with the songs he had written, so instead of subjecting anything to too much corporate influence, recording was just a matter of playing in the studio. Ahmet Ertegun, who by now had produced hits for the label for six years, remembers: 'It was a real lesson to me to see an artist of his stature at work. You could lead him a little bit but you really had to let him take over. For the first time, we heard something that didn't have to be messed around with, it was all there. And he only got better, he got more commercial without trying to make hits. He was doing what he wanted to do naturally, but the music and the songs became better and stronger.' Ray Charles was soul's first paid-in-full genius.

He left Atlantic in 1959, his real influential period now on the wane as soul music became established in the 1960s, but in terms of sales figures he continued to grow as the rest of the world began to catch on. Much of his enormous appeal was due to his skill at immersing himself in other styles, but, while retaining the flavour, putting his own soul stamp on them – along with jazz and blues, in the 1960s he began a lengthy flirtation with country music. It's easy to say that if there had been no Ray Charles there would have been no JAMES BROWN or STEVIE WONDER or OTIS REDDING, but it's true. It all started here.

The Birth Of Soul: The Complete Atlantic R&B Recordings;
Atlantic 82310; 1992

Three-CD box, available widely on import at around £45, that
brings together fifty-three examples of Ray Charles's early soul
stuff in easy-to-follow chronological order. Although most of
this stuff is on the whole out on other albums, to consider it all
together like this is the only way to appreciate what Ray Charles
was doing. And *how* he was doing it, as while it was obvious
that the man's musical vision was his own the building bricks
came from all over the place. Whereas other soul innovators
have worked to refine and filter their material, Charles added
just about everything to the mix – such was his musical understanding there was nothing he couldn't come to grips with, and
then make it work for him. Plot his path through such milestones as 'What'd I Say', 'It Should Have Been Me', 'I've Got A
Woman', 'A Fool For You' and 'The Sun's Gonna Shine Again'.
Then read all about it in the stunningly designed, fascinatingly
informative thirty-two-page booklet.

His Greatest Hits Volume 1; Compact Classics 036; 1990
His Greatest Hits Volume 2; Compact Classics 037; 1990

Two discs of twenty tunes that each comprise Brother Ray's ABC
sessions between 1959 and 1972, which, although far more famous
than the Atlantic recordings (less influential though), have been
unavailable for years. Remastered and compiled by Charles himself, these albums are exactly what he wants to hear and how he
wants to hear it. An offer no sensible person should refuse.
Among the gems unearthed are 'Georgia On My Mind' (the song
he recorded only because his chauffeur kept singing it, and it went
on to sell a million), 'Here We Go Again', 'Let's Go Get Stoned',
'Busted', 'Baby It's Cold Outside' and 'Hit The Road Jack'.

ALSO RECOMMENDED:

Genius + Soul = Jazz; Essential ESSCD009; 1961

Arranged by Quincy Jones, this is instrumental big band jazz
but with a soul seasoning.

*The Right Time; Atlantic 241119; 1987

Just under half the hits of the boxed set, and although this probably represents good value, it's frustratingly short of the full
load.

SEE ALSO: *Atlantic R&B Volumes 2, 3 & 4*; Atlantic 781294/5/6

Arthur Conley

(Born 1946 Atlanta, Georgia)
A journeyman R&B singer who did rather well for himself after
being adopted, in purely a professional sense, by OTIS REDDING. In
1967, after several flops, came the Redding penned and produced 'Sweet Soul Music', a blatant 'tribute' to SAM COOKE's
'Yeah Man', a finger-snapping soul anthem just waiting to happen and, entirely understandably, a huge hit. After such success, Conley assumed a vocal style that was little more than
Cooke and Redding mannerisms – in roughly equal amounts –
but in spite of the impact of his first hit, all that was heard of
him after that was 'Shake Rattle And Roll' (1967) and 'Funky
Street' (1968). A classic example of a soul song taking on far
more importance than its singer.

SEE: Atlantic Various Artist compilations

Sam Cooke

(Born Chicago, Illinois, January 22, 1931)
It can never be said that Sam Cooke's material did the work for
him, even though he wrote or co-wrote much of it. 'Wonderful
World' . . . 'Twistin' The Night Away' . . . 'I Love You For
Sentimental Reasons' . . . if anybody else at the time (except
maybe RAY CHARLES) had done those same songs they would've
sounded just plain dumb. It's a tribute to Cooke's talent and
timing skills that he could get inside that drivel and turn it into
what amounted to a celestial experience, but in doing so – by
simply taking syrupy secular music and ladling unadulterated
gospel attitude all over it – he drew a target at which every

other pop/soul hopeful over the next twenty years would aim. (An enormously successful Jamaican tour in 1960 resulted in nearly every reggae vocalist of the 1960s and 1970s citing Sam Cooke as their major influence.)

Cooke was never going to do anything else though. The apparently incompatible notions of hormone-agitating pop stardom and the service of the Lord came into conflict in his life early in his career. Joining top gospel group The Soul Stirrers in 1951, after a childhood spent performing in churches in groups with his brothers and sister, Cooke became something of a sex symbol among the pews and, not slow to grasp any potential, he itched to try secular music. A big mistake – this was before MARVIN GAYE or Prince, and religion and sex didn't yet mix in public. A couple of singles under the name of Dale Cooke were rumbled immediately by his more God-fearing crowd and he was booed off stage at a subsequent Soul Stirrers show. The record label, anxious not to jeopardise their stake in the gospel market, let Cooke go . . . let him go on to non-religious music and a US number one, 'You Send Me', in December 1957.

After two years and nine consecutive hits on the tiny Keen label, he signed to RCA for the staggering fee, for a black artist, of $100,000 (actually that wasn't bad for any artist in 1960). By the time Cooke signed the deal, the company's black pop sensation, Jesse Belvin, had been killed in a car crash, and all the flim-flam tunes that would have gone his way became earmarked 'Sam Cooke'. Although he managed to spice up his repertoire with the feisty likes of 'Chain Gang' and 'Little Red Rooster', there was a noticeable slide towards bland out. The show, recorded at New York's Copacabana in 1964, included 'Bill Bailey', 'Blowin' In the Wind' and 'The Best Things In Life Are Free'. The world never got the chance to find out if he was actually going to sink as low as Vince Hill covers though, for Sam Cooke was shot dead in a three-dollar-a-night motel room on December 11, 1964. The investigation mentioned 'assault' and 'rape' and was signed off as justifiable homicide.

*The Man And His Music; RCA 7127; 1986

Twenty-eight tracks that go far enough back in his career to include a few numbers by The Soul Stirrers, and then takes things right up to the end. Everything you could want is here, plus a few non-hit surprises, and the remastering has cleaned the sound up to a staggering degree. 'You Send Me', 'Wonderful World', 'Touch The Hem Of His Garment', 'Cupid', 'Bring It On Home To Me', 'Chain Gang' and so on.

Live At The Harlem Square Club; RCA 5181; 1985

Recorded in said club in Miami in 1963, this wasn't released at the time as the lowdown R&B punch packed by Cooke's perfor- mance was deemed out of sorts with the mainstream areas the company had him pointed towards. Ten rip-roaring versions of as many well-known, but in this case only just recognisable, songs: 'You Send Me', 'Twistin' The Night Away' and 'Bring It On Home To Me' among them.

ALSO RECOMMENDED:

The Two Sides Of Sam Cooke; Specialty 2119; 1989

A compilation of Soul Stirrers' gospel and that initial secular stuff that got him in all that trouble way back then.

Lee Dorsey

(Born Portland, Oregon, December 4, 1926)
As a former successful boxer – a lightweight contender under the name of Kid Chocolate, who ran a crash repair workshop and used to be in the navy, Lee Dorsey was one helluva singer. But he would've been a pretty good one anyways, as was proved with his light-hearted New Orleans R&B (he moved to the city as a child) and a succession of scat-sung hits in the early 1960s that proved novelty records didn't have to be cretinous. Through the end of that decade he grew up, sort of, and under the guidance of ALLEN TOUSSAINT, made the kinds of record that proved black soul music could be as much fun as anything the pop charts had to offer – witness 'Working In The Coalmine', 'Holy Cow' and 'Yes We Can'.

During the 1970s he spent more time in his repair shop with a welding torch in his hand than in front of a microphone, only being lured out for live work (The Clash once took him on tour as an opening act!) and TV appearances – in the early 1980s, an overall-clad Lee Dorsey became a staple interviewee for any British film crew making a programme about soul or R&B. He died of emphysema in December 1986.

Great Googa Mooga!; Charly CDNEV3; 1991

Possibly the best title imaginable for an LP, by the man who Allen Toussaint described thus: 'If a smile had a sound it would be the sound of Lee Dorsey's voice.' The forty tracks (it's a double-CD set) run through the New Orleans nonsense of the title track – and other cuts with names like 'Ya Ya', 'O Me-O My-O' and 'Ay-La-Ay' – to the big hits 'Ride Your Pony', 'Acapella', 'Everything I Do Gon' Be Funky', 'Sneakin' Sally Thru The Alley' and, of course, 'Working In The Coalmine'. If a smile could be digital and put on a disc, this is it.

ALSO RECOMMENDED:

Soul Mine; Charly CDCD1115; 1993

A more sensible (slightly) single-CD distillation of the above, concentrating on the better known material.

The Drifters

(The original line-up: Clyde McPhatter, born Durham, North Carolina, November 13, 1933; Gerhard Thrasher; Andrew Thrasher; Bill Pinkney)
Best known for their mid-1960s/early-1970s hits, by that time – though still singing soulfully and applying an R&B theory to their arrangements – The Drifters had long since ceased to be a true part of the soul scene. 'Via Con Dios', 'Memories Are Made Of This', 'Stranger On The Shore'? We are not talking about *any* part of 'cross the tracks cool. It was in the 1950s that the group counted in terms of innovation and influence. Then, they appeared to be able to drive a song for themselves and weren't slaves to their material. Also, to make matters better, in those days said material was much stronger.

The original group was built around Clyde McPhatter, literally as well as musically – he'd acquired a considerable reputation as lead singer with The Dominoes, so when they sacked him in 1952 Atlantic's Ahmet Ertegun tracked him down to offer him a deal provided he could get a group together. The singer roped in a few of his friends, but their first Atlantic session was such an ill-rehearsed shambles that he had to rope in a few more after the first crew walked out. This reserve team ended up as the first Drifters' line-up, and their debut single, 'Money Honey', sold a million.

The song compounded a unique style that had McPhatter's high tenor working around the other voices, instead of on top of them, to create a breadth and versatility of sound, unusual to a black group of the day. This was a deliberate attempt on McPhatter's part to push away from gospel and doo-wop confines, something he'd been unable to experiment with in The Dominoes – 'musical differences' had figured large in his departure. At that time, it was radical and worked well enough to play a significant part in the sculpting of the interactive harmonising of the traditional R&B vocal group.

It was also successful enough for the group to carry it through without McPhatter, who officially left in 1956. Still more line-up changes followed, until by the end of the decade the group was completely different with Ben E. King as lead singer. But the end was in sight. Other groups had adopted the style and were catching them up so, to give them an edge, rock 'n' roll-based writers/producers Leiber and Stoller were brought in – in 1959 so many R&B harmonisers were leaning towards what they saw as a lucrative mainstream market. While the first few tunes had still had a substance to them, the strings and all that went with them were taking over: while 'There Goes My Baby', 'On Broadway' and 'This Magic Moment' had a certain delicate splendour to them, it was but a short step to 'Under The Boardwalk'.

*Let The Boogie Woogie Roll: Greatest Hits, 1953–1958;
Atlantic 7567819272; July 1993

Absolutely the best Drifters' collection. By taking in the McPhatter years the development of the style can be plotted to the ultra-slick 'Adorable' (which was cut with sound-a-like – nearly – Johnny Moore), then, among the thirty-two tracks there's 'Honey Love', 'Such A Night', 'Watcha Gonna Do', 'Bip Bam' and 'Ruby Baby'.

*All Time Greatest Hits And More, 1959–1965; Atlantic 75678191312; 1993

The end of 1958 was something of a watershed year, as manager George Treadwell, who owned the name, sacked the lot of them. He then recruited vocal group The Crowns, with Ben E. King on lead, to be The Drifters. So while the technique is more or less the same, the emphasis can be heard to be switching from the group to the production, from the singing to the whole feel of it. But while this set goes up as far as Bert Berns's out and out pop productions, the early tunes (especially with King, who left in 1961), make it all worthwhile. In fact, in this setting, even the schmaltz is perfectly acceptable after a hard day at the funk face.

The Falcons

An interracial R&B group in 1955? That's what the Falcons were when EDDIE FLOYD and white singer Bob Manardo teamed up in Detroit. It only lasted a year, though, as Manardo was called up and replaced by Levi Stubbs's brother Joe, who was in turn replaced four years later, in 1960, by a very young WILSON PICKETT. Other Falcons alumni include MICHAEL JACKSON's father Joe (a guitarist), and for a time THE OHIO PLAYERS, then called The Ohio Untouchables, were their backing group. The Falcons had two marvellous hit singles, 'You're So Fine' (Stubbs on lead vocal) and 'I Found A Live' (Pickett).

*You're So Fine: The Falcons Story Pt 1; Relic 7003; 1992

Sixteen tracks of rough, very early R&B doo-wop, built round Eddie Floyd and so obviously experimental – in terms of arrangements and what could be done with the style – it's never less than exciting.

*I Found A Love: The Falcons Story Pt 2; Relic 7012; 1992

More of before, but onwards from 1959 and any sophistication born from experience is cancelled out by the addition of Joe Stubbs's somewhat earthier tones. Good to see the sandpaper throat seems to run in the Stubbs family.

Eddie Floyd

(Born Montgomery, Alabama, June 25, 1935)
Say 'Eddie Floyd' to anybody with so much as a passing interest in sixties soul, and the chances are they'll reply, '"Knock On Wood", and . . . and . . .' But there was a bit more to him than that. 'Knock On Wood' wasn't even his only hit – there was a string of them in 1967 and 1968, including 'Bring It On Home To Me', 'Don't Mess With Cupid' and 'I've Never Found A Girl (To Love Me Like You Do)'. It was just that none of them delivered with the naked spirit of 'Knock' or went on to epitomise what Stax Records was all about – indeed Floyd and Steve Cropper had written the song for OTIS REDDING, but after Jim Stewart had heard their storming demo, he let Floyd keep it. An original member of The Falcons, he was actually something of a Stax backbone, because as staff songwriter his was the pen responsible for hits by RUFUS THOMAS, WILSON PICKETT, OTIS REDDING, WILLIAM BELL and SAM & DAVE. But these days, all anybody expects from seeing his name on a record is 'Knock On Wood'.

*Rare Stamps/I've Never Found A Girl; Stax CDSXD 096; 1989

Two albums on the one disc, tracking across 1967 and 1968, Eddie Floyd's most successful time as a performer. 'Knock On Wood' features, and the material runs around that chunky well upfront style he developed at the label. 'Big Bird' and 'Things Get Better' are also here, as are two blistering duets – almost duels – with Mavis Staples.

*Knock On Wood: The Best Of Eddie Floyd; CDSX 010; 1992

Floyd's entire Stax career summed up on one CD is an hour of concentrated down-home funk, displaying a wider range than is popularly imagined and a particular handling of the big soul balled out but with a superbly Stax spin to it.

SEE ALSO: (1) Various Artists; *This Is Soul*; Object FPFCD01; 1989; (2) Stax/Atlantic Various Artist compilations

The Four Tops

(Levi Stubbs, lead vocals, born Levi Stubbles; Renaldo 'Obie' Benson; Abdul 'Duke' Fakir; Lawrence Payton; all born Detroit, Michigan)

In summer 1994, at Wembley Arena, The Four Tops played a note-perfect, stormingly energetic ninety-minute live show. Sitting almost level with the stage it was easy to see their faces and to realise they were genuinely enjoying what they were doing. Remarkable on two counts: first, the gusto with which they approached their task – these guys have a combined age of about 240; secondly that they could possibly still be getting a charge out of doing exactly what they've been doing for the last thirty years.

But The Four Tops are a remarkable group. Initially the most recognisable exponents of the Holland-Dozier-Holland sound, they *were* Motown in the beginning. They were in the forefront of changing that sound too, when 'Reach Out I'll Be There' signalled new instrumentations and arrangements in the Detroit studio. They survived leaving the label when it went to Los Angeles. They survived disco – even had a couple of hits. And they've survived forty-one years together in the same line-up.

What people forget is that they were relatively old when they arrived at Motown. Formed in 1953 (all had previous experience, Stubbs was briefly in The Royals, before HANK BALLARD joined) as The Four Aims, they made a good living in local clubs both on their own and singing backgrounds/opening for big touring acts, then going on tour themselves. In 1959, with their name changed to avoid confusion with the Aimes Brothers, they spent time at Chess, Red Top and Columbia Records without a hit (at CBS they worked with John Hammond, the same producer who had no luck with ARETHA FRANKLIN either). Then

Berry Gordy signed them to develop them as a jazz group, presumably because the almost thirty-year-old Tops were so much older than the other 'kids' he was signing. In fact it was only Eddie Holland, seeing their act in a club one night, who tried out a new song on them, 'Baby I Need Your Loving'. It went top twenty, instantly. 'Just Ask The Lonely' followed. Then 'I Can't Help Myself'. Then 'It's The Same Old Song' . . . At the time of writing, the group were back at Motown and about to be given a lifetime recording contract.

The Four Tops; Motown 5122; 1964

The first album in its original form, and interesting in the audible battle of wills that seems to be going on between The Tops' exuberance and Motown's formula. The group's style clearly hasn't evolved to its fullest yet, but it's got a definite edge, more than enough to let you know something special is happening. Also, it's probably The Tops' LP with the most straight ballads, which, when they're of the calibre of 'Just Ask The Lonely', 'Where Did You Go' and 'Love Has Gone', you wonder why they didn't do more. But the real attraction is that first track, 'Baby I Need Your Loving' . . . All together now, '*Got* to have all your loving.'

The Four Tops' Second Album; Motown ZD72491; 1966

As well as containing most people's fave Tops' song 'I Can't Help Myself', this is a vital set for more than just 'Something About You' and 'It's The Same Old Song'. It represents the closest Holland-Dozier-Holland ever got to the gospel-inspired mayhem that was coming out of Memphis and Muscle Shoals as it follows on from the opening 'I Can't Help Myself' to get the drums kicking, the brass honking and The Four Tops rising to the occasion with a passion. If it hadn't already been established that Levi Stubbs wasn't your usual Motown smoothie then this album left no doubt.

The Singles Collection; Polygram TV 515710; 1992

Not quite comprehensive, but good value all the same as the twenty-one tracks run from 1966's 'Loving You Is Sweeter Than Ever', right up to the post-Motown years and 'Don't Walk

Away', 'Loco In Acapulco' and 'Indestructible'. Of course, because it doesn't start until 1966, it misses out on the first couple of albums. But it's been put together with care – instead of running the tracks chronologically they're arranged to create some sort of flow – and it's interesting to hear The Tops over the years and realise that different styles and producers bent to accommodate them and not the other way round. Which is probably the secret of their longevity.

ALSO RECOMMENDED:

Greatest Hits; Motown WD72280; 1967

The first Motown hit singles.

Tonight!; Casablanca 800049; 1981

A post-Motown celebration that rocks like men of that age have no business doing.

Aretha Franklin

(Born Memphis, Tennessee, March 25, 1942)
'The Queen of Soul'; 'Lady Soul'; 'The First Lady of Soul' . . . Aretha Franklin's been called all of these things, but she very nearly wasn't. The first six years of her career were a virtual write-off, as she became a vivid example of how record companies don't always know what's best for their artists – even if they are an eighteen-year-old preacher's daughter fresh off the bus into New York City.

In 1960, as a reaction to four demos she'd cut, CBS Records gave her a six-year deal and she was assigned to producer/A&R man John Hammond (who was later to be known as the man who 'discovered' Bob Dylan and Bruce Springsteen). Enormously impressed with her vocal range and control, he steered her jazzwards, believing he had stumbled on 'the next Billie Holiday'. Without much success. So he tried big, Broadway-type show tunes. Then blues. Then overly-sloppy torch songs. Then pop. A dozen unfortunate albums later, when her contract was up, Franklin wasn't all that keen to re-sign.

Enter Jerry Wexler with a ticket to Muscle Shoals, Alabama, and the idea that it would take a firing-on-all-cylinders R&B backing to jump start the gospel passion in that voice. At Rick Hall's Fame Studios she was teamed up with WILSON PICKETT's rhythm section, of good ol' Southern boys with an intuitive feel for R&B, to cut 'I Never Loved A Man (The Way I Love You)' and 'Do Right Woman – Do Right Man', *in the first take.* The latter was actually finished in New York after her husband/manager, Ted White, had such a blistering row with one of the horn players that the New Yorkers took an early flight home. It was the culmination of the hostility and resentment White and, to a degree, Franklin felt towards what they saw as a bunch of rednecks trying to tell them about black music. This was a frequent problem when Atlantic's sophisticated, urban-living black artists, many of whom were only one generation removed from sharecropping in the South, first started coming down to use the studios in Memphis and Muscle Shoals (see WILSON PICKETT).

'I Never Loved A Man' didn't suffer though. It sold over 250,000 in the first two weeks of release, to go top ten, the first of twelve million-sellers in a row. The line of Wexler/Franklin hits stretched all the way to 1973, making her, then, the best-selling female recording artist. She won the Grammy Award for Best R&B Vocal Female every year from 1967 to 1975, and three times since then. And while all this was going on in the counting house, her uninhibited way with her voice, her total understanding of how R&B worked as popular music, and Wexler's ability to wring every inch of emotion out of every note she sang, rewrote the rulebook of what the emerging soul style should aim for.

However, even in the midst of her success, when Aretha Franklin stepped outside of this style, things almost went as wrong as they had back in the CBS days, as two recent CD reissues show. 1971's *Aretha Live At The Filmore West* was her introduction to a rock audience and she never sounds remotely comfortable; and *Soul '69* is quite bafflingly titled, as The Queen of Soul opts to wallow in syrupy big band jazz that can't see the shame in the inclusion of 'Elusive Butterfly' (at the time this strange set was attributed to the public falling apart of her marriage to Ted White during the recordings).

Of course, it was only to be expected that Aretha Franklin

should do well in emotive, gospel-based songs, as hers was a grounding little short of illustrious. Her father, the Reverend C. L. Franklin was the biggest preacher of the 1950s, and nicknamed the Million Dollar Voice as a reference to his appearance fees. She taught herself to play the piano, but singing lessons came courtesy of Mahalia Jackson and Marion Williams, friends of the family. It was James Cleveland, who roomed at the Franklin house, and Clara Ward, another acquaintance, who encouraged her to perform. Then, once she'd got over her stage fright with some gospel touring experience, SAM COOKE pushed her towards a secular style and the New York record industry.

Although her association with Wexler finished in 1974, she continued to have hits until the end of that decade with such producers as QUINCY JONES, CURTIS MAYFIELD, Lamont Dozier or herself at the board. But by then times had changed and the relative failure of her *La Diva* album in 1979 (which peaked at US 142) seemed to indicate that one of the most significant eras of soul music was over. ↦

Queen Of Soul: The Atlantic Recordings; Rhino 71063; 1992

At around £50 this four-CD set was never for the casual punter, but if you take into account over five hours of music from Aretha Franklin, and an information-packed booklet by Dave Marsh, it starts to look like a pretty good deal. The eighty-six-strong selection of songs, all cut between 1967 and 1977, run the spectrum of hits and supplement themselves with the more interesting album tracks and B-sides. As well as just being an entirely justifiable indulgence, this set shows the scale of Aretha Franklin's talent even though it stayed within her own parameters, as she handles her own compositions, covers, different producers and varying styles in a way that is completely her own and yet usually surprising – even at the end of the fourth disc.

20 Greatest Hits; Atlantic 7567-81668; 1994

If you don't want to stretch to fifty quid, there are a baffling amount of Aretha Franklin Greatest Hits compilations available, concentrating on the early Atlantic hits. This one is the best value, an hour of music and going up as far as 1974 and her huge hit cover of STEVIE WONDER's 'Until You Come Back To Me (That's What I'm Gonna Do)' and 'I'm In Love', her last top twenty hit of the 1970s. And, naturally, while it's getting there it goes by way of 'Do Right Woman, Do Right Man', 'Think', 'Respect', 'Day Dreaming', 'I Say A Little Prayer', 'Don't Play That Song', 'Rock Steady' and 'Dr Feelgood'.

The First 12 Sides; Columbia 31953; 1989

A dozen tracks cut during those first years at CBS, which, when filtered out to this degree, make you wonder why they still couldn't do anything with her. Still blatantly church, it's got a lot of jazz and raucous blues in there and, thanks to the likes of 'Won't Be Long', 'Sweet Lover' and 'Maybe I'm A Fool', backed by The Ry Bryant Trio, it succeeds as more than just a curiosity or as a case study of the roots of a career. Even though the latter is interesting enough by itself.

Spirit In The Dark; Atlantic 8122-71525; 1970

The inclusion of 'Don't Play That Song', a huge hit that summer, ought to be enough to make this worth investigating, but the clincher is a blistering torch-song reading of 'The Thrill Is Gone', originally the B-side of the title track. The former was her first million-seller for nearly two years, in fact this whole LP is something of a return to form with her piano playing and singing coming together to hit new heights of celebratory soulfulness. Could this have had anything to do with the fact she'd just got married again?

Young, Gifted & Black; Atlantic 8122-71527; 1972

An album that goes beyond the title track's consolidation of Aretha Franklin's position as Queen of African America – 1967's 'Respect' had been taken up as the Black Panther Party's anthem, and she had never denied their references to her as The First Lady – for no other reason than 'Rock Steady' and 'Day Dreaming' are present. But otherwise, it's enjoyable proof of Aretha Franklin's progressive maturity as a singer and musician without sacrificing any initial fire.

ALSO RECOMMENDED:

Lady Soul; Atlantic 7567 81818; 1968

Most 'Retha-est experience – 'People Get Ready'.

I Never Loved A Man The Way I Loved You; Atlantic 7567 81439; 1967

Most 'Retha-est experience – 'Respect'.

Amazing Grace; Atlantic 906; 1972

Gospel with James Cleveland and The Southern Californian Community Choir. Most 'Retha-est experience – all of it.

SEE ALSO: Atlantic Various Artist compilations

Marvin Gaye

(Born Marvin Gay, Washington DC, April 2, 1939)
If any one artist was responsible for dragging Motown Records out of the early 1960s and bobby-soxed, three-minute puppy love dramas – excellently performed and produced as many of them were – it was Marvin Gaye. Before *What's Going On*, and before STEVIE WONDER's 1970s albums, in 1969 Marvin Gaye gave a clear demonstration of how powerful a medium the soul song could be when he completely reconstructed Gladys Knight's 1967 hit 'I Heard It Through The Grapevine'. With the aid of the similarly adventurous Norman Whitfield, his searing, stagger-ingly phrased vocals transformed the innocuous tale of appar-ently adolescent gossip into a dark, almost paranoid saga of deceipt – real and imagined – jealousy, shattered trust, infidelity and deep, deep sadness, surrounding itself with music as over-powering and as angular and shadowy as a gothic mansion. It was the first proper insight into how any Motown performer's mind worked, and was a pretty scary snapshot of Gaye's take on life and love. But it came from the soul.

It also came as more or less a complete surprise, because for five years Marvin Gaye had sung Nat King Cole-style, like a good soldier along The Motown Way. Sure, he had the voice of an angel but the material was never anything special – in fact to get the briefest tastes of what he might be capable of you had to listen to the tunes to the very end, where he's often doing something startling with his fade-out note. It was almost as if nobody was paying too much attention at that point so he felt he could get away with it, which might well have been the case, as Berry Gordy had never wanted Marvin Gaye to be a solo singer in the first place.

Gaye joined the company as a backing singer/drummer – he's tub thumping on SMOKEY's first hits and Stevie Wonder's first single – after being brought in by Harvey Fuqua, Gordy's brother-in-law. A fellow Washingtonian, Fuqua had taken over Gaye's first group, the vocal trio The Marquees, and renamed it The Moonglows in 1959, moving them to Chicago. There, he got them two singles on Chess, but a year later broke the act up and decamped to Detroit where he met Gwen Gordy and became a director of her Anna label (named after another Gordy sister who, coincidentally, was a future Mrs Marvin Gaye), before it was absorbed into Motown. He sent for Marvin Gaye almost immediately, though it was several months before he was given his chance in front of his own microphone. Then the first side he cut was 'Let Your Conscience Be Your Guide'. The idea was that he'd be some sort of answer to SAM COOKE, a high-class supper club artiste, a notion that persisted until 1962 when his first hit was the first record he'd written for himself, which cut him a bit more corporate slack.

Where Marvin Gaye did excel during the 1960s was as part of various duets – Mary Wells, Kim Weston and, most spectacularly, Tammi Terrell – a situation that clearly spurred him on emotionally and laid the foundation stones for the lurrrve soul of the next decade. It was as if actually singing with a woman allowed him literally to act out his feelings through his voice, which went a long way towards the growing up of the Motown Love Song. But even in spite of such gutsy, relatively abandoned (for Motown) two-handers like 'You're All I Need To Get By', 'Ain't Nothing Like The Real Thing' and 'Ain't No Mountain High Enough' nothing had prepared the way for 'I Heard It Through The Grapevine', which sold over two million and was the company's biggest single to that date. It allowed Marvin Gaye much more freedom to explore his musical vision. ↤

Anthology; Motown 530181; 1989

As the only complete pre-1970s Marvin Gaye album still on catalogue is the lamentable *MPG* – Marvin's fluid tones crammed into a constricted croon, with miserable material – this double-disc set gives best access to early period Marvin Gaye (it seems to concentrate on that area, probably because the later albums are still available). Forty-six tracks cover the more inspired solo songs, 'Can I Get A Witness' 'Stubborn Kind of Fellow', 'Too Busy Thinking About My Baby' and 'Grapevine' among them, and a liberal sprinkling of duets. However, as the set runs up as far as 'Mercy Mercy Me', 'Trouble Man' and 'Inner City Blues', it's difficult to listen to the older stuff without a sense of frustration at years he appeared to be wasting as he submerged his own creative bent. Pleasant as most of it is, it's not even hot enough to be considered a warm up for what was to come.

ALSO RECOMMENDED:

The Very Best Of; Motown 5302922; 1994

A selection of the above, likewise 1960s-biased, released to coincide with the tenth anniversary of his death.

SEE ALSO: Motown Various Artist compilations

The Impressions

(Curtis Mayfield, tenor, born Chicago, Illinois, June 3, 1942; Jerry Butler, baritone; Arthur & Richard Brooks, tenors; Sam Gooden, baritone.)
This was the original line-up, but it isn't the one most people know because The Impressions went through all sorts of reinventions, restarts and reformations before they settled down as Mayfield, Gooden and Fred Cash. The trio, who translated hardline black politics into the sweetest gospel harmonies, at a time

in the mid-1960s when that sort of thing just wasn't done, saw out the decade with a soundtrack entirely appropriate to the burning inner cities. But they had a tangled history.

The first quintet formed in 1957, after Gooden and the Brooks brothers quit their five-piece singing group The Roosters, and relocated from Tennessee to Chicago. There, they hooked up with local boys Mayfield and Butler ('boys' isn't far off the mark, they were fifteen and eighteen respectively) and kept their previous group's name. Under CURTIS MAYFIELD's direction, they began to develop a style that maintained the gospel tradition of switching lead vocalist – during a song or even a verse – but applying it to non-secular music. (This is very much at odds with the more rigidly structured harmony groups of the day, but is so commonplace in the Windy City it's often referred to as The Chicago Sound.)

Understandably they attracted attention and signed to Vee-Jay Records in 1958 where they were renamed The Impressions (it was felt, correctly so, that bird names for singing groups were somewhat *passé* by then). Their first single, 'For Your Precious Love', reached number 11 and later assumed soul classic status, deservedly so. Unfortunately it also caused the band to split as its billing of Jerry Butler & The Impressions had prompted Butler to go solo and the others, rather peeved as their style specifically involved no clear leader, did not jump to stop him. Fred Cash, one of the original Roosters, was called up from Tennessee to replace him, but there were no more hits, the company dropped them (it kept Butler though) and they disbanded.

In 1960, Curtis Mayfield, who'd been working with Butler as a writer and guitarist, reformed the group and moved them to New York where it was a year before they had their first hit. But many would say it was worth the wait as this hit was 'Gypsy Woman'. However its success wasn't repeated and in 1963, when Mayfield took the group back to Chicago, the Brooks brothers were sufficiently disillusioned to stay in the Big Apple.

That was it, all that remained was the golden-throated triangle of Mayfield, Gooden and Cash. It was then, back in his native environment, that Mayfield started to rebuild the gospel-type vocal passing game and felt confident enough that it wouldn't be swamped when he boosted his productions with big horn arrangements. Although this worked, success and influence didn't really spread beyond the specialist market, until 'Keep On Pushing' in 1964, a politically flavoured number that perfectly captured a mood of rumbling disappointment with the speed at which the Civil Rights campaign was affecting social change. It hit number 10, and the LP of the same title was their best seller to date.

This set a trend for the rest of the decade: soaring harmonies; full and lively orchestration; and the socially aware songs doing rather better, saleswise. A case in point was 1967's 'We're A Winner', an unambiguous celebration of black strength, it met with a widespread radio airplay ban but still got to number 14 in the charts. In fact, such was The Impressions' reputation for political commentary, that when Mayfield left to go solo in 1970, he rerecorded many of the numbers he'd written for the group as a way of stating his intentions instantly.

Leroy Hudson replaced Mayfield, who continued to write and produce for the trio for a couple of years, but they only had a couple more hits and then pretty much faded from view except to regroup with Mayfield or other original members for nostalgia tours or TV specials.➻ *Curtis Mayfield*

The Definitive Impressions; Kent 923; 1993

For a group that are so well respected and had so much influence on soul singing as it moved from the 1960s to the 1970s – a bigger jump than a mere ten years – The Impressions are woefully under-represented on CD. None of the albums are available in original form, even in Japan where low-quality control and lax copyright laws tend to see most things in digital form. So the best of the Best Ofs is this twenty-eight-track jobbie that gives you everything of note from the 1960s.

For Your Precious Love; Charly CDCD 1105; 1959

Very early VeeJay material – so early it features Jerry Butler and has for a long time been considered 'lost'. The title track is the group's first hit, now considered something of a modern gospel/early soul classic. The album, which concentrates on similarly themed material – love songs – is an interesting example of the

Chicago sound in its infancy, but it's not nearly as exciting as the closely harmonised polemics that were just around the corner.

The Isley Brothers

(Ronald, born May 21, 1941; Rudolph, April 1, 1939; O'Kelly, December 25, 1937; all born Cincinnati, Ohio)

Remarkably, this was a group who were quick to set up their own label and exploit the benefits of leasing recordings to majors; who were at the forefront of absorbing hippie culture into black music disciplines; and who once released, entirely straight-faced, a doo-wop cut of 'The Cow Jumped Over The Moon'. OK, so it was their first record and everybody needs to learn, but at the time they had left home to live in New York and were thus clearly old enough to have known better. But then a lot of what the early Isleys did might have been filed under novelty-dance instructors 'The Snake', 'Surf And Shout', 'Tango', 'Hold On Baby' and so on – all spinning off from their massive R&B hits 'Shout' and 'Twist And Shout'.

They didn't start out as wiggy dance gurus, however. They didn't even start out as a trio. And the most prominent feature of their career is two-year gaps between each flush of success.

In 1955, along with fourth brother Vernon, they broke away from their church choir to tour other churches as a guest quartet – a lucrative business – but stopped for a year after Vernon was killed in a road accident. Coming back as a trio in 1957, they moved to New York and produced 'The Cow Jumped Over The Moon', after which it's surprising it was only two years until their first hit, 'Shout'. This sold a million, attracting serious record company attention, but all that simply led to writers and producers of the Bert Berns and Lieber and Stoller calibre trying to force this raucous threesome into a slick, crossover-oriented package. Again two years passed before they got another sniff of the charts, and then it was with Berns's own composition 'Twist And Shout', a song he figured would bring out the best in them. It also brought out the string of similarly titled sounda-likes that became so much for the Brothers to bear that in 1964 they uppped sticks and started their own label, T-Neck, named after the town in which they were now living – Teaneck, New Jersey.

Not a happy experience. One flop single – 'Testify' now best noted for a pre-fame Jimi Hendrix on guitar. Then nothing, for two years, until Berry Gordy signed them to Motown to team them up with Holland-Dozier-Holland for 'This Old Heart Of Mine', a hit in 1966. But, apart from a UK chart placing for 'Behind A Painted Smile', it was their only hit of note on the label, and after a reasonable amount of time, roughly two years, they left to reactivate T-Neck.

The Isley Brothers were now free to dabble in the rockisms they'd been paying attention to for a few years but were unable to try out: their first album *It's Our Thing* in 1969 made this point with more than the title. It sold over two million and ushered in a new dawn for the thirty-something brothers. ↔

*The Isley Brothers Story, Volume 1: Rockin' Soul (1959–68); Rhino 70908; 1990

Whoever put this album together deserves to sell it, if for no other reason than the sheer hard work involved in compiling twenty tracks from six different record labels. But what it means is a comprehensive collection of the pre-T-Neck Pt II hits, and a few that weren't but are well worth hearing anyway. Like the aforementioned 'Testify', a spirited cover of 'Rock Around The Clock'; and 'Who's That Lady' the foundation stone 'That Lady' was built on almost ten years later. Of course, it's worth the price of a CD just to own 'This Old Heart Of Mine' in glorious digital clarity.

ALSO RECOMMENDED:

*Brothers In Soul, The Early Years; Charly CDCD1107; 1993

A bit of a misleading title, this set ought to be called 'Brothers In Daft Dance Extravaganza'. It's early 1960s stuff, cashing in on 'Twist And Shout' to serve up, among the Bert Berns material, a dozen or so other choppy rhythmed, abandonedly vocal dance 'sensations'. Although the first track 'Twist And Shout' is wonderful, as is 'The Snake' and 'Nobody But Me', and it's New Year's Eve party value is considerable, there's not a lot to be gained from repeated listening to songs with names like 'Spanish Twist', 'Rubber Leg Twist', 'Twisting With Linda' and 'Rockin' McDonald'. What it does give, though, is a good early indication of the Isleys' gift for copping the pop sounds of the day and putting them over with a strong black style in a way that seemed to improve both sides of the coin.

Etta James

(Born Etta Hawkins, Los Angeles, California, January 25, 1938) With one of the biggest, gutsiest R&B voices, Etta James's spiritual and physical resilience is such that she had her biggest hits while bouncing back from a long period of hospitalisation for heroin addiction. It was a career that was never too far away from controversy though, from right back in 1951 when JOHNNY OTIS discovered her and was booking her into LA night clubs at the age of fourteen. Her first single raised a few eyebrows too. In 1955 Otis wrote 'Roll With Me Henry' for her, a direct and bawdy response to HANK BALLARD's 'Work With Me Annie' – but the record company thought that a wee bit too rude so it came out as 'The Wallflower'. Not that anybody seemed to notice, it wasn't a hit.

In fact James had to wait until 1960 for the hits to come, and then, when they did, it was in two clumps – pre- and post-rehab (1960/63 and 1967/69). Although the songs from the second wave, made with Rick Hall at Muscle Shoals, are among the best of that period, it seems that by the time Etta James had achieved the momentum to take it further (the point she was approaching prior to hospitalisation) the world of soul had moved on. It remains open to speculation how far she would have gone if the white horsemen hadn't carried her away in mid-flow. All through the 1970s and onwards, live work showed she still had big soul abilities but nobody took much notice of her intermittent recordings.

*At Last!; Chess 9266; 1960

Etta James's first LP, made after five years of recording and narry a hit among them. And she fairly bursts out of the traps with 'All I Could Do Was Cry', 'My Dearest Darling', 'At Last', 'Stormy Weather' and 'Trust In Me'. Bizarrely, it seems as if she's being pushed towards a pop audience with a full orchestral backing doing its best to sweeten things up. However, the honking brass, red hot R&B rhythm section and the star herself keep it well and truly away from wishy-washy. As the title suggests, there'd been too long a wait for this opportunity to be squandered.

Tell Mama; Chess 9269; 1969

The best of everything she cut at Fame, and here, with the likes of Oldham, Johnson, Spooner, Hood and Hawkins giving it more than merely 'plenty' it's Etta James at her peak. Contained within are the hits 'I'd Rather Go Blind', 'Tell Mama', 'Steal Away' and 'Security', plus 'Just A Little Bit', and 'The Love Of My Man'. Although they're all covers except for the title track, which was written for her by CLARENCE CARTER, there's nothing on this set that doesn't finish up with Owned By Etta James stamped all the way through.

Gladys Knight and the Pips

(Born Atlanta, Georgia, May 28, 1944; The Pips: Merald 'Bubba' Knight; William Guest; Edward Patten)
Maybe it was because she came to Motown late and the corporate pecking order had already been established; or maybe because she was a bit old (at twenty-two) to be promoted as part of the Sound of Young America; or maybe because her group were experienced in the record business and had a fully formed stage act which couldn't readily be moulded into the Motown Way; or maybe because her big, straight up soul voice reminded the executive suite of what they were striving discreetly to distance themselves from. But Gladys Knight never really got the Motown star treatment in anything approaching full effect.

She was only there because, when they were hired on a freelance basis to open the Motown Revues, the response from the crowd was such that putting the group under contract made sense. She'd always been the people's choice: at the age of seven she won $2,000 in an audience vote talent contest. Then from their early teens this extended family group (Merald is her brother, the other two are cousins, as was their first manager James 'Pips' Woods – hence the name) had big hits on small labels with their large, gospel-based vocals, while a stage show that had developed into some of the sharpest-stepped routines made them a popular draw on the live circuit. Even on Motown, where they were on the Soul subsidiary label with JUNIOR WALKER, if they got what wasn't considered premiership material they'd turn it into something quite spectacular – 'I Heard It Through The Grapevine', 'The End Of Our Road', 'Take Me In Your Arms And Love Me'. And cover versions like 'The Nitty Gritty', 'Help Me Make It Through The Night' and 'I Wish It Would Rain' would become their own as the rich old soul tones took over. During the second half of the 1960s, along with Junior Walker and THE FOUR TOPS, Gladys Knight was pig's feet and collard greens on Motown's crusts-cut-off buffet. Although they wore the evening clothes, they were a glorious throwback to that far side of the tracks where The Motown Story started. In 1972, believing they hadn't been getting the support they might have, Gladys Knight & The Pips left Motown. Buddah Records signed them immediately.

*Anthology; Motown 530043; 1993

Goes way back to those pre-Motown records, and right up to 'All I Need Is Time' and 'Neither One Of Us (Wants To Be The First To Say Goodbye)', which were released by the company after the group had left. All that's missing is 'The Nitty Gritty' – a curious omission considering the amount of album tracks and B-sides used to make up the two-CD numbers – and although as time wore on Gladys Knight & The Pips started edging towards the supper club soul of big belting ballads, this is Motown's finest gospeller at her soul tradition peak.

SEE ALSO: Motown Various Artist compilations

Little Milton

(Born Milton Campbell, Inverness, Mississippi, September 7, 1934)

A genuine soul survivor, this man is a walking, singing R&B almanac. As a teenager he backed IKE TURNER in the Kings of Rhythm; he was under contract to Sun through the second half of the 1950s; he signed with Leonard Chess on Checker in 1961; when that company went belly up he shifted to Stax; after the Memphis label went bust in 1976 he stepped over to TK; until they collapsed, when he moved to MCA in the 1980s and from there to Malaco. But all the while he's been making the same slick, oh-so-Southern blues-groove soul he's always done. Indeed, it was during his time at Checker that his records, like 'Grits Ain't Groceries', 'We're Gonna Make It' and 'Who's Cheating Who', were a motivating force in the move towards the soul singing that came out of Stax and Muscle Shoals after large sections of Planet R&B had swung towards rock 'n' roll.

Waiting For Little Milton/Blues 'N' Soul; Stax CDSXD 052; 1992

Two early Stax LPs on the one CD, this shows Milton Campbell taking his raw-boned rural blues approach to a tight Memphis rhythm section and delivering what's best described as cool country funk. Wrap yourself up in 'Tain't Nobody's Biz-ness If I Do', 'That's How Strong My Love Is', 'Hard Luck Blues', 'The Thrill is Gone' and 'Sweet Woman Of Mine'.

ALSO RECOMMENDED:

Blues In The Night; Dillion 2610072; 1992

A selection of Cadet singles.

We're Gonna Make It; Charly CDRED18; 1990

Blues in a soul bag, or is it the other way around? More or less the Best Of Little Milton.

SEE ALSO: (1) Various Artists; *Sweeter Than The Day Before*; Charly CDARC515; (2) Various Artists; *The Art Of The Soul Ballad*; Charly CDCD1096; 1993

The Mad Lads

In the mid-1960s, this Memphis doo-wop group used to be called The Emeralds, but as time wore on and they progressed into R&B and gutsy pre-funk soul, such a handle somehow seemed much too sensible. Although their beautiful close harmonising was never given as distinctive a treatment as, say, Norman Whitfield's with THE TEMPTATIONS around the same time, as one of Stax's top-ranking vocal groups (even if sales never adequately reflected this) they gave the world of synchronised singing some hearty Southern flavour.

*The Mad, Mad, Mad, Mad, Mad Lads/A New Beginning; Stax CDSXD 958; 1990

Two albums from 1969 and 1973 on the same CD, that show the Lads moving into the more gutsily-structured world of post-doo-wop soul harmony, then on to the lush arrangements and big productions that were so much a part of 1970s soul.

SEE ALSO: *Stax Vocal Groups From The '60s & '70s: Just A Little Overcome*; Stax CDSXD019; 1990

Martha & The Vandellas

(Martha Reeves, born, Alabama, July 18, 1941; Annette Stirling; Rosalind Ashford)
As one of the very first Motown girl groups to have hits – only THE MARVELETTES preceded them – the enormous crossover potential of Berry Gordy's musical vision was yet to be realised. In other words, ultra-sophistication hadn't quite become corporate bye-law and this trio was allowed to whoop it up a bit, R&B dance hall style. While theirs wasn't the way that influenced the company's future (in later years Reeves was to complain loud

and long about the preferential treatment Diana Ross appeared to be getting), Martha and the Vandellas were instrumental in establishing the label in the early-1960s as, genuinely, The Voice of Young Black America and not just another wannabe pop fad.

That they signed to the label at all was purely a result of Reeves's patience. The group had split up through lack of success in the late 1950s, and she spent two years as a secretary at Motown, always eager to stand in for absent background singers until she got the chance to put the trio forward as a self-contained backing outfit. After they doo-wopped behind MARVIN GAYE on 'Stubborn Kind Of Fellow' and 'Hitch Hike' they were given a name and a chance, and hit with their second single 'Come And Get These Memories', an uncharacteristically down-tempo number. As their hits progressed through the 1960s, Reeves was the only constant in a line-up that changed with bewildering frequency until the late 1970s. Then, after five barren solo years, Martha re-recruited original Vandellas, Ashford and Sterling, from their day jobs in a hospital and for a phone company, to play a benefit show. It went so well, the trio now tours the nostalgia circuit whenever they can get the time off work.

24 Greatest Hits; Motown 530040; 1991

An essential catalogue of Martha & The Vandellas that covers such magnificence as 'Heatwave', 'Dancing In The Street', 'Jimmy Mack', 'Honey Chile', 'Quicksand' and 'Nowhere To Run'. Spinning them back to back like this, and remembering what an effect they had on the mainstream record buyer, makes you a bit sad that there wasn't room for this sort of raucousness in the Berry Gordy masterplan.

SEE ALSO: Motown Various Artist compilations from the 1960s

The Marvelettes

(Gladys Horton; Georgia Dobbins; Georgeanna Tillman; Katherine Anderson; Juanita Cowart; Wanda Young)
In spite of what you may have read about THE SUPREMES, in all ways this sextet – who were among the very first Motown

hitmakers – were the epitome of that well-publicised Motown Dream: teenage schoolfriends from the Detroit housing projects, they would sing for amusement until they won an audition at Motown as a first prize in a local talent contest. They are also a fine example of how the Motown work ethic sometimes failed to take into account how young and naive many of their acts were. After the first run of hits, one of the group had left through ill-health and another had had a nervous breakdown. They were not yet into their twenties. And their stop-start career serves to illustrate how the company would forget about certain acts to concentrate on others: The Marvelettes were more or less shelved during 1963 and 1964 while the company got behind The Supremes. It was only after that trio was up and running by the mid-1960s that The Marvelettes started to get the support from songs and promotion that was needed to push them back into the charts in the middle of the decade. At the moment it's commonplace to see The Marvelettes in cabaret, quite often in more than one place at the same time. There are several groups of middle-aged black women operating under the name, but none of them contain members with any genuine claim to the moniker.

23 Greatest Hits; Motown 530041; 1990

From the very beginning up to 'My Baby Must Be A Magician', this compilation shows just how brittle the Motown Sound was in its very early days, not yet big enough in the production department to be able to bolster up voices as young and untrained as these. The Marvelettes got round it with the novel step of using two lead vocalists, at the same time. It works, to combine with the infectious optimism of the early hits, to produce a series of tracks that remain impossible to ignore. You try and sit still with 'Please Mr Postman' playing loud in the same room.

SEE ALSO: Motown Various Artist compilations from the 1960s

The Meters/The Neville Brothers

(Aaron Neville, vocals, born January 24, 1941; Art Neville, vocals/piano, December 17, 1938; Charles Neville, sax, December 28, 1939; Cyril Neville, percussion/vocals, January 10, 1950 – all born in New Orleans, Louisiana; Ziggy Modeliste, drums; George Porter, bass; Leo Nocentelli, guitar)

Since 1977 onwards, The Neville Brothers' Cresent City soul singing has charmed the rock establishment to such a degree that Keith Richards, Carlos Santana and Jerry Garcia play on their albums and by the end of the 1980s mainstream support was such they were enjoying enormous commercial recognition. But twenty years before that, as Stax, Atlantic and Motown were on the wane, The Meters played the most singularly kicking small band funk there was, more or less creating a prototype for what was to come in the 1970s. Before that, in 1966, they had marked their place in soul music history after Aaron's achingly beautiful million-selling single 'Tell It Like It Is' was taken up as a Black Power anthem.

With a combined history that involves a stretch in prison for car theft, a marriage at fourteen, a spell in the US Navy and local R&B groups, the Nevilles came together as The Neville Sounds in the mid-1960s, with Modeliste, Porter and Nocentelli, backing Aaron on his single 'Tell It Like It Is'. By the time the band split, Charles had already moved to New York, then Aaron and Cyril departed, leaving Art and the rhythm section to rename themselves The Meters. As a New Orleans top soul session crew, they figured on most of ALLEN TOUSSAINT and Marshall Sehorn's sessions, only starting to record as themselves in 1969. It's now that the group's syncopated, sharply clipped rhythm patterns defined the new soul's stripped down mood. While as it often gave way to sly, hypnotic, slightly left-of-centre groove, it laid down guidelines for the odd, rock-influenced overlays that were to figure large in their music.

Their big time only really lasted a couple of years after their biggest hit, the crisply funky 'Cissy Strut' in 1969, before the rest of the brothers were back in the fold by 1976 and the focus had switched to vocals. The Meters had moved mountains in terms of advancing the music – perhaps more so even than BOOKER T & THE MGS in the previous decade, as this group had aggressively stated the case for the soul instrumental as a valid form, not merely as an alternative to a vocal version, but to put an instrument up in your face with as much right to be there as, say, Otis Redding. It was a major opening of possibilities that went a long way to creating the right environment for funk.

Funky Miracle; Charly CDNEV2; 1991

All The Meters hits on two CDs. Strung together like this, the bridge they form between traditional Southern soul and modern-day, very urban funk is entirely obvious. And the use of lead instrumentation above the chopped out beats are probably closer to what the New York bands did in the mid-1970s than James Brown, who is usually assumed to take total responsibility. That's the theory, and it's probably best not to worry about it too much, just shake the room with 'Cissy Strut', 'Ease Back', 'Look Ka Py Py', 'Here Comes The Meterman', 'Sing A Simple Song' . . .

Uptown Rulers (Live On The Queen Mary!); Sequel NEXCD220; 1992

Maybe the best way to sum up this seriously tight set is to say The Meters take Bread's 'I Want To Make It With You', steep it in New Orleans funk, and turn it into something you actually want to hear. More than once. This is the band in 1975 at their rocking best, lashing their noisily appreciative audience with music, as they literally scorch into 'Fire On The Bayou', turn out a deadly groove on 'Africa' and roll 'Cissy Strut' and 'Cardova' together for a lethal extended play.

ALSO RECOMMENDED:

Original Funkmasters; Charly CDINS5066

The group's finest moments, just less of them than on *Funky Miracle*.

Legacy: A History Of The Nevilles; Charly CDNEV1; 1990

Two-disc compilation that puts together early Art and Aaron Neville solo stuff and a selection of The Meters' best. Although 'Tell It Like It Is' is included here and is a song worth dying for, this remains an interesting rather than vital album.

Willie Mitchell

(Born Ashland, Mississippi, 1928)
The other side of the Memphis soul scene was Hi Records, a
lower profile outfit that had scored a few hits with country
blues by the likes of Ace Cannon and Bill Black (Elvis Presley's
original bass player), but went on to define black Southern Soul
in the 1970s courtesy of AL GREEN, OV Wright, Ann Peebles, SYL
JOHNSON and Otis Clay. Before all that though was Willie
Mitchell, a trumpeter-turned-producer/arranger who during
the previous decade had created the signature swirling organ,
phat brass, swaying sound.

   Mitchell came to the label in 1961, after running his own local
band that at one time or another included half of Booker T's
MGs and numbered Steve Cropper and Donald 'Duck' Dunn
among its followers. Originally, he worked with Cannon and
Black, but as he became more established and started recording
his own instrumental albums he shaped and honed his own
band into an in-house unit to rival those more illustrious ses-
sioneers across town. By the end of the decade he had, quite literally, changed the face of Hi Records as he built up the roster
of talent that was to take the company into the 1970s, and in
1969 all but stopped recording himself to devote time to his new
discovery Al Green. The unique Hi sound he developed came
about through a regular seven-piece horn section – large even
for those days – and deliberately smoothing out the organ
instead of pushing it towards the percussion fill end of things.
When layered on top of the solid, stepping beat and echoes by
the equally melodic wall of horns, it produced a low down,
rather sanctified sound that spoke volumes of Southern
churches and steamy goings on under ceiling-fans. It was at
once far more adult and culturally reminiscent than the hometown flavour it was replacing, and thus fitted perfectly into the
mood of black America during the next ten years.

That Driving Beat; Hi HIUKLP408; 1987

A collection of Mitchell's best sides, mostly recorded during the
second half of the 1960s, during his transformation from marginally countrified R&B to a Memphis soul sound worthy to

take up Booker T's baton. An utterly accurate title, for a set featuring 'Soul Serenade', '20–75', 'Percolatin'' and 'The Crawl'.

ALSO RECOMMENDED:

Solid Soul + Soul On Top; Hi HIUKCD120; 1968/1969

Two late albums on the same disc, mixing up covers and originals to show off Mitchell's gift for layered arrangement to the very best. Includes a compulsively souled-up version of Cream's acid blues 'Sunshine Of Your Love'.

SEE ALSO: *Hi Records: The R&B Sessions + The Soul Years*; Hi HIUKCD 129; 1991

The Orioles

(Original line-up: Sonny Til, born Earl Tilghman, died 1981; George Nelson, died 1968; Alexander Sharp, died 1959; Johnny Reed; Tommy Gaither, died 1950)

Formed in the late-1940s by Earlington 'Sonny Til' Tilghman (who remained a constant in various line-ups for nearly forty years), The Orioles were one of the earliest examples of a tight harmony group approaching doo-wop balladeering from a pure gospel point of view, instead of deliberately smoothing out the soul, hoping to create an instant crossover hit. They remained true too. While the proliferation of later harmonisers adopted a pale pop stance and, except for very few, had sporadic success, The Orioles stayed black and, during the first half of the 1950s, swooped and soared uninhibitedly to a succession of mesmerisingly beautiful hits. More an influence on than actually part of the accepted idea of soul, but none the less important to the big picture.

Greatest Hits; Collectables 5014; 1987

Fourteen tracks and nothing the specialist won't already own, but an excellent Orioles' calling card for the keen amateur. Includes 'Crying In The Chapel', 'It's Too Soon To Know', 'What Are You Doing New Year's Eve' and 'It's Gonna Be A Lonely Christmas'.

Johnny Otis

(Born John Veliotes, Vallejo, California, December 28, 1921)
In spite of Johnny Otis's best-known records being little more than rock 'n' roll-ish novelties, as a catalyst and talent scout his fingerprints appear on so much early soul. After the early 1940s spent touring the West Coast playing vibes or piano with visiting big bands, he set up The Barrelhouse Club in the black Los Angeles district of Watts, as a venue for his newly formed band and a showcase for new talent. *The Johnny Otis Show* gave the first break to, among others, ETTA JAMES, Esther Phillips, T-Bone Walker, Lowell Fulson and The Coasters when they were still The Robins. Such was the operation's success, King Records employed him as A&R, where he signed JACKIE WILSON and HANK BALLARD, and put Leiber and Stoller on Big Mama Thornton's case – the first song they wrote for her was 'Hound Dog'. So whether there's any *Johnny Otis Show* soul on CD or not, there would be a whole lot less by other people if he hadn't been there to start off with.

Freda Payne

(Born Detroit, Michigan, September 19, 1942)
A schoolfriend of Eddie and Brian Holland, Freda Payne tried out for Motown in the very early days, but didn't hang about because she wanted to be a jazz singer and believed R&B to be somewhat beneath her. After the 1960s spent touring with the likes of Louis Bellson, Duke Ellington and Lionel Hampton, but little personal success, she teamed up with the Hollands and Lamont Dozier at their Invictus label to bring her marvellously disciplined voice to bear on the smash hits 'Band Of Gold', 'Deeper And Deeper', 'Cherish What Is Dear To You' and 'Bring The Boys Home', a million-selling anti-Viet Nam number.

Deeper And Deeper (The Best Of); HDH HDHCD005; 1990

Twenty-two tracks on the one CD is probably more Freda Payne than most people thought existed. Not too many of them are wasted either. At this point, and with a female singer who had a serious set of lungs, Holland-Dozier-Holland were keen to prove there was a viable alternative to the diva-dom that was going on elsewhere in Detroit. Thus Freda's large, blue-tinged voice wraps itself round a set of what are really torch songs with attitude to put some real soul into pop soul. Much the same point the trio made with The Four Tops a few years previously. You've got to ask questions as to whether Freda Payne quite warranted her 'Diana Ross of Invictus Records' handle, but 'Band Of Gold', 'Deeper And Deeper' and 'Cherish What Is Dear To You' are enough to make anybody take notice.

SEE ALSO: Various Artists; *Holland-Dozier-Holland Present The Hits Of Invictus & Hot Wax*; HDH HDHCD501; 1986

Wilson Pickett

(Born March 18, 1941, Prattville, Alabama)
The Wicked Pickett. Hardly an inappropriate moniker either, as he was one of the most exciting soul singers ever to stalk a stage, quite literally hurling himself into songs with a gusto that went way beyond the words into a repertoire of yelps, grunts and screams (it wasn't unusual for him to writhe on the floor as a supplement to vocal expression). This enthusiasm came over on plastic too, ending up in a string of late-1960s hits. While off-stage Wickedness involved a reputation for the ladies and a temper quick enough to mean many an exchange of ideas would be settled with a fist fight.

Moving to Detroit as a child, the teenage Pickett sung gospel in The Violinaires before being invited to join local R&B group THE FALCONS after he was heard singing outside his parents' house (MICHAEL JACKSON's father Joe was one of The Falcons' guitarists). The group had no huge success, so in 1963 he quit as lead singer to go solo and, two years later, after three flop singles on LLOYD PRICE's Double L label, was signed to Atlantic. Success wasn't immediate there either, and it took two lacklustre records to convince Jerry Wexler that this singer needed something to work off. He took Pickett to the Stax Studios in Memphis (Atlantic owned Stax by then) and put himself in charge of sessions that were backed by BOOKER T & THE MGS: among the first songs they cut is a Pickett/Steve Cropper composition 'In The Midnight Hour' and as it went top twenty in both the US and the UK, so Wilson Pickett became the Voice of Sixties Soul. Official.

'Don't Fight It', '634 5789' and 'Ninety Nine And A Half (Won't Do)' followed, but Pickett really hit his stride in 1966 when they moved him to Muscle Shoals to work at Rick Hall's Fame Studios. And the edginess that pervades those recordings is rather understandable – the self-styled Wicked One would much rather not have been there. He told an interviewer that when the plane was coming in to land he could see black folks picking cotton, memories of his Southern childhood flooded back and he wanted out. When on the ground he saw Rick Hall, a huge, mean-looking white man, waiting to meet him – he thought it was the law. Although he and Hall became firm friends, he maintains that if he'd seen a picture of him first he wouldn't have made the trip. And the world would have been without 'Land Of 1000 Dances', 'Mustang Sally', 'Everybody Needs Somebody To Love', 'I Found A Love' and 'Funky Funky Broadway'.

When that was over later that same year, he went back to Memphis to work with Chips Moman and BOBBY WOMACK, but the hits were thinning out as the old southern soul sound started to change. Indeed it must be said that Old Wilson tried to change too – in what can only be assumed to be a nod to the Woodstock times, he cut a series of rock-like tracks under the guidance of The Allman Bros' Duane. Ill advised? The only one to do anything was a cover of 'Hey Jude', and the less said about The Wicked Pickett's version of The Archies' 'Sugar Sugar' the better. In fact all that stretched his reputation into the next decade was *Pickett In Philadelphia* ('Engine Number 9' and 'Don't Let The Green Grass Fool You'), an entirely empathetic production by Kenny Gamble and Leon Huff, who were utterly in tune with what had been before, but at the same time knew where soul had to go. Then came street funk and disco – the Voice of the Sixties was becoming increasingly out of step with the seventies. Even a deal with Motown in 1988 failed to restart a career that now concerns itself mostly with nostalgia tours, firearms offences and alcohol-fuelled brawls.

The Sound Of Wilson Pickett; Atlantic 2379; 1967

The Wicked One's fourth LP takes bits from the album before and grafts them on to new material, but in effect puts together a truly classic 1960s soul album. It's all Muscle Shoals recordings, with Tom Dowd, Jerry Wexler and Rick Hall in charge and the studio band of apparent rednecks that had stirred so many preconceptions in the visiting stars are blowing up a storm on every number. Only when playing with fire in the belly could you hope to keep pace with a Pickett whose vocals pull so hard on his gospel roots they add up to what must have been an out-of-body experience. Contained – if that's the right word – within are 'Mustang Sally', 'Everybody Needs Somebody To Love', 'Knock On Wood', 'She Ain't Gonna Do Right' and 'Up Tight Good Woman'. Enough said?

A Man And A Half; Rhino 70287; 1992

A two-CD set that'll give you absolutely everything you've ever wanted by Wilson Pickett in forty-four tracks, from 'I Found A Love' with The Falcons, up to the Philly tracks and taking in some of the lamentable cod-psychedelic cover versions of the very late 1960s. (That's the trouble with 'everything you want', too often there's much you don't need.) But that said, the well-known tracks – all the Atlantic hits feature – are supplemented with less characteristic almost smoochy songs such as 'Let Me Be Your Boy', 'I'm In Love' and 'Jealous Love', plus the inspired likes of 'Minnie Skirt Minnie' and 'Three Time Loser' that never really made it to the UK's turntables. Playing the first disc (up to 1967) through, it's a joy listening to the Pickett pipes evolve from pure gospel to a grade-one screamer to a sometimes rather subtle soulster. A fitting approach to the Voice of the Sixties.

The Best Of Wilson Pickett; Atlantic 81283; 1968

Twelve early Atlantic tracks, 'In The Midnight Hour', 'Mustang Sally', 'Land Of 1000 Dances', '634 5789' among them, but, good as it is, this set will never be anything more than a trailer for *A Man And A Half*.

SEE ALSO: Atlantic Various Artist compilations

The Platters

(Tony Williams, lead vocals, born Elizabeth, New Jersey, April 5, 1928; David Lynch, vocals; Paul Robi, vocals; Herb Reed, vocals; Zola Taylor, vocals.)

During the Second World War, the black population of Los Angeles increased three-fold as manufacturing jobs, inexpensive housing and a relatively liberal atmosphere attracted migrants from all across the South. It was these original 'settlers' who established the black communities of Watts and Compton – now known as South Central – and had children that grew up to provide the city with a wealth of doo-wop singing talent during the 1950s. Although more 'soulful' than the accepted notion of 'soul', this style provided a glossy urban counterpoint to the rawer rural blues that became R&B and is the beginning of the bridge between the first rock 'n' roll – a black form – and soul-as-we-came-to-know-it. Among the best of the black doo-wop crop were The Rivingtons, The Turks, The Olympics, The Penguins, The Robins and The Lamplighters, but The Platters were far and away the most successful of that era.

The group were put together by Williams in 1953, and while singing in clubs as an all-male quartet were signed by Buck Ram, The Penguins' manager. During the next year, Robi replaced one member and Taylor joined to increase the breadth of their range. In 1955 Mercury Records wanted to sign The Penguins after their 'Earth Angel' sold a million on an independent label. Ram agreed on the condition they put The Platters under contract too. Their debut single 'Only You (And You Alone)' got to number 5 in the US, while the follow up, 'The Great Pretender', topped that chart for two weeks. It convinced Ram that the group had enormous potential as ballad specialists and so a career was born.

A career that lasted into the next decade, put thirty-five records into the charts, survived a sex scandal when the male members were caught, kit off, with three nineteen-year-old white girls (this was 1959); and very nearly got past the departure of Tony Williams in 1961. By then, though, times had changed. They left Mercury in 1963 and their last big record was the Motown-influenced 'With This Ring' four years later.

Magic Touch – The Platters Anthology; Mercury 510314; 1991

A two-CD, fifty-track set with all the group's Mercury hits – 'Only You', 'Smoke Gets In Your Eyes', 'Goodnight Sweetheart', 'Sixteen Tons', 'My Prayer', 'The Great Pretender', you know the drill – the best of the B-sides, Tony Williams's solo single, a sprinkling of album cuts and surprisingly little dross.

Lloyd Price

(Born Kenner, Louisiana, March 9, 1934)
If there was a point in the second half of the 1950s at which the post-war, small-group black music style split definitively into R&B and rock 'n' roll then that point was probably Lloyd Price. Based in New Orleans, he'd already staked his claim to the latter style in 1952 when he developed 'Lawdy Miss Clawdy' from a radio jingle he'd written. When he came out of the Army in 1956, he brought all the Cresent City's honky tonk tradition to bear on a series of riveting black dance tunes that hit at the very roots of the goodtime urban blues ethic. Even the pop ones were funky. Also, the man had the ears to recognise something special when he heard it, he signed WILSON PICKETT to his Double L label as far back as 1963.

Lawdy!; Specialty 7010; 1985

A truly classic set that rips through twenty-five tracks as if the band and Price are just playing for themselves – they have to be, R&B of this power, in this concentration, isn't so much a commercial proposition as a potentially lethal weapon. 'Lawdy Miss Clawdy', 'Mailman Blues', 'What's The Matter Now', 'Carry Me Home' . . . If you only ever buy one Lloyd Price album it should be this one. If you still think you need another one then make sure your insurance policies are paid up.

ALSO RECOMMENDED:

Lloyd Price; MCA 1503; 1960

Late-1950s hits, veering into the novelty at times, yet it adds up to a three-dimensional snapshot of what he was about.

Otis Redding

(Born September 9, 1941, Dawson, Georgia)

One-time Little Richard impersonator on the Macon, Ga, club circuit, Redding attempted to get into the music business in Los Angeles in 1960 and ended up working in a car wash. Returning home he rejoined one of his teenage groups – as their chauffeur, taking no more than the occasional singing spot. Which is exactly how he got signed to the Stax subsidiary Volt in 1963: while ferrying the same band, The Pinetoppers, to a session at the label's Memphis studios, the non-productive recording was finished early and Redding persuaded Stax owner Jim Stewart to let him step up to the microphone in the remaining, already paid for, time. One of the two songs he recorded was the self-penned 'These Arms Of Mine', and, in not much more time than it took to play the tape back, Otis Redding came out from behind the wheel and into a recording contract.

Over the next four years, Redding was to define Southern soul, chiselling it from raw-form R&B, sifting out the increasingly awkward rock 'n' rollisms and always remembering its rural roots. The singer's phrasing, timing and inflection were unique, giving vent to an emotional combination of pleading, resignation and dented optimism, that never really changed, yet nobody ever got tired of. Quite simply, such was his talent that every song sounded fresh. He wrote far more songs, for both himself and others, than many people realise.

That first recording was also his first US hit, although three years passed before the UK took any notice – and then, instead of a homegrown, Southern-fried Stax-stormer, it was with a cover of a previous big hit, THE TEMPTATIONS' SMOKEY ROBINSON-penned 'My Girl'. Maybe the Great British public hadn't been quite ready for the real deal, but once they'd made their minds up Redding was to do, relatively, better in this country than he did in the US: indeed, a mere four months after that first hit, the TV show *Ready Steady Go!* devoted a whole episode to his live performance.

But just as he had cracked the European market, Redding would continually try to expand his horizons: in 1966 he started his own production company, Jotis, and among its early successes was Redding's production of 'Sweet Soul Music' for ARTHUR CONLEY. In 1967 he teamed up with RUFUS THOMAS's daughter CARLA for the hit album of duets *King and Queen*, and in June of that year, he successfully took his unadulterated sound to a white hippy audience, as he performed a rousing (and rousingly received) set at that high acid rock weekender The Montery Pop Festival.

Then, on December 10, 1967, a twin-engined plane carrying Otis Redding and THE BAR-KAYS to a concert, went down in one of Wisconsin's freezing lakes. Only one of the band survived. Carrying Otis Redding's coffin were JOE TEX, SOLOMON BURKE, PERCY SLEDGE, JOE SIMON, JOHNNIE TAYLOR, Don Covay and Sam Moore. His career had lasted four and a half years from his first hit (about the time taken between albums by today's big league) and he went on to sell more records after his death than he ever did when he was alive.

Otis Blue; Atlantic 7567-80318; 1966

Otis Redding's first UK chart album, this record is claimed to be *the* Soul Album of the 1960s. And nobody's going to get an argument from me on that. Although the title would point toward the less extrovert end of the Otis Redding spectrum – i.e. deep *deep* sorrow – it was his most varied set up to that point, maybe because it only includes three self-compositions and otherwise draws on a range of writers. In mixing up a fairly faithful reading of 'My Girl' with 'Respect', 'Wonderful World', 'Shake', 'Satisfaction', 'You Don't Miss Your Water', 'Rock Me Baby' and 'Down In The Valley', it shows the Redding style to be just as inspired coming from either a rock, R&B, blues, gospel or just plain party point of view. And that's without mentioning the masterpiece that is 'I've Been Loving You Too Long'. True, it's not too cheerful, but by itself it's worth the price of a CD. Then there's the most frequently overlooked aspect of this LP, which is the towering contribution made by his regular backing band. In fact, it's with such inspiration that they support and spur on their leader, that *Otis Blue* could, hand on heart, be described as Booker T & The MGs' greatest record.

Pain In My Heart; Atlantic ATCO80253; 1967

A dozen of the deepest Southern soul stirrers, made up of the earliest Redding recordings on Atlantic. Equally balanced between cover versions such as 'Lucille', 'The Dog', 'Pain In My Heart' and 'You Send Me' and originals like that first hit, 'Something Is Worrying Me' and 'Hey Hey Baby' (the other song he recorded at that try-out session) it shows that before the singer was niche-marketed as Mr Pitiful, he could take it far wider and still keep it unique.

Otis! The Definitive Otis Redding; Atlantic 8122-71439

A four-CD box set that truly lives up to its subtitle, and in it's lavish packaging and comprehensive booklet seems less of a shock to the wallet (don't expect much change out of a fifty). It's all here, right from the word go. Every key track in Otis Redding's brief career, with the puzzling exception of that first UK hit 'My Girl' – no, the reading of it on the *Otis Live* disc simply doesn't count. But other than that, start at the Little Richard wannabes 'She's Alright' and 'Shout Bamalama' and move as slowly as possible through to the countrified classic that became Otis Redding's epitaph, the posthumously released 'Dock Of The Bay'. In between is a heartwarming journey through the very best the South had to offer.

With Carla Thomas; King And Queen; Atlantic 7567-82256; 1967

Like one of those rapidly-becoming-regulation Motown couplings, but with all the rough edges put back on, Carla proved she could tear it up as good as any guy, while Otis, if not actually intimidated, was determined not to give an inch. It's what would come to be called sexual chemistry, but back in the day it was just two singers in a good-natured, wholly respectful but serious-as-a-heart-attack cutting contest as they brought songs like 'Bring It On Home To Me', 'It Takes Two', 'Tell It Like It Is' and 'Knock On Wood' to life. But vividly. And even then nothing could have prepared the listener for the battle royale they made out of Tramp.

Otis Redding Live In Europe; Atco 80318; 1967

Recorded on the 1967 Stax/Volt European tour (played Hammersmith Odeon and Finsbury Park Astoria), this is a stunning example of an old-time soul show in full flow – Redding used to top so many Best Vocalist polls in Europe, it felt he put something extra into shows there. The twelve tracks include 'Can't Turn You Loose', 'Try A Little Tenderness' and 'I've Been Loving You Too Long'.

Remember Me; Stax 8572; 1989

A posthumous LP that has nothing to do with the terms 'rip off' or 'cash in'. Among the previously unreleased material are alternative takes of 'Dock Of The Bay', 'I've Got Dreams To Remember' and 'Try A Little Tenderness', and some totally funky covers including 'Cupid' and 'There Goes My Baby'.

ALSO RECOMMENDED:

It's Not Just Sentimental; Stax CDSXD041; 1990

The 'missing' tapes. All previously unissued material, featuring alternative takes, out-takes, covers and a direct cut of 'Stay In School'.

The Immortal Otis Redding; Atco 80270; 1968

Steve Cropper produced, taken from the 'Dock Of The Bay' sessions and expanding the style into such songs as 'I've Got Dreams To Remember' and 'Hard To Handle'.

Love Man; Rhino 70294; 1969

More from the last sessions, recommended for a spirited reading of 'Your Love Has Lifted Me Higher'.

SEE ALSO: Stax/Atlantic Various Artist compilations

Smokey Robinson & The Miracles

(William 'Smokey' Robinson, Detroit, Michigan, February, 1940; Ronnie White; Pete Moore; Bobby Rogers; Marv Tarplin, guitarist) 'I had composed over a hundred songs by that time. Berry [Gordy] tore each one apart and showed me what was wrong with them. Then he told me how to develop a basic plot and stick to it. He explained how every song should be a complete story. Berry Gordy has been the greatest thing that ever happened to me.'

Smokey Robinson's memories of his first days as an eighteen-year-old novice songwriter at the fledgling Motown Records. But he did his bit for Berry Gordy too: The Miracles' contract with End Records and their first single 'Got A Job', co-written by Gordy and Robinson and an R&B number, was what pushed Gordy into giving up his day job at the Ford production line to go into music full time; The Miracles' 'Shop Around' in 1961 was Motown's first pop hit; and as a songwriter and producer, in spite of Berry Gordy's early critique of his work, Smokey Robinson advanced Motown music from lightweight R&B to an innovative pop soul force – he is the direct link between Motown's popularist vocal approach of the mid-1960s and the previous decade's black doo-wop tradition. Or maybe that was *because of* his new boss's harsh words, as a singular mainstream selling point of Robinson's writing was his lyrics, concerning themselves more with narrative storytelling than with just what the words sounded like, which is the true scat-rooted black doo-wop way that has continued right up to rap.

As much as Berry Gordy was the businessman, in those early days Smokey Robinson was the artistic base upon which Motown Records was built. In 1957, Robinson, a celebrated high school basketball and football player, opted against a career in sport to concentrate on the other talent that was getting him noticed – singing. He and his group of schoolfriends, having changed their name from The Matadors to the Miracles, were turned down by JACKIE WILSON's manager, who suggested them to Berry Gordy, the man who wrote 'Reet Petite' and wanted to be a manager. Within two years of Motown's founding, Smokey Robinson, still only in his twenties, was writing, producing and arranging songs for the growing roster of young artists. Presumably with the dressing down from Gordy still in his mind, Robinson's songs became mini-operas of emotional narrative, while the music was equally dramatic: he was the nearest thing Motown had to Phil Spector, creating lush orchestral gestures, sweeping strings into peaks and troughs, utilising deft rhythmic devices to pace and climax internal movements, while some of the most startling tone and tempo changes ensured the story's flow stayed interesting. It was over this he set vocal arrangements of pure doo-wop, then pushed them harder and harder to keep up with what was going on behind them. He would go for strength rather than covering the entire scale as the music would plug any holes.

Robinson was largely responsible for THE TEMPTATIONS' ground-breaking style, and THE MARVELETTES, MARVIN GAYE and MARY WELLS all owe him and his magic pen a great deal. But on a more general level, Smokey Robinson's willingness to experiment with arrangements and vocal/musical balance did much to move harmony singing into the 1960s and by doing so establish Motown as The Sound of Young Black America. At that time, as Civil Rights gained momentum, the idea of a traditional black street-corner style (doo-wop) assimilating the sophistication of downtown night clubs, yet still being controlled by a black man in Detroit, was very attractive. Of course he had his own successes too. Since 'Shop Around' earned Motown its first gold disc, Smokey's falsetto led the group to some two dozen US top forty hits before he left the group to go solo in 1972. Always performed to a unique, ballet-like choreography – unlike other groups of the day, The Miracles sang round one mic, and would thus would move in a triangular configuration instead of in line, a delicately timed joy to watch – these hits include some milestones in modern-day soul: 'Tracks Of My Tears', 'Abraham, Martin & John', 'You've Really Got A Hold On Me', 'I Second That Emotion' and 'Tears Of A Clown'. ↦

*The 35th Anniversary Collection; Motown 37463-6334; 1994

At around forty quid for a four-CD set, this might prove too much Smokey for some people, and they'd probably have a point. While Robinson may have written ninety-seven brilliant songs for other people, he didn't record anywhere near as many for himself, thus putting that number out back to back like this was bound to end in tears. And it does. By disc four (into the 1970s and beyond The Miracles) his chaste, lightweight love ditties are sounding worryingly wet when set against what else was going on ('Let Me Be The Clock'!). However, as so little Smokey

Robinson is available on CD in the UK, this is the best way into a comprehensive romp through the group's 1950s and 1960s.

The first disc (up to 1961) contains more almost straight doo-wop than any other style, and shows the Smoke's songwriting developing and the group's vocal patterns changing. Then discs two and three are the best of what he blossomed into as the hits are supplemented by the better album tracks and B-sides, some so long-forgotten they might as well be new. As to even approach this level of Smokedom would involve buying the double CD *Anthology*, currently only available on import and therefore not much under £35 (and that doesn't have this one's handsome packaging and lavish sixty-four-page booklet) maybe *The 35th Anniversary Collection* isn't such a bad deal after all.

The Greatest Hits; Motown 530121; 1992

Like the above but less so, this is the only other Smokey Robinson & The Miracles CD on catalogue in Great Britain. While it's got 'Going To A Go-Go', 'Tears Of A Clown', 'Tracks Of My Tears', 'You've Really Got A Hold On Me' and 'I Second That Emotion', it's up against *35th Anniversary*, so it's really just a taster.

ALSO RECOMMENDED:

Tears Of A Clown; Motown 5156; 1965

Readily available import of the re-issued Tamla album featuring 'My Girl', 'More, More, More Of Your Love', 'Hunter Gets Captured By The Game' and 'I'm The One You Need'.

Going To A Go-Go; Motown 5269; 1964

Likewise, in from the USA, and containing some of the group's best: 'Tracks Of My Tears', 'Ooh Ooh Baby', 'My Girl Has Gone' and the title track.

(Up until a few years ago these two albums were on release in this country on the same CD. It's still possible to find a copy.)

SEE ALSO: Motown Various Artist compilations

Sam & Dave

(Sam Moore, born October 12, 1935, Miami, Florida; Dave Prater, May 9, 1937, Ocilla, Georgia)

One night in 1958, professional singer Moore was performing in a Miami night club, when the uninvited, somewhat exuberant Prater, a member of the audience, jumped on stage to join him for a couple of numbers. Surprisingly, the twosome clicked, the crowd loved it and Dave was asked to come back and stage-invade the next night. And the next. And so the duo that would come to be known as Double Dynamite was born.

After a couple of years playing clubs, developing their foot-stomping 'preachin' and singin' ', and an unsuccessful stint on Roulette Records where their none-too-special gospel-based R&B material never lived up to the excitement they could create on stage, the pair signed to Atlantic. There, they were immediately despatched to Memphis to record as part of the company's newly acquired Stax set up. Which means ISAAC HAYES and David Porter wrote and produced for them, while BOOKER T & THE MGS played their music and everything fell into place. The result was, quite simply, the most storming twosome ever to explode on to vinyl – the nickname was not just a snappy alliteration – with a flow of hits that took them from 'You Don't Know Like I Know' in 1966 to 'Soul Sister Brown Sugar' in 1969 and an acrimonious split in 1970.

It was no secret that, as time went on, Sam and Dave grew to hate the sight of each other, so when solo success eluded them and they were forced occasionally to reform to trot out the old hits as a means of paying the bills, they would tour without actually speaking to each other. In 1987, Prater was fined and put on probation after being caught selling crack cocaine, and on April 9, 1988, he was killed when the car he was driving left the road and hit a tree. Meanwhile, Sam still tours using a succession of substitute 'Daves'.

*Hold On, I'm Comin'; Atlantic 80255; 1966

The duo's Atlantic debut, and even in a vocal style as committed to the idea of giving a song absolutely everything, you can hear a raw enthusiasm that didn't make it to the next set, *Double*

Dynamite. This more or less reproduces their stage act – which, remember, hadn't gone far beyond the oh-so-funky ghetto club scene – for the benefit of the tape recorder and in its wild unsophistication it drew a new set of guidelines for aspirant soul singers. Included here are 'You Don't Know Like I Know', 'I Got Everything I Need', 'I Take What I Want', 'Ease Me' and, naturally, the true soul classic title track.

*Sweat & Soul: Anthology 1968–1971; Rhino 812271253; 1994

Everything you've ever wanted from Sam and Dave. On one handy double-CD set. 'Soul Man', 'Soothe Me', 'You Got Me Hummin'', 'I Thank You', 'Soul Sister Brown Sugar', 'You Don't Know Like I Know', 'Hold On I'm Comin'', 'Soothe Me', 'You Don't Know What You Mean To Me' . . . alongside the lower profile likes of 'When Something Is Wrong With My Baby', 'A Place Nobody Can Find', 'Said I Wasn't Gonna Tell Nobody' and 'Can't Stand Up For Falling Down'.

SEE ALSO: (1) Various Artists; *This Is Soul*; Object FPFCD01; 1989; (2) Stax/Atlantic Various Artist compilations

Percy Sledge

(Born Leighton, Alabama, 1941)
When, late in 1965, this former hospital porter and part-time singer – formerly of gospel group The Singing Clouds and later doo-woppers The Esquires – made the trip to Rick Hall's Fame Studios and cut 'When A Man Loves A Woman' as an audition demo, even the heard-it-all-before session crew, including Chips Moman, Dan Penn and Spooner Oldham, were staggered. Close to tears even. The kid had a soul voice so slow and heavy it might have been standing still, but the depth of emotion wrung out at the mic was almost supernatural. It seems the rest of the world agreed, and Percy Sledge's debut Atlantic single went to number 1 in the US and sold millions all over the world. It was the start of a three-year relationship with Muscle Shoals that resulted in some of the most devastating deep soul records ever to melt a turntable. He flowed over such master-

pieces as 'Warm And Tender Love', 'It Tears Me Up', 'Out Of Left Field' and 'Dark End Of The Street', but was unable to move on so when the style became *passé* he was swiftly consigned to that drawer marked 'nostalgia'.

The Ultimate Collection; Atlantic 80212; 1991

Percy Sledge stayed with Atlantic until 1974, and this twenty-track collection goes up to 'Sunshine' (later a hit for the O'Jays) in 1973. When put back to back like this – over an hour of concentrated Percy – the intensity is almost damaging, but its an ideal situation to let the listener immerse themselves in that voice and drift off to a better place. It's also a fine spot from which to observe Atlantic soul's relationship to country music: while his gospel roots were undeniable, there were few on the label with more straw on their vocal chords than Percy Sledge. The collection includes all his hits, plus the less successful but no less desirable numbers such as 'You're Pouring Water On A Drowning Man', 'Cover Me' and 'I Had A Talk With My Woman Last Night', and has four bonus tracks not on the vinyl ('Sudden Stop', 'That's How Strong My Love Is', 'Put A Little Lovin' On Me' and 'You Really Got A Hold On Me').

SEE ALSO: (1) Various Artists; *This Is Soul*; Object FPFCD01; 1990; (2) Atlantic Various Artist compilations

The Supremes

(Florence Ballard, born June 30, 1943; Diane Ross, March 26, 1944; Mary Wilson, March 6, 1944.)
Perhaps the most remarkable thing about this group is that although they became Motown's first act to be so totally 'accepted' that people forgot they were black, Berry Gordy initially passed on them and they didn't start having hits until Holland-Dozier-Holland, the staunchest R&B team in the company, started writing for them. But that is more or less all that is interesting about The Supremes – apart from the apparently non-stop bitching, if various biographies and autobiographies are to be believed, and half a dozen or so blistering pop soul

classics like 'Stop In The Name Of Love', 'Baby Love', 'When The Lovelight Starts Shining Through His Eyes', 'You Can't Hurry Love', 'I Hear A Symphony' and so on. These records managed to avoid the desperate-to-please-the-mainstream agenda that resulted in such artistically suspect ventures as *The Supremes Sing Country, Western And Pop*, *A Little Bit Of Liverpool*, *The Supremes Sing Rodgers & Hart* and *We Remember Sam Cooke*. As the 1970s were ushered in, Diana Ross leaving to become a 'Goddess' didn't resoul The Supremes, it just meant their material got (even) worse. In 1976, after numerous line-up changes, Mary Wilson, the only original member, decided to call it a day and Motown could no longer see a future for the group.

*Diana Ross & The Supremes: Anthology; Motown 530196-2; 1987

Going back as far as two of those first flops – 'Your Heart Belongs To Me' and 'Let Me Go The Right Way' – and beyond La Ross to 'Floy Joy', while this double disc set takes in nearly everything you'd want it manages to dwell far too long on that dismal mid-period when the songs didn't even have enough character to be disliked: 'Some Day We'll Be Together', 'A Hard Day's Night', 'Some Things You Never Get Used To'. You know the drill.

*Greatest Hits & Rare Classics; Motown 530050; 1991

Post-Ross. 'Up The Ladder To The Roof' is probably the best song. And while the 'Rare' is entirely understandable, 'Classics' doesn't sit quite so easily.

SEE ALSO: Motown Various Artist compilations

Johnnie Taylor

(Born Crawfordsville, Arkansas, May 5, 1938)
A no-nonsense, gravel-voice, testifyin' soul shouter from the old school – he took a brief break from music in the late 1950s to try his hand at preaching – Taylor was actually Stax's biggest-selling male singer following the death of OTIS REDDING. Formerly

with The Soul Stirrers, where he'd replaced SAM COOKE, he auditioned for Stax as a spur of the moment thing in 1966, having just moved to Memphis. There was nothing casual about the string of hits though. From 'Who's Making Love' in 1968, to 'We're Getting Careless With Our Love' in 1974, through 'I Am Somebody', 'Testify (I Wanna)', 'Jody's Got Your Girl And Gone' and 'Steal Away' he kept his essentially unchanged style in fashion by backing it up (never swamping it) with whatever slick funk rhythms were carrying the swing of the day.

*Chronicle: The 20 Greatest Hits; Stax CDSXE 084; 1993

Taylor's mainstream profile was never as high as a few of his labelmates, but from 1967 up to the company's demise eight years later he was Stax's most consistent hitmaker. This has twenty reasons why, as there was never any doubt as to who he was making records for. All the familiar country blues themes are accounted for: money, religion, and mostly infidelity – his biggest hit was built around the line 'Who's making love to your old lady, while you're out making love?' His vocal style that elevated the songs' narrative to what you'd expect to hear from the pulpit, ad lib punctuated with all sorts of 'tell me now's and 'let me say's. And a beat that doesn't know when to stop.

*Raw Blues/Little Bluebird; Stax CDSXD 051; 1990

Two early Stax albums (*Raw Blues* was his first) back to back, showing Taylor to have been sure-footed and tuff-throated from the off. If anything, some of these first recordings that were never intended for single release, are a revelation of raw, even on Taylor's gravelly yardstick. A release vital for the live cuts of 'Steal Away' and 'Jody's Got Your Girl And Gone'. Or at least that's just one of the reasons. 'Hello Sundown' and 'Part Time Love' are two more.

The Temptations

(Eddie Kendricks, born Birmingham, Alabama, December 17, 1939; Otis Williams, born Otis Miles, Texarkana, Texas, October 30, 1939; Paul Williams, Birmingham, Alabama, July 2, 1939;

David Ruffin, Meridan, Missouri, January 18, 1941; Melvin Franklin, born David English, Montgomery, Alabama, October 12, 1942)

SMOKEY ROBINSON may have been in charge; THE FOUR TOPS had more bring-it-on-home credibility; STEVIE WONDER, well, he was 'a genius'; but for sheer mindblowing mid-sixties Motown smooth The Temptations ruled. Sophistication on ten legs, all of which moved in perfect unison. And they had the best dances too – none of that 'Mickey's Monkey'-style ape walking here, or all the sweating involved in 'I Can't Help Myself'. The Temptations, you felt, didn't even have to try, just the downwards sweep of a hand – twenty-five fingers moved in time – glide a foot back and still get the best-looking girls. If you were fifteen years old and just blown your first three wage packets on an £11 mohair suit, all you wanted to do was wear it in front of your bedroom mirror and be a Temptation. A kind of uptown version of the kid with the tennis raquet and the Led Zep record.

This would be The Temptations Pt 1, 1963–1968, who, like nobody else on Motown, except for maybe very early SUPREMES, exactly achieved the corporate ideal of being able to take soul from the street corner and sell it in supper clubs like The Copacabana as if it belonged there. Nobody was going to count the spoons after the dinner-jacketed Temptations had eased through, yet, and this was a very important point, they made sure the street corner stayed with them inasmuch as it was always gutsy enough for their first fans not to feel excluded. It was perfect for the time – dressing like, carrying on like and moving in an upmarket world like The Temptations, yet regularly tipping a sly wink to the folks back home, just to let them know you know what time of day it is, was perceived as incredibly liberating back before Civil Rights.

Well balanced or otherwise, this incarnation of the group wasn't the first. They'd come together as The Elgins, out of two Detroit groups The Primes (Kendricks, Paul Williams and Cal Osborne, who had come up from Alabama together and worked with 'sister' group The Pimettes, who later became THE SUPREMES) and The Distants (Franklin, Richard Street, Otis Williams, Elbridge Bryant, Albert Harrell), when in 1960 Osborne quit The Primes, Harrell and Street left The Distants and the remaining members joined up.

After three years on the label, being written for and produced by Berry Gordy, all they had was a name change (Otis Williams suggested The Temptations), a new member (when Bryant left to be replaced by David Ruffin) and no hits whatsoever. In 1964, SMOKEY ROBINSON took over to precipitate a run of success that lasted well into the next decade and established the band as the new face of harmony soul. Doo-wop for the next generation. A state of affairs taken almost literally by their next producer Norman Whitfield, who, by the end off the decade, was starting to drag the group – somewhat uncomfortably if sleeve photos are anything to go by – into the post-acid, politically aware, altogether less dinner-jacket world of post-1960s black music. ⤏

Greatest Hits Vol. 1; Motown WD72646; 1967

The group's first UK hit album, running to their first twelve hits (up to 'I Know I'm Losing You'), and although the change from Smokey Robinson to Norman Whitfield (in partnership with Eddie Holland) takes place two-thirds of the way through it's barely noticeable: 'The Way You Do The Things You Do', 'My Girl', 'Get Ready' and 'Since I Lost My Baby' are representative of the former, while 'Ain't Too Proud To Beg', 'Beauty Is Only Skin Deep' and 'I Know I'm Losing You' weigh in for the latter.

The Temptations Sing Smokey; Gordy 374635052; 1965

Many of the early hits, plus a few that weren't and some B-sides and album tracks – while this will never be a vital album it's one of the best examples of Smokey Robinson's poetry of soul, both music and lyrics. Curiously, the arrangements and combinations of voices in this setting does more for the material than Smokey's own group does in many cases.

Cloud Nine; Motown ZD72460; 1969

By now, David Ruffin's silky baritone has been replaced by the more flexible, slightly wilder-sounding Dennis Edwards (Ruffin wanted a return to traditional deep soul), Norman Whitfield is in sole control of the group, has formed a partnership with writer Barrett Strong and they're starting out in a new direction as this set finds them dabbling in black politics, social consciousness, studio technology and hallucinogenic-style mixing technique. 'Runaway Child, Running Wild', 'Cloud Nine' 'Hey Girl (I Like Your Style)' were all considered very radical for Motown at the time (the release of the title track was held up in the UK for six months as it was believed to be too progressive), but were all US top ten hits, as was the album. It was a taste of things to come, and while others may have been thinking about what was going on in the rest of the world by then, they were the only Motown act to go into the seventies with any acknowledgement of the revolutions that had happened in the sixties.

ALSO RECOMMENDED:

Anthology; Motown WD72525; 1989

Two CDs, forty-two tracks, thirty-two pages in the booklet.

Live At The Copa; Motown ZD75201; 1969

Big hits, pop chestnuts and a live show excitement that even 'Old Man River' don't manage to squash.

SEE ALSO: Motown Various Artist compilations from the 1960s

Joe Tex

(Born Joe Arrington, Rogers, Texas, August 8, 1933)
One of the very few artists to take soul through from the rawest R&B of the 1950s to the rougher end of disco over two decades later, and not to lose his sense of humour while he was doing it. But for all the rambunctious 'Show Me's, 'I Gotcha's and novelty-type 'Skinny Legs And All's or 'Ain't Gonna Bump No More (With No Big Fat Woman)'s, Joe Tex had a dictionary-definition wicked soul voice, as was demonstrated on ballads like 'Hold What You've Got' or straightforward dance frenzies like 'Show Me'. And he was capable of writing songs for such discerning clientele as James Brown and Jerry Butler. Joe Tex died of a heart attack in August 1982, less than a week after his fiftieth birthday.

*The Very Best Of Joe Tex; Charly 133; 1990

Twenty-five tracks from the mid-1960s, which prove you don't
have to be po-faced to be soulful, but, thankfully, they don't go
up as far as the disco novelty items he offered in the next
decade. All the hits are there – 'S.Y.S.L.Y.F.M. (The Letter
Song)', 'I Want To (Do Everything For You)', 'A Sweet Woman
Like You', 'Show Me' and the one that started it all off, 'Hold
What You've Got' – and the spectrum is rounded out with the
lesser known 'You're Right, Ray Charles' and 'Don't Let Your
Children Pay (For Your Mistakes)'.

Carla Thomas

(Born Memphis, Tennessee, December 21, 1942)
RUFUS's daughter, who started out duetting with Dad as a
teenager, then got in the mainstream charts in 1961 with the
pop-flavour of 'Gee Whiz (Look At His Eyes)'. This was an
important record in the Story of Soul, as it was Stax's first big hit
after they'd signed with Atlantic, and the music industry attention Carla attracted was enough to persuade the new owners to
take this Memphis cottage soul industry seriously. From there,
thanks to 'B-A-B-Y' and a string of hits both on her own and as
duets, she became the label's official Queen of Soul.

*The Best Of Carla Thomas: The Singles Plus! 1968–1973;
Stax CDSXD

Not the most accurate album title ever written, as it goes back to
that important 1961 hit, and then as it progresses to her last big
record for the company, 'I Like What You're Doing (To Me)', it
manages to avoid 'B.A.B.Y.', 'Let Me Be Good To You' and
'Tramp', the blistering duet with Otis Redding. That said – and
they are available elsewhere – this set is the best single document of Carla Thomas's wonderfully versatile voice that covers
sweet ballads, belting blues and all points in between.

SEE ALSO: (1) *You Thrill My Soul, Female & Girl Groups From
The Early Stax Sessions*; Stax CDSXD088; (2) *Stax/Volt Live
In Europe, London To Paris*; Stax CDSXCD; 1966; (3)
Stax/Atlantic Various Artist compilations

Irma Thomas

(Born Irma Lee, Panchatla, Louisiana, 1941)
A classic New Orleans balladeer, her way with a torch song was as breathy as the genre required, but stayed strong enough not to tip over into 'gush'. Also, in the tradition of that city's R&B she never forgot that it was the narrative that moved the song along. But in spite of a couple of her best efforts doing much better when somebody else sung them – 'Time Is On My Side' was covered by The Rolling Stones and 'Ruler Of My Heart' became OTIS REDDING's 'Pain In My Heart' – she made a series of serious tunes in the first half of the 1960s.

Fact fans may appreciate the music business cliché of Irma Thomas's discovery: she was singing to herself while working as a waitress when she was overheard by band leader Tommy Ridgeley. He had her record the local hit 'You Can Have My Husband (But Please Don't Mess With My Man)' the very next day.

*Time Is On My Side: The Best Of Irma Thomas; EMI 97988; 1991

Probably all the Irma Thomas anybody below fetishist level is going to want – twenty of the cream of that early-sixties period, penned by such notables as ALLEN TOUSSAINT, VAN MCCOY and Randy Newman – and four previously unissued numbers. As expected, her handling of the slow stuff is superb, but the quicker-paced 'Break Away' proves she can swing a bit to, while the original version of the title track makes it obvious that although Mick Jagger may have tried to copy the original, note for note, he never really came close to getting inside the song's meaning.

Rufus Thomas

(Born March 12, 1917, Collierville, Texas)
Remember a fifty-five-year-old black man with snow-white hair and a pink short-pants suit on *Top Of The Pops*? Go on, think hard. He's doing a dance that was like a kind of (marginally) cooler version of The Birdie Dance? That was Rufus Thomas

and his 1972 hit 'Do The Funky Chicken', just one of a whole menagerie of successful exploitations of popular dance crazes that included 'Do The Funky Penguin', 'Walking The Dog' and 'Can Your Monkey Do The Dog?'. But was it soul? Of course it was, because it was Rufus Thomas. He wasn't just some silly old bloke in an even sillier whistle, he was Mr Soul.

Originally a stand-up comedian, he became a Memphis radio deejay with a far-reaching and influential R&B show through the 1930s and 1940s, running talent contests where he 'discovered' such monster artists as IKE TURNER, Bobby Bland, ISAAC HAYES and B.B. King. His radio show was entirely supportive of Jim Stewart's fledgling local record company, and Thomas's unstinting exposure of that product was undoubtedly a big factor in Stax growing to the force it became. Thomas recorded his fair share of straight R&B during the 1950s and 1960s too, some with Sam Phillips at the Sun Studios, gaining hometown acclaim and a contract at Stax when it was still Satellite Records. The plan there was to cut duets with his daughter CARLA THOMAS, but after one hit, 'Cause I Love You', she teamed up with OTIS REDDING and Dad got down with the daft dances.

What shouldn't be forgotten, though, is that just as Rufus Thomas had pushed R&B music in the thirties, forties and fifties, so his high-entertainment factor in the late-sixties and early-seventies did much to present soul music in a light other than as black nationalist propaganda-with-a-bassline, which is what many in the mainstream began to see it as, a perception not helped by a sense of loss for the good old days when those artists 'knew their place'. And, most importantly, Rufus Thomas's success helped convince the record industry and radio producers that more soul music than Motown and the pop end of Atlantic had wide appeal.

The Best Of: The Singles 1968–1975; Stax CDSXD094; 1994

Although the best-known tracks were cut in the 1970s, the very idea of Rufus Thomas and these songs belongs to the previous decade. The set doesn't go back as far as any of the straight stuff so this is purely Penguins, Monkeys, Dogs, Robots, Walks, Chickens and the Mississippi, each one about as funky as it can get. Backed by THE BAR-KAYS, it doesn't let up in its greasy, pumping, Southern soul power and shows Rufus Thomas at his irre-pressibly boogie-ing best. Anything less and it would have got boring.

ALSO RECOMMENDED:

Crown Prince Of Dance; Stax CDSXE 054; 1974

A bunch of stuff that didn't make it on to *The Best Of*, including a track announcing Rufus as 'The Funkiest Man Alive'. Well, are you going to argue?

Allen Toussaint

(Born New Orleans, Louisiana, January 14, 1938)
A piano player who formed his first professional group when he was just fourteen, Allen Toussaint played on a lot of the Ace sessions as a teenager and, after a spell in the Army in the early 1960s, hooked up with Marshall Seahorn to become the archi-tect of New Orleans soul. Toussaint wrote, produced and arranged those tricky shuffle beats and swamp-funk rhythms that did so much for LEE DORSEY, IRMA THOMAS, Ernie K-Doe, AARON NEVILLE and Betty Harris, while The Meters perfected their craft under him as his house band. Their Sea-Saint Studios promoted the Cresent City contribution to post-1960s music to such a degree that soon his Sansu Productions were sought out by the likes of Paul McCartney, Paul Simon and The Band. And, on Allen Toussaint's admission, his own recordings lapsed into 'easy listening soul'.

From A Whisper To A Scream; Kent CDKENM 036; 1985

Allen Toussaint's own records were never quite as interesting as the ones he put together for other people. However, this makes the most of his crisp piano style by concentrating on instrumental versions of some his best-known songs – 'Working In The Coalmine', 'Everything I Do Gonna Be Funky', 'Number Nine' and the title track among them.

NB This album has exactly the same tracklisting as the Charly CD *Mr New Orleans*.

Ike & Tina Turner

(Ike Turner, born Clarksdale, Mississippi, November 5, 1931:
Tina Turner, born Annie Mae Bullock, November 26, 1939,
Brownsville, Tennessee)
For all the impact Ike and Tina Turner had on 1960s soul, they
left behind them a surprisingly slim legacy of recorded music.
Even less on CD, but, handily, one of them is 1965's *Live! The Ike
And Tina Turner Revue*. Because that's where Ike and Tina were
at home, on stage and all the way live. It's how they met, when
one night in a club in East St Louis, in 1956, Ike Turner, leader of
The Kings of Rhythm, offered the microphone to Alline Bullock.
The girl was too shy to get up and sing, but her sister Annie
Mae, a talent-show regular who'd been unsuccessfully pester-
ing Turner for weeks, took the stage instead. The guitarist was
impressed with the seventeen-year-old's 'stuff' in general, and
when he asked her for a date the most tempestuous relationship
in soul (both professionally and privately) was out of the traps.

Using all the blues and soul experience he'd picked up as guitarist with B. B. King and Howling Wolf and as a session player
at Sun Studios, over the next few years he transformed The
Kings of Rhythm into the Ike and Tina Turner Revue. (They
married in 1958.) Boosted by a series of R&B hits, the act toured
almost constantly to increasing crowds as Tina's stage presence
and vocals became wilder and Ike constructed music to match it
that wasn't afraid of rock 'n' rollisms. But the real big break
came in 1966 when Phil Spector spent $20,000 putting up a wall
of sound in front of which Tina was to bawl 'River Deep
Mountain High'. The record was a hit all over the world except
the US – where it staggered to number 88. It was said that
Spector's disappointment with what he considered to be one of
his finest songs was a big factor in his shutting down Philles –
his record label – shortly afterwards.

It was success the duo never built upon either – they didn't
have another significant record until the early 1970s when
'Proud Mary' and 'Nutbush City Limits' rescued them from a
late-1960s of ill-advised (and even less successful) blues albums
and residencies in Las Vegas hotels.

Tina walked out on Ike in 1976, over a year after their last
chart single together, amid tales of the most appalling domestic

violence. He went on to various court appearances for a range of charges running from drugs to tax offences to defrauding the phone company. She became a 'rockin' grandmother' and is now a film.

Live! The Ike And Tina Turner Revue; Kent CDKEND 102; 1965

The songs might not be the most obvious, as this was pre-'River Deep Mountain High', but that also means it's pre-Phil Spector, and therefore gives an accurate idea of what they were about without all the frills. And it is clear what had made this show one of the biggest draws on the 'chitt'lins circuit' (small R&B clubs and bars) in the first half of the 1960s, indeed what had attracted Spector. It is, quite simply, a no-holds-barred stormer of a performance, with Tina in classic R&B a-sweatin' and a-testifyin' mode, with Ike, as slick as he used to be, leading a band that is determined not to be left behind. Such specialist market hits as 'You Should Have Treated Me Right', 'Am I A Fool In Love' and 'It's Gonna Work Out Fine' get the treatment, plus there's numbers from Bobby Montgomery, Vernon Guy and Venetta Fields.

Proud Mary: The Best Of Ike & Tina Turner; EMI 95846; 1988

A twenty-cut journey through classic Ike and Tina, starting at the very early R&B of 'It's Gonna Work Out Fine' and 'A Fool In Love', continuing to 'Acid Queen'. By way of 'Nutbush City Limits', 'Proud Mary' and 'River Deep Mountain High', with an entertaining detour around a rather zonked out cover of 'Come Together'. This is loud music at it's hand-clappin', foot-stompin', mojo-shakin' best. Go on, annoy the neighbours. They might even like it.

ALSO RECOMMENDED:

It's Gonna Work Out Fine; Collectables 5137; 1990

The best of the Sue tracks cut between 1960 and 1962.

Too Hot To Hold; Charly CDCD1042; 1992

Movin' On; Charly; CDCD1135; 1993

Junior Walker And The All Stars

(Born Autrey DeWalt Walker II, Blythesville, Arkansas, 1942; Willie Woods, drums; Vic Thomas, organ; James Graves, drums) One of the few acts Berry Gordy bought fully formed, instead of signing them up and developing them in the corporate image. They arrived as part of the assets when Gordy took over his brother-in-law Harvey Fuqua's Harvey label, and, as they were hot off a local hit 'Cleo's Mood', they were more or less left alone. Which may account for why Junior Walker's parping, rasping sax and singular presentation style – a stage set involved generous helpings of sweating, lewdness and rolling on the floor – were allowed to stomp all over The Motown Way with size twelve boots. It was always more roadhouse than house on the hill, but people seemed to like it – maybe it was a piece of shrewd thinking on Gordy's part that a funky black R&B honker like Junior Walker on the books proved he hadn't forgotten where he 'be coming from'. The group blew up a storm from 1964 until the end of the decade, by which time they'd chilled down a bit from the bolt-you-to-the-wall likes of 'Roadrunner' and 'Shotgun' to the well-on-the-way-to-mellow 'Walk In The Night' and 'What Does It Take (To Win Your Love)'. But no matter how well he kept a rough edge on this new cool, Junior Walker's time had come. Today, he and his sax still make a good living from session playing, and he isn't afraid to take it out on the road every so often.

*Greatest Hits; Motown 5208; 1969

The Junior Walker spectrum, such as it was, taking it from that first hit 'Cleo's Mood' up to 'These Eyes' in 1969. (An irritating record because dance hall deejays would play it as a slow record, which in theory it was, but it was never quite right to dance with a girl to – if you had made a successful move, you'd usually end up making a fool of yourself.) 'Walk In The Night' isn't on this, but as it's got 'Roadrunner', 'High Heel Sneakers', 'Shotgun', 'Come See About Me' and 'Pucker Up Buttercup', nobody's going to miss it.

*Live!; Motown 5465; 1970

Eight of his biggest, put out with the sort of extra punch and eye for an improvisation you don't expect from 1960s Motown acts. Excellent cleaned-up sound quality, an ideal opportunity to check out the true soul of Junior Walker.

ALSO RECOMMENDED:

Shotgun; Motown 5141; 1965

Eleven early cuts of funk so raw it's still dripping blood.

SEE ALSO: Motown Various Artist compilations from the 1960s

Mary Wells

(Born Detroit, Michigan, May 13, 1953)
In 1960, the sixteen-year-old Mary Wells walked into Motown Records with a song she'd written and wanted Berry Gordy to get it to JACKIE WILSON. By way of a demo, she sung 'Bye Bye Baby' in the hall of the house Motown used as an office and Gordy signed her on the spot. The song was her first single, and the album of the same name was the company's first LP. Then SMOKEY ROBINSON set to work writing and producing for her, and starting with the next year's 'I Don't Want To Take A Chance', she racked up ten chart records in a row to be known round the company as 'Little Miss Hitmaker'. Although her voice was never as big as GLADYS KNIGHT's or Martha Reeves's, or her delivery as captivatingly dramatic as Diana Ross's, she became the template to which those who followed her into the company conformed. But further to that as the first to adopt the glamorous evening-gown look, she was Motown's first female superstar – indeed, at the start of the 1960s to talk about The Motown Way in a female context would be to talk about Mary Wells.

She hit the peak of her fame in 1964 with 'My Guy', the song she'll always be best known for (she was also known for opening US shows for The Beatles). It was the year she turned twenty-one and could renegotiate her contract with the company, which she did, but unsatisfactorily. Later that year she opted for Los Angeles, where an attempt to get into the movies came to nothing more than a contract with Fox's record label 20th Century. And the start of a rapidly lowering profile.

*My Guy; Charly CDCD1146; 1964

Half Little Miss Hitmaker's Motown hits on the one LP, but they're the half you want – 'You Beat Me To The Punch', 'Two Lovers', 'What's Easy For Two Is So Hard For One', 'Two Lovers' and the title track. Also find enclosed 'Sunny' and the one that got it all started for her, 'Bye Bye Baby'. It's interesting, on the earlier stuff, to listen to that soon-to-become-familiar Motown girlie sound finding its feet.

SEE ALSO: (1) Various Artists; *This Is Soul*; Object FPFCD01; 1990; (2) *Hitsville USA – The Motown Singles Collection 1959–1971*; Motown 530129; 1992

Jackie Wilson

(Born Detroit, Michigan, June 9, 1934)
Spectacular and successful as Jackie Wilson was, he's also one more example of how, back in the pre-Atlantic/pre-Motown days, soul and R&B wasn't taken seriously as a style in itself, but assumed to be some sort of stepping stone for its more talented exponents to move on to something else. Why else would CBS have wasted all those years on Aretha? And why would Jackie Wilson have been given so much of the rank material he had to put up with. 'Danny Boy'? 'Rags To Riches'? *St Therese Of The Roses*? An LP of cheesy Christmas songs? True, he did a creditable job – Jackie Wilson singing is always worthwhile – but this stuff isn't exactly Funky Broadway, and the constriction is audible. What made up for the years in MOR wilderness, however, were the songs that worked. Most of these were recorded during the late-1950s or the mid-1960s and are soul singing at its best.

Jackie Wilson could have been a boxer, he was good enough as a teenager, but his mother wanted him to stay in school and then find a less risky profession. (As it turned out, he was nearly killed in 1961 when an over-ardent female fan broke into his apartment and shot him in the stomach as he stopped her shooting herself after he had rejected her advances.) He took up singing, joining first The Thrillers (HANK BALLARD was a fellow member), then, on JOHNNY OTIS's recommendation, The Dominoes, where he progressed to lead singer after Clyde McPhatter was fired. Peeved that although he was lead singer the group was called Billy Ward & The Dominoes, he went solo and started off in 1957 with a song co-written by his old boxing buddy Berry Gordy. 'Reet Petite (The Finest Girl You Ever Want To Meet)' was actually a much bigger hit in the UK (number 6), but it was the first in a series from the Gordy pen which culminated in the writer taking his royalties and starting a record company, while Wilson carried on having big-time R&B hits that crossed over into the mainstream.

The difference was that in 1960 Wilson changed management and while he continued to cut enough tough stuff to keep the R&B market serviced, he was being pushed firmly towards an upmarket white audience. And without Berry Gordy's intuitive writing, pretty soon the blahs got the upper hand. It wasn't until the second half of the decade that Jackie Wilson got back on course, when after a move to Chicago the Windy City's unique soul sound collided with his volatile R&B to produce a storming run of singles culminating in '(Your Love Keeps Lifting Me) Higher And Higher'. But by the 1970s it's back to simplified pop fodder.

On September 29, 1975, Jackie Wilson had a heart attack on stage in New Jersey. He hit his head as he fell, going into a coma and suffering brain damage as a result of lack of oxygen. He never fully recovered and was in permanent care until his death nine years later. The soul world lost a considerable talent, and you wonder what that would've become if he'd stuck with Berry Gordy back in 1958.

The Very Best Of Jackie Wilson; Ace 913

Twenty-four tracks, and a title that doesn't lie. This compilation sorts out much of the cabaret-inclined drivel and concentrates on the best of his R&B repertoire. It starts at 'Reet Petite', progresses through the other Gordy co-compositions – 'To Be Loved', 'I'll Be Satisfied' and 'Lonely Teardrops' – then on to 'Doggin' Around', 'Whispers (Getting Louder)', 'Higher And Higher' and the Van McCoy-written 'I Get The Sweetest Feeling'. It goes all the way to his final US single 'You Got Me

Walking' and is really all the Jackie Wilson anybody ought to need.

ALSO RECOMMENDED:

Mr Excitement; Rhino 70775; 1992

A three-CD set taking in everything on the above, but as it stretches to seventy-two tracks, it runs from recordings made with Billy Ward & The Dominoes and takes in a great deal of less than soulful material. Some say this other stuff demonstrates Wilson's versatility; there's another school of thought that believes it just gets in the way.

Stevie Wonder

(Born Steveland Judkins, Saginaw, Michigan, May 13, 1950)
Stevie Wonder's contribution to the advancement of soul music can be taken as read. Indeed it usually is, with the word 'genius' often in close attendance. However, when people talk about Stevie Wonder the innovator they often take great pains to distinguish this 1970s manifestation from the lovable moppet in the grown up suit or the gauche teenager with the baby afro. In other words it's as if all the singer was famous for in the previous decade was selling truckloads of records and performing in venues he was too young to have been allowed in as a punter. 'Twelve-year-old genius' comes with a completely different set of artistically credible baggage than 'just plain genius'. But of course Stevie Wonder didn't simply wake up one morning in January 1970 and look in the mirror and say, 'Enough with the pop soul schlock. After breakfast I'm going to alter the course of black music.'

Blind since birth, his family moved to Detroit when he was very young and he started playing piano and harmonica at the age of five. Brought to Motown by Miracle Ronnie White in 1960, his first records came out two years later, the initial hits ten months after that. Already displaying a marvellous natural voice and a gift for understanding music beyond just playing it – how it actually works inside the songs – his first compositions in 1966 and 1967 showed he was not dovetailing precisely into The Motown Way.

He'd already spent much time learning music theory and composition, in braille, and would later continue to study these subjects at the University of Southern California. His new ideas were soon apparent: 'Uptight', 'I Was Made To Love Her' and 'Signed, Sealed, Delivered' were not traditional Motown records, they owe a great deal to the more orchestral side of rock music, yet still show re-emphasis on traditional R&B instruments within their Big Sound structure. But what they announced was that Stevie Wonder was prepared to experiment with different rhythmic ideas and take a wider approach to instrumentation and arrangement. That they sold meant he was allowed to carry on – albeit within certain guidelines. The final couple of years of the 1960s were more a statement of intent of the fully fledged musical revolution he was going to instigate in the next ten years. ⟶

The Essential Stevie Wonder; Motown 530047; 1987

The early Stevie Wonder albums are all off catalogue in this country, but that doesn't really matter in the light of this truthfully titled set. This genuinely is the essential pre-genius Stevie Wonder. It tracks him from when he was 'Little' and not yet having hits ('I Call It Pretty Music But The Old Folks Call It The Blues') through adolescence and into such grown-up stuff as 'Signed, Sealed, Delivered'. Every big track is here, plus a few B-sides and the more interesting album tracks (this is why the deletion of the LPs doesn't matter – he wasn't yet making albums so there was a lot of filler). While the musical progression is obvious what is frighteningly in place from the word go is his confidence as a performer.

SEE ALSO: Motown Various Artist compilations

VARIOUS ARTIST COMPILATIONS

The Stax Revue Live At The 5/4 Ballroom, 7 & 8 August 1965;
Stax CDSXD 040; 1965

Booker T & The MGs, Green Onions, You Can't Sit Down,
Summertime, Soul Twist, Boot-leg; **The Mad Lads**, Don't Have
To Shop Around; **The Astors**, Candy; **The Mar-Keys**, Last
Night; **William Bell**, You Don't Miss Your Water, Any Other
Way; **Carla Thomas**, Every Ounce Of Strength; **Rufus Thomas**,
Do The Dog, Walking The Dog.

Stax/Volt Live In Europe, London To Paris; Stax CDSXCD;
1966

Booker T & The MGs, Red Beans & Rice, Hip Hug Her, Boojer-
Loo, Green Onions; **The Mar-Keys**, The Philly Dog, Last Night;
Carla Thomas, B.A.B.Y., Let Me Be Good To You, Yesterday,
Something Good (Is Going To Happen To You); **Eddie Floyd**,
Knock On Wood, I Don't Want To Cry, Raise Your Hand; **Otis
Redding**, Fa-Fa-Fa-Fa-Fa (Sad Song), Day Tripper, My Girl,
Respect, Shake, Try A Little Tenderness.

Really, the only way to appreciate the excitement of Stax was to
see it on stage, and these wonderful (for the time) recordings are
the next best thing. While the latter album scores highly for calibre of track and Emperor Rosko's manic MC-ing at the London
gigs, the former, set in a big night club in South Central Los
Angeles, has the edge when it comes to sheer power.

*Various Artists; 1000 Volts Of Stax: Rare & Unreleased Tracks
From The Golden Era Of Soul*; Stax CDSXD042; 1992

Booker T & The MGs, Hide Away, Sittin' On The Dock Of The
Bay; **Albert King**, Don't You Lie To Me; **Otis Redding**, Cupid,
I've Got Dreams To Remember; **Bobby Marchan**, Don't Worry
About Tomorrow; **Rufus Thomas**, Walking The Dog; **Carla
Thomas**, Run Around; **Floyd Newman**, Floyd's Beat; **Ruby
Johnson**, When My Love Comes Down On You; **William Bell**,

She Won't Be Like You, Never Let Me Go; **Mabel John**, Sweet Devil; **The Mad Lads**, Cloudburst; **The Mark-Keys**, Hippy Dippy; **Rufus & Carla Thomas**, Don't Mess Up A Good Thing; **The Astors**, Just Enough To hurt Me; **Eddie Floyd**, Knock On Wood.

*Various Artists; 2000 Volts Of Stax: Rare & Unreleased Tracks From The Golden Era Of Soul; Stax CDSXD074; 1992

Booker T & The MGs, Kinda Easy Like, Say A Little Prayer; **Albert King**, Crosscut Saw; **Otis Redding**, Pain In My Heart, Try A Little Tenderness; **Deanie Parker**, How About You; **Rufus Thomas**, Ride Your Pony; **Carla Thomas**, Try Me; **Ruby Johnson**, It's Not That Easy; **Eddie Kirk**, I Found A Brand New Love; **William Bell**, You Don't Miss Your Water, Never Let Me Go; **Mabel John**, Sweet Devil; **The Mad Lads**, She's The One; **The Mark-Keys**, Slinky; **The Astors**, Come Out Tonight; **Eddie Floyd**, Bark At The Moon; **The Bar-Kays**, Hot Shot; **The Tonettes**, Please Don't Go.

Two entertaining, if not vital, sets, consisting of alternative takes of well-known songs, instrumental versions, unreleased tracks, studio playfulness and the occasional bold experiment that didn't quite come off.

*Stax Vocal Groups From The '60s & '70s: Just A Little Overcome; Stax CDSXD019; 1990

The Mad Lads, No Strings Attached, Make This Young Lady Mine, These Old Memories, I'm So Glad I Fell In Love With You; **The Dramatics**, Your Love Was Strange, Highway To Heaven, Since I've Been In Love; **The Newcomers**, Open Your Heart (Let Me Come In), Girl This Boy Loves You, Mannish Boy; **The Nightingales**, I'm With You, Just A Little Overcome, Baby Don't Do It; **The Temprees**, Your Love (Is All I Need), Whole Bit Of Love; **The Stingers**, I Refuse To Be Lonely; **Ollie & The Nightingales**, Showered With Love, The Mellow Way (You Treat Your Man); **The Limitations**, All Because Of You;

The Epsilons, The Echo; **The Leaders**, Anyone Can; **United Image**, Love's Creeping Up On Me.

Sweet harmony singing wasn't something that immediately sprang to mind when the words 'Stax' and 'soul' came up in conversation. *Just A Little Overcome* redresses matters to an almost embarrassing degree.

**Stax Gold Hits 1968–1974*; Stax DCSXD043; 1992

Booker T & The MGs, Soul Limbo, Time Is Tight; **William Bell & Judy Clay**, Private Number; **Johnnie Taylor**, Cheaper To Keep Her, Who's Making Love; **Eddie Floyd**, Bring It On Home To Me; **William Bell**, I Forgot To Be Your Lover; **Carla Thomas**, I Like What You're Doing To Me; **Rufus Thomas**, Do The Push And Pull Pt 1; **Jean Knight**, Mr Big Stuff; **The Dramatics**, Whatcha See Is Whatcha Get, In The Rain; **The Staple Singers**, I'll Take You There, Respect Yourself; **Isaac Hayes**, Theme From Shaft; **The Bar-Kays**, Son Of Shaft; **Frederick Knight**, I've Been Lonely For So Long; **Mel & Tim**, Starting All Over Again; **Shirley Brown**, Woman To Woman; **The Soul Children**, I'll Be The Other Woman; **The Emotions**, So I Can Love You; **Mavis Staples**, I Have Learned To Do Without You; **The Temprees**, Dedicated To The One I Love; **Veda Brown**, Short Stoppin'.

The ultimate Stax sampler. For the cost of just one CD, this skilfully supplies compiled highlights of the label's transition from hick soul to slick funk. And a lot of dance hall memories from the very early 1970s, when Motown was starting to lose it and Stax was carrying the inner city swing.

**You Thrill My Soul, Female & Girl Groups From The Early Stax Sessions*; Stax CDSXD088

Carla Thomas, Same Thing, Here It Comes Again, I Can't Stay, Ain't Enough Hours In The Day, Gosh I'm Lucky, Do Boys Keep Diaries; **The Tonettes**, Heavenly Angel, Stolen Angel, Unhand That Man, Tell Me, Come To Me; **Wendy Rene**, Gone For Good, The Same Guy, Love At First Sight, He Hasn't Failed Me Yet, Crying All By Myself, Last Love, Crowded Park, Can't

Stay Away; **Barabra Stephens**, If She Should Ever Break Your Heart, Love Is Like A Flower; **Deanie Parker**, Just One Touch, Heartbreaker.

It seems Motown didn't have the monopoly on girlie groups and singers. These cuts, deservedly dug out from the Memphis vaults, prove it's possible to put a Southern spin on the notion of the shimmery evening gown and still keep it sweet.

The Complete Stax/Volt Singles Volume 2; Stax 9CSD 4411; 1993

Quite literally what the title says it is. Every single released on the Stax and Volt labels during the first three post-Atlantic years (1968–71). It adds up to a staggering 216 songs across nine CDs, complete with a handsome booklet. At the wallet-lightening price of £110, and not available individually. For the true Stax maniac only, thus it's a waste of space to list all the titles as anybody interested enough to be considering splashing out on it will have them all committed to memory anyway.

Various Artists; *Soul Hits: Dance Party*; Charly QSCD6005; 1991

Sam & Dave, Soul Man; **Eddie Floyd**, Knock On Wood; **Clarence Carter**, Patches; **Rufus Thomas**, Walkin' The Dog; **Fontella Bass**, Rescue Me; **Dobie Gray**, The In Crowd; **Barbara George**, I Know; **Al Wilson**, The Shake; **The Olympics**, Western Movies; **Sam Cooke**, Sweet Sixteen; **Bob & Earl**, The Harlem Shuffle; **Joe Simon**, You Keep Me Hangin' On; **Bobby Womack**, That's The Way I Feel About Cha; **Joe Tex**, Hold On To What You've Got.

Various Artists; This Is Soul Vol 2; Charly CDCD1176; 1994

Jackie Wilson, Higher And Higher; **Joe Tex**, One Monkey Don't Stop No Show; **Benny Spellman**, Lipstick Traces; **Ernie K-Doe**, I Cried My Last Tear; **Betty Everett**, You're No Good; **The Tams**, Hey Girl Don't Bother Me; **Etta James**, I'd Rather Go Blind; **Chuck Jackson**, Any Day Now; **Jerry Butler**, He Will Break Your

Heart; **Billy Stewart**, Summertime; **Sugar Pie Destano**, Soulful Dress; **Johnny Adams**, Reconsider Me; **Peggy Scott**, Every Little Bit Hurts; **Timi Yuro**, Hurt; **Solomon Burke**, Boo Hoo Hoo; **Percy Sledge**, When A Man Loves A Woman; **Robert Parker**, Barefootin'; **Syl Johnson**, Dresses Too Short; **Irma Thomas**, Ruler Of My Heart; **Bobby Womack**, Looking For A Love.

*Various Artists; This Is Soul Vol 1; Charly CDCD1026; 1992

Practically a duplication of Charly's *Soul Hits: Dance Party*, but with the notable inclusions **Jimmy Castor**'s 'Troglodyte', **Brenton Wood**'s 'Gimme Little Sign' and 'B.A.B.Y.' by **Carla Thomas**. But, and this could be the deciding factor, *sans* 'Harlem Shuffle'.

*Various Artists; The Chess Story Vol 3: From R&B To Soul; CDCD1125; 1993

Jan Bradley, Mama Didn't Lie; **Sonny Boy Williamson**, Help Me; **Tommy Tucker**, Hi Heel Sneakers; **Sugar Pie DeSanto**, Soulful Dress; **Jackie Ross**, Selfish One; **Mitty Collier**, I Had A Talk With My Man Last Night; **The Radiants**, Voice Your Choice; **Tony Clarke**, The Entertainer; **Little Milton**, We're Gonna Make It; **Ramsey Lewis**, The In Crowd; **Fontella Bass**, Rescue Me; **Billy Stewart**, Summertime; **Bobby Moore & The Rhythm Aces**, Searching For My Love; **Laura Lee**, Dirty Man; **Etta James**, I'd Rather Go Blind; **The Dells**, Stay In My Corner; **Pigmeat Markham**, Here Come The Judge.

A wonderfully educational compilation – the last in a series that moved from *Blues To Doo-wop* (CDCD1123) and from *Doo-wop To R&B* (CDCD1124) – showing the gradual transformation of the music that took place at Leonard and Phil Chess's Chicago label. How it ended up at Pigmeat Markham's robust comedy, however, is anybody's guess.

*Sweeter Than The Day Before: 28 Classic Soul Cuts From The Chess Label; Charly CDARC515; 1993

Herb Ward, Strange Change; **Maurice McAllister And The Radiants**, Baby You've Got It; **Gene Chandler**, Such A Pretty

Thing; **Bobby Moore**, Chained To Your Heart; **Denise LaSalle**, A Love Reputation; **Marlena Shaw**, Let's Wade In The Water; **The Dells**, Make Sure (You Have Somebody To Love You); **George Kirby**, What Can I Do; **Harold Hutton**, Lucky Boy; **Andy Mack**, Later Than You Think; **The Valentinos**, Sweeter Than The Day Before; **Tammy Montgomery**, If I Would Marry You; **Timiko**, Is It A Sin; **Joan Garnett**; Whole New Plan; **Terry Callier**, Look At Me Now; **Johnny Nash**, Strange Feeling; **The Vashionettes**, A Mighty Good Love; **Johnny Williams**, My Baby's Good; **Little Milton**, Sometimes; **The Carltons**, Can't You Hear The Beat; **The Seminoles**, I Can't Stand It; **Doug Banks**, Just Keep On Dancing; **Etta James**, Payback; **Mitty Collier**, Pain; **Tony Clarke**, Landslide; **The Dells**, Thinkin' About You; **Sunday**, Ain't Got No Problems; **Billy Stewart**, Count On Me.

*The Story So Far: Essential Argo/Cadet Grooves, The Sampler; Charly CDARC517; 1993

Sonny Stitt, Slick Eddie; **New Rotary Connection**, I Am The Blackgold Of The Sun; **Daniel Salinas**, Straussmania; **Terry Callier**, Ordinary Joe; **Jack McDuff**, The City Bump; **Marlena Shaw**, California Soul; **Grady Tate**, Moondance; **American Gypsy**, Golden Ring; **Frank Foster**, Samba Blues; **Baby Face Willette**, Mo' Blues.

*Action Line; Charly CDARC518; 1992

Dorothy Ashby, Action Line; **Odell Brown**, The Thing; **Etta James** Out On The Streets Again; **American Gypsy**, While It's Cold Outside; **Ramsey Lewis**, Afro Boogaloo Twist; **Lou Donaldson**, Soul Gumbo; **Odell Brown**, Raising The Roof; **Ramsey Lewis**, Function At The Junction; **Jack McDuff**, Black Is; **Dorothy Ashby**, Soul Vibration; **Lou Donaldson**, I Feel It In My Bones; **Odell Brown**, Free Delivery; **American Gypsy**, Stuck On You; **Odell Brown**, Nitty Gritty.

Three volumes from the vaults of the Chess label (and its subsidiaries) that give a good jumping off point into Chicago Soul of the 1950s and 1960s. Always more jazz-influenced and instrumental-based than its Southern counterparts, it struggled for public recognition against the likes of Stax and Motown in its second decade as it failed to establish personalities among its artists. Before the mid-1960s, when the company started sending artists down to Muscle Shoals to record with Rick Hall, Chess developed a very up-tempo style of intricate musical arrangements that came over here as Northern Soul and perhaps suffered in London because of this association. Fact fans will appreciate that Maurice White, later of Earth, Wind & Fire, was Ramsey Lewis's drummer.

Various Artists; The Art Of The Soul Ballad; Charly CDCD1096; 1993

Sam Cooke, You Send Me; **Etta James**, At Last; **Percy Sledge**, Warm And Tender Love; **Billy Stewart**, Sittin' In The Park; **Barbara Lewis**, Hello Stranger; **Eddie Holman**, Hey There Lonely Girl; **Betty Lavette**, Let Me Down Easy; **Joe Simon**, Misty Blue; **Brook Benton**, Rainy Night In Georgia; **Peggy Scott**, Every Little Bit Hurts; **Aaron Neville**, Tell It Like It Is; **Luther Ingram**, If Loving You Is Wrong (I Don't Want To Be Right); **The Ad Libs**, Giving Up; **Jerry Butler**, Make It Easy On Yourself; **Johnny Adams**, Reconsider Me; **Irma Thomas**, I've Been Loving You Too Long; **Bobby Womack**, That's The Way I Feel About Cha; **Gladys Knight & The Pips**, Either Way I Lose; **Chuck Jackson**, Anyday Now; **Little Milton**, Stand By Me.

British Motown Chartbusters; Motown 530066; 1967

Stevie Wonder, Blowin' In The Wind; **Diana Ross & The Supremes**, You Keep Me Hangin' On; **Four Tops**, Standin' In The Shadows Of Love, **Marvin Gaye and Kim Weston**, It Takes Two; **The Marvelettes**, When You're Young And In Love; **The Temptations**, (I Know) I'm Losing You; **Jimmy Ruffin**, What Becomes Of The Brokenhearted; **Diana Ross & The Supremes**, The Happening; **Four Tops**, Seven Rooms Of Gloom; **Junior Walker & The All Stars**, How Sweet It Is To Be Loved By You; **Martha & The Vandellas**, I'm Ready For Love; **Diana Ross &**

The Supremes, Love Is Here And Now You're Gone; **Jimmy Ruffin**, Gonna Give Her All The Love That I've Got; **Stevie Wonder**, I Was Made To Love Her; **Gladys Knight & The Pips**, Take Me In Your Arms And Love Me; **Martha & The Vandellas**, Jimmy Mack.

British Motown Chartbusters Volume 2; Motown 530067; 1968

Marvin Gaye & Tammi Terrell, Ain't Nothing Like The Real Thing; **Diana Ross & The Supremes**, Reflections; **Smokey Robinson & The Miracles**, If You Can Want; **Four Tops**, You Keep Running Away; **The Temptations**, I Could Never Love; **Gladys Knight & The Pips**, I Heard It Through The Grapevine; **Stevie Wonder**, I'm Wondering; **Jimmy Ruffin**, I've Passed This Way Before; **Diana Ross & The Supremes**, Some Things You Never Get Used To; **R. Dean Taylor**, Gotta See Jane; **Stevie Wonder**, Shoo-Be-Doo-Be-Doo-Be-Doo-Dah-Day; **The Temptations**, You're My Everything; **Martha & The Vandellas**, Honey Chile; **Four Tops**, If I Were A Carpenter; **Smokey Robinson & The Miracles**, I Second That Emotion; **Marvin Gaye & Tammi Terrell**, I Could Build My Whole World Around You.

Motown Chartbusters Volume 3; Motown 530068; 1969

Marvin Gaye, I Heard It Through The Grapevine; **Diana Ross & The Supremes & The Temptations**, I'm Gonna Make You Love Me; **Stevie Wonder**, My Cherie Amour; **The Isley Brothers**, This Old Heart Of Mine; **Marv Johnson**, I'll Pick A Rose For My Rose; **Diana Ross & The Supremes**, No Matter What Sign You Are; **The Four Tops**, I'm In A Different World; **Martha & The Vandellas**, Dancing In The Street; **Stevie Wonder**, For Once In My Life; **The Temptations**, Get Ready; **Edwin Starr**, Stop Her On Sight (S.O.S.); **Diana Ross & The Supremes**, Love Child; **The Isley Brothers**, Behind A Painted Smile; **Junior Walker & The All Stars**, (I'm) A Road Runner; **Smokey Robinson & The Miracles**, The Tracks Of My Tears.

Motown Chartbusters Volume 4; Motown 530059; 1969

Jackson 5, I Want You Back; **Marvin Gaye & Tammi Terrell**, The Onion Song; **Marvin Gaye**, Too Busy Thinking About My Baby; **The Supremes**, Up The Ladder To The Roof; **Four Tops**, I Can't Help Myself; **Jimmy Ruffin**, Farewell Is A Lonely Sound; **Junior Walker & The All Stars**, What Does It Take To Win Your Love; **Four Tops**, Do What You Gotta Do; **Diana Ross & The Supremes**, Some Day We'll Be Together; **The Temptations**, Cloud Nine; **Stevie Wonder**, Yester-me, Yester-you, Yester-day; **The Temptations**, I Can't Get Next To You; **Diana Ross & The Supremes & The Temptations**, I Second That Emotion.

Hitsville USA – The Motown Singles Collection 1959–1971; Motown 530129; 1992

DISC ONE: **Barret Strong**, Money (That's What I Want); **Smokey Robinson & The Miracles**, Shop Around; **The Marvelettes**, Please Mr Postman; **Eddie Holland**, Jamie; **Mary Wells**, The One Who Really Loves Me; **The Contours**, Do You Love Me; **The Marvelettes**, Beechwood 4-5789; **Mary Wells**, You Beat Me To The Punch; **Marvin Gaye**, Stubborn Kind Of Fellow; **Mary Wells**, Two Lovers; **Smokey Robinson & The Miracles**, You've Really Got A Hold On Me; **Martha & The Vandellas**, Come And Get These Memories; **Marvin Gaye**, Pride & Joy; **Stevie Wonder**, Fingertips Pt 2; **Martha & The Vandellas**, (Love Is Like A) Heatwave; **Smokey Robinson & The Miracles**, Mickey's Monkey; **Eddie Holland**, Leaving Here; **The Temptations**, The Way You Do The Things You Do; **Mary Wells**, My Guy; **Shorty Long**, Devil In A Blue Dress; **Brenda Holloway**, Every Little Bit Hurts; **The Four Tops**, Baby I Need Your Loving; **Martha & The Vandellas**, Dancing In The Street; **Carolyn Crawford**, My Smile Is Just A Frown (Turned Upside Down); **The Velvelettes**, Needle In A Haystack; **Diana Ross & The Supremes**, Baby Love; **Marvin Gaye**, How Sweet It Is To Be Loved By You.

DISC TWO: **The Temptations**, My Girl; **The Velvelettes**, He Was Really Sayin' Somethin'; **Four Tops**, Just Ask The Lonely; **Martha & The Vandellas**, Nowhere To Run; **Brenda Holloway**, When I'm Gone; **Smokey Robinson & The Miracles**, Ooh, Baby

Baby; **Four Tops**, I Can't Help Myself; **The Contours**, First I Look At The Purse; **Smokey Robinson & The Miracles**, Tracks Of My Tears; **Four Tops**, It's The Same Old Song; **Martha & The Vandellas**, Love (Makes Me Do Foolish Things); **Kim Weston**, Take Me In Your Arms (And Rock Me A Little While); **Stevie Wonder**, Uptight (Everything's Alright); **The Marvelettes**, Don't Mess With Bill; **The Elgins**, Darling Baby; **The Isley Brothers**, This Old Heart Of Mine (Is Weak For You); **The Monitors**, Greetings (This Is Uncle Sam); **Shorty Long**, Function At The Junction; **Junior Walker & The All Stars**, (I'm) A Road Runner; **The Temptations**, Ain't Too Proud To Beg; **Jimmy Ruffin**, What Becomes Of The Brokenhearted; **Junior Walker & The All Stars**, How Sweet It Is To Be Loved By You; **Chris Clark**, Love's Gone Bad; **Diana Ross & The Supremes**, You Can't Hurry Love; **The Temptations**, Beauty Is Only Skindeep; **The Elgins**, Heaven Must Have Sent You.

DISC THREE: **Four Tops**, Reach Out I'll Be There; **The Temptations**, (I Know) I'm Losing You; **Four Tops**, Standing In The Shadows Of Love; **Marvin Gaye and Kim Weston**, It Takes Two; **The Marvelettes**, The Hunter Gets Captured By The Game; **Martha & The Vandellas**, Jimmy Mack; **Four Tops**, Bernadette; **Marvin Gaye & Tammi Terrell**, Ain't No Mountain High Enough; **Smokey Robinson & The Miracles**, More Love; **Gladys Knight & The Pips**, I Heard It Through The Grapevine; **Smokey Robinson & The Miracles**, I Second That Emotion; **The Temptations**, I Wish It Would Rain; **Rita Wright**, I Can't Give Back The Love I Feel For You; **Bobby Taylor And The Vancouvers**, Does Your Man Know About Me; **Marvin Gaye & Tammi Terrell**, Ain't Nothing Like The Real Thing; **Diana Ross & The Supremes**, Love Child; **Stevie Wonder**, For Once In My Life; **The Temptations**, Cloud Nine; **Marvin Gaye**, I Heard It Through The Grapevine; **Smokey Robinson & The Miracles**, Baby Baby Don't Cry; **Edwin Starr**, Twenty-five Miles; **David Ruffin**, My Whole World Ended (The Moment You Left); **David Ruffin**, What Does It Take (To Win Your Love); **The Temptations**, I Can't Get Next To You; **The Originals**, Baby I'm For Real; **The Supremes**, Up The Ladder To The Roof.

DISC FOUR: **Jackson 5**, I Want You Back; **The Originals**, The Bells; **Rare Earth**, Get Ready; **Jackson 5**, ABC; **The**

Temptations, Ball Of Confusion; **Jackson 5**, The Love You Save; **Stevie Wonder**, Signed, Sealed, Delivered; **Edwin Starr**, War; **The Motown Spinners**, It's A Shame; **Diana Ross**, Ain't No Mountain High Enough; **The Four Tops**, Still Water (Love); **Jackson 5**, I'll Be There; **Smokey Robinson & The Miracles**, The Tears Of A Clown; **The Supremes**, Stoned Love; **Gladys Knight & The Pips**, If I Were Your Woman; **The Temptations**, Just My Imagination (Running Away With Me); **Marvin Gaye**, What's Going On; **Jackson 5**, Never Can Say Goodbye; **The Supremes**, Nathan Jones; **Gladys Knight & The Pips**, I Don't Want To Do Wrong; **The Undisputed Truth**, Smiling Faces Sometimes; **Marvin Gaye**, Mercy Mercy Me (The Ecology); **Rare Earth**, I Just Want To Celebrate.

Unsurprisingly, these two coinciding methods of buying Motown by the yard – original form *Chartbuster* albums, or the big box set – must bring a tear of joy to a marketing man's eye: although *Hitsville*'s Disc Four set is virtually *Chartbusters Five* (see 1970s section) with bits of *Four* thrown into a different running order, practically nothing else crosses over. Thus to get the full Motown story (which both formats imply they offer) you've got to buy the whole lot. The most remarkable thing about setting them alongside each other like this is the amount of truly enormous Motown songs that *weren't* on the *Chartbusters* albums, yet at the time nobody (and every home had them in the late-1960s) seemed to notice – 'Baby Love', 'The Tears Of A Clown', 'My Girl', 'I Second That Emotion' 'For Once In My Life' and so on. But that was back in the days when people used to buy singles.

Blues Brother, Soul Sister; Dino DINTVCD56; 1993

John Lee Hooker, Boom Boom; **Erma Franklin**, (Take A Little) Piece Of My Heart; **Sam & Dave**, Soul Man; **Etta James**, I'd Rather Go Blind; **Booker T & The MGs**, Green Onions; **The Isley Brothers**, Shout; **Aretha Franklin**, Think; **The Staple Singers**, Respect Yourself; **Bob & Earl**, Harlem Shuffle; **Al Green**, Take Me To The River; **Muddy Waters**, Mannish Boy; **Fontella Bass**, Rescue Me; **Wilson Pickett**, In The Midnight Hour; **Eddie Floyd**, Knock On Wood; **Little Milton**, Stormy

Monday; **Dobie Gray**, Drift Away; **Betty Everett**, It's In His Kiss; **Fleetwood Mac**, Need Your Love So Bad; **Anne Peebles**, Gonna Tear Your Playhouse Down; **Ben E King**; Stand By Me.

Blues Brother, Soul Sister Vol 2; Dino DINTVCD61; 1993

Martha & The Vandellas, Dancing In The Street; **John Lee Hooker & Bonnie Raitt**, I'm In The Mood; **James Brown**, It's A Man's Man's Man's World; **Aretha Franklin**, Soulville; **Albert King**, Born Under A Bad Sign; **Al Green**, I'm So Tired Of Being Alone; **Ike & Tina Turner**, The Night Time Is The Right Time; **Junior Walker & The All Stars**, (I'm) A Road Runner; **Etta James**, I Just Want To Make Love To You; **Aaron Neville**, Tell It Like It Is; **Tommy Tucker**, High Heeled Sneakers; **Aretha Franklin**, Today I Sing The Blues; **John Lee Hooker**, Dimples; **The Staple Singers**, I'll Take You There; **B.B. King**, The Thrill Is Gone; **William Bell & Judy Clay**, Private Number; **Howlin' Wolf**, The Red Rooster; **Maxine Brown**, Oh No Not My Baby; **Nina Simone**, I Put A Spell On You; **Percy Sledge**, When A Man Loves A Woman.

Blues Brother, Soul Sister Vol 3; Dino DINTVCD85; 1994

James Brown, I Feel Good; **Aretha Franklin**, Respect; **BB King**, Ain't Nobody Home; **Arthur Conley**, Sweet Soul Music; **Gladys Knight**, Midnight Train To Georgia; **Wilson Pickett**, Mustang Sally; **Percy Sledge**, Warm And Tender Love; **Howlin' Wolf**; Smokestack Lightning; **Ray Charles**, What'd I Say?; **Ike & Tina Turner**, Nutbush City Limits; **The Isley Brothers**, That Lady; **Muddy Waters**, Got My Mojo Working; **Al Green**, I'm Still In Love With You; **Carla Thomas**, B.A.B.Y.; **The Temptations**, My Girl; **Mary Wells**, My Guy; **John Lee Hooker**, Serves You Right To Suffer; **Dorothy Moore**, Sittin' On The Dock Of The Bay.

Although 1960s soul compilations tend to draw from a very limited pool – i.e. they're starting to repeat themselves by now – this one is worth examination. In its bid to put a unique spin on its presentation of those 'classic' tracks, it's mixed them up with blues to provide a useful take on the relationship between southern soul and the blues. Don't let the idea that it's TV advertised put you off.

Various Artists; This Is Soul; Object FPFCD01; 1989

DISC ONE: **Sam & Dave**, Soul Man; **The Drifters**, There Goes My Baby; **James Brown**, Papa's Got A Brand New Bag; **Gladys Knight**, Operator; **Percy Sledge**, Warm And Tender Love; **The Tams**, Hey Girl Don't Bother Me; **Sam & Dave**, Hold On I'm Coming; **Brook Benton**, Kiddio; **Eddie Floyd**, Knock On Wood; **Gladys Knight**, So Sad The Song; **George McRae**, Rock Your Baby; **Brook Benton**, It's Just A Matter Of Time; **The Moments**, Look At Me I'm In Love; **Sam & Dave**, Soul Sister Brown Sugar.

DISC TWO: **The Drifters**, Saturday Night At The Movies; **Sam & Dave**, I Thank You; **Brook Benton**, Rainy Night In Georgia; **James Brown**, Please Please Please; **Gladys Knight**, Every Beat Of My Heart; **Percy Sledge**, When A Man Loves A Woman; **The Drifters**, Under The Boardwalk; **Archie Bell & The Drells**, Tighten Up; **Soul Survivors**, Expressway To Your Heart; **The Moments**, Girls; **The Tams**, What Kind Of Fool; **Wilber Harrison**, Let's Stick Together; **Dobie Gray**, Drift Away.

DISC THREE: **The Drifters**, Up On The Roof; **Mary Wells**, My Guy; **Percy Sledge**, Try A Litle Tenderness; **Sam & Dave**, Respect; **Martha & The Vandellas**, Nowhere To Run; **Bob & Earl**; Harlem Shuffle; **Ben E King**, Stand By Me; **Sam & Dave**, Sweet Soul Music; **Percy Sledge**, You Send Me; **Martha & The Vandellas**, Quicksand; **Brook Benton**, So Many Ways; **George McRae**, I Can't Leave You Alone; **Ben E King**, Supernatural Thing.

DISC FOUR: **Ben E King**, I Who Have Nothing; **Martha & The Vandellas**, It's The Same Old Song; **The Drifters**, On Broadway; **Ben E King**, Spanish Harlem; **Percy Sledge**, Behind Closed Doors; **Martha & The Vandellas**, Dancing In The Street; **Jerry Butler**, Only The Strong Survive; **Harold Melvin & The Blue Notes**, The Love I Lost; **Martha & The Vandellas**, In The Midnight Hour; **George McRae**, It's Been So Long; **The Tymes**, You Little Trustmaker; **Brook Benton**, Baby You've Got What It Takes; **Martha & The Vandellas**, Get Ready; **Harold Melvin & The Blue Notes**, Satisfaction Guaranteed.

This four-CD box is budget priced – i.e. you should pay no more than £20, but don't expect much in the way of attractive packaging and even less when it comes to sleeve notes. However, it's a better than simply pennywise proposition as it takes tracks from a number of record labels, thus providing a superb sixties soul starting point. In fact it's even worth suffering the Brook Benton numbers.

*Various Artists; Holland-Dozier-Holland Present The Hits Of Invictus And Hot Wax Records; HDH HDHCD501; 1986

Chairmen Of The Board, (You've Got Me) Dangling On A String; **Honey Cone**, Want Ads; **Glass House**, Crumbs Off The Table; **Honey Cone**, Stick Up; **Chairmen Of The Board**, Give Me Just A Little More Time; **Honey Cone**, Girls It Ain't Easy; **100 Proof**, Somebody's Been Sleeping In My Bed; **Chairmen Of The Board**, Everything Is Tuesday; **Freda Payne**, Band Of Gold; **Laura Lee**, Women's Love Rights; **The 8th Day**, She's Not Just Another Woman; **Laura Lee**, If You Can Beat Me Rockin'; **Chairmen Of The Board**, Finders Keepers; **Flaming Ember**, Mind, Body & Soul; **Honey Cone**, While You're Looking Out For Sugar; **Freda Payne**, Bring The Boys Home; **Flaming Ember**, Westbound # 9; **Freda Payne**, Deeper And Deeper; **Chairmen Of The Board**, Chairmen Of The Board; **Honey Cone**, One Monkey Don't Stop No Show; **Chairmen Of The Board**, On My Way To A Better Place.

The biggest hits from the two labels set up by Lamont Dozier and the Holland brothers Eddie and Brian, after their acrimonious departure from Motown in 1966.

*Atlantic Soul Classics; Atlantic 241138; 1987

Arthur Conley, Sweet Soul Music; **Wilson Pickett**, In The Midnight Hour; **Eddie Floyd**, Knock On Wood; **Aretha Franklin**, Respect; **Sam & Dave**, Soul Man; **Don Covay**, See Saw; **Solomon Burke**, Everybody Need Somebody To Love; **The Bar-Kays**, Soul Finger; **Ben E King**; Stand By Me. **Carla Thomas**, B.A.B.Y.; **The Drifters**, Under The Boardwalk; **Otis Redding & Carla Thomas**, Tramp; **Percy Sledge**, When A Man

Loves A Woman; **William Bell**, Tribute To A King; **Otis Redding**, (Sittin' On) The Dock Of The Bay.

*Various Artists; Atlantic Soul Ballads; Atlantic 2411336; 1988

Otis Redding; Try A Little Tenderness; **Aretha Franklin**, I Say A Little Prayer; **The Drifters**, Save The Last Dance For Me; **Wilson Pickett**, I'm In Love; **Percy Sledge**, Warm And Tender Love; **Clarence Carter**, Patches; **The Persuaders**, It's A Thin Line Between Love And Hate; **Ben E King**, Spanish Harlem; **Sam & Dave**, When Something's Wrong With My Baby; **Otis Redding**, My Girl; **Major Harris**, Love Won't Let Me Wait; **The Drifters**, On Broadway; **Barbara Lewis**, I'm Yours; **Brook Benton**, Rainy Night In Georgia; **Wilson Pickett**, Hey Jude.

*Atlantic R&B Volume 1 (1947-1952); Atlantic 781293-2; 1987

Joe Morris, Lowe Groovin'; **Tiny Grimes**, That Old Black Magic; **Tiny Grimes**, Annie Laurie; **Tiny Grimes**, Midnight Special; **Joe Morris**, Applejack; **Sticks McGhee**, Drinkin' Wine Spoo-dee-o-dee; **Frank Culler**, Coleslaw; **Ruth Brown**, So Long; **Ruth Brown**, I'll Get Along Somehow; **Professor Longhair**, Hey Little Girl; **Professor Longhair**, Mardi Gras In New Orleans; **Harry Van Halls**, Tee Nah Nah; **Joe Morris**, Anytime, Anyplace, Anywhere; **Ruth Brown**, Teardrops From My Eyes; **Sticks McGhee**, One Monkey Don't Stop No Show; **The Clovers**, Don't You Know I Love You; **The Cardinals**, Shouldn't I Know; **Big Joe Turner**, The Chill Is On; **Big Joe Turner**, Chains Of Love; **The Clovers**, Fool, Fool, Fool; **The Clovers**, One Mint Julep; **The Cardinals**, Wheel Of Fortune; **Big Joe Turner**, Sweet Sixteen; **Ruth Brown**, 5-10-15 Hours; **The Clovers**, Ting-a-Ling; **Willis Jackson**, Gator's Groove; **Ruth Brown**, Daddy, Daddy; **Ray Charles**, The Midnight Hour.

*Atlantic R&B Volume 2 (1952-1955); Atlantic 781294-2; 1987

The Diamonds, Beggar For Your Kisses; **Ruth Brown**, Mama, He Treats Your Daughter Mean; **The Clovers**, Good Loving; **Ruth Brown**, Wild Wild Young Men; **Ray Charles**, Mess

Around; **Big Joe Turner**, Hush Hush; **Clyde McPhatter & The Drifters**, Soul On Fire/Money Honey; **Clyde McPhatter & The Drifters**, Such A Night; **Professor Longhair**, Tipitina; **Clyde McPhatter & The Drifters**, White Christmas; **Clyde McPhatter**, Honey Love; **Clyde McPhatter,** Whatcha Gonna Do; **Big Joe Turner**, Shake Rattle & Roll; **The Chords**, Sh'Boom; **Tommy Ridgley**, Jam Up; **Ray Charles**, Tomorrow Night/Twedlee Dee/I Got A Woman; **The Cardinals**, The Door Is Still Open; **Big Joe Turner**, Flip Flop And Fly; **Ray Charles**, A Fool For You; **Ray Charles**, This Little Girl Of Mine; **The Drifters**, Play It Fair/Adorable; **The Robins**, Smokey Joe's Cafe.

*Atlantic R&B Volume 3 (1955-1958); Atlantic 781295-2; 1987

The Drifters, Ruby Baby; **The Cookies**, In Paradise; **Big Joe Turner**, Chicken And The Hawk; **The Clovers**, Devil Or Angel; **Ray Charles**, Drowing In My Own Tears; **Ray Charles**, Hallelujah I Love Her So; **LaVerne Baker**, Jim Dandy; **The Coasters**, Down In Mexico; **Big Joe Turner**, Corina Corina; **Clyde McPhatter**, Treasures Of Love; **The Clovers**, Love, Love, Love; **Chuck Willis**, It's Too Late; **Ray Charles**, Lonely Avenue; **Lloyd Hunter**, Since I Met You Baby; **Ruth Brown**, Lucky Lips; **Clyde McPhatter**, Without Love; **The Drifters**, Fools Fall In Love; **Big Joe Turner**, Midnight Special Train; **Ivory Joe Hunter**, Empty Arms; **Chuck Willis**, C.C. Rider; **The Bobbettes**, Betty And Dupree; **Chuck Willis**, What Am I Living For; **Chuck Willis**, Hang Up My Rock 'N' Roll Shoes; **The Coasters**, Yakety Yak; **Clyde McPhatter**, Lover's Question; **Ray Charles**, I Cried A Tear; **Ray Charles**, The Right Time; **Ray Charles**, What'd I Say (Pts 1&2); **The Drifters**, There Goes My Baby

*Atlantic R&B Volume 4 (1958-1962); Atlantic 781296-2; 1987

The Coasters, Along Came Jones; **Ray Charles**, Let The Good Times Roll; **The Coasters**, Poison Ivy; **The Drifters**, Dance With Me; **Ray Charles**, Just For A Thrill; **Ray Charles**, This Magic Moment; **Ray Charles**, Save The Last Dance For Me; **The Coasters**, Shopping For Clothes; **Ben E. King**, Spanish Harlem; **Ben E. King**, Young Boy Blues; **Ben E. King**, Stand By Me; **Carla**

Thomas, Gee Whiz; **Solomon Burke**, Just Out Of Reach; **The Coasters**, Little Egypt; **Ben E. King**, Amor; **The Mar-Keys**, Last Night; **The Ikettes**, I'm Blue (The Gong Gong Song); **William Bell**, You Don't Miss Your Water; **The Falcons**, I Found A Love; **Solomon Burke**, Cry To Me; **Ben E. King**, Don't Play That Song; **Booker T & The MGs**, Green Onions.

Atlantic R&B Volume 5 (1962–1966); Atlantic 781297-2; 1987

The Drifters, Up On The Roof; **Ben E. King**, I Who Have Nothing/See See Rider; **Solomon Burke**, If You Need Me; **Otis Redding**, These Arms Of Mine; **Barbara Lewis**, Hello Stranger; **The Drifters**, On Broadway; **Doris Troy**, Just One Look; **Nat Kendricks & The Swans**, Do The Mashed Potatoes (Pts 1&2); **Chris Kenner**, Land Of A Thousand Dances; **Chris Kenner**, Wlaking The Dog; **Esther Phillips**, Release Me; **Don Covay**, Mercy Mercy; **The Drifters**, Under The Boardwalk; **Esther Phillips**, And I Love Him; **Joe Tex**, Hold What You've Got; **Otis Redding**, Mr Pitiful; **Barbara Lewis**, Baby I'm Yours; **Willie Tee**, Teasin' You; **Otis Redding**, I've Been Loving You Too Long; **Wilson Pickett**, In The Midnight Hour; **Don Covay**, See Saw; **Otis Redding**, Respect; **Sam & Dave**, You Don't Know Like I Know; **Percy Sledge**, When A Man Loves A Woman; **Sam & Dave**, Hold On I'm Coming; **The Capitols**, Cool Jerk; **Jimmy Hughes**, Neighbour Neighbour.

Atlantic R&B Volume 6 (1966–1969); Atlantic 781298-2; 1987

Wilson Pickett, Land Of A Thousand Dances; **Eddie Floyd**, Knock On Wood; **Otis Redding**, Try A Little Tenderness; **Wilson Pickett**, Mustang Sally; **Sam & Dave**, When Something Is Wrong With My Baby; **Arthur Conley**, Sweet Soul Music; **Sam & Dave**, Soul Man; **Aretha Franklin**, I Never Loved A Man (The Way I Loved You); **Aretha Franklin**, Do Right Woman, Do Right Man; **Joe Tex**, Show Me; **Otis Redding & Carla Thomas**, Tramp; **Wilson Pickett**, Funky Broadway; **Booker T & The MGs**, Hip Hug Her; **Aretha Franklin**, Respect; **Aretha Franklin**, You Make Me Feel Like A Natural Woman; **The Bar-Kays**, Soul Finger; **Aretha Franklin**, Baby I Love You; **Joe Tex**, Skinny Legs And All; **Aretha Franklin**, Chain Of Fools; **King**

Curtis, Memphis Soul Stew; **Otis Redding**, (Sittin' On) The Dock Of The Bay; **Otis Redding**, Tighten Up; **Clarence Carter**, Slip Away; **Aretha Franklin**, Think; **Roberta Flack**, The First Time Ever I Saw Your Face; **R.B. Greaves**, Take A Letter Maria; **Ray Charles**, Rainy Night In Georgia; **Donny Hathaway**, The Ghetto.

*Atlantic R&B Volume 7 (1969–1974); Atlantic 781299-2; 1987

Walter Davis, Turn Back The Hands Of Time; **Les McCann**, Compared To What; **Aretha Franklin**, Don't Play That Song; **King Floyd**, Groove Me; **Clarence Carter**, Patches; **The Beginning Of The End**, Funky Nassau (Pts 1&2); **The Persuaders**, Thin Line Between Love And Hate; **Aretha Franklin**, Rock Steady; **Roberta Flack & Donny Hathaway**, You've Got A Friend; **Betty Wright**, Clean Up Woman; **The Spinners**, Could It Be I'm Falling In Love; **Roberta Flack**, Killing Me Softly With His Song; **Roberta Flack & Donny Hathaway**, Where Is The Love; **The Spinners**, I'll Be Around; **Roberta Flack**, Feel Like Makin' Love; **The Spinners**, Mighty Love; **Major Harris**, Love Won't Let Me Wait.

Sensibly available as individual albums instead of as an optimistically marketed eight-CD box, this series traces Atlantic Records' soul involvement right from the roots. It's not just a collection of thoroughly enjoyable music either, the compilation is comprehensive enough to make a few important points: put in a context such as this, Ray Charles's influence can be seen to be as enormous as it was; it goes back to trace soul's blues roots to prove this side was as important as gospel; it contains the originals of many songs made famous in cover version form, giving good opportunity to see what it was that attracted the mainstream to this music in the first place; and, a little unfortunately, demonstrates that Atlantic lost the plot in the early 1970s, when Planet Soul started spinning in a street funk orbit.

NB *Volume Seven* deserves particular consideration as it may well be the only way to get a full-length version of Beginning Of The End's 'Funky Nassau' on CD. And as it's on the same CD as The Persuaders' 'Thin Line Between Love And Hate' . . . you owe it to yourself.

*Hi Records: The R&B Sessions + The Soul Years; Hi HIUKCD 129; 1991

Willie Mitchell, That Driving Beat; **Don Bryant**, It Ain't Easy, Clear Days And Stormy Nights, Sure Looks Good To Me; **1+1**, I Will Be True; **Willie Mitchell**, The Champion (pt 1); **Norm West**, Hey Little Girl; **Janet & The Jays**, Love What You're Doing To Me, Without A Reason; **Gene 'Bowlegs' Miller**, The Goodest Man; **James Fry**, Mama's Boy, I've Got Enough; **Five Royales**, Help Yourself, Roll With The Punch; **Al Green**, Strong As Death; **Syl Johnson**, Back For A taste Of Your Love; **OV Wright**, I Don't Do Windows; **Bobo Mr Soul**, She's My Woman; **Willie Mitchell**, Teenie's Dreams; **Quiet Elegance**, After You, You Got My Mind Messed Up; **Otis Clay**, Trying To Live My Life Without You; **Ann Peebles**, I've Been There Before; **Phillip Mitchell**, Turning Over The Ground; **The Masqueraders**, Wake Up Fool; **Joint Venture**, When The Battle Is Over; **George Jackson**, Let Them Know You Care, Aretha Sing One For Me.

A cross-section of Willie Mitchell's production work at Hi, starting in the late 1960s and moving into the next decade. The musical base on which Al Green's success was built.

1970s

By the beginning of the 1970s, soul music was a revolution waiting to happen. It was as if all the bits of the jigsaw had been found and set out on the table ready to be put together to make a picture.

The politics of the 1960s had changed not only the way white people looked at black people, but had altered black people's perception of themselves. To varying degrees up and down the US, it was now more than just all right to look 'Mr Charley' in the eye, it was damn near obligatory. Angela Davis-type afros, dashikis and hand-carved wooden clenched black fists worn as jewellery had more than simply sartorial value, the idea was to make a fashion statement that could in no way be confused with trying to look white. The social change that had swept the country meant this was far more likely to be at least tolerated if not accepted. While tolerance comprised a large portion of the hippie agenda, events of the 1960s, shown on national television, served to shame much of middle America into rethinking their approach to life in general.

The corporate structures for soul music to take a more introverted approach were falling into place too, as the labels that had shaped R&B into soul ten years earlier were losing interest and influence. They were either being swallowed up by the majors at the expense of creative independence (King); going bankrupt or heading that way (Chess and Stax, respectively); or crossing over to the far more lucrative world of white rock (Atlantic and, surprisingly, Motown tried to tread that route). All of which left a door open for a new strata of independent record labels, studios and production companies, eager to follow the old Black Panther party maxim and take care of their own business for themselves. Even without the efforts of The Fairplay Committee, the music business had long been viewed, by those inside and outside it, as the most blatant example of post-slavery black exploitation.

A new style soul music represented sound commercial sense too. Black *owned*, as opposed to just black, radio stations were on the increase, so the music would be guaranteed empathetic air time, and the money was there for the records to be bought. The overall prosperity of the 1970s meant there was, proportionately, more money in the black communities, and, as a result of the recently improved opportunities in employment and education, the Black Urban Professional, or Buppie, came into large-scale being at this point. This fiscal security meant it was possible to sell enormous amounts of records without a mainstream hit. Consequently, soul music was, perhaps for the first time, under no obligation to conform to anybody else's idea of what it should be or do. An opportunity nobody wanted to squander.

Before the first year had come to a close, James Brown had opened proceedings with 'Sex Machine'. This five-minute almost primal groove swept all before it, clearing the way for the whole Street Funk Method, a powerful, repetitively rhythmic style that based itself on a strong beat which allowed all sorts of musical showing off and influences to go on on top, without compromising the essential blackness. At the time, most 'serious' mainstream music fans dismissed this style as being simple-minded, pointless even, never coming to terms with why it should be working so hard just to celebrate its own being there, never stopping to think how tough it had been to get to this point in the first place. It became something of a knee-jerk reaction for groups to make their sound tougher, less mainstream accessible, as an expression of how down with the cause they were.

As the decade went on we had jazz/funk (Kool & The Gang, Roy Ayers, The Crusaders); acid/funk (The Temptations, Rick James), orchestral funk (Philly), Latino funk (War), P-Funk (a law unto itself) and, of course, street funk as it developed into instrumental-type jams courtesy of Brass Construction, The

Fatback Band, BT Express, Mandrill and so on. New sub-styles were formed practically every day, but with one common denominator – they were musician led. The players themselves were in charge, not some aging producer entirely responsible for artists' output, but young, adventurous, out-to-prove-themselves artists with ever-open ears. This was really soul's belated assimilation of what had been rock groups' right since The Beatles – to be self-contained writing/producing/quality-controlling units. But such was the benevolent feudalism that traditionally ran through black music, it had taken a revolution to gain such independence.

Such a wide creative spectrum naturally meant a rapid evolution of style, and such was the speed at which things were turning over that Sly Stone's groundbreaking Woodstock funk/rock-isms were looking dated by about 1971. It was as if once he'd made the point that it was cool to mess about with rock, it loosed a tidal wave of young black musicians eager to have a try. Not so young, but well to the fore of this development (that ran in perfect harmony with street funk) was George Clinton's Funkadelic, delivering exactly what the group name promised, building their rock nuances around a much darker, spookily zonked-out modern day blues. At the same time Motown staffer Norman Whitfield took full advantage of the advancements in studio technology to explore post-psychedelia from a traditional soul point of view. At that company Stevie Wonder was also redefining soul parameters as the Moog Synthesiser (on the market from early in the decade) allowed him the means to realise his musical visions. Likewise Marvin Gaye, who was taking the very rock-based approach to making albums rather than a collection of singles.

Then there was The Sound of Philadelphia. The brainchild of writer/producers Kenny Gamble and Leon Huff, it was the pop/soul of the 1970s, the new sound of young black America. Based on Philadelphia's vocal harmony traditions it wove strings and melodies around hard funky rhythms, to create an arrangement that was light enough for mass appeal but never forgot where it was coming from or who its base audience were. And although the roots of disco can be heard in the Philly arrangements, in true 1970s style the lyrics were never quick to shy away from soul's social conscience.

Each of these occurrences did a great deal to win mainstream credibility for soul music, as they appeared to be playing by pop/rock rules. But they also served to underline one of the highest profile casualties of the 1970s, Motown Records. The groundbreaking projects from the above artists were actively obstructed by this company as it was felt nobody would be interested. Indeed such was the corporate lack of judgement that while the world turned around them they tried in vain to extend the glory days of well-behaved artists in gleaming bee-hive wigs and matching mohair suits.

It served as an apt metaphor for how society had moved on. The well-behaved negroes of ten years hence (when Berry Gordy's aspirational game plan had been liberating in itself) were now up in people's faces. And proud to be there, a notion that continued throughout the decade, as soul strived to stay ahead of a mainstream that constantly sought to adopt the current black styles. It wasn't really anything new, this sort of artistic theft had been going on since Benny Goodman appropriated big band jazz and called himself The King of Swing. But given these new circumstances something could be done about it.

As the decade came to a close, post-*Saturday Night Fever*, street funk had been so totally co-opted by disco it was almost a dirty word. What was called for was a style so innately inner city it would be a long time before the mainstream got their heads round it, let alone ripped it off. In December 1979, an unknown group from New Jersey had an enormous hit with a track called 'Rappers' Delight'. And suddenly the 1970s were over and done with.

Ashford & Simpson

(Nickolas Ashford, born Fairfield, North Carolina, May 5, 1943; Valerie Simpson, born The Bronx, New York, August 26, 1948) Even with Berry Gordy's well-documented failure to come to terms with what MARVIN GAYE and STEVIE WONDER were doing at the turn of the decade, Motown closed off another avenue of advancement in 1972 when they allowed Ashford & Simpson to leave: while the former situation demonstrated how the label was losing touch with Young Black America, the latter made it much more difficult for them to service their existing fans as they grew older. If anybody was likely to pull the beleaguered corporate approach out of bobby sox and into some serious lingerie – where it could have enjoyed a future beyond mere nostalgia – it was this husband and wife writing/production team. They had an understanding of the Motown Sound and how it functioned (they'd been on the staff since 1967), yet possessed earthy black church roots that refused to lie down quietly and had a firm grasp of adult culture and themes uptown. In songs like 'Ain't No Mountain High Enough', 'I'm Every Woman', 'Landlord', 'Bourgie Bourgie', 'Ain't Nothing Like The Real Thing', 'Remember Me' and 'You're All I Need To Get By' they structured a classy, committed, but entirely tough blend of music and narrative. The fiery orchestrations, intense lyrics and sophisticatedly sanctified arrangements were worlds removed from Smokey's charmingly naive tales of teen angst. In many ways their work reflected their own relationship: though obviously passionate for each other – an evening in their company almost twenty years after they first met was enough to see that – the blazing rows across the mixing desk are soul music legend.

Keeping them sweet would have been no more complicated than letting them perform some of their own songs and giving them as big a push as the artists for whom they wrote. But it was a measure of how the rigid demarcation system at Motown was becoming increasingly at odds with the times that they didn't get that break. It's not as if Berry Gordy would have been taking an enormous risk either.

Ashford and Simpson met as performers in a Harlem church gospel group in the early 1960s – he would later maintain he only joined because he had his eye on her; around that time Nick cut a couple of jazzy singles for Verve; in 1964 they recorded together as Val & Nick; and, according to Marvin Gaye, towards the end of Tammi Terrell's life, Valerie Simpson was singing more and more of her vocal parts. Thus it seems strange that Valerie's two solo Motown albums – the nearest thing they had to a performing career on the label – were virtually buried. Even more stange considering they had a run of strong-selling albums on Warner Bros throughout the 1970s, leading to even bigger hits on Capitol in the first half of the next decade. While their stunning live shows redefined the then fad for male/female duet singing, they sang to each other so blatantly their words of love were far more than theoretical – on a good night it was as if the audience were intruding on a series of intensely private moments.

However, slick and sensuous as the couple's albums were, it was providing for other people – first as employees, then under their own Hopsack & Silk Productions banner (a little joke on how they saw each other) – that they made the most impact. They wrote their first songs in 1964 for no other reason than to see if they could, then, astonishment out of the way, figured they might have a career in it when they sold six for $75. Early recipients of the Ashford & Simpson fairy dust include Maxine Brown, Chuck Jackson and RAY CHARLES ('Let's Get Stoned'), while their finest Motown moments were with Marvin Gaye & Tammi Terrell and a post-SUPREMES Diana Ross. From that point it would have been more than interesting to see how far they could have taken it in an organisation such as Motown once was, i.e. totally geared up to marketing black music. As it was, Ashford & Simpson were still responsible for some sublime moments in lowdown, grown-up soul both as themselves and with CHAKA KHAN, THE BROS JOHNSON, GLADYS KNIGHT and TEDDY PENDERGRASS.

Solid; Capitol CDP746662; 1984

As the stunning Warner Bros album *Is It Still Good To Ya?* is at the time of writing no longer available, this first Capitol set is the best original A&S LP on the shelves, and it does run *Good To Ya?* a very close second. Not least because it proves the couple to be utterly adept at incorporating a lightly cut up hip-hop flavour into their usual luxurious framework, intensifying the emotional and in no way muddying up the deep velvet pile of the orchestrations. Then, while the title track, 'Cherish Forever More' and 'Honey I Love You' declare their devotion in almost armour-plated terms, it still finds space for concern with the socially aware 'Babies'. It showed the couple continuing to grow into the 1980s.

The Best Of Ashford & Simpson; Capitol C285015; 1993

Only the best of the Capitol years, but together with the highlights of *Solid* there's such cause to get excited as 'High Rise',

'Love Or Physical' and 'Found A Cure' – one of the best late disco tunes that didn't have the name Chic attached to it. All that lets this set down, really, is the couple of numbers from the *Real Love* album, which, held up next to the rest, are noticeably weedy.

Average White Band

(Alan Gorrie, born Perth, Scotland, July 19, 1946, bass/vocals/clarinet; Steve Ferrone, drums; Hamish Stuart, guitar; Roger Ball, saxes; Malcolm Duncan, saxes; Onnie McIntyre, guitar)
Without wishing to appear unduly chauvinistic, it hardly seems likely that Perth, in Scotland, would be home to one of the most vital bands of the mid-1970s street funk scene. But yes, that's where Alan Gorrie, a bass player with the dryest sense of humour, put together the Average White Band in 1972. After working as support to Eric Clapton, one unsuccessful album and their drummer overdosing on heroin, the band recruited Steve Ferrone behind the kit and signed to Atlantic Records, who recognised their heavyweight potential by putting them with top US producer Arif Mardin. The result was an eponymously titled LP that went to number 1 in the US and top ten in the UK, followed by two more American top ten LPs and a succession of hit singles both here and over there. Sharp as these were, though, the song that counted was the million-selling 'Pick Up The Pieces', off that second LP in 1975. A sweat-inducing classic of epic proportions, all growling horns, jangling guitar breaks and the thumping back-beat that will, without exception, still move an older crowd in a way that would stop an osteopath's heart. In fact, such was its status on London's black soul scene twenty years ago that dance floors would respond to the first few bars with exaggeratedly weary shouts of 'Average! Average!'

Any ironic statement was lost on JAMES BROWN though: presumably affronted by the notion of a British group who went under such a remorselessly provocative name dominating American black radio, he and The JBs cut a reasonably successful, determinedly funky single titled 'Picking Up The Pieces One By One' and called themselves The Above Average Black Band.

Average White Band; Atlantic 7815152; 1974

Although they went on to make eight albums in as many years, and the follow up, *Cut The Cake*, was the one that everybody seemed to own, this is the only album that's survived on CD. While it's funky all the way through, it's got 'Pick Up The Pieces' on it, which is really the only AWB tune anybody wants to get misty-eyed about. It's worth whatever it costs for that number alone.

SEE ALSO: Various Artists; *Classic Funk Mastercuts Volume 1*; Mastercuts CUTSCD6; 1992

Roy Ayers

(Born Los Angeles, California, 1940)
It's entirely appropriate that vibraphonist/vocalist Roy Ayers should still be packing 'em in in such jazz-oriented London nightspots as Ronnie Scott's or The Jazz Café, quite literally leading his audience a merry dance on such tunes as 'Running Away', 'Poo Poo La La' and 'Can't You See Me'. Ayers is one of jazz/funk's founding fathers – in its truest sense. As opposed to established jazzers pausing to dip a toe in something prospectively far more commercial, or later exponents who arrived at an established style, Ayers worked skilfully to incorporate soul and funk rhythm structures, arrangements and, most importantly, attitude into the vibraphone playing he'd learned with the likes of Herbie Mann, Chico Hamilton and Wayne Henderson.

In many ways, such fusion was hardly surprising. He'd studied classical piano and, while still in his teens, translated the experience to the vibes. In his twenties, and based in New York, the social upheavals of that decade didn't pass him by – he remains an upstandingly conscious brother as he cruises through his fifties – and as the loudest expressions of black pride were from the soul crowd it was natural for him to look in that direction: in spite of a solid jazz grounding, by 1968 he had put out an album called *Solid Soul Picnic*.

But it was in the 1970s, with his regular group Ubiquity, that his experiments found a footing. Riding Black America's early 1970s mood, he made a sunny instrument like the vibraphone the centre of such dark brooding pieces as his *Red, Black & Green* album (the colours of Black America's 'national' flag), 'Sensitize Your Mind', 'The Theme From Mash', an almost spooky take on Bill Withers' 'Ain't No Sunshine' and handled 'Feel Like Making Love' in a way that turned the ROBERTA FLACK ballad into a startling display of musical climaxes. Even after appearing to mellow out and concentrate on vocals and lighter arrangements, Roy Ayers stayed down by experimenting with African sounds and musicians – including Fela for his *Africa, Center Of The World* LP in 1981.

'Discovered', and thus given a new lease of life, by a UK club audience in the late 1970s, high-profile 1980s tracks were tailored to a post-disco dance floor crowd. Simplified as they seemed compared with what had gone before, the less prominent album tracks were clever enough to prove continued dedication to the complex structures of his jazz days. And besides, who was going to begrudge a solid soul trooper like Roy Ayers his time in the spotlight? Especially when it was those Roy Ayers club hits that provided a welcoming door for so many new arrivals to delve a bit deeper into jazz.

Rare, Volume II; Polydor 8437582; 1990

Replacing Volume I, this collects much of the best from those early days, showing Ayers at his most potent. The tunes mentioned above, plus a celebratory cover of Stevie Wonder's 'Don't You Worry 'Bout A Thing' and the ultra-soulful 'When Is Real Real?' show his genuinely intriguing blend of straight funk bass 'n' drums with jazz lead lines to bring a new dimension to the music. It's evocative enough to express the feeling of the day without recourse to any more lyrics than it takes to sing a chorus, or a smoochy smoove that just oozed lurrrve.

Hot; Jazz House JHCD021; 1993

Very nearly a Greatest Hits Part 2, this puts together some of the best – i.e. not the most uncomplicated – of his club hits and a few interesting album tracks. That it contains 'Running Away', 'Can't You See Me' and 'Love Will Bring Us Back Together' makes it a solid proposition. Yet it's got 'Everybody Loves The Sunshine' as well.

Africa, Centre Of The World; Polydor PD1627, 1981

This album came about after Ayers toured the motherland in 1980 and, using local pick-up musicians to supplement his regular players, began increasingly to incorporate African sounds into his arrangements. As the tour progressed he was using Fela as a featured player and learning all he could about how the sounds worked and would work with his western jazz. The LP is an attempt to get what he learned down on to wax, again using African musicians, and while it's never less than interesting it appeared a bit too self-indulgent to have a huge commercial value.

SEE ALSO: Various Artists; *Classic Jazz/Funk Mastercuts Volume 2*; Beechwood CUTSCD4; 1991

The Bar-Kays

(Mark II line-up: James Alexander, bass; Lloyd Smith, guitar; Michael Beard, drums; John Colbert, vocals; Charles Allen, trumpet; Harvey Henderson, sax; Winston Stewart, keyboards; Frank Thompson, trombone; Sherman Gray, percussion; Mary Bynham, keyboards)
➥The 1967 plane crash that killed OTIS REDDING left two of The Bar-Kays alive – trumpeter Ben Cauley, the accident's sole survivor, and bass player James Alexander who was late for take off and got left behind. It was Alexander who put together a new young group under the old name, which came to sum up 1970s Stax as a modern proposition, while still paying heed to the label's musical traditions. These guys had been listening to more acid rock than SAM & DAVE, were experimenting with guitars and electronic effects, could keep what they were learning hard by putting it on top of a stripped back funky rhythm, and knew the best way forward was to get up in your face. Oh yes, they also knew what it meant to be black and heading into 1970, and celebrated ghetto culture with a pimp swagger attitude and titles like 'Black Rock', 'Jivin' Round', 'Funky Thang', 'Cold Blooded' and 'Money Talks'. A new currency indeed. As the new house band, and successful in their own right, they were

the vanguard of a wind of change down in Memphis. A new era that saw the better behaved soul singing stars of the 1960s replaced with bands. Bands who called themselves Black Nasty, 24-CARAT BLACK, Sons Of Slum and Sho Nuff. They were part of the Stax that went on show in 1972 at the 'Black Woodstock' of nationalistic pride, Wattstax.

Probably the best known Bar-Kays record is 'Son Of Shaft'. Apt really, considering that by far the most famous example of their work, and a worthy illustration of how sharp they were, is as ISAAC HAYES's backing band (a regular gig of theirs) on the original 'Theme From Shaft'.

Money Talks; Stax CDSXE0233; 1978

A late album, really the band's swan-song before they lost heart in the 1980s, to see out their time as just-another-competent-funk-band. But what a way to go. Quite apart from the storming cold-cash-gettin'-paid approach on the title track, there's 'Holy Ghost': big, brassy, wild and in a remix version too, that pushes this seminal funk even further.

Gotta Groove/Black Rock; Stax CDSXD962; 1969/1971

Two for one that show the group developing what they ended up doing so well – in true Booker T style, there's a cover of 'Hey Jude' that manages to keep itself from sounding cheesy, like-wise a bizarre Memphis take on 'Montego Bay'. But however embryonic some of this is, there's more than enough guitar and horn funk in workouts like 'Humpin'' and 'In The Hole' to make up in imagination what they might lack in expertise.

SEE ALSO: (1) Stax Various Artist compilations; (2) Various Artists; *Wattstax*; Stax CDSXE2079; 1972

The Beginning Of The End

If you're only going to have one hit then that hit really ought to be powerhouse, 1971 big band-style early funk. Like 'Funky Nassau'. That way nobody will ever forget you and the record will still move parties today. Even if, at the time, the public didn't know you were a Bahamian group who'd had a hit in the islands with the same song before Atlantic picked it up in the USA. But as, at the time, your brighter deejay strung this in a sequence with 'Hey America' and 'Move On Up', you didn't really have to think about much.

SEE: *Atlantic R&B Hits Volume Seven, 1969–1974*; Atlantic 781229; 1987

Archie Bell & The Drells

(Archie Bell, born Houston, Texas, 1949; Lee Bell; James Wise; Willie Pernell)
Archie Bell & The Drells made the sort of record that people were always really glad to hear but would never actually come up and ask you to play. You know, the kind of tunes everybody was pleased to own but nobody could remember buying. In other words grooves like 'Tighten Up', 'Let's Groove' and 'Soul City Walk', that had a definite and important place on the scene of the time, but were always at the top of the second division, never quite making it into the first. Maybe this was because while they never actually did anything wrong, they were far too rooted in the 1960s to be entirely relevant in the 1970s.

Bell formed the group in 1965 when they were all still at school, putting it together along classic post-doo-wop harmony lines and it never really changed. They were among Gamble and Huff's first successes several years before Philadelphia International, and even on that label in the mid-1970s they were never really typical – their still-traditional style was simply polished up by McFADDEN & WHITEHEAD.

An interesting Archie Bell fact: 'Tighten Up', a US number 1, was originally the B-side of their debut Atlantic single 'Dog Eat Dog' in 1968, which was released, with little success, just as the group's leader was drafted to Viet Nam. While he was away, radio deejays flipped the record and he came home on leave to discover the flop he'd left behind had sold over a million copies. Apparently he had a hard time convincing his regiment that he was one of the biggest soul stars in the country.

SEE: Philadelphia International Various Artist compilations

George Benson

(Born Pittsburgh, Pennsylvania, March 22, 1943)
In Great Britain in 1994 think of George Benson and you'll bring to mind pastel-coloured polo shirts, Ford Escorts, superannuated suburban soul boys and arena-sized venues taking on the 'vibe' of such pasteurised night spots that have names that end in 's'. You know, Bogart's, Bailey's, Lacey's and so on. Think a bit harder and you'll be looking at a suspiciously smooth-faced character putting down his guitar to croon comfortingly in front of a full-scale orchestra. It wasn't always like that, though.

True, Benson's first recording contract in the mid-1960s had him down as a vocalist as well as guitarist, but at the beginning of the next decade he took note of the emerging jazz/funk scene to bust some powerful Wes Montgomery-type fretwork. By now he was with the altogether more nurturing CTI label, home of Hubert Laws, Bob James and Freddie Hubbard – he could keep up with all of them too. In fact the Benson pipes only came back into serious play in 1976, and even then there were more than a few killer jazz/funk tunes put out before the cabaret clarion was clearly heard. Then, when he went for the big time, he did it in *the* biggest way – at one point George Benson's collection of Rolls-Royces was well past double figures and when looking for somewhere to live 'within easy reach of LA, but not too close to the business', he bought a Hawaiian island. A few years later he was instrumental in converting MICHAEL JACKSON to a Jehovah's Witness.

Breezin'; Warner Bros K256199; 1976
Give Me The Night; Warner Bros 256823; 1980
In Flight; Warner Bros 256327; 1977

The one that's missing – no longer available – from the classic Benson jazz/funk foursome is *Weekend In LA*, but while that means we're missing out on 'On Broadway' and 'Lady Blue', there was so little musical development between these three sets it won't leave too much of a hole. What they show is George Benson at his silkily soulful best, kicking up a hard-boiled rhythm and nimble guitar licks out front of a lush orchestra, yet never losing sight of the fact that this was jazz-based dance music. 'Love X Love', 'This Masquerade' 'The World Is A Ghetto', 'Breezin'' and 'Give Me The Night', each one of them well aware of where they be coming from.

ALSO RECOMMENDED:

Early Years – The Best Of George Benson; CTI 8136 592; 1983

The pick of the far jazzier Creed Taylor material. Hardly geared up for the dance, but worth listening to, if for no other reason than 'White Rabbit', something of a cult item at the time.

The Blackbyrds

(Kevin Toney, keyboards; Keith Killgo, drums; Joe Hall, bass/ vocals; Orville Saunders, guitar; Barney Perry, guitar; Stephen Johnson, saxes; Allan Barnes, saxes; Perk Jacobs, percussion)
There was a moment, the best part of twenty years ago, at what used to be the Hammersmith Odeon, when near the end of an absolutely storming set The Blackbyrds settled back into a bass 'n' drum groove and called ex-Art Blakey trumpeter DONALD BYRD on stage. This wasn't a rock 'n' roll-style carefully rehearsed 'spontaneous' jam – in fact the then portly veteran didn't even have his instrument with him. It was simply a case of 'Come out and take a bow, some of this applause is yours.' Respect due, you might say. And, to thunderous cheers and stamping, Byrd came out, waved almost sheepishly, then backed off smiling proudly.

Or was that smile paternal? It might well have been. Donald Byrd was more than merely The Blackbyrds' mentor – hence the name. As chair and active lecturer in the Black Music Department at Howard University in Washington, he was the core group members' teacher. He put the group together, originally, as part of a project studying jazz and its place in modern black music, then as they clearly demonstrated life beyond the classroom he was instrumental in getting them a deal with Fantasy Records in the early 1970s. Whereas Byrd himself made a huge contribution to the soul scene's sideways expansion by coming at funk from a jazz perspective, these kids, barely out of their teens, were steeped in street funk culture, and were introduced to jazz with that as their background. An uncommon occurrence at the time – KOOL & THE GANG were about the only other act to be treading this path so early – as it was a far more subtle proposition and thus could have presented a much longer route to stardom. However, once again as with Kool, The Blackbyrds scenic route to funk paid off in spades.

By the time they arrived at their self-titled first album in 1974, they'd been together long enough to have a total understanding of what it was they had to do. The need for directness was ingrained, and they weren't afraid of the repetition involved in creating a solid anchor. Just as well, because the soaring flight-paths of guitar, brass and keyboards that Donald Byrd layered intricately on top – his own trumpet style had evolved into lines that always flew way above the rhythm section – needed a firm rooting. But as this artful dodger melody section was never in any doubt that the beat came first, The Blackbyrds' groove wasn't so much jazz/funk as pure funk constructed from a jazz rule book. Black London clubland couldn't get enough.

Although nothing else they did had remotely the impact of this first set, they maintained their status for two more albums which made up for an overall drop in quality with such marvellous soul classic high spots as 'Rock Creek Park' and 'Walking In Rhythm'. As they assumed a life of their own in the second half of the decade, two factors conspired to knock them off the top: first, by growing increasingly distant from Donald Byrd, too much conventional melody was creeping in, dulling their edge; and second, now their groundbreaking technique was tried and tested, the rest of the world was catching up and they seemed unable to raise their game to move on. The Blackbyrds continued to release LPs to steadily diminishing returns until their split in 1981. Today they occasionally get together, touring either with Donald Byrd or on their own.

The Blackbyrds/Flying Start; Fantasy CDGP086; 1974/1975

Quite superb value. The first album, which for years could only be found as ludicrously priced second-hand vinyl, is *the* stunning example of what The Blackbyrds were capable of. There's so much more on this set than the two hits 'Do It Fluid' and 'Gut Level', as right across the board Byrd's construction works to add multi-part subtext to each rhythm, while the lads' street funk ideals turned these quasi-melodic phrasings into interior-type grooves. Riffs within riffs. So what you saw first was a big phat basic beat, then if you blinked and looked in closer it revealed a series of smaller beats coming together as one hard-hitting tune. Never less than abrasive. Some of which had been smoothed out by *Flying Start*. However, any LP that contains, 'Blackbyrds' Theme', 'The Baby' and 'Walking In Rhythm' isn't going to get too many complaints from me.

SEE ALSO: *Classic Funk Mastercuts Volumes 1 & 2*; Mastercuts CUTSCD6/14; 1992/4

Bohannon

(Born Hamilton Bohannon, Newman, Georgia, 1942)
Serious a proposition as early-1970s soul was, it had its lighter moments. Often the two combined, as with Hamilton Bohannon and his thumping 1975 club hit 'South African Man'. On the one hand, the song was comfortably filed away with Jimmy Castor's 'Bertha Butt Boogie' or KOOL & THE GANG's 'Funky Granny', as solid enough for the average dancer, but too novelty to want to be heard too often (although the naked beat of 'South African Man' was so irrestistible that 'not too often' was more often than some); but pay attention to something other than the drums and you had an international conscience-pricker that greatly pre-ceded the higher-profile pronouncements on the subject. Even if Bohannon wasn't perhaps blessed with GIL SCOTT-HERON's com-mand of language, you've got to give props to anybody who'll run an unadorned club stomp with the rhythmically repeated lyric 'South African man, give him a helping hand . . . South African man, give him a helping hand . . .'

It's entirely likely that STEVIE WONDER had a great deal to do with Bohannon's politicized dance floor approach, after the two came into contact when the Motown star visited the college where, in the mid-1960s, Bohannon was taking a music degree. Impressed with the youngster's tub-thumping prowess, Wonder offered him a job as his drummer once he'd completed his course. A promise that held good too, and Bohannon occupied that particular stool for five years until, in 1972, he left to build his own career. At present, as a result of his big clean drum sounds and percussion riffs being ideal sampling material, there's something of a vintage Bohannon revival going on.

Bohannon – Essential Dancefloor Artists Volume 3; Sequel DGPCD699; 1994

More or less a Bohannon's Greatest Hits, and probably all the Big Bo' Beat anyone will ever need. Whereas 'Let's Start The Dance' and 'Pimp Walk' remain tricky enough to be worth it, such later successes as 'Disco Stomp' and 'Foot Stompin' Music' genuinely were novelty records. In fact nothing else he did ever really meant as much to his base audience as 'South African Man', contained here in all its powerhouse glory.

Brass Construction

(Randy Muller, born, Brooklyn, New York, 1952, keyboards/ flute; Wayne Parris, trumpet; Michael Grudge, sax; Jesse Ward, sax; Morris Price, trumpet; Wade Williamson, bass; Larry Payton, drums; Joseph Wong, guitar; Sandy Billups, congas)
The biggest, phattest blast of funk in 1975 was the opening chord of the opening track of Brass Construction's opening album, *Brass Construction*. It would rip out of a club sound system, grab dancers and then . . . and then nothing. A couple of beats of empty space, followed by a keyboard line so weedy it made you wonder if you'd imagined that opening salvo. Then, as the undernourished plinking died away, a five-piece brass section strode into the arena on a bass line so powerful it could have the uninitiated begging for mercy. 'Movin' ' was eight minutes of total New York horn groove, and it proved Brass Construction to be unsurpassed masters of the rhythm-driven, vocally-chanted built-from-the-floor-upwards, down-tempo seventies funk. Under the guidance of band leader Randy Muller, who put them together in 1974, and producer Jeff Lane (who also took care of business for fellow Brooklyn funkateers BT EXPRESS), they showed themselves capable of working up this steamroller head of steam whenever they fancied it

– 'Changin'', 'Party Line', 'Walkin' The Line', 'Ha Cha Cha' meant they dominated UK dance floors for nearly ten years. The trouble was, though, they didn't seem to fancy it nearly often enough, never more than once or maybe twice on each album. Often LPs were too full of keyboard-led filler or second division ballads for Brass Construction to ever be perceived as much more than a top-notch singles band.

*Movin': The Best Of Brass Construction; Syncopate; SYLP6002; 1988

For the above reasons, this is much the best way to approach Brass Construction in the CD age. Kicking off with full-length album versions of 'Movin'' and 'Changin'' – the tunes that made that first album so special, and the best value – it delivers the other eight essentials, storming through to 1985. Set in chronological order, it's easy to hear how the band's sound changed when Muller took over production from Lane and – economics being a factor here – eased them away from the five-man horn attack to a more synthesized approach with little discernable loss of funkiness. The only dead wood is a frantic late-eighties remix of 'Movin'' which, up against the real one, comes over as entirely redundant. Why re-invent the wheel when it can only end up square?

SEE ALSO: *Classic Funk Mastercuts Volume 2*; Mastercuts CUTSCD14; 1993

James Brown

➡️If ever there was a line drawn across the sands of soul it was in the summer of 1970, when James Brown unleashed 'Get Up I Feel Like Being A Sex Machine'. 'Unleashed' is exactly the right word too. It was a beast of a tune, that rampaged through soul's inner sanctum to emerge fangs dripping with blood and leaving behind a music genre that would never be the same again. Whereas the advances made by the likes of Norman Whitfield, SLY STONE and ISAAC HAYES were groundbreaking to the max, at the time they came over as so wild that they were sidelined by mainstream critics and so-called taste-shapers – treated as some sort of odd fad, not really what 'proper' soul was about.

But a character such as James Brown was never going to allow himself to be marginalised. His musical revolution didn't introduce anything new-fangled or other-worldly to soul, or create any kind of new category – he took what already existed – R&B-based soul with a sanctified approach to vocals – turned it in on itself about a half a dozen times, then kept picking away at it until all that was left was its essence. Sure, he'd created funk as a form in itself (as opposed to merely an adjective), but he'd done that by first establishing its definition, rather than coming up with some handy theory after the event. As he created it, in strictly musical terms, funk wasn't about what you put in, but what you took out.

Although it was impossible for anything to prepare you fully for the first-time hearing of 'Get Up I Feel Like Being A Sex Machine' (the spectacular clumsiness of the title certainly wasn't going to give you any clues), it was obvious James Brown had been moving towards this higher rhythmic state for some time. As far back as 1968 and 'Say It Loud, I'm Black And I'm Proud', he was blatantly edging out the melody to overload the rhythm section – indeed, with hindsight, it seems as if such 1969 sides as 'Funky Drummer' and 'Ain't It Funky Now' were, if not rehearsals for 'Sex Machine', then certainly warm-ups. Opening acts, if you like, for a refinement of the music that looked to sacrifice everything on the Altar of the Good Groove. Melodies? Pah, who needs 'em? The idea was to strip a tune down so that it carried no spare flesh, then build it back to juggernaut proportions as the different beats pile on top of each other. While these multi-levels of rhythm are built on the bass, drums and percussion (your traditional rhythm section), instruments that ought to be carrying the tune are press-ganged into service as supplementary percussive devices: horns – group them together and have them play stabbing points of sound; keyboards – arch those fingers and bang out riffs rather than phrases; guitar – hit it rather than strum it, just clipping the strings for that choppy, pre-wah wah scratch that will become known as 'James Brown Guitar', even though he wouldn't have known one end of the instrument from the other. Also, as it's expected to have some sort of vocal in there somewhere, get the lyrics to sound as much like a chant as possible while still being able to call it a song. But whenever possible degenerate actual words into screams, yelps and grunts that can be used to accentuate different beat patterns.

Stitching together all these percussive attacks Brown formed grooves that have no end because, unlike songs, they have no middle or beginning, they merely keep themselves from getting boring (and keep the party on its toes) with an assortment of time changes and mini loops. It seems simple and throwaway, but only looks that way because it's so complex internally.

The importance of what James Brown was doing at this moment cannot be overstressed. THE FATBACK BAND's funk, KOOL & THE GANG's funk, BRASS CONSTRUCTION's, even P-FUNK's funk can all be directly traced back to this moment.

It also marked a personal watershed for James Brown, as he broke ties with the past by getting rid of most of The Famous Flames, his touring and studio band of some fifteen years. He replaced them with a bunch of modern-thinking young whippersnappers called The JBs, some of whom, such as bassist William 'Bootsy' Collins, were just half his age. 'Sex Machine' proved him to be right back on the block as far as his own community was concerned too. Just as Ray Charles had done roughly ten years previously, as James Brown stood on the verge of enormous crossover success he reinvented himself to make sure he was keeping his primary audience served. In fact it marked the start of a spell of open consciousness that made 'Say It Loud' look ambiguous. Words were as hard as the music, and tracks like 'King Heroin', 'Down And Out In New York City', 'The Payback', 'Superbad' and 'Hey America' hit the head, the heart and the feet, while 'Hot Pants', 'There It Is' and 'Make It Funky' showed there was still room for relaxation.

He funked up his sidekicks too. In a previously unprecedented burst of democracy, The Godfather of Soul (or, as he was given to describing himself, The Minister of New New Super Heavy Funk) allowed the supporting cast of The James Brown Revue to make their own albums. During the first half of the 1970s, The JBs, Lyn Collins, Maceo Parker and Fred Wesley all cut LPs that were every bit as funky as anything their boss ever did – hardly surprising really, since James Brown wrote,

produced, arranged and (in some cases) performed on them. As
Maceo Parker once told me: 'Although they were our albums,
there was never any doubt about who was in charge – count
how many times the name James Brown appears on those
sleeves! It's a wonder his picture isn't on there too.' On a JBs' LP
Doing It To Death, the ratio is 10:2 in favour of the Godfather.

Such an imbalanced approach to credit apportion, plus the
notorious James Brown Discipline Experience proved too much
for his new young crew, and after a few years many of them cut
out to join George Clinton's P-FUNK thang, where the dress code
(and just about every other code) was slightly more, er, relaxed.
Still, this mass defection wasn't enough to stop James Brown's
awesome funk mission which climaxed in the middle of the
decade with *The Payback* double LP and 'Papa Don't Take No
Mess', a track which took up one whole side of the otherwise disappointing *Hell* album. Although James Brown continued to
pump out perfectly respectable funk until the end of the decade,
past these milestones in soul other people were running with his
ball and doing far more interesting things with it. Comparatively,
the glory moments were much fewer and further between.
Although this 1969 to 1975 era is one of the most meaningful
periods in black soul music, it's by far the most underrepresented
section of James Brown's career on CD in the UK. Odd, eh? ↦

The first albums are easily available as US/Japanese import
CDs, and as they are vital to any comprehensive soul music collection they're worth paying whatever is asked. (If it's much
over twenty-five quid, though, it's worth shopping around.)

The Payback; Polydor PD3007; 1974

Without doubt the absolute pinnacle of what this second-stage
James Brown achieved. Using the '40 acres and mule' symbol-
ism (what each freed slave was to have received in order to
make a start in the world) it takes as its theme the substitution
of physical slavery for mental slavery and 'The Payback' of the
title is the storm of revenge on its way. James Brown's most sustained, articulate and ferocious best, never seen to this degree
before or since. And such righteous anger is given wings by the
hardest grooves he ever committed to tape. Just eight numbers,

with the shortest at five minutes, the longest at twelve, there isn't a single note wasted in this textbook display of drilled, empty funk, going under titles such as 'The Payback', 'Forever Suffering', 'Time Is Running Out Fast' and 'Mind Power'. The instrumentation appears to exist for no other reason than to drive the rhetoric, and by rising to the necessary levels of strength it presents itself as irresistibly dark dance floor fodder.

Black Caesar; Polydor PD6014; 1973

With every prominent soul star recording 'blaxploitation' film soundtracks in the early-1970s, it seemed unlikely James Brown was going to resist. As was somehow fitting for the man who made the hardest music, *Black Caesar* was the most nihilistically violent of the genre. Or at least of the ones that got a British release. At the time, it seemed like the soundtrack format was exactly what was needed to push James Brown into making an album instead of just a pretty disparate collection of singles, and this set benefits greatly as, by running the same subliminal musical themes from beginning to end, it builds up the funk to cliff-face proportions. (*The Payback*, James Brown's other cohesive album, had such a strong story it was like a soundtrack without a film.) Also, the different rules for film scoring, as opposed to making hit records, afforded a freedom to experiment that resulted in such classic tracks as 'Down And Out In New York City', 'The Boss' and 'White Lightning'.

Get On The Good Foot; Polydor PD3004; 1972

A bit of a bridging album between the 'Sex Machine'-style songs of 1971 and 1972 and the near psychotic grooves of the coming years, as it manages to reach back and include updated versions of 'Cold Sweat', 'Please, Please, Please' and 'Lost Someone'. But it's more than just interesting for this fact. On what was, on vinyl, a double LP, there are full-length versions of 'Make It Funky', 'Get On The Good Foot' and 'I've Got A Bag Of My Own', all of which became lost James Brown classics, and a wicked long jam that pointed the way forward in no uncertain terms: it was entitled 'Funky Side Of Town' and the main lyrical hook was 'Let's go, let's go . . .'

*MACEO & THE MACKS; Us; People PE 6601; 1974

Essentially The JBs, led by Maceo Parker and produced by James Brown. As expected, the sax quota is well up and working sublimely as it oozes through low-down versions of 'Drowning In The Sea Of Love' and 'Show And Tell' and gets raw funky for a new take on 'Doing It To Death' and the club classics 'Party' and 'Soul Power 74'. But the true funk gem is the swirling, aching, ten-minute long 'Soul Of A Black Man', complete with a lengthy rap from brother James.

*THE JBS; Doing It To Death; People PE5603; 1973

The album for the extended JBs jam and while perhaps a trifle indulgent, it's difficult to accept abbreviated versions of the title track (10.04), 'You Can Have Your Watergate, Just Gimme Some Bucks And I'll Be Straight' (6.27), 'More Peas' (8.27) and 'La Di Da La Di Day' (5.40) when you know there's all this out there waiting for you.

*FRED WESLEY & THE JBS; Damn Right I Am Somebody; People PE6602; 1974

The most direct political statement of all the sidemen LPs, musically this is somewhat restrained by comparison. However, it does contain the totally wild 'bone-led instrumental 'Blow Your Head', while 'Same Beat' and 'If You Don't Get It The First Time' should satisfy most feet. But that's not what it's really about. The original sleeve design repeated the phrase 'Think that you are somebody and you'll be somebody' and the title track is a typically deft piece of James Brown spiritual uplift that we all seemed to need every so often.

ALSO RECOMMENDED:

*FRED & THE NEW JBS; Breakin' Bread; People PE6604; 1974

An album that tended to get lost in the deluge of James Brown related product around that time, but also one that seemed to show they might have overplayed their hand a wee bit. Three tracks make it special, 'Breakin' Bread', 'Rockin' Funky Watergate' and 'Little Boy Black', each one a wiggly, jazzy, trombone-heavy semi-instrumental, but it had none of the truly killer grooves of the other records.

Hell; Polydor PD9001; 1974

This was a double LP with only one worthwhile track on it – the mesmerising 'Papa Don't Take No Mess' which took up all of one side and, judging by its content and execution, was clearly left over from *The Payback* sessions. If there's no other way to get the full-length version of this track (and at the moment it's no longer than five minutes on JB compilations) then it's worth the price of a Japanese import double CD. Probably one of only five soul tracks that are.

Slaughter's Big Rip Off; Polydor PD6015; 1973

James Brown's other violent thriller soundtrack which, although it had a couple of excellent high spots – 'Get Up People And Drive Your Funky Soul', 'Slaughter Theme' and 'King Slaughter' – was very much *Black Caesar*'s poor relation in terms of musical invention. More like tunes he had lying about than material specifically written for the job – maybe he was overworking himself.

UK RELEASES:

James Brown's Funky People Volume 1; Urban 829417; 1986
James Brown's Funky People Volume 2; Urban 835857; 1988

The best of those in the James Brown organisation whose names weren't James or Brown. Not that this second billing should be in any way a discouragement. While providing as good an example of James Brown's singular funk as anything under his own name, these albums represent an ideal sampler before jumping into the deep end of import CDs as they contain a wealth of otherwise hard-to-get-hold-of funk as well as reminders of a few old favourites. Among the cast of characters are The JBs, Maceo & The Macks, Fred Wesley, Lyn Collins,

Marva Whitney, Hank Ballard and Bobby Byrd. Unignorable tracks include, on Volume One, 'Gimme Some More', 'Think (About It)', 'Party (Part 1)' and 'Givin' Up Food For Funk', while Volume Two's got 'Soul Power '74', 'Cross The Track (We'd Better Go Back)', 'Blow Your Head', 'I Know You Got Soul' and 'Supergood'. The unexpected but enormously welcome 'It's The JBs Monaurail' and 'Damn Right I Am Somebody' (Volume One) and 'You Can Have Your Watergate' and 'I'm Paying Taxes, But What Am I Buying' (Volume Two) are previously rare enough to make each set a wise buy.

ALSO RECOMMENDED:

Sex Machine – The Very Best Of James Brown; Polydor 8458282; 1991

Although spanning the entire career, the very early-1970s singles come well represented with the title track, 'Hot Pants', 'Hey America', 'Soul Power', 'Good Foot' and 'Make It Funky'.

Star Time; Polydor 8491082; 1991

The four-CD box set, as discussed in the 1950s/1960s section, but as two discs take it on from 'Funky Drummer' this can work out good value. Especially as there's seven minutes of 'The Payback', over five of 'Doing It To Death' and nearly four and a half of 'Papa Don't Take No Mess'. The only niggle is, much of the chugging 1970s funk tracks appear to have been slightly speeded up from the originals.

SEE ALSO: *Classic Funk Mastercuts Volumes 1 & 2*; Mastercuts CUTSCD6/14; 1992/4

Shirley Brown

(Born West Memphis, Arkansas, January 6, 1947)
One of soul music's great mysteries is why Shirley Brown didn't have the career she threatened to with her blistering, below-the-Mason-Dixon-line-testifying, deep-fried, straight-from-the-pulpit soul narrative 'Woman To Woman'? The album of the same

name seemed to crop up in everybody's record collections back in 1974, sitting entirely comfortably next to *The Payback*, *I'm Still In Love With You* and *Keep On Stepping*. Which is partly what made *Woman To Woman* so remarkable: it was produced by Steve Cropper, and represented one of the very few true examples of Stax Soul being taken into the 1970s – as opposed from 1970s soul being made at Stax – and as such was a genuine updating of that classic Memphis sound. It was all done with attitude: while the music mined that rich Stax seam, an 'Ike's Rap'-style, elongated, elaborated, acted out delivery turned the vocals into a funky black radio play. Told from a woman's point of view and minutely studded with powder-room detail and rich 'cross-the-tracks in-jokes, it was liberating, relevant and entirely in keeping with the times.

It also got her frequently sneered at as some sort of PG-rated MILLIE JACKSON, but that did Shirley Brown an enormous injustice. She was much more a School of Richard Pryor graduate: talking *to* her home crowd rather than performing *for* a wider audience, and dealing in subtleties they could understand. And further contributing to her timid reputation, in a live situation she didn't need to be obscene to make her point or to make you laugh – which, by the way, neither did Richard Pryor.

Unfortunately, just about the time she should have been following up *Woman To Woman*'s enormous success, Stax went to the wall and she never seemed to get the same crack of the whip anywhere else. It was as if those Memphis studio staff were the only ones that knew how both to kick off and contain her massive soulfulness.

Woman To Woman; Stax CDSXE002; 1974

This really is a one-track album, but that track is so strong two or three of them would probably be too much. A perfect example of the 'tell it, girl!' style of blunt emotional commentary, blurring the lines between speaking and singing while the sumptuous band does wonderfully slinky things in the background. It almost doesn't matter that she didn't do anything else overly interesting.

Tom Browne

(Born Queens, New York City, 1959)
If ever a tune had an impact, while the guy who made it was the Invisible Man, it was Tom Browne and 'Funking For Jamaica'. A journeyman NYC jazz/fusion trumpeter during the second half of the 1970s, in 1979 he wrote and released the song as a tribute not to the island but the area of New York in which he lived. Such a picky point was lost on the black British soul scene, in which Jamaica (in the Caribbean) has an enormous cultural presence, the title was misinterpreted, sometimes deliberately so, and the song was a huge and instant hit. Of course its immediately recognisable opening note, its clipped leads and its gut-shaking bass line may have something to do with that too, and it quickly crossed wide enough to become a top ten hit.

The song remains a soul boy, jazz/funk evergreen, on a par with 'Joy And Pain' or 'Ain't No Stopping Us Now', but with the exception of 'Fungi Mama' and (maybe) 'Thigh High (Grip Your Hips And Move)' everything else Tom Browne did was instantly forgettable. Even if you've just played the album.

The Best Of Tom Browne; Arista 260962; 1991

It's got the hits on, which should be enough, but for the true afficionado there is 'Bygones' and 'Rockin' Radio'.

B.T. Express

(Jamal Rasool, vocals/bass; Bill Risbrook, guitar; Rick Thompson, guitar/vocals; Dennis Rowe, percussion; Wesley Hall, lead guitar; Dennis Rowe, percussion; Carlos Ward, saxes/flute; Kashif, keyboards)
The third, not so famous, leg of an unholy trinity of mid-1970s New York street funk – the other two being THE FATBACK BAND and BRASS CONSTRUCTION – they were what producer Jeff Lane did when he got time off from banging out the best of Brass Construction's repertoire. B.T. stood for Brooklyn Transit, by the way, and the B.T. Express was a subway train route, which, thanks to this band, for a brief period assumed the cultural significance of a latter day A Train.

B.T. were easily as hot and hard as Randy Muller's mob, but how it was tickled up was with lead lines rather than pure riffs, a liberal sprinkling of strings and more guitar work than you could shake a wah wah pedal at. Although their early hits came together so crisp you never noticed it wasn't perhaps as horn heavy as it might have been, they never maintained their initial momentum. In spite of still making records well into the 1980s everything after their overwhelming debut was pretty much a total disappointment. Indeed, B.T. Express's last moment of serious clubland glory came with a couple of crisp rhythm attacks on their second album, *Non Stop*, in 1976.

Do It 'Til You're Satisfied; Cleo CLCD00399; 1975

Indispensable. Another snapshot of the times-type cover photo, as the band – in big caps, bigger shirt collars and even bigger flares – crouch on a subway platform waiting for a train. (The B.T. Express?) But what's really important is a track listing that scores nine out of nine as every tune was one that they'd never get close to again. The stupendous 'Do It (Til You're Satisfied)' that builds up from a straight bass 'n' drums to layer on chopping guitar, driving horns, a spiralling organ and pleading vocals to a climax of urgency and innuendo; 'Express', their train whistle-enhanced theme song that was about as easy to stop as, well, a train; 'Do You Like It?', which, as with 'If It Don't Turn You On' and 'This House Is Smokin'', were slippery slabs of irresistible, swirling big-butt funk . . . And so it goes on. The only B.T. Express album still available. But so what?

Donald Byrd

(Born Detroit, Michigan, December 9, 1932)
Probably jazz/funk's founding father, as years before the trumpeter was putting together groups like THE BLACKBYRDS and C.N.N.U. from the classes he taught at Howard and Duke Universities and experimenting with funk beats and jazz arrangements. And even then he was operating on the notion that the best way forward was with an old head on a young atti-

tude – it was another of his students, Larry Mizzell, who convinced him to record what is acknowledged as the new genre's first whole album, 1972's *Ethiopian Knights*. Not that Byrd needed much persuading. Well versed in jazz theory, history and social interaction, Byrd was in no doubt that, by the end of the 1960s, much of the feisty nationalistic spirit of jazzers of ten years since had died down. That the formerly self-serving state of affairs had gone mainstream. Yet he was equally aware, as his college kids kept him up with contemporary black music trends, that post-soul soul music (so to speak) was Afro-America's truly meaningful soundtrack. *Ethiopian Knights* was followed by *Street Lady*, and although this funked-up follow-up was not as resolutely impenetrable as the first, it's not that difficult to see why the mainstream critics panned both of them – Byrd had deliberately set out to reclaim the music they had recently put themselves in charge of, in order to bring it home. It's also easy to see why those two albums quickly became collectors' items.

However, as bold and worthy as this move was, it was a slight miscalculation. Especially with a set structured as ramblingly jazz-styled as *Ethiopian Knights* (it had only three tracks on a fifty-minute LP). His new audience were more tuned into rock and pop's extra-curricular influences than they were to jazz, and his ideals had to be rethought – without being overly compromised – into more conventionally presented tunes. As a result, he took a careful approach that involved building up a complicated beat with a series of individually simple rhythm patterns, then draped it in deceptively tricky solos and lead lines and put it on public display on the *Black Byrd* LP. Instant recognition from the constituency he was aiming at. From then on it was superior jazz/funk anthems ahoy – 'Change (Makes You Wanna Hustle)', '(Fallin' Like) Dominoes', 'Places And Spaces' and so on. Even if nothing was ever quite as deep as those first three LPs, for the rest of the decade he broadened clubland soul's horizon in a way that would never have been dreamed of five years previously.

Donald Byrd still occasionally tours with the reformed Blackbyrds, and has stayed on his chosen course to promote jazz and traditional black American culture down the generational ladder through his work with Guru's *Jazzmatazz* project.

Black Byrd; Blue Note BNZ 294; 1973

The LP in which all Donald Byrd's fusion theories clicked, as keeping the numbers to a more acceptable length and building in the peaks and troughs of conventional musical story, people were far more willing to give it a chance. He held their attention with his jazzman's confidence that meant he was never afraid to make each individual part intricate as he worked in the knowledge that the whole would make perfect (and perfectly accessible) sense. When the tunes hit the sound systems – as their funk gutsy basis ensured they would – they set off tingling frissons of excitement as on initial hearing people were drawn straight in but never quite knew what to expect next. This album's 'Flight Time', 'Black Byrd', 'Love's So Far Away' and 'Sky High' were very special moments and remain just as listenable over two decades later.

Greatest Hits; Blue Note BNZ285; 1992

A jazz/funk jamboree, moving most of the way through the decade and including 'Change (Makes You Wanna Hustle)', 'Wind Parade', '(Fallin' Like) Dominoes' – live and studio versions, 'Street Lady', 'Places And Spaces', 'Lanasana's Priestess', 'Steppin' Into Tomorrow', 'Black Byrd', 'Love's So Far Away' and 'Flight Time'. 'Nuff said.

SEE ALSO: Various Artists; *Classic Jazz/Funk Mastercuts*

The Chi-Lites

(Eugene Record; Marshall Thompson; Robert 'Squirrel' Lester; Creadel Jones; Clarence Johnson)
It seems odd that during all the changes going on as the 1970s rolled around, one group should have done so well by doing little more than what had gone before. Just doing it *very very well*. The Chi-Lites were that group, and led by Record's falsetto (probably the most, and worst, imitated voice in early 1970s soul) their harmony singing pre-dated Motown and Stax to present the classic doo-wop method. That this was their chosen course was hardly surprising, the group *did* pre-date Stax and

the individual members were all professional singers before Berry Gordy opted to change the course of modern soul.

Formed in Chicago in 1960 they were known as The Hi-Lites – the 'C' was added as a hometown salute only after a combo called The HiLites threatened legal action – then became Marshall & The Chi-Lites, spending a decade working that classic Windy City way of using different members as lead singers – often within the same song. And having virtually no success at all on a spectrum of local labels.

What made the difference was Eugene Record being promoted to permanent lead singer in 1970, after it was noticed his leads got the best response from live audiences. By the following year he was the group's writer and producer too, and had come up with '(For God's Sake) Give More Power To The People', a combination of contemporary social commentary and straight old-time singing values that proved irresistible. From that point on, until Record quit in 1975, they reverted to love songs to join the ranks of soul's biggest balladeers.

The Best Of The Chi-Lites; Kent CDKEN911; 1987

The Chi-Lites' success was due, in the main part, to their being both an anachronism and appearing new on the scene – they presented no-frills solid singing at a time when everybody else seemed to be being clever; and they weren't stars from a previous era, thus to be treated with suspicion. A major factor of this approach was a succession of club-friendly smooch singles – for which there will never be a substitute – the likes of which were getting thin on the ground at the time as soul music romped around in its new-found freedom. All of those marvellous singles are on this album: 'Homely Girl', 'Oh Girl', 'Letter To Myself', 'Power To The People', 'The Coldest Days Of My Life' . . .

Chic

(Nile Rodgers, guitar, born New York City, September 19, 1952; Bernard Edwards, bass, born Greenville, North Carolina, October 31, 1952)

'Yowsah! Yowsah! Yowsah!' was a kind of nasally intoned disco rallying call in 1978 that was sort of fun for the first two or three times, then, like the slightly later 'whooop-*whooop*', swiftly became rather tedious. The band responsible were Chic, but it was only their first single 'Dance, Dance, Dance (Yowsah, Yowsah, Yowsah)' and, to give them credit, even though it sold well over a million they didn't do anything nearly so irritating again. What they did do was develop that record's signature rhythms into an easy-going, rolling beat kept bouyant by Rodgers's nagging guitar and made mainstream radio-friendly by sweeping strings. But it stayed close to the ground thanks to Edwards's lolloping bass and odd breaks and tempo changes which meant they were always going to keep dancers on their toes. It was called The Chic Beat and on it they rode the disco boom with credibility and panache.

It wasn't always like that, though. Rodgers and Edwards were perpetually bumping into each other as teenage session players on the booming New York live circuit, when, in 1970, they realised they had a good musical understanding, paired up and began hiring themselves out as a duo. Drummer Tony Thompson joined them two years later and they attempted to peddle a jazz/funk sound under numerous different names including Allah & The Knife-Wielding Punks – that was, Rodgers confessed in later years, 'to try and shock people into taking notice of us'. But by then disco was big in New York and starting to break the whole world over, the Punks did what amounted to a stylistic U-turn, put down the knives, got a girl singer, bought some snappy suits and Chic – a very pro-disco idea of sophistication – were touting demos until Atlantic Records' president personally signed them in 1977 – after his A&R department had already turned the group down.

Chic's days of glory lasted far beyond their own three-year run of chart hits – which, by the way, included Atlantic's biggest-selling single, the four million-plus 'Le Freak' – into Rodgers and Edwards writing and producing partnership as The Chic Organisation. As well as being responsible for Sister Sledge's disco success – 'We Are Family', 'He's The Greatest Dancer', 'Lost In Music' and so on – they unofficially and (at first) uncreditedly supplied the bassline for the first big hip-hop hit when THE SUGARHILL GANG appropriated a large part of 'Good Times' for 'Rappers' Delight'. Then the Chic beat was in demand all across the musical spectrum as, among others, Blondie, Diana

Ross, Duran Duran, Mick Jagger, Madonna and David Bowie engaged Rodgers and Edwards to produce records for them. By the mid-1980s the twosome had parted company, and a reformation in 1992 was not enormously successful.

Chic; Atlantic 756780407; 1978

Apparently recorded in just three weeks, this set shows the band as standing on the verge. Naturally the big ones are there, 'Dance, Dance, Dance', 'Everybody Dance' and 'You Can Get By', but it sets what became a trend for Chic – to pay attention to what else was on the LP so that it wasn't just the hit singles and eight filler tracks. This was, of course, diametrically opposed to how most disco acts operated and might well have contributed to this one's widespread, longer lasting success, but in this instance it definitely provided the surprisingly effective ballad 'Est-Ce Que C'est Chic'. The album sold over a million, again hardly par for the disco course.

C'est Chic; Atlantic 756781552; 1978

This is the one they really hit their stride on. The relationship between Edwards's hydraulic bass and Rodgers' insistent guitar is fully matured and their confidence has grown to use strings in some, at the time, truly inventive ways, considerably raising the stakes for their disco peers. Alongside 'Le Freak' and the slightly less frantic 'I Want Your Love' are such club gems as 'Chic Cheer' and the jazz-tinged 'Savoir Faire'. It's even got LUTHER VANDROSS singing background vocals. Like its predecessor it went platinum, and has since been held up as one of the greatest dance music albums ever made.

WITH SISTER SLEDGE; Freak Out: Greatest Hits; Telstar 229241246; 1987

All the hits from the above, and running on to 'My Forbidden Lover' and 'My Feet Keep Dancing', but also includes the Sister Sledge hits. A bit of a double-edged sword this one – while the album provides a good Chic primer it can't run to their more interesting album tracks; but a grab-bag 'greatest hits' form is the only way to approach Sister Sledge as it avoids the dross that padded out their two albums. And while they're a lot of fun, there simply isn't enough worthwhile Sledge stuff to fill an entire CD.

ALSO RECOMMENDED:

Risque; Atlantic 756780406; 1979

Although a slightly shallower dip in the Chic barrel than *C'est Chic*, essentially the ingredients are all there. Includes 'My Forbidden Lover' and 'My Feet Keep Dancing'.

The Commodores

(Lionel Ritchie, born Tuskegee, Alabama, June 20, 1949, vocals/keyboards; Thomas McClary, lead guitar; William King, trumpet; Ronald LaPraed, bass/trumpet; Milan Williams, trombone/drums; Walter 'Clyde' Orange, drums)

This group was formed – with the express purpose of impressing girls – in the late 1960s at the Tuskegee Institute, a black college in Alabama. Nothing remarkable in that, except that the members kept up their graduate and doctorate studies after turning professional in 1969 and even when, for five years, they were having huge international hits, tours were structured round examination schedules, while recording sessions had study periods built in. More than simply shaking the comfy stereotype of black kids struggling out of social deprivation thanks to raw musical talent, it proved further education and funk need not be mutually exclusive. In interviews The Commodores (a name picked at random out of a flicked-through dictionary) were as valuable as JAMES BROWN as spokesmen for the growing drive for black literacy programmes, anti-drop-out campaigns and the post-social revolution push for education as the means to all newly available ends.

They weren't nearly as influential musically though. The group never quite achieved the promise of their dynamic instrumental debut single 'Machine Gun', as while the album of the same name showed an assured exploration of sophisticated funk structure, after that they seemed to throttle back. The second set, *Caught In The Act*, seemed as if they were trying not to offend anybody, so therefore thought it better not to go too far with anything in particular. As a result they came across as a (very) second-rate EARTH, WIND & FIRE. Shame really, as the *Machine Gun* LP, with its far greater subtlety that most New York street funk – its nearest living relative – represented one of the very rare examples of the successful 'Motown-ising' of the genre. Rather than adopt it as tablets of stone (RICK JAMES) or create something entirely new out of it (STEVIE WONDER, Norman Whitfield), they had taken it and added some extra, sophisticated arrangements without destroying the spark. Just like old Mr Gordy had done so brilliantly with street corner R&B fifteen years previously. This should've been the company's entry into the world of self-contained playing-and-singing soul groups, a state of affairs Gordy seemed only to apply to his growing white rock roster.

As it was, The Commodores got more and more forgettable, until their lead singer briefly reincarnated them (and launched his own solo career) by writing them a series of supremely syrupy ballads during the second half of the decade. With the exception of the crisp 'Brick House', this new force was to dictate the band's soft soul path until Ritchie quit in 1982. At the moment, The Commodores memory that proves embarrassingly durable is of a nearly full Hammersmith Odeon at the very start of the 1990s, with more than a few audience members shouting 'Bring back Lionel.' And less kind comments. Definitely not what they deserved, as the group put a great deal into the community in the beginning, and should probably be remembered for their Marvin Gaye/Jackie Wilson tribute 'Nightshift' – mawkish in the extreme, but wonderfully intentioned. ➻ *Lionel Ritchie*

14 Greatest Hits; Motown CD530096; 1984

A good cross-section of what The Commodores were capable of, going from that first song, and others of its ilk – 'Slippery When Wet' and 'Brick House' – moving on to the more substantial of the slow tunes, while Lionel Ritchie was still out front: 'Easy', 'Three Times A Lady' and 'Sail On' among them.

All The Great Love Songs; Motown 530051; 1984

Exactly what the title says it will be, but on balance with the one above it's not such brilliant value – all the songs you want are on the other one, yet you sacrifice the up-tempo numbers for some decidely un-vital album fillers. However, as seamless background 'mood' music it won't throw any curves.

SEE ALSO: Motown Various Artist compilations

Randy Crawford

(Born Macon, Georgia, 1952)
It always appeared as if Randy Crawford had been given too much bad advice much too often. It was as if somebody kept saying to her, 'Hey kid, here's some ropey songs and a duff producer. Just go though the motions, *act* like a soul singer. Nobody'll know the difference.' But they did, as her first albums attracted interest thanks to one or two high spots then let themselves down with enough filler to be measured in acreage. However, when Ms Crawford got the good material and the right people in the studio with her she proved that leather-lunged soul-belting wasn't a lost art and that real power only comes from total control, like the material she did with THE CRUSADERS – songs that introduced her almost unadulterated gospel soul tendencies to their crafty jazz/funk experiments. Songs that gave her something tight to work off yet were never going to swamp her character as it struggled, blinking, into the light after years of being buried. Songs that sold by the truckload.

Her 1979 *Now We May Begin* album – her first whole set produced and played on by The Crusaders – is possibly one of the most accurately titled LPs known to soul. From there she had a string of wonderfully silky LPs both with that group and Tommy Lipuma, before descending gracefully into the acceptable end of the supper club market.

*The Very Best Of Randy Crawford; Dino DINTVCD58; 1991

Eleven carefully compiled tracks that take only the best from the earlier albums, go all the way up to 'Knockin' On Heaven's Door' and get there via 'One Day I'll Fly Away', 'Rainy Night In Georgia', 'You Might Need Somebody', 'Almaz' and, of course, 'Street Life'. The one glaring omission would be 'Last Night At Danceland'.

Secret Combination; WEA K256904; 1980

The nearest we're going to get to an original album from Randy Crawford's golden period is this, her first produced by Tommy LiPuma. That wasn't meant to sound disparaging, as there's still a lot of the old Crusaders-stoked fire in her approach, and the orchestrations had some edge to them. Besides, as well as the title track and 'Rainy Night In Georgia', this LP features Randy Crawford at her most full-on seductive, singing 'You Bring The Sun Out'.

SEE ALSO: Various Artists; *Classic Funk Mastercuts Volume 1*; Mastercuts CUTSCD6; 1992

Creative Source

(Don Wyatt; Steve Flanagan; Barbara Berryman; Barbara Lewis; Celeste Rose)
It's hard to think of a group who made a bigger splash on the early-1970s street soul scene with just one song. And almost impossible to imagine how that group could have come up with something as brilliant as 'Who Is He And What Is He To You?' on their first, eponymously titled album and then never make another record worth a damn in a three-album, three-year career. Mind you, if the album sleeve was anything to go by – they're kitted out in symbolic-type face paint and zodiac signs – they were odd in the most Los Angelean of ways.

But what a tune. It was written by Bill Withers, nearly twelve minutes long and had a tambourine intro that would regularly be used to tease club crowds as deejays would fade it in then cut back to another record just as the dancers took notice. Such was the popularity of 'Who Is He' that this wind up could be repeated several times, each taste increasing the anticipation. Then, once it kicks off properly, its almost surreal horn layers – some stretched to impossible length and others compressed into needle points – duck in and out of a chopping keyboard, a strung out lead guitar, a bass line that doesn't quit and a flute that manages to hold its own with surprising vigour. The harmony vocals are pretty much an optional extra. Then it's all over much too soon.

SEE: **Various Artists;** *Classic Funk Mastercuts Volume 1;* Mastercuts CUTSCD6; 1992

Crown Heights Affair

(Bert Reid, saxes; Raymond Reid, guitar; Phillip Thomas, vocals; William Anderson, guitar; James Baynard, trumpet; Muki Wilson, bass; Howie Young, keyboards; Raymond Rock, drums/ percussion)

Put together in, and taking their name from, a section of Brooklyn, NYC, now known as Crime Heights, Crown Heights Affair are probably the best example of what disco started off as – when it was New York street funk's hyperactive younger brother; before other people got hold of it and it still had a depth of purpose and a first-hand knowledge of where it began. Sure, 'Foxy' and 'Dreaming A Dream' in 1974 – off their first album after four years of playing live and cutting the odd single – were frantic enough to be marked down as dangerous, and they wore the most ridiculously flared and spangle-trimmed suits. But the difference was they kicked it with such genuine excitement that even your toughest-posing *Maggotbrain* fan would be forced into putting aside his darkness and dropping some foot. With a smile on his face too. Then, as they progressed and the disco scene grew they were shrewd enough to put different cuts of the same song on albums in an early example of the old uptown and downtown mixes gag. And they were good enough at what they did to last ten years and almost as many albums. Long after they ceased to have any base audience relevance.

Crown Heights Affair – Essential Dancefloor Artists Volume 1; Sequel DGPCD665; 1994

Nine tracks, including all the big ones – 'Dreaming A Dream' , 'Foxy', 'You Gave Me Love', 'Far Out' and 'Say A Prayer For Two', and if it had a few of the alternative cuts on it this LP would be the perfect Crown Heights collection.

The Crusaders

(Joe Sample, keyboards; Wilton Felder, saxes; Stix Hooper, drums; Wayne Henderson, trombone; Larry Carlton, drums)
This band didn't really change the shape of anything, as their jazz/funk was approached so squarely from a jazz point of view it was too far removed to interact properly with 1970s soul – it was really just a post-post-bop with flattened out rhythm patterns. Yet during the first half of the decade they shifted such enormous amounts of records to self-styled sophisticated soul fans that they became integral to the scene without actually being part of it. A quick spin of Crusaders' albums *Southern Comfort*, *Chain Reaction* or *Those Southern Knights* makes this odd state of affairs as clear as crystal. Further, they were responsible for that extended version zenith of post-disco still-credible soul, 'Street Life'. In fact, The Crusaders were so downright funky, in the way you imagine jazz is supposed to be, that even if they hadn't unleashed that gut-churning big-butt boogie spectacular 'Stomp And Buck Dance', they still would have earned their entry in this book.

Southern Comfort; GRP 01362; 1974

The first of the group's trio of funk-friendly outings, and a good choice as the only one still available in original form. A double on vinyl, featuring just twelve satisfyingly stretched out tunes, it is fresh enough in what it's doing not to have any set ideas yet and so runs a number of interesting experiments. They veer between downright dance floor – 'Stomp And Buck Dance', 'Well's Gone Dry' and the Fred Wesley-ish 'Time Bomb' – the oozingly smoove instrumentals 'Ballad Of Joe Louis', 'Lilies Of The Nile' and 'Greasy Spoon'. What makes them stand out, though, is at this stage they were unable to avoid sounding like a jazz band playing soul.

Street Life; MCA MCLD 19004; 1979

Artistically this is pretty much diametrically opposed to *Southern Comfort*, as it proves the band to have entirely mastered the genre and puts them over as a slick disco-oriented jazz/funk outfit. With a featured vocalist, no less. However, they were never less than shrewd to use their understanding of what they were doing to give them considerable freedom within the genre. As well as the title track, 'Rodeo Drive', 'The Hustler' and 'Night Faces' are superior in both confidence and invention.

The Golden Years; GRP 50072; 1992

A comprehensive CD set, spanning the group's 1970s hits and running to thirty-two tracks, should fail to satisfy only those Crusaders completists who are beyond hope. Quite simply every single, club classic or upper bracket album track is here.

SEE ALSO: (1) Various Artists; *Classic Funk Mastercuts Volume 2*; Mastercuts CUTSCD14; 1993; (2) *Classic Jazz/Funk Mastercuts Volume 2*; Beechwood CUTSCD4; 1991

The Delfonics

(Ritchie Daniels; William Hart; Wilbert Hart; Randy Cain; Major Harris)
Although this group had its big hits in the 1960s, they're in this section because they made far more difference to what was going on *after* their success than during it. Working in Philadelphia (three were from there, the Hart brothers out of nearby Washington DC), they were the first group that Thom Bell wrote for and produced, and it was their classic interpretation of that city's street corner harmony style – interchangeable lead vocalists, and much closer layers of sound behind than traditional West Coast doo-wop – that forms the basis for the Philadelphia International vocal sound that stole the pop/soul swing from Motown during the 1970s. After working them up to the hits 'La La Means I Love You', 'Didn't I Blow Your Mind This Time' and 'Ready Or Not Here I Come', Bell must have felt he'd developed these vocal arrangements far enough to put them with a younger more marketable group, and left them to continue with THE DETROIT SPINNERS and THE STYLISTICS. The Delfonics never had another serious success.

*Echoes – The Best Of The Delfonics; Arista 260627; 1991

As this is probably the only way you're going to be able to buy 'Didn't I Blow Your Mind This Time' on CD, this has to be of greater value than just as a vaguely interesting chapter in the evolution of the Philly Sound.

The Detroit Emeralds

(James Mitchell; Abe Tillman; Ivory Tillman; Marvin Willis)
In 1977, Mitchell and Willis branched out with two other singers to serve up twelve minutes of, er, floating, that's known to millions as a Creme Egg commercial, but then was simply known as 'Float On'. But don't hold it against them. A few years previously, they'd worked out how to harness Detroit's fast emerging, apparently indigenous, left field funk and apply it to 1960s soul's vocalisations. That is, take things a few steps further from where Holland-Dozier-Holland or Motown had left them, but stay in sight of the source. 'Feel The Need', 'Baby Let Me Take You' and 'You Want It You Got It' were just three of their entirely grown-up soul songs that worked a pretty wild funk backing as hard as the singing to put across a very 1970s way of doing things while still appearing to play it straight. It was exactly this kind of undercover method that gave them a huge disco hit in 1977 with a deeply funky extended remake of 'Feel The Need'.

*Do Me Right/You Want It You Got It; Westbound
CDSEWD 067; 1993

The first two Emeralds albums on one CD gives you the three biggest hits and shows the development of their sound from virtually bog-standard harmonics to pimp-strutting, giving-it-plenty funk. In more ways than two contrasting album sleeves.

*I'm In Love With You/Feel The Need; Westbound
CDSEWD 068; 1993

Another twofer, and although not quite as swaggeringly exciting as the other one, you'll find 'I Think Of You' and the magnificent second version of 'Feel The Need', coupled up with a few more quite bearable disco outings.

SEE ALSO: Various Artists; *Classic Funk Mastercuts Volume 2*; Mastercuts CUTSCD14; 1993

The Detroit Spinners

(Henry Farnborough; Phillipe Wynne; Bobbie Smith; Billy Henderson; Pervis Jackson)

Christmas Eve 1970, and at a particularly cooking North London dance hall the mistletoe tune was The Detroit Spinners' 'It's A Shame'. A smooch supreme that, together with seasonal cheer, was definitely working overtime in its job as romantic respite from the likes of 'Sex Machine', 'Superbad' and 'Move On Up'. The deejay dropped it three or four times, licking it back more than once. Produced by STEVIE WONDER, falsetto-led and enveloping without being cloying, it proved the group had so mastered the art of genuinely exciting harmony singing they could do anything with it. But when their next record wasn't a hit, Motown dropped them.

On the recommendation of fellow Detroiter ARETHA FRANKLIN, they were signed to Atlantic, and put with Thom Bell who, fresh from THE DELFONICS, pushed the group along the lines laid down by THE DETROIT EMERALDS. He turned their slick harmony hands to some solid Motor City funk, topical social themes and the occasional risque love song and the group kicked five years' worth of the best 'last record' and bouncy-tempo soul harmonic in the business. A run that went on until lead voice Wynne joined FUNKADELIC in 1977 (his is one of the prominent straight background voices on *One Nation* and *Uncle Jam*). 'Working My Way Back To You', 'I'll Be Around', 'Could It Be I'm Falling In Love', 'Mighty Love', 'Ghetto Child', 'Rubberband Man' and 'Love Or Leave' are just a few of their hits and unavoidable examples of how Motown of the day was far from sure of what they should be doing.

SEE: (1) Various Artists; *Motown Chartbusters Volume 5*; Motown 72675; 1971; (2) Various Artists; *Atlantic R&B Volume 7 (1969–1974)*; Atlantic 781299; 1987

William DeVaughn

'Diamond in the back/sun roof top/digging the scene from the gangster lean/woh-oh-woh-oh/gangster whitewalls/TV antennae . . .' Now that's what you call a soul anthem. If you were really hip in 1974 you could sing all of William DeVaughn's 'Be Thankful For What You've Got'. If you were really stupid you attempted to drive your car from the gangster lean – slumped so low you looked through the steering wheel instead of over it.

But the point is, if you ever hear this song you'll want to sing it. You may even end up crashing your car. And to think that when William DeVaughn wrote and recorded his only really significant record he was a Jehovah's Witness.

Be Thankful For What You've Got; Start CHELD1002; 1989

Once you bring yourself to play the rest of the album – which also includes 'Give The Little Man A Great Big Hand', the other William DeVaughn song people have heard of – it's quite easy to see how religion was the singer's driving force. Even the hit was really about how 'Diamond in the back/sun roof top/digging the scene from the gangster lean/woh-oh-woh-oh . . .' *wasn't* the most important thing in life. Maybe that was why he never made another record. Pity, it only needed to be half as good as 'Be Thankful' and he would have cleaned up. No one would have minded who he was cleaning up for.

The Dramatics

(Ron Banks; William Howard; Elbert Wilkins; Larry Demps; Willie Ford)
Just as 'Respect' became a 1960s black theme song, so did The Dramatics' 'Whatcha See Is Whatcha Get' in the post-Panther early 1970s. Like Aretha's hit, there was more than one 'definitive' interpretation of the lyric; it contributed to, as well as borrowed from, street slang of the day; and it was spot on stylistically, as the deeply layered music wove in out of itself as well as the vocal. But as a mark of how things had moved on in under two years, whereas 'Respect' demanded a change, 'Whatcha See's sentiment was the then entirely relevant 'Here

we are. And this how we're gonna do things.' In one of the most moving sequences ever committed to film, the song is played during the opening credits of the *Wattstax* movie, against a background of footage of the Watts riots spliced in with the stage being built for the concert, by a virtually all black crew.

Like The Spinners and The Emeralds, The Dramatics were another Detroit vocal group that moved into the vacuum Motown was allowing to occur. Almost literally. When Motown staff producer Don Davis left and went to Stax in 1968 – he felt he would be allowed more freedom there – he came back up north to sign Banks's group who, for some reason, hadn't been picked up by local companies. Their three immediate hit singles and two big-selling albums for the company (on Volt) more than justified Davis's journey. In spite of their impact though, internal problems led to a split after the first album, that resulted in two groups both calling themselves The Dramatics and working at the same time. After Stax's decline the faction made up of Banks, Demps and Ford, with the addition of L.J. Reynolds and Lenny Mayes, signed with ABC but couldn't maintain the early momentum.

*Watcha See Is Whatcha Get/A Dramatic Experience; Stax CDSXD 963; 1971/1973

The first album is the one you want – the original Stax line up and, as well as the title track, the hits 'In The Rain' and 'Get Up And Get Down', as well as a series of chunky Detroit-meets-Memphis grooves. The second one is Banks's Dramatics after the split and while it's perfectly respectable it lacks the first one's fire and, under these circumstances, is not much more than a bonus.

SEE ALSO: (1) Various Artists; *Classic Mellow Mastercuts Volume 2*; Mastercuts CUTSLP8; (2) Various Artists; *Wattstax – The Living Word*; Stax CDSXE2 079; 1972

Earth, Wind & Fire

(Maurice White, born Memphis, Tennessee, December 19, 1944, vocals/drums/kalimba/percussion; Verdine White, bass; Phillip Bailey, vocals; Jessica Cleaves, vocals; Larry Dunn, keyboards;

Al McKay, guitar; Johnny Graham, guitar; Andrew Woolfolk, saxes; Fred White, drums)

'I went to see a Sly Stone show at Madison Square Gardens in 1969 or 1970, and it blew me away. I thought, "Why can't you have that level of production and spectacle with a pure soul show?" Black audiences would love it.' Maurice White is remembering what prompted him to change the name of his band from The Salty Peppers to Earth, Wind & Fire. To expand their horizons to include a 'spiritual philosophy' that would end up grappling with metaphysics, Egyptology and the secrets of the cosmos, while the music got LARGE. In doing so to lay the seeds for stadium funk – elaborately staged, expensive shows aimed at black audiences rather than looking to take it into the rock mainstream as Sly had done. And because this was the 1970s, by the time the group had truly established themselves the term 'spectacle' wasn't nearly big enough to describe what they were doing.

Maurice White maintains he 'wanted Earth, Wind & Fire stage shows to take the audience to another dimension for two hours'. Which may sound like overblown showbiz lip service, but nobody who ever went to one would deny he came pretty damn close. Stage sets fashioned after the burial site of the Giza – not scaled down that much either, just given a kind of sci-fi spin; costumes that must've kept the BacoFoil factory on overtime for months just to cover the shoulder pads; levitating bass players; floating spheres; disembodied pyramids kitted out with all-seeing 'third' eyes; band members disappearing and materialising apparently at will all around the auditorium; and music as overwhelmingly horn-heavily funky as these visuals warranted. All of which spilled over into the albums and their packaging, making Earth, Wind & Fire more some kind of total experience than merely a group. And the remarkable thing was that White managed to immerse himself in all this mysticism (some might say 'mumbo jumbo') of the Cosmic Pyramid and all-knowing, unseen forces, sell enormous amounts of records across the board – eight multi-platinum LPs between 1973 and 1983 – and still not compromise his funky black approach to either music or life.

But White was never going to be run of the mill. While at school, in the 1950s, he was earning money as a drummer in a group with BOOKER T JONES, and at sixteen he entered the Chicago Conservatory of Music to study classical composition and percussion technique. He stayed up north in Chicago to land a job as a Chess Records house drummer – Fontella Bass, ETTA JAMES and Chuck Berry were all beneficiaries of the MW big beat – eventually edging towards jazz and uptempo soul when he became one-third of The Ramsey Lewis Trio. A position he kept for three years, until the hopelessly named Salty Peppers.

At the height of Earth, Wind & Fire he set up ARC – the American Recording Company – his own label, on which he shaped careers for, among others, The Emotions, Deniece Williams and Weather Report, while after the group split up in 1984, his production skills were much in demand by artists as diverse as Barbra Streisand and Jennifer Holliday. Since 1987, the band has reformed every so often to release an album (LPs which usually do OK in the US) or tour (shows at which both the audience and the band themselves are looking back to the good old days). At least they have the good grace to make sure there's always one stunning disappearing trick.

That's The Way Of The World; Sony 80575; 1975

This is the LP that really got it started for the group, when it spent three weeks at US number 1, selling over two million. It was a film soundtrack, thus ensuring exposure, and was the one that concentrated on Phillip Bailey's falsetto, by building tunes around it rather than just putting it on top (e.g. 'Reasons' and the title track), while what had previously just been musical urgency was beginning to pan out into White's broadly funky vision for the future ('Shining Star' and 'Yearnin' Learnin''). If not quite as spectacular as later efforts, it's probably the group's most consistent album.

Gratitude; Sony 88160; 1975

A mostly live set, that takes in nearly every track on *That's The Way Of The World*, a couple of numbers from prior to that and even 'Sun Goddess', a Ramsey Lewis track that White originally produced and played drums on. Even at this early stage, the live reputation that won them 1976's Grammy for Best R&B Group is entirely justified.

All 'N' All; Sony 82238; 1977

It's at this point they got big. Big audiences, big budgets, big productions and big music. The pyramid themes are by now dominating and with the horns and expansive rhythms (percussionist Paulinho DaCosta was drafted in as a featured player), this is a wild journey through an afrocentric take on time, space and the forces that control them. Home to 'Serpentine Fire', 'Fantasy', 'Brazilian Rhyme' and 'Magic Mind'.

I Am; Sony 86084; 1979

The cosmic party rocks on: 'After The Love Is Gone'; 'Boogie Wonderland'; 'Star'; and 'In The Stone'.

Raise; Sony 85272; 1981

Maybe the spaceship was starting to run out of fuel at this point, as between this one and its predecessor, the now deleted *Faces*, they were starting to look much more like a singles band. A pretty sporadic one at that. Mind you, the big single off this was 'Let's Groove' and that buys back an awful lot of credibility. Also along for the ride are 'I've Had Enough' and 'Wanna Be With You'.

I Am/All 'N' All/Raise; Sony 4673882; 1990

A box set of the three original CDs, with no extra material or fancy packaging, just the discs, in their cases in a box. But at around twenty quid, you can't really expect a great deal.

The Eternal Dance; Sony 472614; 1993

A sumptuously packaged three-CD box set that, with fifty-five tracks, plots a course from the very beginning of their CBS days up to 'System Of Survival' fifteen years later. Featuring a dozen unreleased items, both unheard songs and live versions of old faves, a couple of numbers by The Emotions and a forty-five-page book of photos and interviews, even at nearly twice the price of the other set this would represent good value. A flashy box somehow seems appropriate for this group's musical CV.

ALSO RECOMMENDED:

Best Of Earth, Wind & Fire, Volume One; Sony 83284; 1987

The hits from *That's The Way Of The World* and before.

Best Of Earth, Wind & Fire, Volume Two; Sony 46332002; 1991

Ten tracks, taken from *All 'N' All* to *Raise*.

Although these collections are undoubtedly a good introduction, for much of that period in the band's history, the big hits really only give you half the story.

Touch The World; Sony 4604092; 1987

Very late model EWF that only really scores with the tracks that sound like the old ones – 'System Of Survival' and 'Touch The World' in particular.

The Fatback Band

(Bill Curtis, drums/percussion; Johnny King, guitar; Johnny Flippin, bass; Earl Shelton, saxes; Artie Simpson, trombone; George Adams, trumpet; Wayne Woolford, congas; Jerry Thomas, keyboards; Jayne Thomas, backing vocals)
It's hardly unusual for funk bands to talk about having 'a party in the studio' as a way of describing successful sessions. With The Fatback Band though, such a remark was a bald statement of fact. This nine-piece, brassy New York band would round up ancilliary studio personnel, innocent bystanders and passing pedestrians, herd them into the recording chamber, get them hand-clapping, foot-stomping – probably even doing the bump – and then turn this impromptu groovathon into bona fide vocalisms as they took up whatever chant constituted that particular track's lyrics. It was felt that such behaviour gave their records a genuine party atmosphere. And they had a point. There came a succession of joyous club classics from the raucous 'Street Walk' and 'Street Dance' in 1973 through the

acknowledged first rap record 'King Tim III, Personality Jock' in 1977 to the oh-so-smooth 'So Delicious' in 1985.

The group was founded by drummer Bill Curtis in the very early 1970s, intended as the backing band for a planned production operation that would treat different singers to his pumping, brass-heavy notion of soul music. The name owes itself to the style he employed of New Orleans R&B 'fatback drumming', which put the kit so far forward it was almost a lead instrument. But as their very East Coast sound developed by playing these big drums off against enormo-brass, the musicians became far more important than the proposed singers – if any did get as far as a release schedule, they've been long since forgotten – and their basslines, riffs and chants added up to a raw, spontaneous-sounding repetitiveness that came to define the sassiest side of street funk.

During the mid-1970s, The Fatback Band were probably the most consistent New York singles group, but they managed to last so long past street funk by sensing their enormous audience was growing up. Curtis and Co mellowed, and added a vocalist and keyboards in the early 1980s, to produce, albeit sporadically, some entirely respectable easy action grooves – 'Is This The Future', 'She's My Shining Star', 'Come And Get The Love'. Then, just to show they hadn't forgotten their roots, every so often they burst out with such soul weekender rallying songs as 'I Found Lovin'' and 'The Girl Is Fine'.

The Fatback Band is pretty comprehensively represented on CD at the time of writing – although a re-release of *People Music* wouldn't go amiss – but, as I said earlier, they were essentially a singles band. So be prepared to shell out for just two or three serious tunes per LP, and it's a good idea to thumb through 1970s compilation albums.

Keep On Steppin'; Event EV6902; 1974

This was *the* album to have tucked under your arm in summer 1975. The picture on the sleeve of the little girl with the 'trying so hard to be cool' look of concentration, as she does her dance on the pavement of a grafitti-covered street, summed up the whole early-1970s black soul scene. It was about doing it anywhere that took your fancy, and while you were going to give some gusto, you knew you had to look slick. The set's also what two of The Fatback Band's finest call home – 'Wicki-Wacky' and 'Keep On Steppin''. They're the kind of good-time grooves that lock in the bass and drums, only troubling to break it up with some sharp stabs of the horn section and letting the porta-party whoop it up around them. And some of the tunes, notably 'Stuff' and 'New York Style', don't even have that much point to them. It's as good an introduction to The Fatback Band as anybody could ask for.

Yum Yum; Westbound CDSEWM 016; 1975

Not quite as dazzling as the two albums that went before it – simply by now you knew what to expect – but The Fatback Band's penchant for gloriously pointless ideas was still going strong enough to blow up a storm across nearly all of the set. 'Yum Yum (Gimme Some)', 'Put The Funk On You', 'Let The Drums Speak' and that lost chord of North London soul circuit classic '(When You Wanna Boogie) Boogie With The Fatback'.

Hot Box; Spring SP1-6726; 1980

By now they were calling themselves Fatback, and the horns were being phased out in favour of synthesisers. But while this set gives all the clues as to where the band is heading, it's the last to approach their work from the old street funk point of view. In other words, while the top end emphasis is changing, everybody's well aware of the value of The Good Groove. New technology and old soul know how to get together for such full-length stormers as 'Backstrokin'', 'Love Spell'' 'Gotta Get My Hands On Some (Money)' and the title track.

ALSO RECOMMENDED:

While the above do actually pass muster as albums, the following stand up only by virtue of specific tracks. But to the more dedicated funkateer the availability of these tracks alone is enough to make them cheap at any price.

Raising Hell; Westbound CDSEWM028; 1976

'(Are You Ready) Do The Bus Stop'; 'Spanish Hustle'; 'Party Time'.

NYCNYUSA; Westbound CDSEWM030; 1977

'Double Dutch'; 'Duke Walk'.

With Love; Westbound CDSEWM024; 1976

'I Found Lovin' '.

SEE ALSO: Various Artists; *Classic Funk Mastercuts Volumes 1 and 2*; Mastercuts CUTSCD16/14; 1992/1994

Roberta Flack

(Born Black Mountain, North Carolina, February 10, 1939)
Throughout the 1970s, Roberta Flack was the quiet storm to the far sweatier goings on elsewhere. 'Sophisticated' was what people used to say, as if you had to make some sort of excuse if you were caught in possession of a Roberta Flack LP. Maybe this was because, in the UK at any rate, the singer was swiftly adopted by the more liberal end of the mainstream and far more likely to be compared with white soft-rock singers of the day. Curious that, as her credentials were impeccable and her contribution to the soul of the day immense.

She was sufficiently gifted to be allowed to study classical piano and vocal technique at Howard University at the age of fifteen, and only a couple of years later was teaching music at High School level. A living she added to by performing part time – as an opera accompanist, a nightclub singer and all points in between – until being spotted by Atlantic Records in 1969. There, apparently because her musical knowledge and technical expertise intimidated lesser-educated corporate personnel, she was more or less left to her own devices. Which meant she could get hold of a song – any song she liked – and strip it bare, then completely reconstruct it. Put it back together from the drums up, using soft jazz phrasings so subtle it took a vocal know-how such as hers to make it work, then she'd wrap the whole thing up in a projection of emotion that owed as much to blues as anything else. Which is what it was, a modern-day blues, but seldom seen as such because it was always polished to absolute perfection and thus perhaps not as rough as the day's self-appointed guardians liked to think blues should be. It's a style that she's managed to keep going for over twenty years of recording too. By using other writers she stays abreast of modern trends, yet is confident enough in herself and sufficiently skilled in what she is doing to totally Flack-ise a song without destroying its core element – many of Flack's biggest hits have been covers, which are all but unrecognisable from the originals.

First Take; Atlantic 781446-2; 1969

A stunning debut, that finds Roberta Flack similar to Nina Simone (only far less aggressive) in more than just classical backgrounds. The most jazziest of all her releases, it approaches the music with a kind of Duke Ellington-ish symphonic spin and then pares it back to basics, leaving just an impression of an orchestra, to create a series of almost hypnotic soul lullabyes – in particular, 'Hey, That's No Way To Say Goodbye', and 'The First Time Ever I Saw Your Face'. The vocal technique is possibly at its most interesting at this point – although what came later is certainly none too shabby – as her main aim seems to be to satisfy herself. A formidable task. The sleeve too, at the time, was an embodiment of the post-Panther Party, Angela Davis-identifying soul revolution, so how she ever got bagged alongside Carol King remains a mystery.

Chapter Two; Atlantic 3080; 1970

There was clearly something of a confidence surge after the first LP was a hit, as this one is less folksier and far more self-assured. More conventionally 'soul' than anything else the musician did, 'Reverend Lee' proves her as capable of kicking up a storm as any of her sweatier labelmates, while the duets with DONNY HATHAWAY – 'You've Got A Friend' and 'You've Lost That Lovin' Feelin'' – show an intelligent pop sensibility.

The Best Of (Softly With These Songs); Atlantic 756780564; 1994

The most recent repackaging – while it gives you the hits, it perhaps shouldn't have bothered with the housey remix of 'Uh-Uh

Ooh-Ooh Look Out Here It Comes' and dwelt a little longer on the more inventive work from the first five years of her career. However, it would be little short of churlish to take issue with a set of songs that includes 'The First Time', 'Killing Me Softly', 'Feel Like Makin' Love', 'You've Lost That Loving Feeling', 'You've Got A Friend' and the two soaring duets with Donny Hathaway 'Where Is The Love' and 'Back Together Again'.

SEE ALSO: Atlantic Various Artist compilations

Marvin Gaye

➤As if to prove that funk meant more than just a big beat, and fully deserved to be accepted as the Soul Of The Seventies, Marvin Gaye wrote his own chapter of the decade with a string of LPs that went way beyond the accepted parameters of lyrical emotion. Songs that left the likes of 'Dock Of The Bay', 'Chain Gang' and 'Tracks Of My Tears' standing, to move so far into the realms of self-expression and bare nerve exposure, that purely and simply they couldn't help but be funky.

What's Going On was the first, by far the deepest and possibly the most considered statement from this 1970s model Marvin Gaye. Prepared outside the Motown System – the success of 'I Heard It On The Grapevine' and 'Abraham Martin & John' had earned him more autonomy than most – the work was the result of a long period in his life when he began looking at the world beyond Motown's sanitised, feelgood bubble. For some time he'd complained vociferously about his corporate world – he felt Motown didn't afford him sufficient star status – but now he was questioning the real world. Understandable really. His long-term singing partner Tammi Terrell had died on stage in his arms, after a drawn out illness. Distraught, Marvin Gaye went into recluse, during which time his brother Frankie returned from Viet Nam telling tales of destruction, drugs and madness among the black GIs. Gaye's sadness intensified as, removed from the day-to-day business of showbusiness, he noticed the feelings of hopelessness setting into many US inner cities at the turn of the decade as the promises of social reform made during the previous five years weren't carried out quick enough. Addressing the community-devastating issues of drugs, the economy, the ecology, black-on-black crime, generational self-neglect and the war in Asia, he asked, 'What's Going On?'

Although the album offered no solutions – that was never on Gaye's agenda – it is one of the best albums made at any time in any style. It was a watershed record for the company also. More so than anything Norman Whitfield had done, it was a whole album with one centric thread, not just a collection of essentially disparate singles, superior or extended as they might be. And to address such a number of issues was far more serious a proposition than just the one 'maverick' protest song per album. Musically, thematically and appearance-wise it presented a very 'of age' Motown album, totally in tune with the post-hippie developments made in the rock industry. It sold by the million. Immediately.

Yet it only just got released, for Berry Gordy did his best to hold it up, convinced such a radical departure would ruin Gaye's career and have serious repercussions for the company. Motown's current CEO Jheryl Busby cites this turn of events as proof that Gordy was losing his ear for the record business. Interestingly, not because he had failed to spot a hit, but because he let the record come out at all: 'In the old days he would have just said a flat no and that would've been an end of the matter. He never would have allowed something he didn't truly believe in to come out with his company's name on it.'

The sales figures and critical acclaim for *What's Going On* pretty much gave Gaye *carte blanche* within Motown. A liberation he seized with both hands, but not for further socio-political musings as, apart from the single-only release 'You're The Man', this was an arena he wasn't to enter again this decade. Instead – Diana & Marvin excepted – he opened his funky mind far enough to provide access to his every and deepest thoughts on sex and relationships. Very adult, virtual stream-of-consciousness LPs that mirrored his deteriorating, drug-ravaged state of mind. The culmination was the bitter, divorce-set-to-music alimony album *Here My Dear* and the naked paranoia of *In Our Lifetime*.

The end of the decade marked the end of Marvin Gaye at Motown too. It also found the one-time suave superstar broke, doing enormous amounts of cocaine and living in an old bread van on a Hawaiian island. He was, according to people who knew him at the time, still very pissed off by *What's Going On*'s failure to take any Grammy Awards almost ten years previously. That year, LOU RAWLS had won his second Male R&B category gong for the pleasant but hardly innovative *Natural Man*. Listen to that, then give Marvin's oeuvre a spin and it becomes easy to see why the man went downhill so fast. ➻

What's Going On; Motown CD530022; 1971

One of the two or three most important albums in modern-day soul music. A dazzling display of sweeping strings set off by hard, brittle percussion, with bizarre jazz inflections sticking out at angles, coming together in a wealth of texture that reflects its nervy stream-of-consciousness lyrics in a musical picture of utter turmoil. Just below the surface. Just like his life and ghetto life in general. Marvin, Motown and most anybody who heard it would not remain unaffected.

Trouble Man; Motown CD530097; 1972

Marvin's favourite album, and for a long time the only one he wrote and produced entirely by himself. As a blaxploitation film soundtrack (the violent movie got very limited release in the UK), it was a chance for him to explore sounds, effects and sequences without being tied into the conventional demands of a pop song. And a chance he took to create a chillingly brilliant suite of electronic jazz instrumentals that – like the hero of the film's catchphrase – played by his own rules. Bleak washes of synthesizer and piano, chased round by a despairing sax, are urged on by the phattest, most upfront drums of the day. As if the former skinsman was going to make sure he left a percussive mark on his first truly solo project.

Let's Get It On; Motown CD530055; 1973

The sex suite. If Marvin was concerned about the state of mankind, then womankind was a positive obsession. With no need to prick anybody's conscience, this set did not have the spiky jazzisms of *What's Going On*, but continued to prove Marvin's mastery of much bigger musical subject matter, as it flowed from the speakers with all the presence of smoke – could physically wrap you up but was always going to be just out of reach. Smoove × smoove – back in 1973 it was all about holding somebody at a dance and hopefully holding them some more in your car, as the music oozed endorsement of what you had on your funky mind. But kicking it today, knowing what I know about Marvin and with my hormones under control, the taut echoing melancholy and the lyrical pleading of 'Please Don't Stay', 'Distant Lover', 'Let's Get It On' and 'If I Should Die Tonight' sound like the saddest songs ever written. Which kind of makes the album that much more special.

The three above albums can be found as a US imported box set. With a no-frills approach to packaging, their original CD presentations are supplemented with a fourth disc, *Love Starved Heart*, '16 rare and unreleased recordings from the Motown vaults'. The catalogue number is Motown 31453 0320, and expect to pay around £35.

The Very Best Of; Motown CD5302922; 1994

Released on the tenth anniversary of Marvin's death, it is by far the most comprehensive collection available at the moment, if not ever. While the later singles lose a great deal by being taken out of the context of their albums, it's a good chance to contrast them with the much earlier stuff and see if there were ever any clues provided. Also, if there's one or two people on the planet who still need an introduction to Marvin Gaye, this is it.

ALSO RECOMMENDED:

I Want You; Motown CD530021; 1973

The problem with Marvin Gaye albums is each new one was judged against what went before and by this time that recent back catalogue was setting ludicrously high standards. Whereas with anybody else's name on it this would be an album and a half, under these circumstances it was never anything more that *Let's Get It On, Chapter Two*, but without the first set's fire.

Here, My Dear; Motown CD530253; 1978

The divorce album, at last available on CD. Jazz-influenced, bitter, dark, uncomfortable and, at times, unhinged, while it's not the sort of album you think about playing that often, it's not nearly as bad as such a concept might have been. Fifteen years later, it's not even as daunting as most people remember it.

SEE ALSO: Motown Various Artist compilations

Gloria Gaynor

(Born Newark, New Jersey, September 7, 1949)
In 1974, with ten years' nightclub experience under her belt, Gloria Gaynor and her enormous traditional soul voice proved a godsend for producer Tony Bongiovi: she could interpret a tune with guts and character; wasn't afraid to rework a popular classic; yet was quite happy to have him call the shots when it came to artistic direction. As disco emerged from the upmarket New York nightclub scene and still retained some vestiges of soul integrity, she scored huge, and for a sustained period of time too. But as the genre descended into meaninglessness she rather went with it.

*I Will Survive – The Best Of Gloria Gaynor; Polydor 5196652; 1993

Now perceived as little more than a gay disco soundtrack, these HiNRG forerunners are a valid snapshot of that time just before all-out disco, when Gaynor got played (occasionally) in funk clubs as deejays would throw in a few (very) fast ones. As this LP features 'Never Can Say Goodbye', 'Reach Out I'll Be There', 'Honey Bee' and the title track, you'll never have to buy another Gloria Gaynor record.

Al Green

(Born Al Greene, Forrest City, Arkansas, April 13, 1946)
At a time when new soul acts were either putting themselves over as studiedly informal or emerging from the dressing up box looking like the cast of a science fiction film, Al Green came on stage at Finsbury Park Astoria in the early seventies wearing a

very slick three-piece suit (not evening dress, just a crisply cut whistle) and a natty bow-tie. Then, well into the set, he threw long-stemmed red roses into the audience. They went wild. Both the men and the women, as Al Green was one of the surprisingly few lurrrve men who guys were interested in beyond what they might capture if they had a spare ticket to the show or the new album playing in the car – not that either ever did you any good, because after the concert or the record, you still weren't Al Green.

He had universal appeal. The ladies loved him because he loved them enough to put himself entirely in their hands, to let them call the shots – his biggest songs had titles like 'Here I Am (Come And Take Me)', 'I'm Still In Love With You', 'Call Me' and 'I'm So Tired Of Being Alone'. While to the guys there was always something a bit knowing about this apparent vulnerability, we were always certain it was just a means to an end – but one so obviously successful we were lost in admiration. In other words, while our girlfriends wanted to be *with* him, we just wanted to *be* him. Oh yes, Al Green could sing a bit too. And the trademark Hi sound of WILLIE MITCHELL's subtly powerful, textbook sensual arrangements didn't do any harm.

Mitchell, then A&R for the Memphis label, spotted Al Green in 1969 and figured the singer had the voice, the personality and song-writing ability to front his mollasses-dripping, brass 'n' organ swirling, Southern-fried love song ideas. Green jumped at such a chance, having just gone solo after nearly ten years in groups, first with his three siblings on the gospel circuit, under his bass-playing father's guidance, as The Greene Brothers; then as vocalist in the Creatins (later to be called Al Greene & The Soul Mates) a combo of ex-school friends. He'd already written 'Back Up Train', and when it was a Chicago area hit for them in 1968 he wanted to continue in this direction rather than the previous rock/soul course. Musical differences left Greene free to drop the 'e' and move to Memphis.

Although what he did with Mitchell was, in essence, little more than traditional gospel-styled balladeering, Green became one of the four great smooves of the decade. Mitchell composed music to fit Green's voice, so there was never any doubt who was the star, and while the unique instrumentation developed out of a need to keep up with the singer's soaring pipes, it gave him a suitably solid sonic launch pad. Often, and this is the mark of the truly great balladeer, he'd allow himself to be pushed so hard that words would osmose into noises of bare emotion. But for all this, Al Green's agenda was fairly straight-forward – the pursuit of happiness through love and lust. He kept things far more accessible than, say, ISAAC HAYES or MARVIN GAYE, and thus a generation striving to come to terms with the sexual revolution's afterglow found it unfussily liberating.

By the second half of the decade, Al Green was interspersing his very secular stuff with more and more religious material. He claimed he'd started to re-evaluate his life after a deranged ex-girlfriend tipped a pan of hot grits over him while he sat in the bath, then shot herself in his bedroom. The results of any intro-spection became apparent in 1976, when he was ordained the Reverend Al Green and bought himself a church. In 1977 he parted company with Willie Mitchell, and by the end of the decade was recording solely religious material. 'I'd had the call, and I couldn't ignore it no more,' is the furthest he'd elaborate on it at the time.

Green Is Blues/Al Green Next To You; Hi HIUKCD 106; 1969/1971

His first two Hi albums that between them show the emerging style in both singing and playing as Green found his upper reg-ister confidence and Mitchell slowed the beat down. One remarkable aspect is the amount of covers chosen – not some-thing usually associated with these two, but it was the way of the day's more progressive-thinking soul artists to cover rock or pop songs as a means of moving the music forward before it had laid down its own guidelines. One more remarkable aspect of this twofer is 'Tired Of Being Alone'. I can remember a deejay playing it for the first time in a dance, fully expecting the floor to fill with clinching couples. It didn't. People were mes-merised, they just stood there and listened.

Let's Stay Together; Hi HIUKCD405; 1972

If 'Tired Of Being Alone', as a single, had got our attention, this LP established Al Green as the star he deserved to be. Although only the title track was a big hit, the whole set is special as the technique is by now firm and singer and producer are starting to push it in all directions.

I'm Still In Love With You/Call Me; Hi HIUKCD111; 1972/1973

Al Green's two best albums on the same CD is, quite literally, an astonishing proposition. Between them, these sets contain their title tracks, 'Have You Been Making Out OK?', 'You Ought To Be With Me', 'Here I Am (Come And Take Me), 'Funny How Time Slips Away' and 'Love And Happiness'. By now, as well as being into a string of mainstream hits, the sound was strong enough to work in all sorts of other elements from country, blues and mild rock – the readings of 'Oh Pretty Woman' and 'For The Good Times' are sinewey Memphis masterpieces that completely reinvent the originals.

Tokyo . . . Live; Hi HIUKCD104; 1981

Recorded in 1978, it's an hour and a quarter of pre-ordination hits, delivered with a fire and passion that comes through so startlingly on this CD it completes the picture of Al Green, legendary seducer. Nearly as good as being at the Finsbury Park show.

The Supreme Al Green; Hi HIUKCD130; 1992

There are a few Al Green compilations in the shops at the time of writing. This one – eighteen tracks, with a couple of excusable exceptions, all early 1970s lurrrve songs – is the best to be found on a single disc, as it doesn't waste a minute. Think of a big Al Green hit and it's here, but there'll be absolutely nothing you haven't heard of.

ALSO RECOMMENDED:

Livin' For You/Al Green Explores Your Mind; Hi HIUKCD113; 1973/1974

'Let's Get Married', 'Take Me To The River', 'Sha La La', and worth the price of admission for the scorching version of 'Unchained Melody' alone.

Al Green Is Love/Full Of Fire; Hi HIUKCD 114; 1975/1976

There's going to be no such thing as an Al Green twofer that isn't worth the money, but by now there was some indecision about which way he wanted to go. And while the singing's superb, the songwriting suffers.

Herbie Hancock (with The Headhunters)

(Herbie Hancock, born Chicago, Illinois, 1940, electric piano/clavinet/synthesiser/pipes. The Headhunters: Bennie Maupin, saxophones/clarinet/flute; Paul Jackson, bass/marimbula; Harvey Mason, drums; Bill Summers, percussion)

When jazz pianist Herbie Hancock bought himself some very modern electronic equipment and recruited a group of adventurous black session players (The Headhunters) to splash around in funk's wide waters, the 'serious' jazz fraternity threw up their hands in horror. On this side of the tracks, however, it was like a homecoming. The unit created a series of sleek, highly complex albums. Another facet of jazz/funk that would ooze all over the listener in silky-to-the-touch layers, yet had a jazz man's sense of the unexpected by managing some serious mood changes within each piece, keeping it all locked down to the same tight rhythms. It was the coolest, the slickest, a natural instrumental extension of what the lurrrve men were doing at the time. It had intellectual pretensions too, because it was 'jazz'. Yes, most guys had a couple of Herbie Hancock cassettes in their car, just in case they wanted to try to turn a promise into something more concrete.

Headhunters; Sony 65928; 1973

The first of Herbie Hancock's electronic jazz/funk excursions, and although not quite the best – *Man Child* went a bit deeper into funk, at the expense of some of the jazzy improvisation – it's the only original set from that mid-1970s period on catalogue. Only four tracks, but it still sets out his agenda with a stunning clarity, largely through the club hit 'Chameleon', fifteen minutes of chunky groove, and 'Vein Melter', possibly the oiliest ten minutes ever made legal and on record.

The Herbie Hancock Collection; Castle Collector
CCSCD283; 1991

While it's got 'Chameleon', 'Watermelon Man' and 'Maiden Voyage' from this early-1970s period, as a bonus it runs up as far as the next decade's hip-hop experiment 'Rockit'.

Donny Hathaway

(Born, Chicago, Illinois, October 1, 1940)
At the very end of the 1970s, Donny Hathaway fell to his death from a window in New York. It was a tragic end to a career that never got started in the way it had threatened to with his first single, the epic piece of soul-searching 'The Ghetto'. His soul apprenticeship read like something out of a movie too: he was raised by his locally famous gospel-singing aunt; majored in music theory at Howard University, where he shared a room with Leroy Hutson; became a staff producer at CURTIS MAYFIELD's Curtom Records in 1968 (Hathaway introduced Hutson to Mayfield); from there, was a producer at Chess, then Stax; and, when he was just about to turn thirty, secured his own deal at Atlantic. But in spite of his big resonant baritone, his willingness to embrace social topics and an ability to write around his own vocals in a way that gave him a chance to scat and show off, he only seemed to come alive (after that first record) as one half of love-song duets with ROBERTA FLACK. Stunning though they were, you always got the feeling this was only the hors d'oeuvre.

SEE: (1) Various Artists; *Classic Funk Mastercuts Volume 2*; Mastercuts CUTSCD6; 1992; (2) Roberta Flack's albums; (3) Atlantic Various Artist compilations

Isaac Hayes

(Born August 20, 1942, Covington, Tennessee)
When Isaac Hayes was declared bankrupt in 1976, with a reported $6 million worth of debts, and living on the floor of a one-room apartment, it somehow came as no surprise. The 1970s and Isaac Hayes were made for each other in terms of

excess. In all areas. Hayes reinvented a section of soul music on a scale that would make Cecil B. DeMille think twice. He composed suites, not merely tunes. He utilised forty-piece orchestras to supplement his rhythm sections. And put three or maybe four tracks on each album, stretching his own works and cover versions (notably Bacharach & David) into towering narratives of love and betrayal (notably betrayal). To allow the music to swell gently to a point somewhere past 'ludicrous' from a standing start, he prefaced these extravagances with lengthy (five or six minutes was standard) scene-setting, spoken introductions, called 'Ike's Raps'.

Isaac Hayes' stage shows were the sort of thing Busby Berkeley would have approved of too. When he played London in about 1973, he roped in some three dozen members of the Royal Philharmonic just to fill the bits of the stage that weren't already occupied by his rhythm section The Isaac Hayes Movement (a temporarily renamed Bar-Kays), the glamourous backing singers Hot, Buttered & Soul, the twelve-strong Isaac Hayes Dancers and, funkiest of all, a young lady with a shaved head and a lithe figure. Clad in a black leotard, she performed a series of balletic moves in front of the dancers to distract the audience while, as a drawn out intro for 'The Theme From Shaft' pounded out, Ike himself quietly took the stage. Suddenly the spotlight hit him. Completely covered up by a floor-length cloak and a huge floppy hat, he walked to the front of the stage, knelt, the bald woman ceremoniously removed his hat and kissed the top of his similarly hairless pate. Slowly he stood, raising his arms as the cloak fell away from his naked upper body. A sort of James Brown in reverse, and more or less what you'd expect from a man who, in 1972, had titled an album *Black Moses* and packaged the double LP with a nearly lifesize fold-out, cross-shaped poster of himself on a river bank wearing a biblical robe and sunglasses.

Yet Isaac Hayes was an enormous uptown hero for more reasons than 'Shaft': even though the mainstream never took to him – too flash? – all his early-1970s grandiose LPs went top twenty in the USA. Hayes had shrewdly tapped into a vibe that wasn't about to let go of the past – buppies had yet to reach the drawing board – and his narratives were street-talking modern day blues, but the scale and skill of the presentation was perfectly in tune with the post-1960s notion that the good life might be available on both sides of the tracks. The heavy chains he wore, he made a point of explaining, were a reminder that where he grew up slavery was only a couple of generations removed. Yet the entrance he made as the *Wattstax* headliner was pure pimping – driven round the arena and up to the stage cold-lounging in an open-top Caddy, with motorcycle outriders. Isaac Hayes knew exactly what buttons to push with his home crowd.

This wasn't so unexpected. For all his apparent ego-tripping, he'd actually kept one foot on the ground for as long as possible: through the second half of the 1960s, he made Stax's first team as a studio keyboard player, supplementing THE MGS, The Markeys and THE BAR-KAYS to back the likes of OTIS REDDING and CARLA THOMAS, but still kept his day job in a Memphis slaughter-house. In fact he only gave that up after he'd started writing hits for a large percentage of Stax's roster in a partnership with David Porter – a teaming up that grew out of Porter's unsuccessful attempt to sell Hayes life insurance, during which the two had started talking about music. The launch of his solo career was equally unplanned: he and a couple of MGs were fooling about in studio time left over on a session and the results, with a bit of polishing, were deemed good enough to be released in 1968 as *Presenting Isaac Hayes*. This album wasn't successful, however, until a few years later when it was re-released as *Blue Hayes*.

It was Isaac Hayes's commercial and cultural success that made it much easier for the likes of BARRY WHITE, STEVIE WONDER, Norman Connors and MARVIN GAYE to expand the field in the way they did, and his big production numbers did serious groundwork for Gamble and Huff's Philly orchestrations. He also wrote the rulebook for blaxploitation film soundtracks, taking them to a level that only a couple of other artists came anywhere near. So it was a shame that when Stax crashed he never managed to go anywhere other than disco and a rapid decline. Now back from bankruptcy and occasionally touring, Hayes is also showing a deft hand at light comedy acting. Building on his two 1970s action film roles, *Truck Turner* and *3 Tough Guys*, plus a recurring role in TV's *The Rockford Files*, he is steadily growing in range and number of lines spoken. Maybe the whole *Black Moses* trip was just an act too.

Hot Buttered Soul; Stax CDSXE005; 1969
Movement: Stax CDSXE025; 1970
To Be Continued; Stax CDSXE; 030; 1971

The enormous Isaac Hayes trilogy. Songs that redefined soul music by knowing no boundaries. There was no such thing as too big a musical statement or an overly dramatic production gesture in Hayes's book. The stunning depth and density of his compositions for a full orchestra allowed ditties such as 'Walk On By' to be presented as fully formed playlets of staggering emotional intensity. The sonic contrasts and Ike's natural sense of theatre, painted light and shade to a degree that wrung the listener out as the climaxes swelled, fell away sharply then built a little higher. It was an experience you'd already been gently pulled into by 'Ike's Raps', which were nothing like hip hop, just Hayes talking in his deep chocolate voice, telling you his tale as he slipped in and out of the song and the music grew behind him. The first one, *Hot Buttered Soul* (with 'By The Time I Get To Phoenix'), is still the best, but the other two are very close behind.

Shaft; Stax CDSXE021; 1971

The godfather of all blaxploitation film soundtracks. And a double LP that will never get a fair crack of the whip as anything that happens after the first track will be held up against that number's opening sequence. An absolutely fantastic, impossibly extended snatch of hi hat and wah wah guitar that played over the film's opening credits, to put across the swaggering confidence of the leather-coated John Shaft as the camera tracked him through Times Square. *Shaft* was one of the first black action films, thus this sequence was one of the most exciting things to reach Turnpike Lane and the electricity that charged through the auditorium as the scene unfolded gave everybody a lift. For weeks guys walked in an approximation of that same pimp-roll strut, 'The Theme From Shaft' playing in their heads. That alone makes this album something very special, but there's more than enough solid, orchestral jazz-based soul to make this something to listen to, while the cool hustle tempo of 'Cafe Regio's' and the bluesy lament of 'Soulsville' make it well worth owning.

Live At The Saharah Tahoe; Stax CDSXE2053; 1975

The same show as he brought to London, and although you can't actually see the production budget, from the big sound and the pictures on the cover you get the idea. All the best-known songs get an airing.

Joy; Stax CDSXE 047; 1973

For a long time, this was one of the great lost Isaac Hayes albums, as, chronologically, it was far enough removed from the first epics almost to escape notice, yet not late enough to be seen as a comeback. A great pity, as the upbeat title track is a monster. Putting together the orchestra and the soul groove in an extended, sumptuously bouncy jam that couldn't be ignored by anybody who heard it. And probably wasn't forgotten by whoever thought up disco music a few years later. Amazingly, Hayes is almost smiling on the sleeve shot too, but any happiness is short-lived with the wonderfully morbid and suitably drawn out 'I'm Gonna Make It (Without You)'. A fitting close to the Isaac Hayes Soul Era.

ALSO RECOMMENDED:

Black Moses; Stax CDSXE2033; 1971

Although this has its moments – 'Never Can Say Goodbye', 'Man's Temptation' and 'Never Gonna Give You Up' – it was all starting to wear a bit thin. Should never have been a double album.

Isaac's Moods: The Very Best Of; Stax CDSX011; 1980

A fairly comprehensive introduction, but if you've heard the big songs in full effect then the abbreviated versions don't quite make sense.

SEE ALSO: (1) Stax Various Artist compilations; (2) Various Artists; *Wattstax – The Living Word*; Stax CDSXE2 079; 1972

Heatwave

(Johnnie Wilder, vocals; Tommy Harris, drums; Rod Temperton, keyboards; Keith Wilder, guitar; Mario Mantese, bass; Ernest Berger, percussion; Johnny Whitten, guitar)

Formed in Germany, largely from ex-pat and ex-military Americans, Heatwave's history is one of the saddest known to soul. After a string of vibrant soft funk hits (thankfully, given their environment, not too European-sounding), Whitten was stabbed to death in Chicago in 1977; Mantese was paralysed in a car crash in 1978; as was Johnnie Wilder in 1979. In spite of all this, they still managed to achieve something nobody else at the time had quite managed – they united the traditionally opposed funk and reggae factions on the one record. On 'Mindblowing Decisions', they seamlessly blended the two by working them into one another at exactly the same tempo whereby it didn't matter that the beat was slightly different.

Powercuts (All Their Hottest Hits); Epic 4689212; 1991

There are several 'best of' Heatwave compilations on the market at the time of writing. This, put together by the parent company of their GTO Records, has the best reproduction and the most desirable selection of their easy-action disco vibe: 'Too Hot To Handle', 'Boogie Nights', 'Mindblowing Decisions', 'Gangsters Of The Groove' and 'Razzle Dazzle' among them.

SEE ALSO: Various Artists; *Classic Mellow Mastercuts Volume 2*; Mastercuts CUTSLP8; 1992

The Intruders

(Eugene Daughtry; Sam 'Little Sonny' Brown; Robert Edwards; Phil Terry)

More important as an overture for writing/production team Gamble and Huff than for what they actually achieved, even though 'I'll Always Love My Mama' and '(Win, Place Or Show) She's A Winner' were the perfectly acceptable face of post-Motown pop/soul. In 1965 the group were the first act signed to

G&H's Excel Records, where their classically Philly-style harmonising was solid enough to allow the pair to experiment with
the rhythm patterns and arrangements that would become The
Sound Of Philadelphia. But they were more than musical lab
rats – it was only after The Intruders had scored a million-selling single 'Cowboys To Girls' on Gamble Records (as Excel was
now called) that they were secure enough financially to set up
Philadelphia International, where The Intruders were among
the very first acts on the books. Although they didn't achieve
the prominence of, say, THE O'JAYS or HAROLD MELVIN, they never
did anything to disgrace themselves either. The group split up
in 1975, and after ten years driving lorries across America,
Daughtry put together a second line-up to work the oldies circuit.

SEE: Philadelphia International Various Artist compilations

The Isley Brothers

➡➡(Now with the addition of Ernie Isley, guitar; Marvin Isley,
bass; Chris Jasper, keyboards (a cousin); Everett Collins, drums)
Once off Motown and now a self-contained unit, the Isleys were
free to plough their own furrow. And it went West, because,
courtesy of the twenty-something new recruits, they took on all
manner of cool Californian rockisms as they edged further and
further from 'traditional' soul. The 1969 LP *It's Our Thing* was a
clear statement of intent, but what began with headbands,
fringed waistcoats and love beads finished up with an album of
cover versions of such rock chestnuts as 'Fire And Rain', 'Ohio',
'Machine Gun', 'Love The One You're With' and 'Lay Lady
Lay'. It wasn't a pretty sight or sound, as for the most part it was
delivered with a baffling po-faced reverence. They seemed
unsure of how to put their own spin on this hippiness, and so
floundered around derivatively. Once the psychedelic soul
style of the time kicked in fully, though, the group had found
themselves a home. Within a set of guidelines defining where
soul ends and rock begins, they were much more secure to
develop the silky, guitar-powered funk that epitomised their
second coming.

But as the decade played out, so did a string of five consecutive million-selling albums and, quite literally, musical differences led to an acrimonious split in 1984, the younger threesome breaking away to become Isley, Jasper, Isley. Since then, other artists have had more success with their songs than either faction – The Housemartins' 'Caravan Of Love' and The Christians' 'Harvest For The World' to name but two.

*3+3 (Epic 9826512)

The album where it all worked. The epitome of Isley Brothers cool, as the years of experience and two very different approaches – gospel, doo-wop, Holland/Dozier/Holland plus guitar melodrama, street funk awareness and general acid-tinged hippiness – added up, in this instance, to produce an album of staggering invention. For example, they took Seals & Crofts' 'Summer Breeze', powered its lyrics into a three-part harmony that reached a zone of sensual celebration only the likes of MARVIN GAYE and AL GREEN had seemed to know about; they ladled Ernie Isley's Hendrix-steeped guitar solo; set the whole thing off to a discreetly chunky synth-powered beat; and created an in-car classic. Then did more or less the same with such milestones of smoove as 'That Lady', 'Highway Of My Life' and 'Don't Let Me Be Lonely Tonight'. To have your Ford Capri's windows rolled down in the summer of 1973, with 3+3 oozing from the eight-track, was to make quite a statement. Something along the lines of, 'Here I am, girls, and I'm one helluva sensitive guy.' Although this marked the beginning of a long run of success, no other Isley's album had this confident, restrained power all the way through, so it's not as bad as it might be that this is the only original album from this period still available.

ALSO RECOMMENDED:

*Forever Gold; Epic CD32238; 1991

A very brief (seven tracks) 'greatest hits'-type affair, that has 'Harvest For The World' along with 'That Lady', 'Highway Of My Life' and 'Summer Breeze'.

The Jackson 5

(Jackie, born Sigmund Jackson, May 4, 1951; Tito, born Toriano, October 15, 1953; Jermaine, December 11, 1954; Marlon, March 12, 1957; Michael, August 29, 1958. All born in Gary, Indiana)
When, in December 1970, The Jackson 5 stormed to number 1 and number 2 in the US and UK respectively, with 'I Want You Back', it was one of the most significant soul events of the new decade. Firstly, their success revitalised Motown which, after the move to LA and prior to the 1970s-model STEVIE WONDER and MARVIN GAYE, was looking distinctly jaded. Then, far more importantly, the group restored the music's teen entry level and kept this access point open for a number of years. A vital state of affairs. The newly minted social and musical freedoms expressed by street funk, rocked out psychedelic soul, consciousness-raising pride stuff and X-rated lurrrve talk may have been fine for us, but our younger brothers and sisters were getting neglected. The Jackson 5, with their neat afros, vaguely hippified clothes, James Brown dance steps and simple ditties of adolescent love angst, were awareness's equivalent of the mohair 'n' beehive harmonisers of a decade or so before. Remember, this was back when Michael was black. Their phenomenal, instant success served this purpose perfectly: the biggest act in the world in any form of category (The Beatles had by now broken up) were brothers. In every sense of the word. At the time it was a feeling of pride that spread far beyond their target age group, and intensified when The Osmonds appeared as a blatant 'whitebread' version.

What The Jackson 5 also did was set Motown, as a corporate strategy, slightly further apart from what was going on elsewhere. But whatever cleaned-up street jive they kicked in their 1971 TV cartoon series, they were a traditional Motown act through and through: they made pop/soul singles (albeit marginally funky) that were selected and prepared for them; assumed carefully orchestrated 'personalities', both as a group and as individuals within it; they were willing students at the Motown grooming/charm school where, as Marvin Gaye liked to put it, 'We were taught not to act like niggers'; hell, Jermaine Jackson even married Berry Gordy's daughter Hazel. And then there was the group's extraordinary sales figures, which would be waved in the face of would-be avant gardists as conclusive proof of how the old way worked.

Ultimately, of course, this did Motown no favours at all. The group remained commercially buoyant for five years at the company, but by then they'd grown up sufficiently to realise that what they were being asked to do hadn't. In fact they'd stagnated around 1972. In a particularly messy divorce that dragged through the courts into the next decade, they left Motown in 1975, having to change their name (Motown owned The Jackson 5) and lose a member (Jermaine as a Gordy-in-law was obliged to stay). On the plus side, though, The Jacksons – keeping the numbers up with young Randy Jackson – got a much higher royalty rate at Epic (Motown still operated along 1959 guidelines) and a similarly increased slice of creative control.

Ironically, *Get It Together*, the second to last Jackson 5 album, was their most mature on Motown. The one that, mainly due to the title track and the single 'Dancing Machine', put them closer than they'd ever been to any sort of street funk credibility and gave them their biggest hits for years. Interestingly this point wasn't entirely lost on the record company, who took the step of making 'Dancing Machine' the title track of the group's *next* album.

It wasn't that their newly found freedom involved anything particularly risky or tricky either. It just meant they could use different writers and producers than were on offer at Motown. Like Gamble and Huff. Which was enough to make a difference straight away, as with them the group scored their two most widely acknowledged contemporary (in any era) soul albums – *The Jacksons* and *Destiny*. However, as their new deal allowed for increased songwriting input from the brothers, so it became relatively obvious they weren't much good at it. But most telling was their lack of character and the talent as a group to make a so-so song fly – in fact, as he sailed past puberty, it was becoming more and more apparent that the Jacksons were Michael And The Other Four. As for Jermaine, he stayed at Motown until 1984 and it's unlikely even he can remember the titles of any of his astonishingly dreary albums – even the one called, with no recourse to imagination, *My Name Is Jermaine*. Indeed his only sniff of success was the Stevie Wonder-penned disco stormer of a single 'Let's Get Serious'.

*Anthology; Motown CD530193; 1987

Never intended to be anything other than a singles group, this really is the only way to appreciate The Jackson 5. Also, as even their phenomenal success would be stretching a double CD, the chirrupey likes of 'ABC', 'I Want You Back', 'Mama's Pearl', 'Dancing Machine' and 'I'll Be There' are bolstered up with a few of Michael's solo hits ('Ben', 'Rockin' Robin' and 'Got To Be There' among them) and Jermaine's one contribution to Western culture 'Let's Get Serious'. They really were something pretty marvellous, and this CD is the sort of thing every soul fan should own, even if they don't play it very often.

SEE ALSO: Motown Various Artist compilations

Michael Jackson

It's important to remember that during the late-1970s Michael Jackson looked pretty much like a proper person. In fact, should you want to settle arguments with anybody under the age of ten as to what colour Michael Jackson is (or should that read 'was'?) it's best to refer to album sleeves from about then. OK, so by the end of the decade his nose had got straight, his cheekbones stuck out and his chin was growing a dimple, but, as was said at the time, he was simply losing his puppy fat. At the age of twenty-one! What he'd also lost were the awful and acceleratingly inappropriate songs served up to keep his pre-pubescent appeal alive – 'Rockin' Robin', 'I Wanna Be Where You Are' and, one of pop's very few odes to a rat, 'Ben'.

After meeting Quincy Jones, when both were involved in that lamentable 'black' remake of *The Wizard Of Oz, The Wiz* – starring a thirty-four-year-old Diana Ross as Dorothy – the two collaborated on Jackson's first solo album for Epic, *Off The Wall*. It came out in 1979, and neither post-disco pop/soul or that murky world of cosmetic surgery as a leisure activity would ever be the same again.➥

*Motown's Greatest Hits: Michael Jackson; Motown CD530014; 1992

A much more sensible proposition than the MJ anthology, as he didn't have nearly enough solo hits on the label to justify a double album. In fact this one somewhat stretches a point, but its hit/album-filler ratio is comfortingly low.

Off The Wall; Epic 83468; 1979

This album has shifted units well into the eight-figure bracket, and went top ten on both sides of the Atlantic almost immediately. But it never gets talked about much because the one that came next was more of a transglobal event than a mere LP. Ignore *Off The Wall*, though, and your life will be considerably poorer. As both a cohesive musical set and an example of the true power of the best pop/funk it's unsurpassed, and actually stands up as a far more exciting LP than *Thriller*. On numbers like 'Off The Wall', 'Working Day And Night', 'Don't Stop 'Til You Get Enough' and the sublime 'Rock With You' you can feel Jackson shimmering with barely contained emotion. At this point he'd long left Motown and 'Little Michael' behind (physically as well as musically) and after those two far less restrained albums with his brothers, was beginning to find out exactly what he was capable of. His barely contained joy at discovering what he could do comes over in the coltish, edgily energetic readings of the songs that, thanks to Quincy Jones's expertise, communicates all the way to the listener. It's a totally magical experience for all concerned (us as well as him) and one that he's never yet repeated.

SEE ALSO: Motown Various Artist compilations

Millie Jackson

(Born Thompson, Georgia, July 15, 1943)
There's always been a rowdy element involved in western black folk musics – blues, calypso, ska, jump-jive, R&B and so on – and there was no reason to imagine soul should be any exception. However, in the sexually aggressive, on-goingly feminist, enthusiastically permissive 1970s, it was open to debate exactly where your bawdy balladeer would be prepared to take it. And just how far record companies would go along with it. The

answer in both cases was Millie Jackson. Who, in units of distance, went so far *past* the knuckle it was up the arm, across the shoulders and back down to the other hand. And it did the woman concerned – in fact, black women in general – no good at all.

After ten years working live and a further five cutting workaday post-R&B singles, Millie Jackson began to develop properly her modern-day testifyin' style with two pretty straightforward albums on Spring. They did all right, prompting her and producer Brad Shapiro to share production duties and build on ISAAC HAYES's overwrought, overblown narrative-type approach, kicking *Caught Up*. But instead of orchestral flights of fancy being the raison d'etre, this set took a soul soundtrack from way below the Mason-Dixon line and – powerful as it was – used it as little more than a frame for a vividly detailed observation of the eternal triangle. He, she and the other woman, the latter role being Millie Jackson's. It was an elaboration of her live act, the story the most important aspect, with each song forming a different chapter as she spun her emotional tale of doomed love. A soul concept album? Could be. But what it *definitely* was was a marvellous piece of black blues art, combining music, self-depreciation, story-telling tradition, in-joke exclusivity and fierce, raucous humour. At a time when everybody you knew had an import copy of Richard Pryor's *That Nigger's Crazy*, Millie Jackson was a high funk priestess, and her very funny, musically exact stage shows put her up at doctorate-level ghetto-ology.

But as her reputation grew, thanks to two more albums that superbly built on the first, so did her audience. And what was attracting the new crowd wasn't the reflection-of-life subtleties that had got her so revered by her home crowd, but the cussing and graphic sexual description. The garnish. Most tellingly, this wider appreciation seemed to focus on the notion of the overweight, overbearing black woman 'who just won't stop'. And Millie Jackson, for whatever reasons, played up to this idea until her witty, carefully thought out and sympathy-winning Other Woman character became a shallow caricature.

Richard Pryor would regularly find himself in the same situation – his homecrowd-oriented act's genuinely hilarious authenticity won him a much wider following, but he started to tailor how he did it to accommodate the new crowd. The role decided for Millie Jackson became the cornerstone of her act. It was what crowds expected, how record companies wanted to market her and by the end of the decade this fantastic singer, sharp comedienne and talented producer/arranger was best known for what lengths she'd go to to talk about last night's oral sex. In 1989, after years in the doldrums, she even put out an album called *Back To The Shit*. Shame.

Millie Jackson; Westbound CDSEWM009; 1972
It Hurts So Good; Westbound CDSEWM019; 1973

Millie Jackson Phase One, which is superior if pretty much straightforward soul singing. However, her way of stretching out a song's music to allow herself space to expand the lyric into an emotional, pulpit-worthy pronouncement on a relationship (usually an unhappy one) is starting to take shape. It's also at this point – through songs such as 'I Ain't Giving Up', 'I Gotta Get Away (From Myself)' and 'My Man, A Sweet Man' on the first album and 'It Hurts So Good' and 'Hypocrisy' on its follow up – that Millie Jackson's place as the 1970s guardian of the southern soul ballad tradition becomes obvious.

Caught Up; Westbound CDSEWM003; 1975
Still Caught Up; Westbound CDSEWM027; 1976
Free And In Love; Westbound CDSEWM032; 1976

Phase Two, the Other Woman Trilogy, in which she had enjoyed, regretted and got out of her affair, but at no time felt shy about sharing her feelings with us. Her widescreen, technicolor handling of the Luther Ingram hit '(If Loving You Is Wrong) I Don't Want To Be Right' pretty much dictates the terms as, addressing women everywhere, her anguish spilled out of every pore and all over the record. Very similar to Isaac Hayes's ludicrousnesses inasmuch as she'd rework popular songs beyond all recognition, often redefining what they stood for, and preface the numbers with scene-setting spoken introductions. Perhaps as a result of its less fraught subject matter (the affair's over by now) *Free And In Love* never quite reaches the dizzying heights of the first two which, even two decades later, remain among the dictionary definition of soul.

*Lovingly Yours; Westbound CDSEWM037; 1977
*Feelin' Bitchy; Westbound CDSEWM042; 1977

Phase Three: presumably as she had run out of thematic ideas, the cussing was starting to kick in around this time. However, unlike what was to take her into the 1980s it hadn't yet got totally gratuitous and the music still seemed to mean something to her. The second of the pair even retains some subtlety of wit.

ALSO RECOMMENDED:

*Royal Rappin's (Millie Jackson & Isaac Hayes); Westbound; CDSEWM059; 1978

It had to happen, but the king and queen of the emotional wringer never conspired to out-torch each other. Instead it's a very shiny set of disco duets – including 'Sweet Music, Soft Lights And You' – that remains more a curiosity than anything vital.

Rick James

(Born James Johnson, February 1, 1955, Buffalo, New York)
I was introduced to Rick James once, by a mutual friend in a restaurant in Los Angeles. It was just as 'Give It To Me Baby' was hitting big, so, quite understandably, he was full of himself. He seemed, on that evening, rather full of other substances too, as his eyes were shut. Shut not just as we shook hands, but throughout his entire meal – his astonishingly over-attired companions (more fringed, primary-coloured leather than has any right to exist) had ordered for themselves and their guv'nor, then scarfed theirs down with little conversation while he just sat there smiling to himself from time to time. Presumably he was imagining what might've been on his plate. When Rick James came to Britain to do press (once HM Customs had finished with him and his entourage), he conducted a series of interviews from his bed, opening his eyes only to scope lasciviously the more attractive journalists. On his album sleeves he posed with spliffs, hookers or loin cloths, named the recording studio he had built Le Joint and once had a big-selling album called *Fire It Up*.

Yes, Rick James believed he had to live the funk, not just play it, and as such he threw himself into what he did one hundred per cent. Sometimes it went spectacularly off the rails, and sounded like the confused rag-bag of influences it ultimately was, but when it clicked he was responsible for some of the most belligerent, juggernaut-powered rock-based street funk that *wasn't* made in the 1970s. (Rick James' didn't have serious hits until the 1980s, but in terms of style – both life and musical – his tent is pitched in the decade before.)

Rick James used to call his music 'punk funk' or 'funk 'n' roll', in acknowledgement of rock roots that went back more than ten years before his first hits. In the mid-1960s, after jumping ship from the US Navy in Canada (James joined up at age eighteen, but, rather understandably, the military life was not for him), he settled in Toronto where he shared a flat with Neil Young. They formed the rock band The Mynah Byrds, which were signed to Motown as part of the company's ill-advised forays into the newly emerging acid rock. Nothing was ever released, and the group broke up: James stayed in Detroit producing THE SPINNERS, THE MARVELETTES and Bobby Taylor, while Neil Young became one of the most famous rock stars of his generation. In 1970, James decamped to London and played bass in rock/blues band The Main Line, and worked with other groups in Britain for seven years, periodically visiting Canada and the USA. He was still in London when punk broke, and its penchant for theatrical rebellion cannot have been lost on Brother Rick.

In 1977, James fused his compendium of influences into a lavishly presented pimp-strutting street opera of sex, drugs and brushes with the law. And signed it to Motown, who were by then feeling a bit left behind by the wilder likes of P-FUNK, EARTH, WIND & FIRE and THE OHIO PLAYERS. As corporately sanctioned bad boy, Rick James had found his niche. Although too late in the life of street funk to influence anything (like JAMES BROWN eight years earlier) and never quite musically intelligent enough to take it into new areas (as his one-time friend Prince did), James slipped easily into an established pond without muddying anything up. When his records hit they were enormous, he further applied his successful OTT touch (virtually unchanged) to writing and producing hit albums by Teena Marie, The Mary Jane Girls and his backing group The Stone City Band.

Rick James may have arrived late and not done much that hadn't been done before, but he certainly did it well enough to deserve the place he occupies in funk legend. The problem was, however, when it's a way of life, as it was to this singer, it's difficult to know when to switch off. By the mid-1980s the bad boy had become so bad he'd lost his corporate approval, and he left the company after much bitterness in 1985. His initial success as an independent producer (Eddie Murphy's first, huge-selling, musical album) didn't last though, but it seems Rick James continued to live the funk – or at least the drugs and women end of things – and has recently been best known for courtroom productions. Not all of them as fortunate as the one in 1990 when he won a case for royalty payments from MC HAMMER, after the rapper had appropriated the bass line from his 'Super Freak' as a hook for his 'U Can't Touch This'. At the time of writing he has just given a rare press interview – from his prison cell.

Street Songs; Motown 530218; 1981

This was on the US charts for over a year, reaching sales well into the seven-figure bracket and for the first time (it was his fifth album) showing James as coming completely to grips with what he wanted to do. That is, he moved the rock to one side, established a solid funk foundation with his bass, a phat horn section and a motor of a synth player, then sparingly spooned the pop/rockisms back on to lighten the load slightly (compared with, say, FUNKADELIC) and provide a more welcoming entrance hall. Also, songs with titles like 'Super Freak', 'Ghetto Life', 'Below The Funk (Pass The J)' and 'Give It To Me Baby' provide an apparently glamorous instant primer to what life is like on the other side of town. In the same way that ICE CUBE now sells enormous amounts of albums to white college kids, so in 1981 it was perfectly usual to see middle-class middle-American high school kids hanging about outside ice cream parlours, doing their best to look cool and chanting, 'Give it to me baby/Give me that stuff that funky stuff' at passing, er, chicks. But while this brought the massive sales returns, Rick James's skill lay in the fact that as well as working on that level, it had an uptown appeal that placed it as one of perhaps a dozen absolutely vital funk albums. Not only were the beats crisp enough (he'd by then worked out that the key was to use all the instruments rhythmically, including the ones that were handling the melodies), but most of us assumed his dumb street life tales to be a bit of wind up. He couldn't possibly mean it. Perhaps if he hadn't he might've stayed the distance a bit better.

Throwin' Down; Gordy Z2474; 1982

This was never really more than *Street Songs Pt II* – in 1986, Motown put out the two LPs on the same CD and one plays into the other absolutely seamlessly – and as such, a mere twelve months later, was naturally subject to the law of diminishing returns. Commercially as well as creatively. But still, it's no slouch as the singles 'Standing On The Top', 'Dance Wit' Me' and the title track are all far above average. But what makes the LP special is the use of THE TEMPTATIONS, not really as backing or lead singers more as another instrument, woven in and out of the mix to perpetually startle and push things along. It's much the same way Norman Whitfield worked with them ten years previously and here represented the sort of progression Motown really should have made more of.

ALSO RECOMMENDED:

Reflections Of Rick James; Gordy 71274; 1984

The hits. All of the best-known tracks from the above, plus a trip back in time to 'Mary Jane', 'You And I', 'Bustin' Out' and a couple of ballads of the bewildering *Garden Of Love* LP.

The Brothers Johnson

(George, born Los Angeles, California, May 17, 1953, guitar; Louis, April 13, 1955, bass)
'Lightning Licks' and 'Thunder Thumbs', respectively, are what Mrs Johnson's lads liked to call themselves when their star shot to prominence with a run of four hit albums in the mid-1970s. And maybe such important-sounding aliases were justified. Although their styles were never particularly original – George's was little more than competent, quick-picking

jazz/rock runs, and Louis's slap and pop technique had been around for roughly ten years – what they did with them stood out. On tunes like 'Get The Funk Outta My Face', 'I'll Be Good To Ya' and 'Strawberry Letter 23', their playing was set within very straightforward muscular frameworks, which not only gained immediate dancefloor appreciation but also made the lead lines (both bass as well as guitar) seem that much fancier so it all came together as one intricate enough funk/rock statement. They looked the part, too, which was an enormous bonus for instrumentalists, and were suitably musically ambitious to hold their own in the rapidly changing 1970s soul scene – from the start of the decade they'd progressed from being regular LA pick-up players for the bigger visiting soul acts, to backing and writing for Billy Preston, to studio work with Quincy Jones. It was Jones who got them their record deal, and played as big a part in their success as almost any amount of Lightning Licks and Thunder Thumbs.

The Brothers Johnson's four killer albums – *Look Out For Number One, Right On Time, Blam!* and *Light Up The Night* – were Quincy Jones creations. And it showed. From the mid-1970s onwards, the producer's jazz/orchestral background had been introducing new dimensions of depth to the already increasing layering going on within the music while not compromising the existing premise. Such technique did a lot to 'legitimise' hard funk in the post-*Saturday Night Fever* years, as it made it more accessible, thus providing a soul survival route that wasn't so lame it needed crutches. The stuff he did with The Brothers Johnson is a clearly defined bridge between street funk and the gutsy pop/soul work Jones would come to do with MICHAEL JACKSON. It did more than many might realise to fight jazz/funk's corner too: although ol' Thunder and Lightning were never going to be racked alongside Cedar Walton or Ronnie Laws, the arrangements of the middle two albums were little more than scaled down versions of the big band stuff on which Jones cut his teeth in the 1950s.

Going into the 1980s, a combination of their continued success and Jones's new friend Michael's impact, the Bros J opted to write and produce for themselves. Not a wise move. In fact it pretty much confirmed who was the brains of the operation. Although they put out several LPs during the 1980s, their most prominent musical adventure of that period was Louis's credit as bass player on the biggest selling album ever. *Thriller*. A Quincy Jones production.

At the time of writing, there are no Brothers Johnson CDs – originals or compilations – on anybody's catalogue anywhere in the UK. We can only assume this is because the sensible person was out of the office when they drew up the release schedules, and that the situation will soon be rectified.

SEE: *Classic Jazz/Funk Mastercuts Volume 4*; Beechwood CUTSCD16; 1993

Syl Johnson

(Born Mississippi, 1939)
When people draw up lists of those eloquent black soul spokespersons of the 1970s, such names as SLY, MARVIN, JAMES BROWN and CURTIS tend to dominate, but there was a host of other less obvious names chipping away with a righteous lyric here, a conscious song there. Like THE O'JAYS, DONNY HATHAWAY, THE CHI-LITES and Syl Johnson. He kicked it large with a truly heart-rending slab of up-dated blues called 'Is It Because I'm Black'. The tune was an ideal vehicle for the still functioning late-model Memphis soul sound – as practised by WILLIE MITCHELL at the deeply Southern Hi Records – as the bass and organ low end resonance was just right for such a cry of pain and served to make the most of Johnson's apparently bottomless baritone. A wonderful example of the naked power still alive in soul, it cropped up as a single in better-dressed record collections everywhere. Curiously, though, never on the CD compilations that celebrate the rest of Johnson's work after he joined Hi to work with Mitchell.

Music To My Ears; Hi HIUKCD117; 1990

A twenty-five-track amalgamation of the best of Johnson's three Hi albums, which are probably better demonstrations of what Mitchell was about, as Johnson's voice isn't nearly as dominating as AL GREEN's. It's still a pretty marvellous set of pipes, though, as the mildly countrified hybrid of gospel, jazz and blues will testify: 'Diamond In The Rough', 'We Did It', 'Back For A Taste Of Your Love', 'I Hear The Love Chimes' and 'Take Me To The River'.

Eddie Kendricks

(Born Birmingham, Alabama, December 17, 1939)
An original TEMPTATION, who stayed with the group until 1971 – his was the lead vocal on 'Just My Imagination' – Kendricks's 1973 solo single 'Keep On Truckin'' could have been an important record for Motown. Featuring just the one voice as part of a mildly wiggy, synthesiser backing, it was very close to what had, by then, a bog-standard self-contained funk band sound, as opposed from, say, The Temps' cathedral-like arrangements or the more traditional Motown methods of clear demarcation between singers and layers of instruments. This was a couple of years before THE COMMODORES, and thus might have been a bit ahead of its time for the company because rather than build on its success they just . . . did nothing. 'Keep On Truckin'' was a killer club track at the time; with hindsight, though, it's one more example of that company's staggering miscalculations.

SEE: Motown Various Artist compilations

Frederick Knight

(Born August 15, 1944, Birmingham, Alabama)
A Stax house writer and producer just after the company's golden days, Knight was equally anachronistic when he scored with his own hit 'I've Been Lonely For So Long'. Back in 1972, this song came over as so hugely enjoyable because it was a very simply constructed throwback to the easy-going mid-tempo ballads of the previous decade, the sort of thing Lee Dorsey might do. It was always good to hear, as a bit of light relief during a more serious soul programme. Knight's other contribution to soul culture was as producer of the massive Anita Ward disco number 'Ring My Bell'. Does this cancel out his own hit?

*I've Been Lonely For So Long; Stax CDSXE099; 1973

There's not really much else going on here, so it's probably better to look out for the track on a Stax compilation.

Gladys Knight & The Pips

→One of the first high-profile acts to leave Motown – in 1973, dissatisfied with the breaks they were getting, in spite of their undeniable success rate – they were also one of the very few (at the time) to do better after leaving the firm. However, top ten singles like 'Midnight Train To Georgia', 'Best Thing That Ever Happened To Me', 'The Way We Were' and 'Home Is Where The Heart Is' were only achieved at a considerable expense – serving up such ready-to-wear supper club nostalgia, at the relatively young age of thirty, will seriously affect your credibility in years to come. But it served as a useful metaphor for how, during this period of drastic social and artistic change, the music world and the world in general viewed pre-funk soul if it refused to come to terms with the 1970s: instant Golden Oldie, with no time off for bad behaviour. To give them their due, Gladys and her cousins managed to breath some life into even the most mundane material – even the CURTIS MAYFIELD-produced *Claudine* soundtrack album was pretty ropey – and they never ever looked like they were particularly enjoying themselves.

*Collection; Castle Collector CCSCD206; 1988

Never a vital set of songs, but a couple – surprisingly 'The Way We Were' among them – aren't as bad as the rest. The best snapshot there is of the mid-career Gladys Knight.

Jean Knight

If you were a one-hit wonder, do you get extra points if everybody who can remember your song – which is most people who ever dropped some foot in soul clubs in the very early 1970s – can remember the album cover too?

Mr Big Stuff; Stax CDSX003; 1971

The hit was 'Mr Big Stuff'. But then you knew that, didn't you? The album sleeve, thankfully retained for the CD, is of the fattest bloke in the world straining the seams of an enormous white suit as he 'eases' into a Cadillac. But then you knew that too. There's a dozen or so other Jean Knight tracks, but nobody knows what they are.

SEE ALSO: Stax Various Artist compilations

Kool & The Gang

(Robert 'Kool' Bell, bass, born Youngstown, Ohio, October 8, 1950; Ronald Bell, saxes; George Brown, drums; Dennis Thomas, saxes; Robert 'Spike' Mickens, trumpet; Claydes X Smith, guitar; Rick Westfield, keyboards)
The whistle as an expression of funky solidarity was getting some pretty bad press by the end of the 1970s. Hardly surprising, as at that time it had become a standard component of some of the direst disco music or the most superficial pop/soul, to such a degree that a prog rock 'n' punk-led music media was – since *Saturday Night Fever* had been and gone – sneeringly confining all black music that wasn't reggae to a bin marked 'Take Out Your Funky Whistle And Blow'. Years before that, though, came if not the first then certainly the most prominent example of the whistle as a bona-fide funk instrument, Kool & The Gang's 'Funky Stuff'. It was definitely the best loved. About two in the morning, midway through and when the crowd was starting to slow down, this piercing blast of a New York traffic cop's whistle could pep up an entire party. It was like reveille. Then having grabbed their attention, there were a couple of beats of absolutely nothing before the first chord of the tune came in, during which time the deejay could lean out and almost touch the anticipation while the crowd were poised to start bouncing again.

And with or without this magical moment, Kool & The Gang were groovemasters. Up there with BRASS CONSTRUCTION and THE FATBACK BAND as the third point of that Unholy Trinity of East

Coast Funk. They had the strongest musical background of all the young groups of the time too: the Bell brothers' father was a Theolonius Monk sideman. When Robert formed the group at high school in New Jersey (all members were in their mid-teens) they were called The Jazziacs and, musically speaking, appropriately flavoured. The name Kool & The Gang evolved over a period of time – through such handles as The Soul Music Review, The New Dimension, The New Flames and Kool & The Flames – during which they continued to play live, locally, as a straight jazz band, but once they began recording they became crucial to soul's evolution. As far back as 1969 they were playing kicking instrumental soul by jazz's rules, inasmuch as a tight rhythm and disciplined players is the only environment that truly encourages wildness, but as teenagers growing up while rock 'n' roll osmosed into rock they fully understood that such wildness had few limits. Indeed. A year or so after SLY STONE and a couple of the others had let on it was OK for black guys to come at it from a rock-type point of view, sassy teenagers Kool & The Gang screamed, quite literally, into the charts with 'Funky Man'. Sample lyric, delivered at a larynx-endangering level: 'Watch out! Watch out! here come that funky man/You better run 'cause he's gonna blow your mind . . .' It was musical mayhem kicking in all directions at once and firing on more cylinders than were believed possible: stabbing horn riffs piled on top of one another; short sharp swirling guitar patterns; vocals that were never more than a happening, chanting, yelling and cheering; all locked in place with an unshakeable bass and drum groove. JAMES BROWN to the soul power of ten, assembled so intricately it looked like it was casual.

At this point in time Kool & The Gang specialised in instrumentals. They could play fast 'n' furious or ultra cool, and they were immensely funk influential from 1969 onwards. While James Brown was stripping it down, they were putting this subtle stuff together, music that sent out clear signals to a post-soul world that clever-clever need not compromise rump-shaking potential. In the aftermath of the singer-obsessed 1960s, they championed the instrumental, and, in so doing, proved how jazz/funk could be a perfectly legitimate expression of jazz arrived at from funk as well as the other way around. Kool's glorious early albums – *Good Times*, *Music Is The Message* and

Live At PJs – had as important an effect on groups like WAR, THE OHIO PLAYERS, BOOTSY'S RUBBER BAND and even the late-model JBs as James Brown ever did.

But it wasn't until 1974 that the band went overground. With the *Wild & Peaceful* album it was as if the previous five years had been a rehearsal. 'Funky Stuff', 'Jungle Boogie', 'Life Is What You Make It' and 'Hollywood Swinging' rocked houses on both sides of town, while with the accurately titled title track, 'Heaven At Once' and 'This Is You, This Is Me' proved their delicate touch was still very much in evidence. The latter approach was to indicate their immediate direction for the follow up LP *Light Of Worlds*, a stunningly laid back blend of synthesizer and brass that racked up one more jazz/funk touchstone for the group. And that's in a career that was never short of invention, experimentation and expertise.

But time was running out – disco was catching up fast. Kool & The Gang attempted to tailor their style to suit the changing times, and only succeeded in watering down what had made them so special to start off with. Their hearts didn't seem quite in it, and sales dropped accordingly. In 1978, the group's 1970s effectively came to an end when they recruited James JT Taylor, their first vocalist, and hired smooth, discofied keyboard player/producer Eumir Deodato. A total reinvention.••

Anthology; VSOP CD168; 1991
Best Of Kool & The Gang 1969/1976; Phonogram 5148222; 1993

It seems ridiculous, given their enormous influence on 1970s soul and the enthusiasm which still greets vintage Kool at your better class of party, that no original albums are currently on catalogue, from either side of the Kool & The Gang Career Divide of 1978. Of the apparently limitless amount of Kool compilations in the racks at the time of writing, these are the only two that offer more than a nod to the early years. Both will give you the high-profile singles – 'Funky Stuff', 'Hollywood Swinging', 'Jungle Boogie', 'Let The Music Take Your Mind', 'Rhyme Time People' and so on – but while the latter concentrates on the period to include some contrasting album tracks, the former has more songs on it and will provide a taste of 1980s

Kool too. While neither is a particularly satisfactory way of appreciating a band that had enormous depth to their repertoire, either is better than no Kool at all.

SEE ALSO: Various Artists; *Classic Funk Mastercuts Volumes 1 and 2*; Mastercuts CUTSCD6/14; 1992/1994

Denise LaSalle

(Born Denise Craig, Greenwood, Mississippi, 1948)
The more stage-friendly name derived from La Salle Avenue in Chicago, the city Denise moved to as a teenager. But it was back down south in 1971, under the production guidance of WILLIE MITCHELL, that she began having hits. Through 'Trapped By A Thing Called Love', 'Now Run And Tell That', 'A Man Sized Job' and 'The Deeper I Go (The Better It Gets)' and with Mitchell's distinctive' style, she was dubbed The Female Al Green. Absolute nonsense. While she had a broader range of attack than AL GREEN, and although her catalogue is peppered with hot hugging southern funk, it was all rather retro. Thus what she really was was the link between Willie Mitchell's 1960s and 1970s.

*Trapped By A Thing Called Love/On The Loose; Westbound CDSEWD018; 1971/1973

Two albums that cover her best period – before she started producing herself – which feature all the hits and are a prime example of Southern R&B developing into its own brand of funk.

M.S.F.B.

If Gamble & Huff thought up The Philly Sound, then Mother, Father, Sister, Brother were the men and women who made it happen. At risk of understating their case, they were the Philadelphia International Records house band. Very Motown in structure with a regular engine room of a rhythm section, supplemented by string, woodwind and brass players as required (forty-five musicians wasn't unusual), they backed every act on the label. Indeed, there were only a couple of differences from Berry Gordy's set up. Arranged by either Kenny Gamble, Leon Huff, Dexter Wansel or Vince Montana, this orchestra understood 1970s black music and how it was willing to experiment to the degree that strings and woodwind and a nasty funk rhythm section need not be mutually exclusive. This by itself was a big enough difference to mean Philly became the most singularly identifiable soul sound of the first half of the decade, but the adventures in time that came as second nature to such a large outfit laid one of disco's most important foundation stones. The other difference was that Gamble & Huff periodically moved these backroom boys (and girls) up front to cut their own albums.

If the duo had removed the distraction of singers just to show off their skills with a full orchestra, then clever for cleverness' sake has never been so acceptable, with M.F.S.B.'s first two albums, *M.F.S.B.* and *Love Is The Message*. Vital records back in 1973. Textbook examples of how something could hit you in the gut to make you dance, yet at the same time be sumptuous, musically sophisticated, socially aware and sexually encouraging – as a major contributor to the early Hustle soundtrack, M.S.F.B. had a lot to do with getting men and women to touch each other when they danced. In fact in terms of sheer class, it's not surprising that so many snatches of these albums live on, twenty years later, as deejay jingles.

They recorded six more LPs for Philadelphia International, but following the first two, Gamble and Huff's attentions seemed more focused on their singing stars and M.F.S.B.'s output became progressively less interesting. It wasn't until 1980, when Dexter Wansel updated their sound to a less frantic, more jazzy texture – post- rather than pre-disco – that they made further impact.

SEE: Philadelphia International Various Artist compilations

Mandrill

(Carlos D. Wilson, trombone/flute/vocals; Louis Wilson, trumpet/ congas; Wilfredo Wilson, bass/congas/percussion; Ric Wilson, sax; Neftali Santiago, drums/percussion/vocals; Juaquin Jessup, guitar/vocals; Claude Cave, keyboards/vocals)

A wonderful example of three important facets of 1970s funk: (a) that it was not ashamed to draw influence from anywhere it fancied; (b) that whacked out humour would never fall too wide of the mark; and (c) how, even back as far as 1973, the records were starting to outlast the people who made them. Mandrill, put together by the Wilson brothers, forced Latinesque rhythm patterns, wild rock guitars and beserker brass into one of the dirtiest New York street soul grooves, to create the *High Ape* album in 1973. The cover was a ludicrous King Kong take-off, the title track had the chant-a-long-a-lyric 'The ape is high/So am I'.

Kicking as the whole set was, the track 'Fencewalk' took their funk so far it seemed it was only the innate tightness of the players that stopped the production going out of control. For about five years that tune was a deejay's 'must have' – don't even bother showing up without it. A guaranteed floor stormer. A funk/rock touchstone as solid as anything THE OHIO PLAYERS ever did. Then nothing else was heard of the group until the end of the decade and a couple of minor early-disco hits, 'Funky Monkey' and 'It's So Easy Loving You', produced by Jeff Lane of BRASS CONSTRUCTION and BT EXPRESS fame.

SEE: Various Artists; *Classic Funk Mastercuts Volume 1*; Mastercuts CUTSCD6; 1992

Curtis Mayfield

➤Throughout the 1960s, Curtis Mayfield made it entirely clear what was on his mind, but while such sentiments were keenly appreciated it was equally true that THE IMPRESSIONS were never at the cutting edge of fat black funk, or at least not how it was emerging to the sons of soul audiences at the impatient tail end of that decade. Although everybody seemed to own one of the group's albums, they didn't find their way to the turntable that often. So when Curtis – very obviously the driving force – announced he was going solo it made good sense to lose the churchified harmonising that, to the day's determinedly modernist James Brown-obsessed teenagers, seemed to dull the sentiment's sharp edges. Remember, this was at a time when most

West Indian (or West Indian descent) youngsters in the UK were at odds with their parents over going to church.

All the same, no amount of anticipation could have prepared anybody for how Curtis announced himself in 1970. The first words of the first track of the first album of his solo career was an enormous, reverberating 'Niggers . . . Whiteys . . . Jews . . .' and moved swiftly along to ram home the song's title phrase, 'Don't worry, if there's hell below we're all gonna go . . .' Instant and lasting peer group credibility. Up there with anything else the 1970s could throw at the world, Curtis's whole tack succeeded way beyond mere music, even though what he was doing in that department was far more on the case than anything he'd done with The Impressions and out there on its own for the time. Or for any other time, come to that.

Where Curtis added a new dimension to the righteous theories put forward with such power by his peers was in seeming to come at it words first. There was no way even the skinniest of white boys could approach this as dance music and pretend there was nothing else involved – with Curtis's first few LPs, *you had to listen to the words first*. And while it would still be easy to attempt to neutralise it with some sort of quasi-anthropological mumbo-jumbo about 'contemporising the griot-based oral culture traditionalism of the African tribal circle . . .' or something, what was going on here was far more potentially uncomfortable. It was a direct continuation of the above ground speechmaking, angry call to arms oration and revolutionary intellectualising of the previous decade. Far more so than *What's Going On*, these were eloquent examples of black people looking to take care of it for themselves, and were closer to the podium previously occupied by Huey P. Newton and Stokely Carmichael than they were to *Top Of The Pops*.

They also demonstrated a previously unseen breadth of political songwriting. Instead of merely discussing issues or sloganeering with one eye on assimilating into the world in general, Curtis looked inside his community as the place where a great deal of work needed to be done. Let's get our own house in order first, to our own personal specifications, is how he saw it, and his fiercely advocated black pride addressed issues that were of little interest elsewhere. But while encouraging people to 'Move On Up', Curtis Mayfield was very much the black nation's conscience: in the same way as 1970s roots reggae came down hard on 'false dread' so he could be merciless on those he felt weren't pulling their weight. '(Don't Worry) If There's Hell Below', 'I Plan To Stay A Believer' and 'We Are The People Who Are Darker Than Blue' pulled no punches, although 'Freddie's Dead' showed he wasn't completely without compassion for backsliders.

Such a take on life gave Curtis an enormous base audience through much of the 1970s – widespread mainstream appreciation for what he was doing back then is recent, faddish and doesn't, on the whole, go much past *Superfly*. Remarkably, for one who seemed so peaceful later in his career, Curtis's following was viewed as somewhat militant and potentially volatile. And sometimes this could have a curious effect on life. At his Finsbury Park Astoria show, one January Sunday evening in 1972 or thereabouts, PA problems meant very late running and an extended intermission between the support act, Bloodstone, and star time. Dressed in fringed buckskin and carrying his guitar by the neck, Curtis eventually sauntered out at nearly eleven o'clock. 'Sorry about the delay,' he announced, 'but I'm gonna sing until they drag me off.' It was something to one in the morning when he took his final bow, yet, incredibly, the tube station opposite was still open and one line still functioning – the police and London transport had taken an on-the-spot decision to extend operating hours as they weren't keen on the idea of 5,000 vibed up brothers and sisters (there were only about three white people in the house) let loose on the streets at that hour.

Then towards the end of the decade he stopped all this. And started making disco records. Not that there's anything wrong with this *per se*, times had changed and Curtis's brand of militancy and musical style was becoming dated. Or maybe he just wanted to get paid. Literally. Nobody begrudged him that, it's just that said disco records were never very good. And when he brought in outside producers – after he sold his ailing record label, Curtom, to RSO in 1979 – they got worse. If half a dozen of you can remember the *Love Is The Place* album, that's probably because it was you six that bought it. Bet you're still wishing you hadn't.

Soon into the 1980s, though, he realised his past was his best hope for the future, and toured extensively with a show that included little or no material dated later than 1975. This began to bump up back catalogue sales and once again Curtis Mayfield was doing very nicely thank you. No more than he deserved.

Then on August 13, 1990, when on stage at an open air concert in Brooklyn, NYC, a lighting rig was blown down on top of him. He was paralysed from the neck down and it is unlikely he will ever recover any mobility.

Curtis; Charly CPCD8036; 1970
Roots; Charly CPCD8037; 1971

'There will be no light/So there can be no sight/And you'll judge your fellow man/Understand/By what is right/We'll all turn black/So who's to know . . . The underground/The underground/ familar music/familiar sound . . .'

These lyrics come from 'Underground' from the second solo album *Roots*. Forming more or less a matched pair with its predecessor, both so raw in presenting their agenda that the combination of anger, wry humour, unabashed charm and obvious love of the people, has all the elegance and eloquence that made Malcolm so charismatic a figure. But progression is clearly evident. On the second set, such direct statements as 'Keep On Keeping On', 'Beautiful Brother Of Mine' and 'We've Got To Have Peace' were separated by the obliquely conceived numbers 'Underground' and 'Get Down', which in terms of gathering darkness and indirect expression of ideas were intriguingly close to a musical take on Ralph Ellison's 'Invisible Man'.

A complex intellect that was equalled by music that placed Curtis's regular small group as the nucleus of strings, woodwind and brass. A full orchestra underscoring the emotions was a valuable attention-holder – clever string arrangements meant you *felt* what he was telling you, and allowed the aching love songs a conventional framework – but it was built around the street-tuff rhythm section so nothing was ever going to lose its way. Indeed, as far as the floor went, although every self-styled Curtis expert will bang on about 'Move On Up', the truth was it was so uptempo it became outdated even quicker. The true club tracks from these two were 'Wild And Free', 'Get Down', 'Underground'

and '(Don't Worry) If There's Hell Below We're All Gonna Go' –
hipper crowds would join in the opening shouting.

Curtis Live!; Charly CPCD8038; 1971

There is no further proof needed that Curtis Mayfield was the
most brilliant communicator of soul of the 1970s. Although there
are a couple of other Curtis-in-concert LPs on offer, they're but
shadows compared with this work. True, it won't have anything
from *Superfly* on it, but it does have a few tracks he didn't record
solo in the studio and one that doesn't exist in any other form.

With the smallest of groups – two guitars, bass, congas and
drums – in a tinier club but packed to the ceiling with an appreciative home crowd, Curtis Mayfield's wit and warmth beams
out of the stereo with a megawatt glow. Songs from the first two
albums take on a new poignancy, but the real product of this
ambience is in allowing the audience to read between the lines
and bask in the exclusive sense of celebration they put over.
Regardless of what ills some might have detailed. The set also
demonstrated that Curtis Mayfield was a much more aggressive
and effective guitarist than people give him credit for. It's pretty
much the same show he did that Sunday night in Finsbury Park.

Superfly; Charly CPCD8039; 1972

Needs no introduction really, but it could be worth noting that
the main reason this is so frequently held up as one of the best
film soundtracks ever made is because it isn't – isn't a film
soundtrack, that is. Like *Black Caesar*, but unlike *Shaft* or *Trouble
Man*, it's a collection of songs that only relate to a film, so are not
tied to the rules of scoring and can behave how they like. Like
one of the best street funk albums ever made.

Back To The World; Charly CPCD8040; 1973

A soundtrack without a film. The centric theme of this set was
the GIs returning from the Viet Nam war, the problems they
came back to and the habits they brought with them. To have
'made it back to the world' was black soldier slang for getting
home from South-East Asia alive. Set to crisp funky music – the
wah wah guitar was by now something of a Mayfield calling

card – the strings and brass create that familiar sweep that urges his voice on to spin a tale in chapters. Chapters of apparent hopelessness, as songs called things like 'Right On For The Darkness', 'Future Shock', 'If I Were A Child Again' and 'Keep On Trippin'' spell out the mounting frustration these men faced. Although there's a gap of a couple of years, it is a further exploration of the bleaker, intellectually more complex angles he was edging towards on *Roots*, so uncompromising at times it makes it look as if Tom Cruise had it easy in *Born On The Fourth Of July*.

Sweet Exorcist; Charly CPCD8047; 1974

From the spooky painting on the sleeve to the almost frighteningly dark sonic pictures within, this is worlds apart from the sunny optimism he put out on stage a couple of years earlier. In many ways it was an accurate reflection of a growing rage inside Black America as, although events of the 1960s had produced some social change, much of it was too little too slowly and while the country as a whole prospered the gap between the chocolate cities and their vanilla suburbs was widening rapidly. To a background of stretched tight small group funk, Curtis's falsetto talks of political and personal affairs with the same despair: 'Our days have come/Dark days of night' ('Kung Fu'); 'To be invisible/Will be my claim to fame/A man with no name/That way I won't feel the pain' ('To Be Invisible'); 'Can't get hung up no more/And now ain't nothing left/Get up and held yourself' ('Ain't Got Time'). It even features DONNY HATHAWAY, never exactly Mr Cheerful, on one track, so you get the drift. In fact it's not unreasonable to wonder if this fifty minutes of near paranoia was Curtis's own *In Our Lifetime*?

ALSO RECOMMENDED:

Curtis In Chicago; Charly CPCD8046; 1973

Live recording of a TV special, featuring members of The Impressions.

Never Say You Can't Survive; Charly CPCD8049; 1977

The last stop before disco – it's respectable enough but a bit of an emotional lightweight after what led up to it.

Maze

(Frankie Beverly, guitar/vocals/piano; Robin Duke, bass; Billy Johnson, drums; McKinley Williams, percussion; Ron Smith, guitar; Roame Lowry, congas; Sam Porter, organ; Phillip Woo, keyboards)

Maze have always been a mystery to anybody who wasn't actually there at the time. Here was a group that never so much as sniffed a mainstream hit, nobody could actually name more than one of them, yet they could be relied upon to sell out arena-sized venues (on one particular occasion, a full week at Hammersmith Odeon) with virtually no promotional campaign at all, and inspired the kind of unstinting devotion most football teams can only dream of. It wasn't just the UK record industry and rock media that were at a loss either. Indeed, while the former wondered how to translate ticket sales into album revenue and the latter held the group up for derision as the epitome of white socks suburban soul, for years your harder edged funk fan could never work out how come music apparently so inoffensive you could wring it out attracted a following like The Maze Craze. *They even had a name!* Until 1981's double LP *Maze Live In New Orleans*. Listen to that once and it all made sense.

Leaving aside acid funk, hard core politicising, jazz/rock influences or The Cosmic Pyramid, Maze were the personification of straight soul music for the 1970s. Not an updated continuation of the 1960s style, but an extension of its values – musical discipline, lyrical craftsmanship, spiritual uplift and a primary desire to please a live audience – as applied to a post-hippie, self-contained group. Every song was built around audience participation at certain points, to such a degree (unusual in the second half of this decade as disco and ego-fuelled pomp funk came to the fore) that the skilful, soulful construction of numbers like 'Joy and Pain', 'Golden Time Of Day' and 'Before I Let You Go' only truly works when heard as a singalong. It is no coincidence that the only two original Maze albums still on catalogue are both live recordings.

This approach was enough to carry well into the 1980s virtually unchanged, a passage made altogether easier by the fact they were unlikely to fall from fashion as they were never really in it to start off with. A decision Beverly took very deliberately after his first group Raw Soul (which included Lowery and Williams) began making a name for themselves in their native Philadelphia in the early part of the decade. At that time, in that city, the only way forward was through The Philly Sound and rather than compromise his ideas the threesome moved to San Francisco to reform as Maze. The location was picked, the singer would later explain, because it had a conspicuous lack of an associated contemporary black music style so he felt free to do what he wanted; local musicians were removed enough not to be playing a certain way, and yet it was within easy enough reach of Los Angeles to stay in touch with the business. In later years, Maze remained far more popular in the UK than they did in their native land – maybe because of their gentle manner and our inherent love of tradition – and British promoters are frequently (and sometimes successfully) trying to put together the fund to bring them over to tour.

Live In New Orleans; Capitol CDP746659; 1981

The perfect Maze album, more or less the show they brought to Hammersmith in 1980. Finely honed, mellow – if that isn't too naff a description – tunes and lyrics that veer between the vaguely mystic ramblings and silky sonnets of love instead of lust. But it's the three-thousand-voice choruses on 'Joy And Pain' that sum up why this band had such an awesome reputation on stage. As if the mutual warmth bounces back and forth between Beverly and his crowd, it grows stronger with each repetition until it becomes completely unavoidable. Then around that you've got an hour and a quarter free of gimmick or spectacle, focusing on the straightforward skills of a bunch of soul showmen, giving it their all on numbers like 'Feel That You're Feelin'', 'Look At California', 'Before I Let Go' and 'We Need Love To Live'.

Live In Los Angeles; Capitol CDP 746359; 1986

Although lacking the impact by association of its predecessor – Maze albums tended to be bought as souvenirs of memorable evenings spent dancing on a seat, and the early shows are held in higher esteem – all the abovementioned rules are still being obeyed. Then, points in favour of the later scheduling, *Los Angeles* has got 'Back In Stride' and also 'Happy Feelin's' which, due to running time, never made the transition from *New Orleans*'s vinyl to CD.

SEE ALSO: (1) *Lifelines Vol 1*; Capitol CDEST 2111; 1989 (A Maze Greatest Hits, and although they're all there, they're not the live versions. For fanatics only.); (2) Various Artists; *Classic Mellow Mastercuts Vol 1*; Beechwood CUTSCD3; 1991

Van McCoy

(Born Washington DC, 1941)
Long before John Trávolta, way back before dance halls and nightclubs were known as discos, there was The Hustle. A dance that afforded physical contact yet was uptempo enough to avoid any form of commitment and had scope within the mid-tempo shuffle for considerable invention. Gamble and Huff's material was in most cases just right for it, allowing dee-jays to give their crowds a breather without – horror of horrors – 'losing their floor' (having people sit down). But the man who took it the whole distance was Van McCoy, as his orchestral track 'The Hustle' pro-actively exploited these breaks. It was the link between Philly's soul-emphathy credibility and disco's purely superficial excess. An enormous, fully scored sound-scape that entirely understood how a slightly slower beat need-n't sacrifice power, and when it doesn't the instrumentation on top can be as lush and as sweeping as you like. Then, how funny little hooks repeating themselves in odd places can relieve a 4/4 beat yet keep the momentum going. But above all, 'The Hustle' wasn't trying to prove itself as a 'hard' tune with – unlike later derivatives – ten minutes of monotonous pounding. McCoy precisely pre-empted most dancers' need for a little rest during an extended cut and built in all sorts of tempo changes to stop even a two-deck ultra-stretched out version turning into an endurance test. Breaks which gave the more athletic couples a chance to show off with niftily revised step, while turning

what could have been a nothing-more-than-a-dance-tune into something you might want to play at home.

It had everything, including success. And started a tidalwave of similarly named soundalikes – more than a few by Van McCoy himself. But he never did anything remotely this exciting again, which was surprising as he'd shown considerable understanding of symphonic soul in his past life as producer for THE SHIRELLES, JACKIE WILSON and THE MARVELETTES during the 1960s. McCoy's subsequent albums, with such cringeworthy titles as *Disco Baby*, *Disco Kid* and *Lonely Dancer* are, thankfully, not available on CD, but 'The Hustle' crops up frequently on Various Artist Seventies compilations and it's worth sifting through any amount of Disco Tex, Dan Hartman or 'Stayin' Alive' to own even the radio edit. Van McCoy died before the end of the decade.

George & Gwen McCrae

(Born West Palm Beach, Florida, 1944; Pensacola, Florida, 1943 respectively)

It was always a thin line between lively pop soul (which you could admit to liking without being pointed at on Wood Green High Road) and out and out disco music (which you couldn't). One of the very few records to straddle both camps – and that was probably only because, on the whole, disco wasn't established enough in 1974 to have got awful – was George McCrae's 'Rock Your Baby'. Recorded in South Florida, it was the enormous success of this tune that led to that area, Miami in particular, becoming the Memphis/Muscle Schoals for hopeful disco artists. If it wasn't made in New York, it would be cut down there, a factor which has a great deal to do with the music's Latin inflections. Although he continued with a string of hits nothing else was ever accepted by the soul scene with any real degree of conviction. His soon-to-be-ex-wife, however (they split up when he hit big) got far funkier from the middle of the decade onwards with a succession of minor club classics, which culmintated in the sublime 'Funky Sensation' in 1981. A tune that spawned countless rapped-over versions and remains irresistible some fourteen years after the event.

Rock Your Baby – The Best Of George & Gwen McCrae; EMI
CDEMS1493; 1993

This might just be worth the price of admission for the title
track, but it loses all manner of marks for not going up as far as
'Funky Sensation'. However, it's got all those Gwen McCrae
tracks that were changing hands for silly money a few years ago
– '90% Of Me Is You', 'I'll Do The Rockin'' and 'All This Love
That I'm Giving' among them – plus that string of hits George
had during 1974 and 1975, the titles of which don't quite come
to mind.

McFadden & Whitehead

(Gene McFadden and John Whitehead, born in Philadelphia,
1952 and 1951, respectively)
If you could tell people you'd written, produced and recorded
'Ain't No Stopping Us Now', you wouldn't really need a history
as well. You'd have updated the then nearly ten-year-old Sound
Of Philadelphia, by laying down a simpler, disco-friendly beat,
cunningly disguised as a cathedral of soaring, overlapped
sound, but one with subtly fractured melodies that took the polished surface off the label's trademark lushness. And it probably would have been enough to fill your CV: not so former
schoolfriends McFadden & Whitehead. Before becoming
responsible for that awesome slab of late-model Philly soul they
did the business for a great deal of the early stuff: ARCHIE BELL,
THE INTRUDERS, HAROLD MELVIN & THE BLUENOTES, THE O'JAYS were just
a few of the company's acts for whom the duo wrote and produced. And it was hardly a surprise that they could sing as well,
in the late 1960s they were two-thirds of The Epsilons – a regular opening act for OTIS REDDING – and then all of The Talk Of The
Town, who Gamble and Huff signed before it was discovered
they could write a bit too.
    Even if, right after it came out in 1979, you reviled 'Ain't No
Stopping Us Now' as some sort of brain-dead-shaving-foam-
fight-at-a-toga-party Soul Weekender anthem, put a lot of that
down to the merciless over-exposure and give it a spin now. It'll
be obvious that this is the same train of thought that brought

you the far superior 'Backstabbers', 'I'll Always Love My Mama' and 'Bad Luck'.

SEE: *The Philadelphia Years Volume Two, 1976–1983*; Knight, KNCD42002; 1989

Mel & Tim

(Melvin Hardin and Timothy McPherson, both born Jackson, Mississippi)
People seem to forget that amid all that storming soul and memorable, aching ballads coming out of the Deep South in the very early 1970s, there were some acts that were never going to be held up as 'classic' though they made some kicking little records in a low-profile style. Cousins Mel & Tim were one such act and their easy action, light-hearted songs became the mould that mellow would be cast in.

*Starting All Over Again; Stax CDSXE 078; 1972

The title track was a much covered easy ballad, and good as it was, it's the crisper two-part harmonies on slightly livelier material that really grabs. 'Don't Mess With My Money, My Honey Or My Woman', 'Yes We Can Can' and 'Wrap It Up'. You know the drill. Pity Stax didn't licence the really big one they did before they came to the company, the Gene Chandler overseen 'Backfield In Motion'. Did I really say Mel & Tim didn't make any true classics?

Harold Melvin & The Bluenotes

(Harold Melvin; Teddy Pendergrass; Lloyd Parkes; Lawrence Brown; Bernard Wilson)
This was the line-up that were signed to Gamble and Huff's newly formed Philadelphia International Records in 1972, sixteen years and several group members after Melvin had started it as a doo-wop harmoniser band and kept it working through the 1960s as a Motown-wannabe small club live act.

And Melvin himself never was the lead singer. Indeed for the first twelve years or so he wasn't even on stage with them, functioning as manager, choreographer, songwriter and arranger. What changed their luck, prior to the record deal, is one of soul's happiest coincidences. According to Lawrence Brown: 'We were on the road all the time, so had our own regular six-piece backing band, but no time to take care of business that wasn't immediate. When our lead singer John Atkins left we were worried about finding the time to audition a new one, but remembered how we'd heard Theodore, the band's drummer, singing. He had a very hoarse, soulful voice and it was exactly the voice the Blue Notes needed.' Theodore was promoted to Teddy, and suddenly the group didn't sound like they were trying to be THE TEMPTATIONS any more. Add Gamble and Huff and McFADDEN & WHITEHEAD (Blue Note Lloyd Parkes was the other member of their first group The Epilsons) to write and produce and the group's success was instant and sustained. Even Harold himself became part of the performing line-up.

Although the arrangements were obviously Philly at its finest, the tunes themselves were never typical of the label's output. In fact, if ever any proof was needed that Gamble and Huff made black soul music first and foremost, Harold Melvin & The Blue Notes are such evidence. They picked up where the harder Chicago soul vocal groups of the previous decade left off, and led by Pendergrass's rough-hewn style they got serious from the word go: 'Miss You', a lesson in yearning self-pity; 'If You Don't Know Me By Now', heavyweight love gone wrong; 'Wake Up Everybody', slap-in-the-face political statement; 'Don't Leave Me This Way', heartwrenching to the point of paranoia . . . and so on. Each one a welcome reminder that The Sound Of Philadelphia had a darker side to it and that the solid soul tradition could exist within the disco environment without noticeable damage to either.

In 1977, when TEDDY PENDERGRASS opted for a solo career, one of the most remarkable runs of the 1970s came to a close. Remarkable particularly because the band had had to be convinced, at great length, that joining the record company in the first place was the right thing to do – they'd get paid cash-in-hand on the live circuit, so why should they want to cancel dates to make records? Oh, how times have changed.

*Satisfaction Guaranteed – The Best Of Harold Melvin & The Blue Notes; Philadelphia International 4720392; 1992

Although this has all the hits – except the debut 'Miss You', which only made it big on black radio in the US – it's a shame it's the only Harold Melvin album on catalogue, as their LPs were always much more cohesive than most singles acts. 1975's *Wake Up Everbody*, for instance, had enough substance to prove Gamble and Huff could sustain an interest for three-quarters of an hour. For that reason, while this is better than no Harold Melvin at all, equal representation can be found on the larger Philly compilation sets.

SEE ALSO: Philadelphia International Various Artist compilations

The Ohio Players˙

(Leroy 'Sugarfoot' Bonner, guitar/vocals; Marshall Jones, bass; Jimmy 'Diamond' Williams, drums/percussion; Belly Beck, keyboards; Clarence Satchell, saxophones/flute; Marvin Pierce, trumpet; Ralph 'Pee Wee' Middlebrooks, trumpet)

Of course, there was more to soul's sexual revolution than MILLIE JACKSON's cussing, BARRY WHITE's satin sheets and MARVIN GAYE's ethereal sensuality. There was The Ohio Players, 1970s soul's answer to the newsagent's top shelf. It was as if, in 1971, the group decided to take an entirely adult – as in 'X rated' – view on boy meets girl by rewriting it as boy meets girl, they both slip into some chains and studded leather underwear, then she ties him up and whips him before sticking a knife in his back as he nibbles her neck. You know the sort of thing. The trouble was, the sleeve illustrations of their first four albums, *Pain, Pleasure, Ecstasy* and *Climax*, which led you through the above saga of sexual adventure, were always more consistently interesting than the music they contained. It was as if they'd ignored the series *content*, in order to put across the *concept*. In spite of solid club tracks like 'Funky Worm', 'Pain' and 'Pack It Up', their attempts at a dark fusion of rock and soul never really had a sense of purpose, leaving the group to come over as little more than an early-Funkadelic wannabe. And, perhaps unsurprisingly, the sleeve designs, so free from irony that they came over as unpleasantly pervy, worked against them – it wasn't the sort of thing you could leave out by the stereo if your mum was in.

But it was a valid attempt to take black funk into new areas. And it was perhaps understandable that they so miscalculated the current generation of record buyers, for they were a long way removed from it themselves. By the time they were making these records, the early 1970s, they were in their thirties and had been together as a group for more than ten years – as The Ohio Untouchables in the late 1950s they'd been straight instrumental R&B and in the first years of the next decade were the nucleus of the band that backed THE FALCONS on their last hit 'I Found A Love', featuring lead vocals by a teenage WILSON PICKETT. In fact, with a background like this, wicked as the Pickett was, the 1970s probably seemed very confusing to this libidinous bunch of Mid-West geriatrics. So it was doubly remarkable when they screamed back at us in 1974 with *Skin Tight*, the first in a trilogy of hard and horny (in both senses of the word) statements that put them up there with funk's finest for the next five years.

The one big difference between the first phase Players and the group that had the impact was Walter 'Junie' Morrison, funk keyboard genius. He was far out in front of his peers in what he wanted to get out of the developing synthesiser (most other players sounded like they still held BOOKER T as a role model) and he dominated the group's line-up to the degree that his direction was the one they all followed. As at that time there were no wiggy-funk guidelines, he was also getting it wrong as often as he was getting it right. Morrison left in 1972 – later to join Funkadelic, where, working within an established set-up, he soared – and the band restructured to become horn-dominated, but with added depth as keyboard and guitars took a lot of the lead.

The blossoming funk scene was tailor made for a band with their credentials: all were accomplished players – they were originally formed as an instrumental unit; were from an age where discipline of riff was a pre-requisite; they weren't afraid to push the outside of the envelope; and they liked to throw a bit of sex into the mix. With no more than chant vocals, their funk was perhaps the trickiest, most instrumentally complex this side of KOOL & THE GANG. But, although their arrangements were jazz in the way the instruments fired off each other, once they'd anchored things with a killer beat, they built up layers of pure funk that packed each track to capacity but still left enough space within the riffs for everything to be heard. It was the epitome of generous, ensemble playing: so cleverly constructed that lines didn't have a life of their own and either worked as part of the whole or they had no business being there. The writing credits always attributed the whole band too.

Maybe it was that obvious togetherness that lifted their music to that degree, but their club hits – 'Jive Turkey', 'Skin Tight', 'Fire', 'Smoke', 'Honey', 'Love Rollercoaster', 'Who'd She Coo' – were like advanced level funk. Even up against the competition of the day. This musical capability gave them the added bonus of being able to make ballads that were genuinely funky, not just slightly lame down-tempo tunes – 'Sweet Sticky Thing', 'Heaven Must Be Like This' and 'I Want To Be Free' were the same intricate constructions on the same supple bass lines, just slow, steamy and as sexy as hell. Oh yes, they kept up the sleeve art too, only this time they offset any offence by spinning it into cartoon proportions: on the sleeve for *Fire* the artily shot model was naked save for a fireman's helmet and an artfully wrapped hose (suggestive nozzle to the fore); and on *Honey* a similarly clad lady quite literally glowed from the jars of golden stuff she'd had poured over her – at the time, there was talk that once the photographer's lights were switched off and the set cooled down, she'd got stuck to the floor.

What scuppered The Ohio Players was a refusal to bend to the winds of disco in the latter half of the decade. But it was still far from over, as they're touring to this day. In London in February 1994, the old line-up fronted by Sugarfoot, sporting a ludicrous afro-quiff syrup, were joined onstage by Junie Morrison, wheeled out the old tunes and were far more funky than any bunch of fifty-somethings had any right to be.

Orgasm; Westbound CDSEWD062; 1993

A greatest hits collection from the group's Westbound years. It takes the sleeve art from the 1974 *Climax* album (itself a vault trawl of unreleased tracks, put out after the group had left the company), borrows the tracklisting from *Pain + Pleasure =*

Ecstasy compilation and adds a few more for good measure. Although those three albums are available in original form on CD, this is by far the best value package. At least use it to test the water, as the synthesiser-based, largely rock-inspired, none-too-conventionally-funky stuff the band was doing back then might come as a bit of a shock to fans of the later model Ohio Players.

None of the big three albums – *Skin Tight* (1974), *Fire* (1975), *Honey* (1975) – or the not quite celestial but still the business *Contradiction* (1976) are on catalogue in any format in the UK at the time of writing. They are all, however, in bigger record stores as surprisingly reasonably priced US imports (around a tenner). *Skin Tight* is the most skilfully varied of the four, moving from absolutely murderous ballads at one end of the spectrum to the kind of guitar-led, horn-powered dance floor funk that ought to require a licence at the other. Throughout the set, it's difficult to believe that anything could be so wild and so disciplined at the same time.

Fire falls slightly short, simply because it lacks the weight at the slow end of things, while you've got to figure on *Honey* being worth more or less any amount of money for 'Sweet Sticky Thing' alone. Likewise, but slightly less so, *Contradiction* and 'Who'd She Coo', but that isn't to say that each one of these isn't a superb value package – any judgements formed here are made against the monstrously high standard the band set for themselves. If proof is needed prior to purchase, though, also on import is *Gold*, a collection of their greatest moments from those four albums. It's a good taster, but far from the whole story.

SEE ALSO: Various Artists; *Classic Funk* and *Classic Mellow Mastercuts*

The O'Jays

(Eddie Levert born June 16, 1942; Walter Williams, August 25, 1942; William Powell, 1941. All born Canton, Ohio)
The O'Jays were the most significant act on Philadelphia International Records for reasons other than consistently large sales figures. Although not the first act on the label, it was The

O'Jays who gave the company the all-important sense of community identification that allowed the Sound Of Philadelphia to take over from Motown as the mainstream commercial face of Young Black America. While much is made of the Philly beat, and how its uptempo good-time approach, further sweetened with lush sweeping strings, went a long way towards laying the foundations of disco, there was, back in the early days, a deeper, more substantial side to the company. That was The O'Jays, the group that gave Philly a street funk credibility that was extended, by association, as far as The Three Degrees and 'Armed And Extremely Dangerous'. Well, almost.

Firstly there was their far from flimsy voices. The group were that label's equivalent of THE FOUR TOPS inasmuch as they were seasoned professionals when they arrived, and tended to eschew delicacy in favour of the gruffer, more urgently emotional harmonising – witness 'I Love Music', the song's a celebration, yet they almost seem to be trying to frighten you into believing them. Then there was their subject matter, they were the voice of Gamble and Huff's social conscience: the first two albums, *Back Stabbers* and *Ship Ahoy*, were rich in angry diatribe particularly slanted at elements within the community who might not be what they seem. Then there was their powering of such righteous tracks as 'Back Stabbers', 'For The Love Of Money', 'Ship Ahoy' and 'Don't Call Me Brother' into the twitchy masterpieces they remain today, bleak, spooky and sometimes downright freaky funk arrangements of the basic Philly Beat, the like of which weren't applied to any other act on the company.

It all conspired to give The O'Jays a meaning well beyond mere foot-moving capacity. Which they richly deserved, if for no other reason than their innate sense of loyalty – a much respected characteristic among young black British at the time. The group had stuck together since high school in the 1950s (in the beginning there were five of them), recording a few singles, but mostly working as a vocal backing unit for the likes of Nat King Cole and The Ronettes. Their name was a show of loyalty to the Cleveland radio deejay who groomed their performance and acted as impromptu manager in 1961, Eddie O'Jay. In 1972, having worked with Gamble and Huff at the Neptune label a few years earlier, the trio, as they were by then, were being wooed by

Motown and Invictus but opted for Philly because G&H had previously given them a break. Their main condition of signing was that lead singer Eddie Levert wasn't singled out for a solo career or the threesome reshaped as Eddie & The O'Jays.

After William Powell was diagnosed as having cancer, they worked around his treatment schedule and reduced their touring commitment to allow him to remain in the group for as long as possible – indeed it was only when he requested that he leave, a year before his death in 1977, that they auditioned for a replacement.

As the 1970s progressed, and Philadelphia International became more established as *the* mainstream soul organisation, so The O'Jays eased into a less socially concerned groove. But tracks like 'I Love Music', 'Love Train', 'Living For The Weekend' and 'Use Ta Be My Girl' proved they still had a certain fire. And they're still kicking it today, occasionally surprising everybody wifh some scorching piece of political correction such as 1990's 'Something For Nothing'.

Collector's Items; Epic 4689222; 1991

It's not much short of a tragedy that none of The O'Jays Philadelphia albums have made it, in original form, on to CD in the UK. However, even if that wasn't the case this compilation would still be a good deal as the fourteen tracks give a good flavour, going right up to 'Living For The Weekend' in 1976, one of the last records William Powell made with the group. They take in all the hits, plus providing a representative cross-section of attitude: 'Give The People What They Want', 'I Love Music', 'Survival', 'Love Train', 'Back Stabbers' and so on. All with the most inventive, toughest tunes ever to rock on a Philly beat, which can't be bad.

Ship Ahoy; Philadelphia International Records ZK32408; 1973

A US import (the only early album on offer over there) that's not overly prominent in the UK but well worth searching out. Three tracks on this set would have been enough, by themselves, to reserve the trio a spot in soul's Hall Of Fame. The ship

of the title track is a slave trader, and the lyric is a blistering con-
demnation of how that whole period of American history has
been pretty much swept under the carpet – this is fifteen years
before PUBLIC ENEMY remember. Then there's 'Don't Call Me
Brother', a dark warning to those who might have strayed from
the path. And 'For The Love Of Money'. The music on this set is
about as experimental as G&H got within their own confines
too, and the phasing, phrasing and cascading arrangements
running through this album often got the producers talked
about as 'doing a Whitfield'.

SEE ALSO: Philadelphia International Various Artist compilations

P-Funk

(George Clinton, born Plainfield, New Jersey, July 22, 1940)
For people brought up on a diet of post-disco soul, hip hop or
1980s-rooted artistic austerity, the notion of P-Funk, either as a
philosophy or an actuality, is a little difficult to come to terms
with. Describing what it was like has its problems too: to be part
of an audience of 25,000 hyped-up, funked-up P-fans watching
about forty singers and players drifting, apparently aimlessly,
on and off stage, while giving up some of the sharpest, tightest
licks imaginable. The lead guitarist is wearing a nappy, the keyboard player's just brought his mum on stage to take a bow, a
man in a pimp suit and long rubber nose is sulking in the corner
of the stage and in a few minutes a middle-aged black man
wearing a three-foot blond wig and a white fur coat and sunglasses will step out of a space ship and shine an enormous
torch on us. It's a bit like trying to explain smoke to someone
who's never seen it.

It all sprang from, or was refined by, the fertile imagination of
George Clinton, former barber, street-corner harmoniser and
unsuccessful teenage recording artist, who decided on this
larger-than-life career after Motown gave his singing quintet,
The Parliaments, the thumbs down in the early 1960s. 'During
the fifties we'd made a couple of records on local labels that
hadn't done anything, so when Motown set up in Detroit in

1959 that's where about every black singing group in the country headed. We did too, but there was nothing going on for us there. We cut some singles for the company that never got released and I did some production, but mostly we'd wait for them to get round to us.

'We'd perform at local clubs and bars, but it was like we were still auditioning and we had to look like a Motown group in case somebody from the company was in – matching socks, neat dance steps and so on. That was hard for us, most of the time we couldn't even get our suits to match.

'This went on for a few years, until one night when the guys were on stage and I was just about to join them I said, "No more!" The only other thing in the room was a Holiday Inn bed sheet, so I tore a hole in it for my face, took off all my clothes, put it over my head and went out to do the set. I was dancing round the stage lifting up and twirling, and the guys never missed a step of their routines. We were soon told not to bother knocking on Motown's door any more.'

This do-watcha-like attitude exploded into a way of life as the original group adopted a zonked-out street-smart persona – the afro 'n' shades-wearing hippiefied-Black Power approach that was prevalent in the late 1960s – and took on soul-steeped, yet acid rock-inspired musicians to become not one but two self-contained bands. Initially they cut a single as The Parliaments – the original quintet of Clinton, Ray Davis, Calvin Simon, Clarence 'Fuzzy' Haskins and Grady Thomas, augmented with Eddie Hazel (guitar), Tawl Ross (guitar), Billy Nelson (bass), Mickey Atkins (organ) and Tiki Fulwood (drums). Then, when a legal dispute meant they lost use of the name, Clinton renamed the group Funkadelic and signed it to another label. Astonished at how easy this was he did it again by calling the same group Parliament and signed a deal with Invictus.

It was, he claimed, an ideal opportunity to develop two parallel strands of funk. Funkadelic, as the name might suggest, was a deeper, darker, edgier aspect. An often oblique black rhetoric that wanted to push instrumental soul as far as it could go into rock territory yet still stay true. Clinton kept in touch with his soul roots through Funkadelic's delicate harmony vocals – although he did these first, always maintaining they were the basis of the group's approach, this singing was often overlooked by the public in the light of the spectacular playing. Parliament was much brasher, more in your face. A horn-loaded take on the developing street funk, that delivered its beats and message with a kicking optimism. For example, Funkadelic were making statements like *America Eats Its Young* and *Maggotbrain*, while Parliament was rocking houses with *Up For The Down Stroke*.

In the early days, Parliament/Funkadelic represented an enormously attractive proposition for the post-1960s hip black crowd. Their rock and funk explorations maintained that anything musical was relevant and, with a bit of effort, could be adapted to fit their deceptively tight framework. Which offered far more of a challenge to audiences and band members alike. They were as ideologically sound as Curtis and Co, but delivered their black pride with a cynical twist and spaced-out, coded logic that appealed to the acid intellectual. They were down with the streets and could bust some serious funk with any amount of in-joke ghetto humour. And, boy, could they party. In short, there was plenty of everything. For everybody. By the middle of the decade they'd not only attracted a huge home crowd following – and a number of hipper ex-hippies who liked the attendant drug culture – but a broad spectrum of black musicians were signing up. Hendrix- and Zappa-influenced guitarists, conservatory-trained pianists, old-time doo-woppers like ex-Spinner Phillipe Wynne, gospel-rooted girl singers, a keyboard player for whom the OHIO PLAYERS were too middle of the road, and such high-profile James Brown defectors as Bootsy Collins and his brother Phelps, Fred Wesley and Maceo Parker. 'Sucked into a black hole' is how Clinton talked about his new recruits.

Each album slightly reinvented the one before. Elements were stacked up and hung on to killer grooves that allowed all manner of wild behaviour, creating a sound that was totally unique. While it played by all of regular street funk's rules it was never as sparse. George Clinton's production skill was to slap it on with a spoon then sort out the layers so you never quite got to all of them at the same time. You heard different bits at different points on different listens to the same tune, the only constant was the beat. They were almost subliminal, three-dimensional productions that nobody else ever came near. So although their attitude advanced the cause greatly inasmuch as it freed other bands' minds, the Funk Mob were always a branch line by themselves – nobody ever followed them up there because nobody else could get it right. Curiously, large as this act was in the 1970s soul sound system scene, it was only the very straightforward tunes – 'One Nation', 'Flashlight' and 'Knee Deep' – that got played out, as everything was just too off centre to lead into and damn near impossible to follow.

Out there on its own it grew to monster proportions. Funkadelic and Parliament evolved parallel funk operas of earthy ghetto life (Funkadelic) and fantastic extraterrestrial soul power (Parliament). Side men and women launched spin-off projects: Bootsy's Rubber Band; The Horny Horns; Parlet; The Brides Of Funkenstein; Bernie Worrell; The P-Funk All Stars; and The Sweat Band. While it was riding high on its own wave of funk power, there was no such thing as an unexpressed thought. And of course they can't all be brilliant.

Street funk in general was in decline by 1979, which made matters worse for Clinton as by that time Parliament and Funkadelic, the glue that held it all together, were putting out some distinctly patchy albums, and touring a seventy-piece stage show was no longer making economic sense. By the end of the decade, after an unsuccessful attempt to launch his own record label, a welter of legal problems from the web of deals he'd cut for his various troops had stopped him recording. It seemed things had got a lot more complicated since he first sold the same band twice ten years previously. ** *George Clinton*

PARLIAMENT

*The Mothership Connection; Casablanca 824502; 1975

This was the one that broke them through big. The one where it all came together and marked the first appearance of the Mothership, both as a concept and a cover adornment. The theory involves aliens arriving from space, taking one look at our sad funkless state, hijacking the airwaves to deliver a whopping bolt of P-Funk ('pure funk, uncut funk, the bomb'). Which is exactly what they do. Bass lines like a slurpily viscous liquid hold it together as the taut rhythms almost get too much to bear, clipped horns dart in and out and the synth lines wiggle all over the place. But it's the voices that kill you, Clinton sounding sly as a fox as he softly urges us to get 'funked up', Ray Davis's bass chorus of 'Tear the roof off the sucker' and Gary Schider's 'Starchild' telling how he's coming to reclaim the pyramids.

The Clones Of Dr Funkenstein; Casablanca 842620; 1976

Chapter two. This time the story concerns Dr Funkenstein who's cloning funkateers to take over the galaxy. Or something. And this time the rhythms are even snappier, giving numbers like the title track and 'Children Of Production' a wonderful laid-back bounce, while the confidence extends as far as deep funk ballads, which actually work. Musically more adventurous than its predecessor, even if this rather cuts down the naked groove quota.

Funkentelechy Vs The Placebo Syndrome; Casablanca 824501; 1977

By now, Dr Funkenstein and Starchild have joined forces to see off the self-explanatory Sir Nose D'Voidoffunk. Topped an' tailed by the anthemic 'Flashlight' and 'Bop Gun (Endangered Species)' this one walks that fine line between out and out groove and musical interest with great skill. While the former of those two tunes will never, ever, fail to make people dance, the set also includes the completely weird love song 'Wizard Of Finance'. How can something this wiggy be so sexy?

ALSO RECOMMENDED:

The Motor Booty Affair; Casablanca 826212; 1978

Underwater frolics, suitably splashy.

Parliament Live – P-Funk Earth Tour; Casablanca NB7021; 1977

Comes close to capturing the event, and features the now much sampled 'Swing Down Sweet Chariot'.

FUNKADELIC

One Nation Under A Groove; Charly CDGR100; 1978

The instant Funkadelic album. Presumably having learned from Parliament's successes, the basis for this title track was a far more conventional dance riff. Conventional by Funkadelic standards that is, so you know it's never going to be dull, but in these circumstances it allows the supple guitar/synth rock to truly soar. They hit heights of tuneful, billowing funk that makes for one of soul's five magic moments. Although you don't really need anything else from this LP, the rest of it won't let you down: 'Who Says A Funk Band Can't Play Rock', 'Think It Ain't Illegal Yet' and 'Cholly (Funk Getting Ready To Roll)'.

Maggotbrain; Westbound CDSEW002; 1971

The finest example of early Funkadelic at their most whacked-out paranoid. This very dark concoction, built round the spooky Eddie Hazel guitar-led title track, epitomises the disillusionment felt at the end of the 1960s, before the next decade's prosperity had started to take effect. George Clinton broods on the coming of Armageddon on top of the kind of playing most rock bands would kill for. It's a masterfully depressing landscape of bleak rhythms and eerie guitars, enlivened so that it holds the attention like a bad dream. And people still persisted in calling him 'zany'.

The Electric Spanking Of War Babies; Charly CDGR102; 1981

The last Funkadelic album. Clinton was by now in dispute with the record company and delivered what he referred to as 'one for the hard core fans'. What it was was a Funkadelic album of old – all the darkness, the odd ghetto humour, the apparent experimentation – but recorded on up-to-the-minute equipment with very experienced players. Although it served to disappoint those looking for a groove track, it's a marvellous example of the band at their free-flowing, high-stepping pimp-swaggering hard rock best. Even SLY STONE, who is guesting on it, has to work hard to make his presence felt.

ALSO RECOMMENDED:

Uncle Jam Needs You; Charly CDGR103; 1979

Worth it for the hard funk follow up to 'One Nation', 'Not Just Knee Deep' and 'Freak Of The Week'.

Cosmic Slop; Westbound SEW035; 1973

While lighter (just) than what went before it, this still takes global destruction as a theme. But it's a lot less hit and miss musically than others from around this time.

BOOTSY'S RUBBER BAND

Stretching Out In Bootsy's Rubber Band; Warner Bros 2920; 1976

Ex-James Brown, now Parliament bass player, Bootsy began life as a guitarist, and after switching to bass harboured thoughts about turning it into a lead instrument. This was his first attempt, and the popping, slapping, looping riffs and lines he puts down pretty much make his case. Bootsy was always clever enough to lay the solid bass rhythms first, leaving spaces for his flash and dash to take the lead without neglecting its primary task. This gave him room to advance his playful notions of what funk was about – the title track and 'Physical Love' are as deliberately daft as the man's star-shaped sunglasses – and, as had previously been hinted, reveal him as something of a lurrrve god. 'Vanish In Our Sleep' represented a new frontier for the funk ballad.

Aah . . . The Name Is Bootsy, Baby!; Warner Bros 2972; 1977

Bootsy at his stoopid, sexy best. By this point he's reinvented himself as a cartoon – the friendly ghost – but when not playfully frightening children with some dangerously funky bass, comic book lyrics and a deep, malted milk laugh that could thaw icebergs, he's delivering some devastatingly oozesome smoove. 'What's A Telephone Bill' and 'Munchies For Your

Love' prove that a seduction mission need be no barrier to a P-Funk sense of humour.

THE HORNY HORNS

*A Blow For Me And A Toot For You; Sequel NEDCD286; 1977

The Funk Mob are once again all present and correct, and under a different name. This time it's led by the horn players under the delicate arrangements of Fred Wesley and produced by Bootsy. At first hearing it's odd, then it starts to grow on you as the intricate weave of four brass parts adds unexpected dimensions to the tight funk riffing. Kicking it off with a ten-minute version of a P-Funk classic ('Up For The Down Stroke') turns out to be a wise move too, easing you into a spread of work that encompasses dance floor grooves and lullaby fugues. Features a recorded interview with George Clinton.

ALSO RECOMMENDED:

*Say Blow By Blow Backwards; Sequel NEDCD269; 1979

Lacks the direct impact and variety of tone of the first one, but 'We Came To Funk Ya' and 'Say Blow By Blow Backwards' are funk heavyweights. The bonus track is an interview with Bootsy.

The above albums (some of which are on US import) represent a good cross-section of easily available 1970s P-Funk albums. But it's only a cross-section. Not counting recently put together compilations, there were about fifty albums with Clinton's paw-prints that decade and every one of them will offer something for the fan, if not, maybe, for the casual observer. However, such wonders as Parlet's *Pleasure Principle*, Bernie Worrell's *All The Woo In The World* and The Brides Of Funkenstein's *Never Buy Texas* are only available in Japan. I'm loathe to recommend ordering them in this country, as I know one chap – not a million miles from where I'm sitting – who spent £28 on that Bernie Worrell album on Japanese import. That was two years ago and his wife still brings the subject up.

Ray Parker Jr

(Born Detroit Michigan, May 1, 1954)
A long time before 'Ghostbusters', Ray Parker Jr's guitar did much to take the instrument, as applied to funk, out of wah wah or chopped chord riffing and into something much smoother. It's him on STEVIE WONDER's *Innervisions* and *Talking Book*, he was BARRY WHITE's axeman during much of the decade – Parker co-wrote 'The Trouble With Me' – and he supplied fretwork for Cheryl Lynn, Boz Scaggs and LaBelle. Parker's slick demeanour and eagerness to be a star pushed the guitar to the front. And pushed him to the front of his own group, Raydio, who had one monster slow jam, 'Jack And Jill (Back Up The Hill)'. He once had a band, back in the 1960s, called Jeep Smith & The Troubadours, but he probably doesn't talk about that much any more.

*The Collection; Arista 7432113; 1986

Like so many session men made good, Ray Parker Jr never quite had the charisma to match his undoubted expertise. 'Jack And Jill' was a milestone tune in the realms of disco-influenced softer soul – a nice gentle slow hustle – but he never knew how to follow it up. Ballads like 'You Can't Change That', 'Two Places At The Same Time' or 'I Still Can't Get Over Loving You' (all of which are here, along with the G word), were as lush and as silky as you'd want them to be but would only hit if they happened to coincide with public taste at the time, rather than his making them unmissable.

Billy Paul

(Born Paul Williams, Philadelphia, Pennsylvania, December 1, 1934)
Billy Paul was a formally trained jazz vocalist; a sometime member of HAROLD MELVIN's BLUENOTES; he made records for Philadelphia International with subject matter as varied as the eternal triangle ('Me And Mrs Jones'), the struggle ('Am I Black Enough For You?', 'Only The Strong Survive'), love ('Thanks For Saving My Life') and lurrrve ('Let's Make A Baby'); had a

no-holds-barred emotional voice; and really ought to have been far more interesting than he was. But aside from the outstanding songs – such as the above – Billy Paul's usual choice of material was bland in the extreme and too often he was ready to put this stuff over with an overly mannered supper-club croon. So even though some of his parts were among the very best, he never quite added up to the sum of them.

SEE: Philadelphia International Various Artist compilations

Teddy Pendergrass

(Born Philadelphia, Pennsylvania, March 26, 1950)
During the late 1970s, after AL GREEN had got God, ISAAC HAYES had changed his style, MARVIN GAYE's behaviour was becoming increasingly erratic and BARRY WHITE was on the wane, Teddy P. pretty much ruled the bedroom. It was right, really, that a Gamble and Huff produced balladeer should be on top, as White's orchestral approach, which was acknowledged as taking lurrrve to new heights of bearskin rug-ness, owed a great deal to the Philly sound. But whereas the big man took it three steps closer to disco, even the uptempo Pendergrass stuff stayed well away from any flapping white flares. He was never going to do it any other way though, his gruff, churchified style of singing was far too unrefined to have sat comfortably with what disco music had become by 1977. And, rhythmically sensuous as his singing might have been, he was the world's worst dancer – to see Pendergrass 'getting down' on stage with all the fluid grace of a cement mixer gave hope even to the most arthritic of would-be groovers.

But none of this came as a surprise, as before he'd ever cut a record on his own Pendergrass had been singing testifyin'ly and moving awkwardly as frontman for HAROLD MELVIN & THE BLUENOTES. In fact it was his addition to the line-up that kicked off the group's success back in 1970: he was the drummer with their backing band, The Cadillacs, when lead singer John Atkins walked out in the middle of a tour of the West Indies and Teddy was offered the chance to come out from behind the kit. Surprisingly modest for somebody who would progress to crooning about hot oil rubs, shared showers and so on, he didn't take his singing that seriously – his mum was a nightclub singer and that was her job, but he was a musician and singing was just a hobby, something he'd done for fun since going to church as a child.

There was nothing casual about his determination to seduce, though. At this point, 1977, there was far less smoove around than there had been five years previously, as disco, it seemed, had no truck with anything below a certain tempo – in the UK, black deejays were mixing in dub-rock and lovers' reggae to compensate for the decline. Thus it was into a progressively asexual atmosphere that Teddy P. launched his campaign with records that stretched the bounds of innuendo: 'Turn Off The Lights', 'Close The Door' and 'Come Go With Me', while jerking on heartstrings with 'The Whole Town's Laughing At Me' and 'I Don't Love You Any More'. They were sumptuous, very grown up ballads or spicily up-tempo tracks that would've stood up among the best that the earlier lurrrve legends had to offer. But his master stroke was a Ladies Only concert tour – shows starting at midnight, every audience member handed a chocolate teddy bear on the way in and tickets selling out as fast as they could be printed.

Then one night in 1982, as he returned from a basketball game in Philadelphia, his Rolls-Royce skidded into a crash barrier leaving him paralysed from the neck down. At the time, rumours circulated that his female companion was in fact a man in drag, and that this popular ladies man actually preferred the men. None of this was ever substantiated, but when he came back two years later, although the album he recorded from his wheelchair proved his voice had in no way suffered, it wasn't the triumph it might have been. Teddy P. is still recording, but his material is mostly spiritual.

*Greatest Hits; Philadelphia International Records
ZK39252; 1984

The only vintage Pendergrass album on catalogue in the UK is probably the best way to appreciate him – each original set was never a whole LP proposition, and this provides the best moments from his days with Gamble and Huff. Most remarkable is the not-so-high-profile, in the UK, 'Love TKO', an arrangement which holds back on the strings 'n' things to provide a wonderfully unobscured example of his voice.

SEE ALSO: Philadelphia International Various Artist compilations

Lou Rawls

(Born Chicago, Illinois, December 1, 1937)
Lou Rawls was the sort of artist you had lying around in your record collection to give it a bit of class. His albums were the funkateer's equivalent of the coffee table book – having them on show impressed the ladies, but rarely did they ever get used. Which was his fault as much as anybody's. Lou Rawls was blessed with a wonderful baritone voice and a way with his phrasing that brought out a deep blue passion, while keeping it lively with a sprinkling of jazz sensibilities. But, after trying and failing in the 1960s to take up the baton from Nat King Cole, he opted for a dreary kind of cocktail-jazz style. He never seemed to rise above his material. Until he signed to Philadelphia International. There, G&H once again proved their ability to write around an artist, incorporating and capitalising on what makes them special, but still not subverting the Philly groove. They gave Lou Rawls some proper rocking mid-tempo soul songs and he flew, his combination of earthiness and sophistication turning 'You'll Never Find Another Love Like Mine', 'Lady Love', 'Groovy People' and 'I'll See You When I Get There' into some of the greatest tracks to come out of that company. Most recently Rawls has been recording for Blue Note and the jazz-based company is bringing out the best of that side of him.

SEE: Philadelphia International Various Artist compilations

Minnie Riperton

(Born Chicago, Illinois, 1947)
Minnie Riperton had a five-octave vocal range, as a child wanted to be an opera singer, and came into soul music at a time when nobody quite knew what to do with women who

weren't (a) MILLIE JACKSON; (b) Diana Ross; or (c) GLADYS KNIGHT. That is to say women who didn't fit the accepted categories of outrageous sex machine, OTT glamourpuss or sanctified soul sister. Minnie Riperton was just plain sexy, and with her breathy tone and absolute control could be as sensual as any of the lurrrve men. Which might have been the problem, for though the sexual revolution was upon us, in the soul world of 1975 it still wasn't quite done for women to take the lead. Although this didn't stop her having a hit so huge it became part of a Richard Pryor stand-up routine – it featured (sung by the comedian in exaggerated imitation) as an instant cure for impotence – it might have come between her and the career many thought she deserved. She was diagnosed as having malignant breast cancer in 1977 and, after spending a year as Chair of The American Cancer Society, she died in 1979.

Minnie Riperton was one of the few soul music stars ever to be attacked by a lion: she was posing with the supposedly docile beast for the cover shot of her *Adventures In Paradise* album, when it turned on her. She was not seriously hurt.

*Capitol Gold – The Best Of Minnie Riperton; Capitol CDP7805162; 1993

Contains the minor hits such as 'Can You Feel What I'm Saying', 'Give Me Time' and 'Young, Willing And Able', and such interesting album cuts as 'Adventures In Paradise' and 'Here We Go', but it would be worth it at whatever price they put on this just for that one track 'Lovin' You'.

Smokey Robinson

➻When Smokey Robinson left The Miracles in 1972, after a six-month farewell tour, he claimed he wanted to retire and spend more time with his wife and family. Apparently he'd been looking to leave for three years, as he'd felt uncomfortable with the internal resentment his top-billing had brought. But while the departure effectively meant the end of The Miracles, Smokey did anything other than retire. He was persuaded to move out to Los Angeles, where Motown had relocated, and given an office and the position of Vice President – from the early days he'd always been pretty much Berry Gordy's right-hand man – but by the end of the next year he'd put out his first solo album *Smokey*.

Like its follow up, *Pure Smokey*, it was overly sentimental and not very good, and it's on these two disappointing sets that people have tended to judge his whole solo career. Big mistake. By 1975, Smokey Robinson had settled down into solo life and was turning out some of the most mature, sophisticated soul music made during that decade. Instead of trying to compete with funk's sharp young gunslingers, or replicate the past exactly how it was, he'd gone back to the melodies and story-telling songs he was best at and given them real weight. He'd reinvented his mellow soul for his original audience, but taken on board the fact that they were by then well past adolesence. The albums *A Quiet Storm*, *Where There's Smoke* and *Being With You* featured jazzy, far more complicated arrangements and, subtly, kicked the tempos up to avoid tipping over into slush. It was old-style Motown updated – not rewritten – representing an album's approach to corporate policy that would have been just right to keep hold of existing fans as they moved on out of the singles market.

But although these sets sold respectably in the US, and were an important contribution to soul's evolution, the company didn't focus on them as albums. By the mid-1970s it seemed their way of selling albums and keeping the old crowd was to repackage the hits of the past, and Smokey continued to be sold as a singles artist, with high-profile pushes on tracks from the LPs into an increasingly distanced market – it's unsurprising he didn't have a top ten hit until 1980, as taken out of their context and put up against disco music his intricate, laid back repertoire looked a bit on the lame side. It was also small wonder he went into the next decade with a serious drug problem.

Over that by the middle of the 1980s, he continues to record, but appears to have very little fire left in his soul.

*Being With You; Motown 530219; 1981

This was Smokey Robinson's only top ten solo UK album, so it's hardly surprising it's the only one still on catalogue. Pity, because while all the above-mentioned qualities of warmth and sophistication apply, and it's got the title track hit, it doesn't quite do it in spades like a couple of the other sets.

SEE ALSO: (1) Motown Various Artist compilations; (2) The Smokey Robinson box set

Rose Royce

(Gwen Dickey, vocals; Kenny Copeland, vocals/trumpet; Lequient Jobe, bass; Henry Garner, drums; Michael Moore, saxes; Freddie Dunn, trumpet; Walter McKinney, guitar; Michael Nash, keyboards; Terral Santiel, percussion)

Back in the summer of 1977 *Car Wash* was a sharp, sketch-based comedy film, set among the black employees of a Los Angeles car wash – everybody had seen it at least once. A big contribution to the movie's success was the soundtrack of top drawer, disco-with-attitude numbers, written and produced by Norman Whitfield, and performed by Rose Royce, a group who, up until a few months previously, had been called Total Concept Unlimited and were the touring band for Edwin Starr, THE TEMPTATIONS and The Undisputed Truth. It was while working with these artists early in the decade that they had met Whitfield. He'd been commissioned to provide the music for this film and he needed a self-contained band for the project.

It couldn't have come at a better time for either party: Whitfield had left Motown a couple of years back and was looking to progress from the now anachronistic psychedelic soul he'd invented with The Temptations; and the group must've been wishing they could *stop* being Total Concept Unlimited. He brought in large-ranged vocalist Gwen Dickey to give them a focus up front, and set about adapting disco to take in his multi-layered visions and acquire real depth. He did this so well on the *Car Wash* soundtrack that instead of swamping disco's essential good-time feel, the added substance was so skilfully constructed it greatly enhanced the sense of celebration. Which is probably why it did so well on both sides of town.

After this hit, the group and their producer were off and running, and saw out the 1970s with a series of killer tracks.

Grooves or smooves, Whitfield would put together deceptively simple backings that were little more than rhythms, but so complex a blend of beats this wasn't immediately apparent, the actual melody being carried by Dickey's remarkable singing, so it would come over as slightly removed from the music. Just as Whitfield had blended traditional soul with the sounds of the moment at the turn of the decade, he was doing the same thing now as disco appeared to be taking over black music. In 1981, both Dickey and Whitfield parted company with Rose Royce and they never had another big hit.

Greatest Hits; Atlantic 923457; 1989

A complete snapshot of the life and times of Rose Royce, dating from 'Car Wash' and 'Put Your Money Where Your Mouth Is' through 'Love Don't Live Here Any More', 'Do Your Dance' and 'Wishing On A Star', right up to 'Is It Love That You're After' and 'Ooh Boy'. Altogether now: 'ha-a-ay ha-a-a-ay, get your car washed toda-a-a-y . . .'

Jimmy Ruffin

(Born Colinsville, Mississippi, May 7, 1939)
As the 1970s got into gear, it wasn't all post-hippie psychedelic soul, hard-hitting street funk or wildly sensuous sheet music, there was some straight old-fashioned stuff that still went down well. Jimmy Ruffin was one such performer, with Motown ballads that really hadn't changed since about 1965, but seemed to have more guts to them than so much else the label was putting out. Maybe because so much of it was sad and you had this notion of it helping you to win women's sympathy vote. Indeed, pre-AL GREEN, 'Farewell Is A Lonely Sound', 'What Becomes Of The Broked Hearted' and 'I've Passed This Way Before' were North London smooch specials.

Motown's Greatest Hits; Motown 530057; 1981

Sixteen tracks, the above-mentioned hits plus 'I'll Say Forever My Love' and 'It's Wonderful', a couple of duets with his brother David, and silky readings of 'Gonna Keep On Tryin'', 'Til I Win Your Love' and a woefully trite take on 'This Guy's In Love With You'.

Rufus

(Chaka Khan, vocals, born Yvette Stevens, Great Lakes, Illinois, March 23, 1953; Bobby Watson, bass; Andre Fischer, drums; Tony Maiden, guitar; Nat Morgan, keyboards; Kevin Murphy, keyboards)

If there were any direct – as opposed to indirect – descendants of SLY STONE, Rufus would be one of them. Although blessed with a slightly more jazzy feel than Sly's straight soul, they took the soul of the day and laced all sorts of rock mannerisms around it to push it towards the mainstream, but with their basic black music integrity still intact. So while they presented a soul fusion from an almost entirely rock perspective, it was built on funk foundations that, in 1974, were strong enough to give them a series of club hits. Mostly from the album *Rags To Rufus*.

But while this set was another fine example of how, once left to itself, soul music had become a more versatile art form than practically any other pop subsection, Rufus didn't have the strength of personality to walk the line between rock and funk with any degree of consistency. Follow-up albums rarely managed to blend the styles with such skill, and tended towards limp funk or directionless rock, wasting Chaka Khan's big soul voice behind a wall of guitar/keyboard sound. The band opted for straight rock by the end of the decade, and she went solo, where the results were just as spotty – such wonderful tuff-rocking singles as 'I'm Every Woman' (1979), 'What 'Cha Gonna Do' For Me' (1981), 'Ain't Nobody' (1983) and 'I Feel For You' (1984) showed how she could bring her buoyant, sexy glow to just about any soul style, but they were part of a CV that included a monstrous amount of dross.

*Rags To Rufus; MCA MCLD19135; 1974

Without doubt, Rufus's finest hour: 'Tell Me Something Good' (written for them by STEVIE WONDER), 'Smokin' Room', 'Swing

Down Sweet Chariot' and 'You Got The Love', to name but four, are grooves strong enough to stand anything laid on top of them and still come out with funk flying. It's a mesmerising example of Chaka Khan's singing, too, and serves to underline the shame so few bands seemed to pursue up-beat funk/rock fusion for more than a couple of albums. Signs here are it could've developed into something truly spectacular.

Salsoul

Not by any stretch of the imagination does the Salsoul Sound – music as recognisable as Philly or Hi – qualify as a development of soul music. It's more like some sort of mad second cousin, as it didn't even evolve out of disco but from Latin Disco, itself a branch line of the genuine article. Salsoul was the name of a record label founded in the mid-1970s by brothers Ken, Joe and Stanley Cayre, to exploit the Latin flavour that was finding favour in the discos. They wanted to marry traditional salsa and New York funk – Salfunk as a name would've sounded daft – and as such a deep bottom end was needed to underscore a music as soaring as salsa, the early compositions were built on the kind of bass lines any self-respecting funk fan ignored at his peril.

The label's first release, in 1975, was Joe Bataan's cover of 'The Bottle' and was enough to get our attention. Kept it too. At this point in time, disco was still more or less playing by funk's rules so it wasn't hard for the The Salsoul Orchestra to step back a couple of paces on the evolutionary tree and establish their trademark balance of uptempo string overkill with percussion and horns that inspired the rhythm track to work that little bit harder, by deploying all sorts of modern-day soul flourishes. It had a Latin joyousness that gave it a genuine heart, something lacking in so much disco music. Through tracks like 'Ten Percent', 'You're Just The Right Size', 'Ooh I Love It' and 'I Got My Mind Made Up', Salsoul gave us some real let's-get-wild dance tracks – double-time hustling was for the very brave or the completely daft only – and was about as much disco as a hard-core funk crowd needed. Or wanted, for that matter.

Salsoul continued cutting much the same sort of records well into the 1980s, about four or five years past its sell-by date really, but by then the sound was thinner and its largest constituency was the gay disco market. In the last five years or so, Salsoul has made a considerable comeback as prominent bits of the label's finest moments have been cropping up as the musical basis for some of house music's biggest hits: 'Love Sensation' was 'Ride On Time' *and* 'Good Vibrations'; 'Let No Man Put Assunder' is very similar to 'Jack You Body'; bits of 'Just As Long As I Got You' surfaced on 'Looney Tunes Volume 2' and so on.

Gil Scott-Heron

(Born Chicago, 1949)

'I see myself as a modern-day version of the African Griot. He was the member of the tribe to whom was given the responsibility for looking after the family history, a man known throughout the Continent for upholding the oral tradition. We started from some simple premises that related to the traditional African delivery of poetry and conga. It seemed the most practical within a system where very few of our people can read with the type of interpretive perception necessary to deal with straight poetry.'

What Gil Scott-Heron is neglecting to mention is that he was funny too. While CURTIS MAYFIELD and MARVIN GAYE, SLY STONE and JAMES BROWN were articulating black frustration in ways that had far more depth than mere 'protest' music, nobody was making us laugh while they did it. Except Richard Pryor, Franklyn Ajaye and Gil Scott-Heron. The unique, and entirely attractive, element of his approach was its searing aggressiveness. While Sly was confrontational, James Brown was stirring, Curtis was laid-back intellectual and Marvin Gaye was, well, Marvin Gaye, Gil Scott-Heron was intent on not just castigating 'The Man' for his down on black America, or pointing a finger at those who weren't quite true to the cause, he wanted to ridicule them. His lyrics were soul's closest thing to a verbal pillory, setting up situations and people just to rip the piss out of them with a command of the language that flexed its muscles at every turn: 'What Nixon knew, Agnew/But Ag didn't knew enough to stay out of jail' ('H2Ogate Blues'); 'He's a legend in his own mind/God's gift to women/But God wasn't giving up a thing' ('Legend In His Own Mind'); 'He acted like an actor/Acted like General Franco when he acted like governor of California/Then he acted like somebody was gonna vote for him for president/Now we're acting like 26 per cent of the registered voters is actually a mandate/Guess we're all actors' (on Ronald Ray Gun in 'B Movie'); and you don't really need to go much further than the titles of 'Whitey On The Moon' and 'The Revolution Will Not Be Televised' to get the idea.

Even in ordinary conversation Gil Scott-Heron can't resist twisting, reinventing and subverting the meaning of anything remotely open to interpretation for he has a long-standing love of words. His mother was a librarian – his Jamaican father was a professional footballer, who had a successful spell at Celtic, in Glasgow, going by the nickname of The Black Arrow – but his exposure to books came from his grandmother who raised him to adolescence in Tennessee. She had no television so he read avidly, and had progressed to writing his own detective fiction by the time he moved to New York as a teenager. It was there, exposed to the chill wind of urban injustices and the radical creativity of the 1960s, that he put aside the thrillers to write more directly relevant material. By the time Gil Scott-Heron was nineteen he'd had two novels published, *The Vulture* and *The Nigger Factory* – both subtly savage indictments of racism – and a book of poems, *Small Talk At 125th & Lennox*. The poems were essentially a celebration of black life and all it means, and the shift to this medium was to allow a greater freedom to play with words.

Whether this is the grass roots of rap or not is open to debate, but what this wonderful lyricism shouldn't obscure is that Gil Scott-Heron made some killer music too. He could've been rocking a house with the tight Latin groove 'The Bottle' – the first time I heard that tune was in 1974 in The Tropical Cove night club in Bedford-Stuyvesant, Brooklyn, where, sandwiched between 'Cosmic Slop' and 'Skin Tight', the place *bounced* rather than just rocked, and it remains burned into my brain as a Great Moment In Funk – or charming an audience with wit, warmth and some artful, intricately jazzy, stretched-out funk. Courtesy of, first, Brian Jackson, whom he met at university, The Midnight Band, and later Amnesia Express. In each case, the restrained tones, led by Scott-Heron's piano and Jackson's flute, were really just scene-setters, an aural framework for vocals that slid from singing to speaking to create some of the most striking contemporary blues.

Although never without a recording contract until the early 1980s, few of his fourteen albums achieved enormous crossover success and as a result, at the time of writing, very little is available on UK-release CD. Curiously, not much more on US import either.➤➤

Glory; Arista 353913; 1990

A two-hour, two-CD Best Of that runs to twenty-six tracks and still only manages to scratch the surface. The biggest tracks are all present and correct – 'Johannesburg', 'The Bottle', 'The Revolution Will Not Be Televised', 'Angel Dust', 'B Movie' and 'We Almost Lost Detroit' – but there was always a depth to each album that went way beyond the singles. Miss 'Home Is Where The Hatred Is', 'Bicentennial Blues', 'A Very Precious Time Of' and 'Is That Jazz', and you miss Gil Scott-Heron at his angriest, funniest, sunniest and most griot-like respectively. While *Glory* remains an excellent value package, there's enough missing from it to justify a Volume Two. At the very least.

The Revolution Will Not Be Televised; Bluebird ND86994; 1974

His fourth album, and the one that broke through large – to a black audience – mainly thanks to the title track's stingingly funny indictment of black people who'd rather stand on the sidelines than do their bit in taking things to the street: 'The revolution will not be right back after any messages about a white tornado, white lightning or white people/The revolution will not be televised. Brother.' 'Sex Education – Ghetto Style' and 'Whitey On The Moon' were just funny. The Scott-Heron/Jackson partnership was beginning to show real breadth now as they explored jazz sounds and rules, the wistful 'Pieces Of A Man', the fiery 'Home Is Where The Hatred Is' and the just plain beautiful 'I Think I'll Call It Morning' stand out.

Winter In America; Strata East SES197542; 1974

The fact that it's got five minutes of 'The Bottle' and a further eight of 'H20gate Blues' ought to be enough to make you pay the extra couple of quid for this US import – the only one that seems to be available. But it's also the best, most consistent, Gil Scott-Heron and Brian Jackson album. By now their musical partnership had matured to the point that it was confident enough to have a life of its own, but still knew its place as subordinate to the lyrics. 'Rivers Of My Fathers', 'Peace Go With You' and 'A Very Special Time' are staggering examples of how this restrained jazz/funk works in long-format tracks, by ebbing and flowing behind the words to build up some of the most drop-dead soulful, well-rounded expressions of blackness to come out of the 1970s.

Shalamar

(Jeffrey Daniel, born Los Angeles, California, August 24, 1955; Jody Watley, Chicago, Illinois, January 30, 1959; Howard Hewett, Akron, Ohio, October 1, 1955)

If, in strict terms of soul's development rather than the arrival of rap, there's any one event that signals the end of the 1970s and the dawn of the next decade, it's Shalamar in 1979. The trio were recruited by Dick Griffey, the producer of US TV's *Soul Train*, to front the name Shalamar, which had already been applied to the minor hit 'Uptown Festival', a discotized Motown medley performed by anonymous session players under Griffey's guidance. The trio, who were all featured dancers in *Soul Train*'s hip young audience, were signed to Griffey's newly formed S.O.L.A.R. label (The Sound Of Los Angeles Records) and had a string of hits stretching up to 1983.

As a definite post-disco soul act, they embodied such alarming trends as the group members being less important than the producer – these three didn't know each other, were musically and vocally limited, and had been picked largely on dancing ability. In addition to this they were *of* Los Angeles as well as just being based there. It was widely accepted that the centralising of the entertainment industry in LA in the second half of the 1970s did much to kill funk's quirkiness of spirit and has been held in evidence of Motown's decline, while the sounds that remained true to their original characters all stayed in their native environment – Philly, P-FUNK (Detroit), CURTIS MAYFIELD (Chicago) and so on. The image seemed to mean more than the sound. Not that this meant they weren't a valuable and exciting contribution to soul's rich tapestry – being part of the audience at the open-air concert at the Hollywood Bowl in 1980, we were mesmerised by Jeffrey Daniel's body popping and moonwalking. (Daniel introduced these street dance staples to a mainstream audience three years before Michael Jackson.) Just as their songs, like their frontiers-of-fashion (some might say 'victim') image were carefully constructed for maximum impact, so they worked as lively celebrations of, er, nothing in particular. And as Griffey and producer Leon Sylvers were old enough to know they needed some soul basis to hold it all together, they managed to exploit disco without totally immersing in it and thus the tracks always had more weight than at first might be supposed. The missing link between soul of the 1970s and soul of the 1980s.

What they weren't, though, was long lasting. The problem with constructing a group like this is there's no guarantee they're going to like each other. Shalamar didn't, that much was soon obvious. Then if they're successful, there's always the chance they're going to want to have a bit of control. Shalamar certainly did, with each member eager to take the act in a different direction. In 1983 they exploded in spectacular style, with various members of the trio telling different journalists that the group had split, a few days before they informed the record company. It must be testament to the threesome's musical skills that none of the ensuing solo careers have amounted to a great deal.

Here It Is – The Best Of Shalamar; SOLAR 4720402; 1990

Exactly how Shalamar deserve to be remembered – a collection of rip-roaring singles, not to be flattered with an original album. And all the usual suspects are here: 'There It Is', 'Take That To The Bank', 'Right In The Socket', 'I Can Make You Feel Good', 'Second Time Around' and so on. How could you hope to have a party without it?

Sho Nuff

(Freddie Young, keyboards/vocals; Lyn Chambers, bass; Bruce Means, drums; Lawrence Lewis, guitar)
Sho Nuff's album *From The Gut To The Butt* was one of the last LPs to come out on Stax before it folded in 1976, and if they'd done more like this sooner it might not have gone to the wall. This was Memphis's take on street funk, and very credible it was too. The band were young enough and sufficiently full of themselves just to want to be black and bad with no half measures – the ghetto slang name, the album title dedicated to the dance and a close-up picture of two bumping butts on the sleeve. This was the kind of hip teen statement the label hadn't made enough of and so lost touch with a generation.

*From The Gut To The Butt; Stax SXD092; 1976

This album means more by what it represents – too little too late – than what it actually is, which is solid, old-fashioned hit-you-in-the-guts-and-make-you-do-the-bump (or something) funk. Among the rump-shaker tracks are 'Steppin' Out', 'Funkasize You', 'Watch Me Do It' and . . . Hey, maybe this isn't so bad after all.

SEE ALSO: Stax Various Artist compilations

Joe Simon

(Born Simmesport, Louisiana, September 2, 1943)
By the time soul progressed into the 1970s, the straight country influences were rapidly diminishing. Joe Simon was holding the hayseed end up though, with a deeply rural soul style that served him solidly if unspectacularly in the 1960s but, by itself, may have been a wee bit anachronistic by this point. However, such was Simon's gut-wrenching way with a ballad that once he was hitched to producers that could give it a modern spin without damaging the essence, he was unstoppable. 'Drowning In The Sea Of Love', produced by Gamble and Huff in 1971, is a case in point. A moment of sheer, celestial magic, creating a

instant in which the most hardened funk fan could wallow in old-time Southern soul without feeling uncool. It remains much covered and never faded. Then, as if to further prove the point that all it took was the right man at the board, Joe Simon had a couple of big dance hits ('Get Down, Get Down, Get On The Floor' and 'Step By Step') a few years later with disco producer Rae Gerald. Credible as they were, they couldn't hold a candle to 'Drowning'.

Drowning In The Sea Of Love; Westbound CDSEWM021; 1971

All you need to know about this LP is the title. But apart from that there's some very pleasant gently simmering country soul stew, and the added bonus of 'Pool Of Bad Luck'.

ALSO RECOMMENDED:

Get Down; Westbound CDSEWM013; 1975

It's got that big hit, but really it's for true fans only as his wonderful voice is applied to some wastefully treacly material.

Sly And The Family Stone

(Born Sylvester Stewart, Dallas, Texas, 15 March 1944)
If there hadn't been a Sly Stone then, arguably, there wouldn't have been a GEORGE CLINTON, a RICK JAMES or an ISLEY BROTHERS. And there would definitely have been no Terence Trent D'Arby, no Lenny Kravitz and no Brand New Heavies. Acknowledged as the pioneer of rock and soul fusion, he was always much more than that – Sly's plan amalgamated the two styles head on, he didn't just play soul from a rock perspective or, as was common, do it the other way round. Both soul and rock elements fuse without actually merging, thus both can be heard, quite distinctly, and his more vibrant albums get separately described, completely, accurately and honestly, as both rock and soul. What this allowed him to do, and why he was such an enormous influence, was to loosen soul's constraints to explore previously unconsidered possibilities of arrangement and

instrumentation, instead of constricting rock by locking it down to too rigid a set of disciplines.

Of course it took his delicate ear for production detail to realise this with any success, but once he was kicking it was enormous. Enormous in a rock world, because by not basing himself in anything too dark and scarey – like, say, Funkadelic or THE OHIO PLAYERS – it offered a rock audience a significantly new and rather exciting flavour. Remember, this was a crowd that had just had so much fun coming to terms with Jimi Hendrix and weren't about to pass up on another exotic-looking black man bearing wild music and all sorts of substances. After a triumphant set at Woodstock, where Sly and his band exploded as a vibrant, funky sunburst amid a number of jaded-looking more traditional rockers, the hippies adopted him, his music and multi-racial approach as some sort of symbol of the times. But Sly never fell too far for that one. No matter how he came to be perceived, he never lost his ghetto credentials, as he was always willing to look his new audience straight in the eye and tell them 'Don't call me nigger, whitey.'

In many ways, this isn't too surprising for Sly Stone's CV reads like a culture clash waiting to happen. He made his first recording at four years old, singing a gospel song; moved into doo-wop harmony groups; was producing pop acts for the Californian label Autumn at age nineteen – Bobby Freeman, The Beau Brummels, The Vejitables, The Mojo Men among them; deejaying on the less formally formatted San Franciscan radio station KSOL a couple of years later – his rhythmic scat patter, on air and over the records, has been taken as the earliest example of rapping; and formed a multi-racial band, The Stoners, with a female trumpeter in 1966. Soon after, on inclusion of his sister Rosemary and cousin Larry Graham on bass, the name changed to The Family Stone.

Once signed to Epic Records in 1967, the group smothered their R&B foundations with the hippie values Sly had steeped himself in as a deejay in San Francisco. Stir in the flash and showmanship fast becoming de rigueur as rock's new first division began spending the money it was earning, to which Sly quite rightly figured he was just as entitled, and the band blew up with 'Dance To The Music', a top ten hit on both sides of the Atlantic in 1968.

But his influence would far outlast his actual contribution. In five years time, Sly Stone was best known for cancelled shows, half-full auditoriums, bankruptcy – real and creative – drug busts, court cases and violence. In spite of attempts by the likes of BOBBY WOMACK and George Clinton to rehabilitate his career by using him on records and taking him on tour, too much of the music business regards him as a potential liability to invite him back in.

Greatest Hits; Epic 4625242

Although this 1970 album is a collection of Sly's finest moments between then and 1968, it's really much more a part of the following decade in its entirely ghetto-centric approach to a collision of black soul and white rock. Detached from the early, often comparatively flabby, album tracks, it presents a sharply focused snapshot of what made Sly so special, both artistically and culturally. It's a total immersion in his complete understanding of the attendant ludicrousness of both styles at that time – R&B's repetitiveness, rock's regulation *san frontiers* – his willingness to exploit same and then to run it all the way to wire. If not further. 'Dance To The Music'; 'I Wanna Take You Higher'; 'Stand!'; 'Everybody Is A Star'; 'Thank You (Falettinme Be Mice Elf Again)'; 'Hot Fun In The Summertime' . . . It's never been more apparent that while there's obviously something serious going on, funk is still F.U.N. with a K.

There's A Riot Goin' On; Columbia 3670632

If *Greatest Hits* is a summary of Sly's pre-Woodstock career, then *Riot* epitomises what came next. Gone is the light touch and shiny optimism, this is a deliberately alienating deconstruction of years of supposed desegregation. And few LPs have been more accurately titled: as a diatribe of black rage, it was scarily representative of the post-Civil Rights era pessimism as inner cities started to fall apart; and by its release in 1971 Sly's life was beginning to crumble under a welter of drug-related problems – said riot was happening internally and externally. With a narrative thread that often degenerates into horribly stoned ramblings, he broods on subjects ranging from black nationalism, the Nixon era, Viet Nam and, if 'Family Affair' is taken at face value, incest, then sets it to the kind of smokey grooves that, while lying back to horizontal, are heavy enough to anchor lead instruments weaving in and out like a spaced out dream. This album remains deeply uncomfortable, but is still as darkly fascinating as it was when it was Sly Stone's only American number 1.

ALSO RECOMMENDED:

Fresh; Edsel EDCD232; 1973

Riot's far sunnier follow-up was deleted on CD in 1983, but copies of it are still knocking about and worth looking out for. More relaxed in terms of lyrical content and the easy-going funk of much of the music, it can come as a bit of a disappointment after its broodingly brilliant predecessor, so play it after *Greatest Hits* instead.

The Soul Children

(Anita Lewis; Sheila Bennett; John Colbert; Norman West)
This is what ISAAC HAYES and David Porter did in their spare time – you know, in the odd hour or so when they weren't creating lavish, over-wrought emotional soul epics. They put this vocal group together at the end of the 1960s and wrote and produced for them a series of stunning gospel-based traditional soul harmonies. Light and apparently uncomplicated, the songs seemed diametrically opposed to what the duo were doing with Hayes's solo career, but The Soul Children's style had a deceptive depth to it, which carried them into the next decade, allowing them to survive all manner of change going on around them. It's also a useful reminder of the power of matching male and female vocals, something which happened so rarely in the same group. Yet nobody ever seemed to wonder why not.

Soul Children/Genesis; Stax CDSXD056; 1969/1973

A fine value twofer, that pairs their first two albums and between them utilises the production talents of Hayes, Porter, Al Jackson and Jim Stewart. It's such a straightforward Stax affair – The MGs backing and the vocals arranged with a big shout to Southern Baptist Church – that it relates far more directly to the 1960s. But don't let that put you off – like the name would suggest, this is a definition of soul harmony singing in itself.

Friction/Best Of Two Worlds; Stax CDSXD056; 1971/1974

More in touch with the decade they came out in, these albums prove a subtle but definite progression, with spunkier funk and more than a few modernisms creeping into both the arrangements and how they sit within them – it's more within than on top of at this point. But as their sweet soul stirrings remain more or less unaffected, this is one of the very few examples of an updating of the old Stax approach.

SEE ALSO: Stax Various Artist compilations

The Staples Singers

(Pops, born Roebuck Staples, Winoma, Mississippi, December 28, 1915; Cleotha, born Drew, Mississippi, 1934; Yvonne, born Drew, Mississippi, 1939; Mavis, born, Chicago, Illinois, 1940)

The wonderful thing The Staples Singers did was to get over a very churchified approach to their music, but present it with an entirely secular wardrobe. While their whole gameplan was small group-gospel harmonising behind Mavis's gutsy contralto and lapsing into well sanctified call-and-response chorus lines, it had a crisply funked-up backing and sentiments that weren't obviously to do with the scriptures or praising of any form. This had such popular funk crowd appeal in the UK, because in the early 1970s most of the actively clubbing teenage soul patrol had been taken to church for much of their lives by their immigrant parents. All sorts of post-adolescent domestic rebellion had gone on to discontinue the habit, thus the last thing any of them wanted to hear in dance halls were what amounted to hymns, yet at the same time the music style was deeply ingrained. Songs like 'Respect Yourself', 'Be What You Are', 'I'll Take You There' and 'People Come Out Of Your Shell' managed to walk the line between upful and trite with verve and confidence too, so the whole package suited the optimism that still existed. And the singles were one hundred per cent kicking dance tracks.

They should have been, too, for the group had had enough experience: Pops organised his daughters into a group as far back as 1951, starting their recording career just two years later. (Originally, son Pervis had been part of the act, but when he joined the Army in 1959 he was replaced by Yvonne.) However, although making waves on the gospel circuit, and doing quite well as a folk quartet (a connection that meant they were one of the few black acts to play Bob Dylan and The Band's 'farewell' concert in 1976) it wasn't until they joined Stax in 1968 that anything began to happen. By then, they'd settled down with Mavis as lead singer, Pops gruffly underscoring her and chivvying things along with sharp guitar licks and Yvonne and Cleotha rounding things out. After a couple of barren years there, Al Bell brought them over to Muscle Schoals and came back with, among others, 'Respect Yourself'.

This started a run of hits that lasted beyond the demise of Stax up to the CURTIS MAYFIELD written and produced 'Let's Do It Again', a powerful, restrained piece of funk for the film of the same name in 1976.

But that was about it. Further efforts both as a group and Mavis as a solo singer really only threw up (probably the right word too!) the discofied 'Slippery People' in 1984 and a recent collaboration with Prince that shows how even a voice as special as hers is nothing without the right material.

Respect Yourself – The Best Of; Stax CDSX006; 1975

There was always a great deal of filler wrapped around The Staples Singers' killer album cuts, so this is definitely the best way to appreciate them. Twenty tracks go from their first hit 'Heavy Makes You Happy' to their final outing with Stax 'City In The Sky' and includes 'Respect Yourself', 'If You're Ready (Come Go With Me)', 'I'll Take You There' and 'Oh La De Da'. The most remarkable thing, when hearing such an anthology, is the lack of development during their six years on the label. While the tag they earned of only being as good as whoever was producing them is a little unfair – nobody could direct Mavis's voice, it's much too strong for that, Bell simply kick-started it – you do wonder about how much input they were having in terms of material and direction.

ALSO RECOMMENDED:

Bealtitude: Respect Yourself; Stax CDSXE001; 1972

Although not as consistently hot as the compilation, it's a cooking set and gets a lot of points for nostalgia value as it seemed that every black household in North London had a copy of it at the time.

The Stylistics

(Russell Tompkins Jr; Herb Murrell; Airrion Love; James Dunn; James Smith)
In 1972 in a world of revolutionary funk, jazz/rock fusion, mind-expanding studio technology, acid-drenched arrangements, butt-kicking street soul and all sorts of aural-visual challenges, it was nice to come home to something normal every once in a while. Like The Stylistics and their tuxedoes and their smoothly harmonised pop/soul love songs that were so comforting they were more likely to get up and put another log on the fire than get up in anybody's face. Sad to say, though, what brought an entire generation of soul fans to The Stylistics was being able to taunt any remotely overweight girls by singing the group's first hit 'You're A Big Girl Now' at them.

That apart, through the first part of the 1970s, under the guidance of Thom Bell and Linda Creed at Gamble and Huff's Sigma Sound Studio, The Stylistics were astonishingly successful with a string of hits that ranged from aching ballads to chugging mid-tempo hustles. It seemed in each case the Philly production – although they weren't on the label, the work going on here was a big part in the sound's development – was giving them a lift while not interfering with their basic naffness, which is what their appeal was based on. A falsetto lead taking on songs of unadulterated slush – 'Betcha By Golly Wow', 'You Are Everything', 'I'm Stone In Love With You', 'Stop Look Listen

(To Your Heart)' . . . get the picture? – but doing it with such assurance you fell in step and quite welcomed the chance not to have so many extraneous aspects of a song to consider. It proved a delicate balancing act too, as once they switched producers to VAN McCOY, what looked like exactly the same formula just stopped working. Although the records continued to sell respectably (if decliningly), 'I Can't Give You Anything (But My Love)' was the only post-1974 tune that had any go in it. Today, the group's greatest hits packages are always strong sellers and they are regulars on the cabaret circuit.

The Best Of The Stylistics; Mercury 842936; 1990

About the most recent and the most comprehensive package, giving you all those dumb hits, from both the Creed/Bell period, including – a bit of a personal fave – 'Rockin' Roll Baby', and the Van McCoy days so you'll also be getting 'Let's Put It All Together', 'Star On A TV Show' and 'Funky Weekend', which are about the best of the second spell.

The 24-Carat Black

(William Talbert, organ; James Talbert, electric piano; Ernest Latimore, guitar/vocals; Princess Hearn, vocals; Valerie Malone, vocals; Kathleen Dent, vocals; Tyrone Steele, percussion; Ricky Foster, trumpet; William Gentry, trumpet; Jerome Derrickson, tenor sax; Gregory Ingram, alto sax; Larry Austin, bass; Dale Warren, piano/vibes)
This enormous band made an appropriately large impact on the hard-core soul crowd, as they epitomised early 1970s ghetto funk on more than one level. Unsurprisingly since they were from Detroit, where – post-Motown – the densest, most imaginative new soul came from, and they were direct descendants of early-Funkadelic (*Maggotbrain*, *America Eats It Young*, that end of things). Their dark, moody, organ-and-guitar upfront sound assumed the freedom of prog-rock's apparent free form, but anchored it in solid soul rhythm patterns and tight arrangements. As the name might suggest, they aimed themselves squarely in the one direction. They were determined to enjoy

the freedoms afforded to self-contained units and further supplemented themselves with woodwind and a large string section, incorporating a delicate quasi-classical touch. And they were so completely uncompromising that – until a few years ago and the so-called Rare Groove Scene – they were completely ignored by everybody outside their constituency.

Ghetto: Misfortune's Wealth; Stax CDSXE090; 1973

Appreciating the notion that, by the 1970s, soul had become an albums genre this – their only record to get to the UK – is far more about listening than wigging out. Exploring the mood of the time that pushed the urban environment forward as grittily glamorous – a very tight in-joke, that stretched back as far as the satirical plays performed more-or-less ad lib in plantation slave quarters – this entire LP celebrated the notion that such conditions were a cultural diamond mine. Hence their name and the title. Through tracks like 'Poverty's Paradise', 'Foodstamps', 'Mother's Day', 'God Save The World' and the title track (chunks of which crop up on ERIC B & RAKIM's *Let The Rhythm Hit 'Em* LP), it runs the spectrum from piano-acompanied poetry to multi-layered orchestral pomp and burbling instrumental funk, but all of it laced with an subtle and wholly appropriate sense of menace. If this was a one-off 'concept' album it gets serious props for hitting it and quitting it ('Strike and fade' was an old Black Panther Party slogan), but if there are any more can we have them? Pleeease.

The Tavares

(Ralph, Antone, Feliciano, Arthur and Perry Lee Tavares. All born in New Bedford, Massachusetts, in the 1940s)
Always rather unfairly earmarked as a disco act, but the fact that this five-piece harmony group found favour on the North London soul sound systems must've meant they had more going for them than that. They did. It was a combination of Freddie Perren, a Motown producer of the old school, five brothers singing together with a gusto that was matched only

by the urgent up-tempo orchestra and an arrangement that knew its way round a rhythm section.

And to think it once might not have happened for them, for they began their working days in the mid-1960s calling themselves Chubby & The Turnpikes ('Chubby' was Antone Tavares' nickname and The Turnpikes was in honour of life on the road). It's unlikely that a cross-section of seriously cool soul boys would have been seen in daylight buying records by Chubby & The Turnpikes, so it was just as well that on a tour of Europe at the end of the decade they opted for a slightly less oblique band name. Not long after that they signed a deal. Coincidence?

Less open to question, though, is what Perren did with them from 1975 onwards. It's quite obvious when approaching such tunes as 'Heaven Must Be Missing An Angel' and 'Don't Take Away The Music' he'd listened long and hard to Philly and Salsoul. But working five almost equally weighted (in terms of in-the-mix-importance) voices to the degree these guys were singing could add a dimension that even THE O'JAYS were pushed to come close to. It considerably took the heat off the music and allowed all sorts of room underneath for Perren to muck about with tricksy stop-starts and tempo changes, to let the bass line breathe a little, and drop things down to the sparsest of rhythm breaks without it suddenly becoming empty. And it was driven along with real funk power, to bring a new dimension to orchestral soul. One that disco could really only dream about. Indeed, such was its longevity that when 'Heaven' and 'It Only Takes A Minute Girl' were rereleased in 1986, they went top ten again.

*Capitol Gold: The Best Of The Tavares; Capitol C289380; 1993

What you really want to know is what's on this. Roll back the rug, get the neighbours round, take a deep breath and here goes: 'Heaven Must Be Missing An Angel', 'Whodunit', 'It Only Takes A Minute Girl', 'Remember What I Told You To Forget', 'Don't Take Away The Music' and 'More Than A Woman'. It must be that *Saturday Night Fever* connection that got them the disco tag, but that shouldn't put you off the earlier stuff by the best Philly act not on the label.

The Temptations

➻The Temptations' 1970s had really begun a year early, in January 1969, with the mildly whacked-out 'Cloud Nine' as their first record with new lead vocalist DENNIS EDWARDS, who'd replaced David Ruffin. But whatever concern it may have caused on and around Planet Motown – indeed, the main reason Ruffin quit was because he felt the band was deviating too far from its traditional soul roots – there had been no need to worry. At that time. True, Norman Whitfield was flexing some in-house clout by bending a few rules, but he wasn't breaking any – 'Cloud Nine' was still, in essence, a good honest Motown record with all those good honest values and we took it on board (when it eventually got released) as such. Quite liked it in fact, as did about a million or so people who bought it, and the Grammy Awards committee who awarded it Best Group R&B Performance for that year. Motown's first ever victory at these so-called music business Oscars.

The six-month delay on the UK release was because the UK branch of the company thought it was 'too progressive' – it must be said, that these offices were run entirely by white eager-to-preserve-the-'entertainment-factor' status quo of Motown's role in the changing world. Their consternation must've turned to apoplexy as the decade moved on. Once sales figures and industry awards had done a great deal to ease US corporate nervousness, it became clear that 'Cloud Nine' was little more than Norman Whitfield's warm up. As the new decade opened, he went on a run that, as well as making all sorts of spikey social comments, would explore modern studio technology to the degree that the vocal group – the very essense of those formed-in-the-late-fifties Motown values – became just another toy in his electronic playpen.

Of course there were still the 'Just My Imagination's and 'Gonna Keep On Tryin' Till I Win Your Love's but from 1970 onwards there were just as many titles like 'Slave', 'Ball Of Confusion (That's What The World Is Today)', 'Message From A Black Man', 'Ungena Za Ulimwengu (Unite The World)', 'Smiling Faces', 'Take A Look Around', 'Plastic Man' and 'Papa Was A Rolling Stone'. Whitfield radically altered the Temps' sound too, by having each member sing lead, in turn, on the same record. This was essential for the tunes he was putting together, as his strategy was to deconstruct a standard Motown orchestral piece and build it back up, virtually brick by brick, moving the various instruments and sections to the front, then dropping them back and moving them across the hi-fi channels in a three-dimensional weaving process that slowly swelled to a number of increasing mini-crescendoes until it hit the final climax. He treated the voices just like the other instruments, fading them in and out and becoming part of the tapestry rather than sitting on top of it. To take them as five separate entities gave him much more breadth than as strictly lead and background.

This style has often been bagged along with SLY STONE as some sort of acid rock, probably because the whole effect was more than slightly stoned, but it was never that. It was more like acid doo-wop – the results of modern technology and modern attitudes applied respectfully to that very traditional style as, regardless of how subordinate they may have been to the music, it was still built for five voices singing in harmony. Curiously, how firmly rooted it was showed up enormously in live performance: although the mixes had to be greatly simplified for an orchestra to play them on stage, the whole structure was tailor made to bring out the best in The Temptations' dancing, as they wove in and out of the line, coming into the light for a line then fading back, using the whole stage and visibly becoming part of the music in the same way Whitfield had made them part of it on record. All of which combined to make this far blacker than anything Sly had been doing, and, unsurprisingly attracted a far blacker fan base. The notion that The Temptations had something to say and were articulating it interestingly, restored a credibility that had been slipping towards the end of the previous decade.

In fact people seemed to like what Whitfield was doing, as the group had their most significant run of success between 1969 and 1974. Three Grammy Awards – one for Best Instrumental for a section of 'Papa Was A Rolling Stone' – half a dozen million-selling singles and seven top twenty albums; interestingly, the LP that fared the worst was the noticeably un-modern *Live At The Talk Of The Town*. But it always seemed that this behaviour was being tolerated at Motown rather than applauded, or even encouraged. No other producers or artists appeared to be learning from what was going on at Norman's house, and when he left at the end of 1974 The Temptations went back to tuxedoes and uncomplicated boy-meets-girl ditties. If it hadn't been for the cupboard full of trophies and gold discs, a year or so later it could have seemed like one of the most vibrant periods in the company's history had never happened – indeed the only other record they've made since then that anybody has taken any notice of, 1985's 'Treat Her Like A Lady', was produced by Norman Whitfield.

Given the impact it made, surprisingly little of this Temptations' golden period has made it to CD intact. It's been suggested that although such albums as *Solid Rock* and *Sky's The Limit* sold extremely well and continue to be highly rated pieces of music, because they were never as accepted by the mainstream as, say, STEVIE WONDER, they're not being taken entirely seriously. And who am I to argue with suggestions?

Masterpiece; Motown 530100; 1974

If all albums were this accurately titled it would save an awful lot of trouble. It's quite clearly the one Whitfield spent five years rehearsing for, and saved some of his best material for. Although it opens with the traditional, if vastly superior, 'Hey Girl I Like Your Style', once that's out off the way it kicks into a title track that involves thirteen minutes of gloriously self-indulgent adventures on the mixing board. It stitches together an orchestral epic confident enough to ignore the vocals for longer than a conventional single's entire length, then, just when you think he's forgotten them, individual voices pop through holes in the arrangements with stark condemnations of ghetto life, and as things progress they come together to deliver some scorching diatribe as the music powers to a peak of spectacular, panicky force. It won their third Grammy for Best R&B Group Performance. What really stands this album apart, though, is that while the supporting tracks are necessarily secondary, there're no fillers. 'Plastic Man', 'Hurry Tomorrow' and 'Law Of The Land' are all killers in their own right and it's only a towering slab such as 'Masterpiece' that can put them remotely into the shade.

All Directions; Motown 530155; 1972

Built around 'Papa Was A Rolling Stone', and while there's other tracks on the set that are interesting – 'Run, Charlie, Run', 'Funky Music Sho Nuff Turns Me On' and a cover of 'The First Time Ever I Saw Your Face' in particular – I don't know anybody who bought it for anything other than that central cut. And to own the full twelve minutes it's cheap at almost any price.

ALSO RECOMMENDED:

Anthology; Motown 530184; 1987

Although they're the abbreviated singles cuts, this double-CD set runs through many of Norman's magic moments. (It's been updated since the 1973 double album of the same name – this goes all the way up to 'Treat Her Like A Lady'.)

SEE ALSO: Motown Various Artist compilations

The Trammps

(Earl Young, vocals; Jimmy Ellis, vocals; Dennis Harris, guitar; Doc Wade, guitar; Michael Thompson, drums; Stan Wade, bass; John Hart, organ; Ron Kersey, piano; Roger Stevens, trumpet; John Davis, sax; Fred Jointer, trombone)
Forget *Disco Inferno* and *Disco Party*, when The Trammps were kicking it was way back in 1974, when they sounded like a Motown group gone to New York, fallen in with bad company and come back with their nice shiny stuff all funked up. On their album of that year, they hit two tunes that sounded like the rhythms were on steroids and the music was so big and urgent it would have given Levi Stubbs pause for thought. They even had the sheer brass neck to call themselves The Fabulous Trammps, after they'd arrived at the name as a comment on their combined wardrobes. But from the sound of that first album, they were so completely tuff that nobody was going tell them otherwise.

*The Legendary Zing Album; Kent CDKENM088; 1974

It's got those two tracks – 'Zing Went The Strings Of My Heart' and 'Hold Back The Night' – and has just been made available in original form. It really does live up to the title. Well, what are you waiting for?

War

(Lonnie Jordan, keyboards/vocals, born Leroy Jordan, San Diego, California, November 21, 1948; Howard Scott, guitar, San Diego, California, March 15, 1946; Charles Miller, saxes/clarinet, Olathe, Kansas, June 2, 1939; B.B. Dickerson, bass, born Morris Dickerson, Torrance, California, August 3, 1939; Harold Brown, drums, Long Beach, California, March 17, 1946; Papa Dee Allen, keyboards, born Thomas Allen, Wilmington, Delaware, July 18, 1931; Lee Oskar, harmonica, Copenhagen, Denmark, March 24, 1946)

In summer 1994 Marmite's TV advertising campaign used a snatch of the backing tracks of War's 'Low Rider' as the music for a nifty catchphrase that went 'My-mate-Mar-mite/My-mate-Mar-mite . . .' I didn't know whether to resent this as a travesty of funk, or approve of the music being given some sort of platform. In the end I didn't think anything other than it was quite funny and nice for the band to be getting a few quid.

The group themselves probably would have had a fight about it. During the 1970s War had a fearsome reputation on the funk circuit for being ready to slug it with just about anybody for more or less any reason. Although that world was never as all-out mellow as some music genres, War's name was entirely accurate (apparently it was deliberately picked to jar against the peace 'n' love 1960s) as other acts would describe them as 'more like a gang than a group' – one prominent funk star who toured with War as his group's support act told me, 'If they couldn't find anybody else to beat up on, they'd beat up on each other. First few times it used to frighten us, because they'd be knocking lumps out of each other in the dressing room five minutes before they were due on stage, but then they'd go out there like nothing had happened.'

Maybe the group had such a volatile approach to life because they were Eric Burdon's backing group for a couple of years. The ex-Animal had been in Los Angeles trying to get a foot on the movie ladder when he was advised to check out a jazz/blues bar band called Night Shift. He liked them, took them on and changed their name. The second album he cut with them, in 1971, was called *Black Man's Burdon* and perhaps unsurprisingly, group and singer parted company shortly afterwards. It's not known if this enormously dumb album title was behind the split or if it resulted in any form of mental scarring, but the band temperament that emerged – perpetually on edge and passionately loyal as a unit – meant they gave up some classic and entirely unique funk.

In fact, once free of their Burdon, it was as if 1970s funk had been designed for them. Part of moving together as 'a gang' resulted in a tightness of the War rhythm section that was astonishing, even when held up against JAMES BROWN's JBs – there was no such thing as a sloppy beat either on record or on stage. And such syncopation allowed the sort of experimentation that cut up the rhythm patterns into choppy, Latinesque tempos, to put a whole new spin on basic street funk. Already jazzy, they had a penchant for instrumentation and improvisation, and these solid anchors provided all manner of scope for big soaringly harmonised vocals and fascinatingly woven solo-ing. They had an excellent understanding of LA street culture – at the height of their fame they'd still find time to hang out with their longtime homies – and while spinning oblique love songs and wry social commentary, could kick the kind of cultural stupidness that meant something only in the ghetto. In rump-shaking up-tempos or in woozy, hypnotic grooves they were equally crisp.

It was a very Los Angelese style: full of Hispanic as well as black references, a laid back approach to ending a track (ten minutes wasn't unusual) and Latin rhythms. It was certainly very different from what was being made in New York. It used to be said that nobody else could emulate this sound because War were, in the early 1970s, about the only LA funk band with a record contract, but the truth was nobody else was good enough. War's songs appealed to the album buyer in us because as well as rocking parties they were also cool to stretch out on the sofa with. They delivered three absolutely vital funk albums, but then disco overtook the style and, beyond the twelve-inch mix of 'Galaxy', they were never really comfortable any more.

It'll probably come as no surprise that they split up in the late 1980s – apparently into two factions that would only communicate by lawyer – however, during the 1990s, interest in the group increased beyond mere nostalgists like myself, as their taut beats and odd sounds became widely sampled. Maybe such acknowledgement had something to do with it, but at the time of writing a band reunion was taking place with pretty definite promises of a new album.

Best Of War . . . And More; Chord CDLAX100; 1988

As the only War album on any catalogue anywhere in the UK at this time, it has to be up for consideration – even if it beggars its own title by not including 'The World Is Ghetto'. All the other key tracks are listed, though: 'Slipping Into Darkness', 'Cisco Kid', 'Me And Baby Brother', 'All Day Music', 'Galaxy' and 'Low Riders'. But they're the edited versions and shouldn't really count.

The following can be found on import in most megastores and although a little pricey (£14 is to be expected) each is well worth it as a record of this unique funk experience.

The World Is A Ghetto; Rhino R271043; 1972

The title track has been much covered, here you get the original ten-minute version that manages to be busy and lazy at the same time – vividly bringing to life the contrast of brothers just lounging as life bustles all around them – while laying down one of funk's finest ever open-ended grooves. 'Cisco Kid' is a chugging Latin work-out, and 'City, Country, City' and 'Four Cornered Room' are the sort of elongated jazzy doodles that would be irritating if it was anybody else.

Deliver The Word; Rhino R271049; 1973

The band's dark album. The whole of the first side a bleak windswept suite that seems dedicated to hopelessness while wanting to beat you up with some very hard music. Side two lightens up a wee bit – 'Me And Baby Brother' and 'Southern Part Of Texas' – but the title track is a twitchy eight minutes of down-tempo funk. Probably the band's best overall set.

All Day Music; Rhino R271037; 1971

Although 'All Day Music' is exactly what you'd expect from LA – kicked back, easy and none too serious – the key track here, 'Slipping In To Darkness', which goes on for seven minutes, is quite disturbingly violent. Maybe this nihilistic side is a regional trait, hence gangsta rap twenty years later. Although those two and the urgent, aching groove of 'That's What Love Will Do' make this set completely special, it is the spottiest of this trilogy.

ALSO RECOMMENDED:

Galaxy; Rhino R271192; 1977

Worth it for a full-length cut of 'Galaxy', one of the few records that proved disco had some sort of potential, had it been handed over to street-tuff musicians.

The Whispers

(Walter and Wallace Scott; Leavil Degree; Marcus Hutson; Nicholas Caldwell, all born in Watts, California, in the late 1940s) In 1994 The Whispers celebrated their thirtieth anniversary as a group – the Scott twins formed the act (with all but one of the lasting line-up) at high school in 1964. But the most remarkable thing about them is that it took over fifteen years before they had any large-scale success; up until 1980 they had little more than minor US R&B Chart hits. When they did break through, it was as the first act on Dick Griffey's SOLAR label (*see* SHALA-MAR). After an appearance on his *Soul Train* TV show in 1977, Griffey had signed them to his company of the time, Soul Train Records. Although they didn't have a hit there either, when Griffey established SOLAR, he took them with him.

Once established, The Whispers became the label's firm traditionalists, singing the same kind of solid harmonising they'd done for years and providing a down-to-earth balance on the label's more modern roster. They provided a valuable post-Philly continuation of the old-time style, too, as producers Griffey and Leon Sylvers set up the backing with a very light disco-influenced touch, then used it to drive heavyweight seasoned vocals. The entirely pleasant results – 'And The Beat Goes On', 'It's A Love Thing', 'Rock Steady' and 'I Can Make It Better' among them – set up a run of pop/soul success that endured well into the middle of the next decade.

*30th Anniversary Anthology; Sequel NEDCD267; 1994

Probably more Whispers than even their immediate family would want, as the thirty-two tracks on this double CD go back to the year dot and include a lot of stuff people didn't even buy twenty-five years ago. However, the CD also goes up as far as the mid-tempo, relaxed hustle stuff of the early 1980s, and as it has space to stretch as far as the lesser known likes of 'Contagious', 'Keep On Loving Me' and 'Emergency' it's worth owning whatever else you're expected to put up with.

Barry White

(Born Galveston, Texas, September 12, 1944)
The remarkable thing about Barry White – or *one* of the remarkable things about him – is that he really is an OG. An Original Gangster. Back before the Crips and the Bloods, when he was in his mid-teens, he ran with a Los Angeles street gang and devoted much of his leisure time to violent crime. It was after an incident involving his mother's garage full of stolen tyres and one of the big guy's crew ratting him out that he ended up in reform school.

At this juncture in his life he realised he had two options: keep his head down, do his porridge, get out and waste the punk who shopped him, thus stepping on to a cycle of revenge and counter-revenge that could only end in an LA morgue; or he could keep his head down, do his porridge, get out and become a Lurrrve God. Luckily for us he took the latter option.

Which is more or less how The Walrus Of Lurrrve came into being. His life was starting to get serious – in years to come his younger brother was killed in gang-related activity – and the only other thing he knew was music, having learned to play a number of instruments and sung in the choir when he did go to school. By the time he turned twenty, Barry White had arranged 'Harlem Shuffle' for BOB & EARL, was Earl's touring drummer and road manager after the duo split and was a regular LA sessioneer on piano and organ. He moved on to produce Felice Taylor and became A&R man at a small record company where he signed a trio called Love Unlimited. He managed the group and married the lead singer Glodean James.

While producing their first record, 'Walking In The Rain (With The One I Love)' White took that first tentative step on the road to Lurrrve Godness: the record contains a phone chat break, and Barry's bass tones can be heard on the line. The record sold over a million and radio stations and the record company were overwhelmed with salivating enquiries from women as to who owned that come-to-bed voice.

At this point he realised: 'I thought I should try to make my own records. Apart from music, the only other thing I knew about [presumably he'd got a bit rusty on the armed robbery] was women, I always understood them and from the age of about thirteen I'd be giving advice to older people about their relationships. So I figured I'd sing about the ladies, and if I wrote my own songs I could write them for my bass voice – nobody else at the time was singing with a bass voice, so it had to make them special.'

What they were was phenomenal: his string of top twenty hits lasted until 1978 – and they were slightly more complicated than just a bass voice. With a drummer's unerring sense of how a beat shouldn't be lost regardless of what's going on on top, Barry White built on the orchestrations previously the property of ISAAC HAYES or the Philly label and crafted some of the lushest bounciest smoove ever recorded. Over his single-minded rhythms, he cascaded layers of melody that did all their interesting stuff in the arrangements, rather than overcomplicate the tune. Thus it was tricksy enough to hold your attention, but made sure it was accessible. It became the link between Philly Soul and out and out disco, which, cleverly, allowed his music to keep its credibility while racking up over a dozen pop hits in a row.

Then there was the man himself. Hardly looks like your text-book Lurrrve God. Yes, of course his voice was like chocolate under chocolate sauce, dripping with chocolate syrup, but it was his whole approach that set him apart. Here was a man who so clearly loved the 'lay-deeez'. His love – sorry, his lurrrve – was the biggest and there was no lengths he wouldn't go to please. The guys loved him for it too because he had them eating out of his hand. Not that he ever took them up on it. Apparently. He once told me that among the various sackloads of mail he still gets from ladies, offering him all sorts, was one sad creature prepared to put up herself and her three daughters – all he had to do was live with them and they'd devote the rest of their lives to his pleasure. In what must have been a flashback to his amateur counselling days, he spent an hour on the phone to her telling her, in the gentlest possible way, to get a life. And his marriage to Glodean has survived over twenty years of this sort of thing.

In fact it's going as strong as the big man's career. Although the 1980s saw a rapid decline in his record sales, and even now it's only the occasional single that charts, he regularly fills 10,000-capacity venues. On such a night, nostalgia rules, for he'll not do a song younger than fifteen years old, but the forty-piece orchestra, his oozing tones and whole notion of unconditional lurrrve can turn even the most hangar like of venues into an impromptu boudoir.

Although there are some Barry White original albums on offer on CD, they're from 1980 and beyond, a period that, in comparison with the previous decade, wasn't very good.

The Collection; Mercury 834790; 1988

Fourteen tracks from the glory years and the two most recent hits, 'Sho You're Right' and 'The Right Night'. On offer here are 'You're The First, The Last, My Everything', 'Can't Get Enough Of Your Love, Babe', 'Walking In The Rain (With The One I Love)', 'Just The Way You Are', 'Never Never Gonna Give You Up', 'Let The Music Play' and so on. It's a marvellous sampler to the bard of the bedroom, but that's all it is compared with . . .

Just For You; Phonogram 5141432; 1993

Weighing in at about thirty quid, this is exactly the sort of deal a man of Barry White's girth, abilities and general over-the-top outlook on life deserves. Three CDs, sumptuously packaged with a thirty-two-page booklet, provide thirty-nine full-length versions of classic tracks that cannot fail to, er, satisfy even the most ardent fan. Think of a desirable Barry White song and you'll find it here, even 'All Around The World' sung in a duet with Lisa Stansfield, which isn't nearly as dodgy as you might at first imagine.

Bill Withers

(Born Slab Fork, West Virginia, July 4, 1938)
Considering the man has been part of the US soul music scene for the last twenty-five years, it seems remarkable that the sum of Bill Withers records on catalogue in the UK at the moment is a ten-track CD best of. But Bill Withers's low-down credentials are never in question, as two things qualify him for a certain funky immortality: (a) when he first got a record deal he kept his day job for a while – installing toilets on aircraft at the Lockheed factory in California; and (b) he co-wrote 'Who Is He And What Is He To You'. He wrote a lot more too: 'Ain't No Sunshine', 'Lean On Me', 'Lovely Day', 'Use Me' and 'Grandma's Hands'. All of which have been done by other people, from THE TEMPTATIONS on down, but few have done them better (except for CREATIVE SOURCE of course). His is a warm, earthy, light blue voice that takes these songs and bounces them off uncluttered, supple instrumentation. It lets the emotion beam out, making the most of an acoustic guitar and coming over like a kind of funky folk music. It's happy, uplifting stuff – he always had an enormous smile on record sleeve photos – that is completely at odds with somebody who spent nine years in the armed forces.

The Best Of Bill Withers; CBS 32343; 1988

Hearing songs such as those mentioned above, performed how they were written, is always a worthwhile experience.

Bobby Womack

(Born Cleveland, Ohio, March 5, 1944)

Bobby Womack was one of those acts that you'd never slag off, because they'd done too much that was worthwhile, but who put out so much duff stuff as well that they made it kinda difficult to give them props. And for every *The Poet* or *Across 110th Street* or *Communication* or *Understanding*, there was a *Womagic*, a *BW Goes C&W*, a *The Last Soul Man* or *The Poet II*. It was as if he had a problem picking material or when it came to writing his own he sometimes got sloppy and tried to coast it on his reputation. Mind you, such was the strength of that reputation you'd be surfing on it, not just coasting. A performer since the late 1950s, he was in a gospel/R&B group with SAM COOKE, The Valentinos; a session guitarist sought after by both rock and soul stars alike – he was a regular on the Muscles Schoals first team during the 1960s; wrote The Rolling Stones' hit 'It's All Over Now', WILSON PICKETT's 'I'm A Midnight Mover' and GEORGE BENSON's 'Breezin''; and was SLY STONE's right hand man when it came to pharmaceutically-fuelled rock 'n' roll excess during much of the 1970s.

Maybe it was a combination of all of these things that made for Womack's erratic catalogue – as he'd dabble in so many different styles and situations it must've been easy to lose his bearings every so often. But when he did get it right it was spot on. He had a gruff, bare-wire emotional soul voice that came correct through touring since the age of fourteen and years of dedicated abuse. His guitar playing had brought the instrument up for R&B through soul and into funk. He could write songs that were rough or smooth. And, significantly, he had an attitude: he would chuckle as he told white journalists, anxious to exploit his friendship with The Rolling Stones and claim him as their own, that he wanted to call *BW Goes C&W* 'Move Over Charlie Pride And Give Another Nigger A Chance'. The joke was the shocked faces as they tried to work out if he was serious or not.

*Womack Winners; Charly CDINS5074; 1989

The greatest hits, and the only surviving record of Bobby Womack's best period, the 1970s. 'Across 110th Street',

'Communication', 'That's The Way I Feel About Cha', 'Harry Hippie', 'Woman Got To Have It', 'Lookin' For A Love', 'Nobody Wants You When You're Down And Out' and fourteen more. And the kind of faultless funky soul music that, when concentrated on a CD like this, makes the other side of his output so much more difficult to deal with.

ALSO RECOMMENDED:

So Many Rivers; MCA MCLD19136; 1985

Unsurprisingly not as good as back-to-back vintage hits, but it's a better than average soul album for its time. It's increased in value at the moment, as nearly every other original Womack album is deleted.

Stevie Wonder

➻Stevie Wonder steamed into the 1970s as if it was always going to be his time. Admittedly the decade got off to a slow start, as all he did in 1970 was release *Signed, Sealed, Delivered* (an album with a sleeve photo that had him sitting in a big cardboard box grinning like a jackass) and get married to Syreeta Wright, another company secretary turned singer. In 1971, though, maybe with that cretinous LP cover shoot still in his mind, he kicked some butt in a way the Motown corporate posterior had never been treated in the past. Stevie Wonder had just turned twenty-one and, no longer a juvenile, was in need of a new, grown-up contract. He made no secret of the fact that other record companies were courting him long and strong, and pulled off a deal that effectively rewrote the Motown Book Of Artist Terms And Conditions. He got a higher royalty rate; freedom to set up his own publishing and productions companies; and, this is the big one, total creative control. No more big cardboard boxes, from now on he'd record what he liked, when he liked, how he liked and would drop it off to the company when he felt like it. And they'd put it out.

By 1972, *What's Going On*, *Sky's The Limit* and *Psychedelic Shack* had made the point that Motown needn't be about shimmering gowns, trite lyrics and twee orchestrations. And an artistically unshackled Stevie Wonder doesn't need to be told twice. The synthesiser had been on the market for a couple of years at this point, and Wonder was already hanging out with Moog specialists Robert Margouleff and Malcolm Cecil, finding his way around the instrument and exploring its potential. His series of albums for the rest of the decade did more to change the mainstream perception of Motown than those of any other single artist. The titles say exactly what was occurring – *Where I'm Coming From, Music Of My Mind, Talking Book, Innervisions, Fulfillingness' First Finale* and *Songs In The Key Of Life* – an intelligent young black man, with musical ability, was free to look inside himself and express his thoughts on the world and his place in it. This time it was personal.

Stevie Wonder's 'final cut' deal made sure they stayed that way too, as he could (and did) write, produce and arrange them, with the technology keeping outside influence to a minimum. Which is what made them so special. Not merely the sythesiser sound – in theory anybody could have done that – but that the path between Stevie Wonder's mind and the tape spool was now as short and direct as possible. His ideas were being recorded virtually unadulterated and the stream of consciousness possibilities this opened up from track to track, as thoughts spun off each other, meant the albums were entirely cohesive. Themes expounded included racial and social injustice, love lost, looked for and found, spiritualism, celebration and mental doodles about nothing at all. A broad church, that hung together in these LPs in much the same way as enjoyable, spirited conversation might – hopping from topic to topic but always with a flowing tone so that everything relates to everything else. It was this musical and intellectual overview on each set that positioned the songs far closer to the rock world's idea of what an LP should be than the traditional soul mentality, which is largely why they became so attractive to the mainstream. That and the fact they were better than just about anything else on offer on that side of the tracks.

But once again, as with MARVIN GAYE and THE TEMPTATIONS, the company didn't seem to learn anything from the critical and commercial success they were having, by simply leaving an artist to get on with it. As Stevie Wonder finished up the decade having grown from the boy in the box to one of the biggest stars in the world – for more reasons than sales figures – Motown were still devoting their efforts to looking for another young group they could shape to replace the departed JACKSON 5.♦♦

The following are the classic 1970s Stevie Wonder albums, individually each is as valuable as the other – different albums have different hits and different quirks – but it's best to appreciate them as a whole body of work. It's really the only way that Stevie Wonder's journey through the decade makes real sense.

Music Of My Mind; Motown 530028; 1972

The first one is very obviously the starting point, simply because the technology sounds so, er, unpolished and the songs are still very traditionally structured. However, the tracks most people remember, 'Superwoman (Where Were You)' and 'Love Having You Are Around', are starting to move the goalposts, making this a vibrant statement of intent.

Talking Book; Motown 530036; 1972

Only a matter of months later, but the rough edges are disappearing fast. It's altogether smoother and more confident in its moodswings, from the sun into the dark more than once. Noticeably, he's good enough by now to put together a tune like 'You Are The Sunshine Of My Life' without it getting sloppy.

Innervisions; Motown 530035; 1973

This was where he really hit his stride. Song constructions have taken on a very individual flavour and the whole essence of the album is one of spirituality and gentle optimism. It's as if with clearly less to worry about in the electronic environment, he's given himself far greater freedom of expression. 'Too High', 'Living For The City', 'Higher Ground', 'Don't You Worry 'Bout A Thing' . . . If this series has a peak, this would be it.

Fulfillingness' First Finale; Motown 530105; 1974

Aptly titled, an album of true beauty. More like straight love songs, but put together with such artistry – both the technology and Wonder's way with it has come on in leaps and bounds in the preceding two years – they have a depth you can drown in. It's not tricky, it's not showing off the system, it's just a textbook example of how techno music can achieve greater warmth than its 'genuine' counterpart.

Songs In The Key Of Life; Motown 530034; 1976

It's as if this double LP was an end-of-term paper for everything he'd learned during the last four years – go back to the sort of song parameters you were using five years ago, but do them with a synthesiser and make them sound both modern and heavyweight. He does it too, as at no point does it flag, and it presents some of the simplest ideas in a form that remains intriguing yet doesn't detract from their subtlety: 'Sir Duke' and 'I Wish' to name but two.

The Secret Life Of Plants; Motown 530106; 1979

This was never as bad as the critics said it was. OK, so there's a bit of showing off involved, but it's got far more humour and quirkiness than most ambient music. In other words you can't quite ignore it if you put it on in the background at that dinner party. Hell, it's even got a couple of numbers you might get up and dance to.

Charles Wright & The Watts 103rd Street Rhythm Band

A sprawling, nine-piece Los Angeles funk band, whose approach to the music was an apt illustration of the stripped down West Coast style: a groove so loose-limbed it was sometimes hard to see how it actually got anywhere; vocals that happened to be passing and were quite content to make it up as they went along; and lead instruments that played, er, stuff, in the enormous spaces that seemed to crop up all over the place. Like so much Californian jazz, it was what you *didn't* do that was most important, and laid back was where things started. Then you proceeded to relax. Of course, anything this minimal can easily go off the rails and just come across as bone idle, but Charles Wright came so correct in 1970 with 'Respect Yourself

Part One' and 'Part Two' (curiously, on different albums) it somehow didn't matter that he never even got close after that.

SEE: Various Artists; *Classic Funk Mastercuts Volume Two*; Mastercuts CUTSCD14; 1993

VARIOUS ARTIST COMPILATIONS

*Classic Funk Mastercuts Volume One; Mastercuts CUTSCD6; 1992

Creative Source, Who Is He And What Is He To You; **The Fatback Band**, Wicki-Wacky; **The JBs**, Gimme Some More; **The O'Jays**, For The Love Of Money; **The Ohio Players**, Fire; **Curtis Mayfield**, Pusherman; **Fred Wesley & The New JBs**, Blow Your Head; **Mandrill**, Fencewalk; **Average White Band**, Pick Up The Pieces; **The Blackbyrds**, Rock Creek Park; **Kool & The Gang**, NT; **James Brown**, Stone To The Bone.

*Classic Funk Mastercuts Volume Two; Mastercuts CUTSCD14; 1993

Brass Construction, Movin'; **The JBs**, You Can Have Your Watergate; **Kool & The Gang**, Funky Stuff/More Funky Stuff; **The Ohio Players**, Jive Turkey; **The Detroit Emeralds**, Baby Let Me Take You; **The Blackbyrds**, Do It Fluid; **Charles Wright & The Watts 103rd St Rhythm Band**, Express Yourself Part 1; **Eddie Harris**, It's Alright Now; **The Fatback Band**, Keep On Stepping; **Donny Hathaway**, The Ghetto; **James Brown**, The Boss; **The Crusaders**, Stomp And Buck Dance.

It's impossible to overpraise these two compilation albums – as I compliled them! However, in content, presentation, running order and sleeve notes they are, undisputably, what they say they are: Classic and Funky. A worthy addition to anybody's collection. I could go on.

Classic Salsoul Mastercuts Volume One; Mastercuts
CUTSCD10; 1993

Double Exposure, Ten Per Cent; **Ripple**, The Beat Goes On And On; **Loleatta Holloway**, Love Sensation; **First Choice**, Let No Man Put Assunder; **Leroy Burgess**, Heartbreaker; **Loleatta Holloway**, Dreaming; **Instant Funk**, I Got My Mind Made Up; **The Salsoul Orchestra**, Nice And Nasty; **The Salsoul Orchestra Featuring Loleatta Holloway**, Runaway; **Candido**, Jingo; **The Salsoul Orchestra**, You're Just The Right Size; **Joe Bataan**, The Bottle.

Classic Salsoul Mastercuts Volume Two; Mastercuts
CUTSCD13; 1993

First Choice, Dr Love; **Double Exposure**, My Love Is Free; **Inner Life**, Ain't No Mountain High Enough; **Eddie Holman**, This Will Be A Night To Remember; **Love Committee**, Just As Long As I Got You; **Moment Of Truth**, Helplessly; **Silvetti**, Spring Rain; **Inner Life**, Moment Of My Life; **Gaz**, Sing Sing; **Loleatta Holloway**, Hit And Run; **The Salsoul Orchestra**, Ooh, I Love It (Love Break); **Candido**, Dancin' And Prancin'.

Classic Jazz/Funk Mastercuts Volume One; Beechwood
CUTSCD2; 1991

Lonnie Liston Smith, Expansions; **Ronnie Laws**, Always There; **Gil Scott-Heron**, The Bottle; **Donald Byrd**, Change (Makes You Wanna Hustle); **Wilton Felder**, Inherit The Wind; **Spyro Gyra**, The Shaker Song; **Azymuth**, Jazz Carnival; **Johnny Hammond**, Los Conquistadores Chocolates; **Eddie Henderson**, Say You Will; **John Klemmer**, Brasilia; **Harvey Mason**, Till You Take My Love; **Dizzy Gillespie & Lalo Schifrin**, Unicorn.

Classic Jazz/Funk Mastercuts Volume Two; Beechwood
CUTSCD4; 1991

Idris Muhammad, Could Heaven Ever Be Like This; **George Duke**, Brazilian Love Affair; **Al Jarreau**, Easy; **Donald Byrd**, Dominoes; **Ned Doheny**, To Prove My Love; **B. Baker**

Chocolate Co, Snowblower; **Roy Ayers**, Poo Poo La La; **Tania Maria**, Come With Me; **Herb Alpert**, Rotation; **David Sanborn**, Chicago Song; **Benny Golson**, The New Killer Joe; **The Crusaders**, Keep That Same Old Feeling.

Classic Jazz/Funk Mastercuts Volume Three; Beechwood
CUTSCD7; 1992

David Bendeth, Feel The Real; **Al Di Meola**, Roller Jubilee; **Herbie Hancock**, Saturday Night; **Donald Byrd**, Love Has Come Around; **Ramsey Lewis**, Spring High; **Roy Ayers**, Love Will Bring Us Back Together; **Bob James**, Westchester Lady; **Kool & The Gang**, Summer Madness; **Ramsey Lewis And Earth, Wind & Fire**, Sun Goddess; **Steve Khan**, Darlin' Darlin' Baby; **Aquarian Dream**, You're A Star; **Lenny White**, Best Of Friends.

Classic Jazz/Funk Mastercuts Volume Four; Beechwood
CUTSCD16; 1993

Weather Report, Birdland; **Herbie Hancock**, I Thought It Was You; **Roy Ayers**, Can You See Me; **Atmosfear**, Dancing In Outer Space; **Arthur Adams**, You Got The Floor; **Deodato**, Whistle Bump; **Sergio Mendes**, The Real Thing; **Chico Hamilton**, Magic Fingers; **The Brothers Johnson**, Strawberry Letter 23; **Wally Badarou**, Chief Inspector; **Tom Browne**, Funkin' For Jamaica; **The Crusaders**, Street Life.

Classic Mellow Mastercuts Volume One; Beechwood
CUTSCD3; 1991

Luther Vandross, She's So Good To Me; **Keni Burke**, Risin' To The Top; **The Gap Band**, Outstanding; **Maze**, Joy And Pain; **Leo's Sunship**, Give Me The Sunshine; **Billy Griffin**, Hold Me Tighter In The Rain; **Arnie's Love**, I'm Out Of Your Life; **Hi-Gloss**, You'll Never Know; **Bobby Caldwell**, What You Won't Do For Love; **Al Johnson & Jean Carn**, I'm Back For More; **Jeannie Reynolds**, The Fruit Song; **Lowrell**, Mellow Mellow Right On.

Classic Mellow Mastercuts Volume Two; Beechwood
CUTSCD8; 1992

Dennis Edwards, Don't Look Any Further; **Womack & Womack**, Baby I'm Scared Of You; **Heatwave**, Mind Blowing Decisions; **The Mary Jane Girls**, All Night Long; **The Ohio Players**, Sweet Sticky Thing; **Barry White**, It's Ecstasy When You Lay Down Next To Me; **Mtume**, Juicy Fruit; **The Dramatics**, Watcha See Is Watcha Get; **Marlena Shaw**, Yu-Ma/Go Away Little Boy; **Paris**, I Choose You; **Fatback**, So Delicious.

Classic Mellow Mastercuts Volume Three; Beechwood
CUTSCD17; 1994

Luther Vandross, Never Too Much; **Bo Kirkland & Ruth Davis**, You're Gonna Get Next To Me; **The Jones Girls**, Nights Over Egypt; **The O'Jays**, Now That We've Found Love; **Jean Carn**, Don't Let It Go To Your Head; **Shirley Jones**, Do You Get Enough Love; **Norman Connors**, You Are My Starship; **Earth, Wind & Fire**, Reasons (Live Version); **Freddie Jackson**, Rock Me Tonight (For Old Time's Sake); **Eugene Wilde**, Gotta Get You Home Tonight; **Anita Baker**, Sweet Love; **Al Jarreau**, We're In This Love Together.

The Philadelphia Years Volume One, 1971–1976; Knight, KNCD42001; 1989

The Ebonys, You're The Reason Why; **Harold Melvin And The Blue Notes**, I Miss You; **The O'Jays**, Backstabbers; **The Intruders**, (Win, Place Or Show) She's A Winner; **Harold Melvin And The Blue Notes**, If You Don't Know Me By Now; **Billy Paul**, Me And Mrs Jones; **The O'Jays**, 992 Arguments; **The O'Jays**, Love Train; **Bunny Sigler**, Tossin' And Turnin'; **Harold Melvin And The Blue Notes**, Yesterday I Had The Blues; **Billy Paul**, Am I Black Enough For You; **The Ebonys**, It's Forever; **The Intruders**, I'll Always Love My Mama; **The O'Jays**, Time To Get Down; **Harold Melvin And The Blue Notes**, The Love I Lost; **The Three Degrees**, Dirty Ol' Man; **The Intruders**, I Wanna Know Your Name; **The O'Jays**, Put Your Hands Together; **The Trammps**,

Love Epidemic; **Billy Paul**, Thanks For Saving My Life; **M.S.F.B.,** T.S.O.P.; **The Three Degrees**, Year Of Decision; **Harold Melvin And The Blue Notes**, Satisfaction Guaranteed; **The Ebonys**, I Believe; **The O'Jays**, For The Love Of Money; **The Trammps**, Where Do We Go From Here; **Bunny Sigler**, Love Train Part 1; **The Three Degrees**, When Will I See You Again; **M.S.F.B.**, Love Is The Message; **The Three Degrees**, Get Your Love Back; **Derek And Cyndi**, You Bring Out The Best In Me; **Harold Melvin And The Blue Notes**, Where Are All My Friends; **The O'Jays**, Sunshine; **Billy Paul**, Be Truthful To Me; **The Three Degrees**, I Didn't Know; **Harold Melvin And The Blue Notes**, Bad Luck; **The O'Jays**, Give The People What They Want; **M.S.F.B.**, Sexy; **Harold Melvin And The Blue Notes**, Hope That We Can Be Together Soon; **Soul Survivors**, City Of Brotherly Love; **Archie Bell And The Drells**, I Could Dance All Night; **The Three Degrees**, Take Good Care Of Yourself; **People's Choice**; Do It Any Way You Wanna; **The Three Degrees**, Long Lost Lover; **The O'Jays**, Let Me Make Love To You; **Harold Melvin And The Blue Notes**, Wake Up Everybody; **The O'Jays**, I Love Music; **M.S.F.B**, The Zip; **People's Choice**, Nursery Rhymes; **Archie Bell And The Drells**, Soul City Walk; **Billy Paul**, Let's Make A Baby; **Archie Bell And The Drells**, Let's Groove; **Harold Melvin And The Blue Notes**, Tell The World How I Feel; **The O'Jays**, Living For The Weekend; **Dee Dee Sharp**, I'm Not In Love; **Lou Rawls**, You'll Never Find Another Love Like Mine.

*The Philadelphia Years Volume Two, 1976–1983; Knight, KNCD42002; 1989

Archie Bell And The Drells, Don't Let Love Get You Down; **The Three Degrees**, The Toast Of Love; **The O'Jays**, Message In Our Music; **Lou Rawls**, Groovy People; **The Jacksons**, Enjoy Yourself; **The O'Jays**, Darlin' Darlin' Baby; **Harold Melvin And The Blue Notes**, Don't Leave Me This Way; **Jean Carn**, Free Love; **Archie Bell And The Drells**, Everybody Have A Good Time; **The Jacksons**, Show You The Way To Go; **Teddy Pendergrass**, The Whole Town's Laughing At Me; **The Jacksons**, Going Places; **Billy Paul**, Only The Strong Survive; **Lou Rawls**, Lady Love; **People's Choice**, Jam Jam Jam (All Night Long); **The O'Jays**, Used Ta Be My Girl; **Lou Rawls**, One Life To Live; **Teddy Pendergrass**,

Close the Door; **Dexter Wansel**, All Night Long; **The O'Jays**, Brandy; **Teddy Pendergrass**, Only You; **Jerry Butler**, (I'm Just Thinking About) Cooling Out; **Lou Rawls**, Let Me Be Good To You; **McFadden & Whitehead**, Ain't No Stopping Us Now; **Billy Paul**, Bring The Family Back Together Again; **The Jones Girls**, You're Gonna Make Me Love Somebody Else; **Teddy Pendergrass**, Turn Off the Lights; **Archie Bell And The Drells**, Strategy; **Frantique**, Strut Your Funky Stuff; **Dexter Wansel**, The Sweetest Pain; **The O'Jays**, Forever Mine; **Jerry Butler**, The Best Love I Ever Had; **Lou Rawls**, You're My Blessing; **The O'Jays**, Girl Don't Let It Get You Down; **Teddy Pendergrass**, Can't We Try; **Jerry Butler**, Don't Be An Island; **McFadden & Whitehead**, I Heard It In A Love Song; **The Stylistics**, Hurry Up This Way Again; **Teddy Pendergrass**, Love T.K.O.; **The Jones Girls**, I Just Love The Man; **M.S.F.B**, Mysteries Of The World; **The Stylistics**, And I'll See You No More; **Dee Dee Sharp**, I Love You Anyway; **Teddy Pendergrass**, I Can't Live Without Your Love; **Teddy Pendergrass**, You're My Latest, My Greatest Inspiration; **The Jones Girls**, I Found That Man Of Mine; **The Jones Girls**, Nights Over Egypt; **The O'Jays**, Put Our Heads Together; **Patti Labelle**, If Only You Knew; **Patti Labelle**, Love, Need And Want You.

Each volume of *The Philadelphia Years* is a fifty-six-track, four-CD set, complete with detailed booklet. Although appropriately priced, together they provide about as comprehensive a history of the label as anyone could ask for. Even if Volume Two does include all those Jones Girls Tracks at the expense of The O'Jays's rather wonderful 'Now That We've Found Love'.

**Philadelphia Classics*; Philadelphia International 4689912; 1991

M.S.F.B., Love Is The Message; **M.S.F.B. & The Three Degrees**, The Sound Of Philadelphia; **The Three Degrees**, Dirty Old Man; **The O'Jays**, I Love Music; **Harold Melvin & The Blue Notes**, Don't Leave Me This Way; **The O'Jays**, Love Train; **The Intruders**, I'll Always Love My Mama; **Harold Melvin & The Blue Notes**, Bad Luck.

Far from comprehensive, an ideal toe-dipper for those two or three people who've never heard a Philly record.

Motown Chartbusters Volume 5; Motown 530060; 1971

Smokey Robinson & The Miracles, The Tears Of A Clown; **Edwin Starr**, War; **Jackson 5**, The Love You Save; **The Temptations**, Ball Of Confusion; **The Four Tops**, All In The Game; **Stevie Wonder**, Heaven Help Us All; **Jimmy Ruffin**, It's Wonderful (To Be Loved By You); **Diana Ross**, Ain't No Mountain High Enough; **Stevie Wonder**, Signed, Sealed, Delivered I'm Yours; **The Supremes**, Stoned Love; **Marvin Gaye**, Abraham, Martin & John; **The Four Tops**, Still Water (Love); **Martha & The Vandellas**, Forget-Me-Not; **The Motown Spinners**, It's A Shame; **Jackson 5**, I'll Be There; **Jimmy Ruffin**, I'll Say Forever My Love.

Motown Chartbusters Volume 6; Motown 530061; 1971

Diana Ross, I'm Still Waiting; **Smokey Robinson & The Miracles**, I Don't Blame You At All; **Stevie Wonder**, We Can Do; **The Jackson 5**, Never Can Say Goodbye; **The Velvelettes**, These Things Will Keep Me Loving You; **R. Dean Taylor**, Indiana Wants Me; **The Supremes & The Four Tops**, River Deep, Mountain High; **The Temptations**, Just My Imagination Running Away With Me; **The Supremes**, Nathan Jones; **The Four Tops**, Simple Game; **The Elgins**, Heaven Must've Sent You; **The Temptations**, It's Summer; **The Jackson 5**, Mama's Pearl; **Smokey Robinson & The Miracles**, (Come Round Here) I'm The One You Need; **The Four Tops**, Just Seven Numbers (Can Straighten Out My Life).

Motown Chartbusters Volume 7; Motown 530062; 1972

The Supremes, Automatically Sunshine; **Gladys Knight & The Pips**, Just Walk In My Shoes; **Michael Jackson**, Rockin' Robin; **The Temptations**, Take A Look Around; **The Supremes & The Four Tops**, You Gotta Love In Your Heart; **Diana Ross**, Surrender; **Michael Jackson**, Ain't No Sunshine; **The Temptations**, Superstar (Remember How You Got Where You Are); **Martha Reeves & The Vandellas**, Bless You; **The Supremes**, Floy Joy; **Jr Walker & The All Stars**, Walk In The Night; **Diana Ross**, Doobedood'doobe, Doobedood'ndoobe,

Doobedood'ndoo; **The San Remo Strings,** Festival Time; **Mary Wells**, My Guy; **Michael Jackson,** Got To Be There.

*Hitsville USA, Motown Singles Collection, Volume Two; Motown 530263; 1993

DISC ONE: **Michael Jackson,** Got To Be There; **The Supremes,** Floy Joy; **The Four Tops,** Simple Game; **Jr Walker & The All Stars,** Walk In The Night; **Michael Jackson,** Ben; **The Temptations,** Papa Was A Rolling Stone; **Valerie Simpson,** Silly Wasn't I; **Stevie Wonder,** Superstition; **Gladys Knight & The Pips,** Neither One Of Us (Wants To Be The First To Say Goodbye); **Diana Ross**: Touch Me In the Morning; **Marvin Gaye,** Let's Get It On; **Eddie Kendricks,** Keep On Truckin' (Part 1); **Eddie Kendricks,** Boogie Down; **The Jackson 5,** Dancing Machine; **The Miracles,** Do It Baby; **The Dynamic Superiors,** Shoe Shoe Shine; **Syreeta,** Harm Our Love; **Willie Hutch,** Love Power; **GC Cameron,** It's So Hard To Say Goodbye To Yesterday; **The Miracles,** Love Machine (Part 1); **David Ruffin,** Walk Away From Love.

DISC TWO: **Smokey Robinson,** Quiet Storm; **Diana Ross,** Love Hangover; **Marvin Gaye,** I Want You; **Thelma Houston,** Don't Leave Me This Way; **Marvin Gaye,** Got To Give It Up (Part 1); **Stevie Wonder,** Sir Duke; **The Commodores,** Easy; **High Energy,** You Can't Turn Me Off (In The Middle Of Turning Me On); **The Commodores,** Brick House; **Rick James,** You And I; **The Commodores,** Three Times A Lady; **Switch,** There'll Never Be; **Bonnie Pointer,** Heaven Must've Sent You; **The Commodores,** Sail On; **Smokey Robinson,** Cruisin'; **The Commodores,** Still; **Billy Preston & Syreeta,** With You I'm Born Again; **Jermaine Jackson,** Let's Get Serious; **Teena Marie,** I Need Your Lovin'; **Smokey Robinson,** Being With You.

DISC THREE: **Diana Ross,** Upside Down; **Rick James,** Give It To Me Baby; **Michael Jackson,** One Day In Your Life; **Teena Marie,** Square Biz; **The Commodores,** Lady (You Bring Me Up); **Rick James,** Super Freak (Part 1); **Bettye LaVette,** Right In The Middle (Of Falling In Love); **The Dazz Band,** Let It Whip; **Lionel Richie,** All Night Long (All Night); **DeBarge,** Time Will Reveal; **Dennis Edwards,** Don't Look Any Further; **Stevie Wonder,** I Just Called To Say I Love You; **The Temptations,** Treat Her Like

A Lady; **Rick James featuring Smokey Robinson**, Ebony Eyes; **The Commodores**, Nightshift; **DeBarge**, Rhythm Of The Night; **Rockwell**, Somebody's Watching Me; **The Mary Jane Girls**, In My House.

DISC FOUR: **Stevie Wonder**, Part-Time Lover; **El DeBarge**, Who's Johnny; **The Temptations**, Lady Soul; **Stacey Lattisaw**, Nail It To The Wall; **Chico DeBarge**, Talk To Me; **Smokey Robinson**, One Heartbeat; **The Boys**, Dial My Heart; **Today**, Him Or Me; **The Good Girls**, Your Sweetness; **Stacey Lattisaw with special guest Johnny Gill**, Where Do We Go From Here; **Johnny Gill**, Rub You The Right Way; **Gerald Alston**, Slow Motion; **Another Bad Creation**, Iasha; **Boyz II Men**, Motownphilly; **Shanice**, I Love Your Smile; **Boyz II Men**, End Of The Road.

Wattstax – The Living Word; Stax CDSXE2079; 1972

The Staple Singers, Oh La De Da/I Like The Things About Me/Respect Yourself/I'll Take You There; **Eddie Floyd**, Knock On Wood/Lay Your Loving On Me; **Carla Thomas**, I Like What You're Doing (To Me)/Gee Whiz/O Have A God Who Loves; **Rufus Thomas**, The Breakdown/Do The Funky Chicken/Do The Funky Penguin; **The Bar-Kays**, Son Of Shaft/Feel It/I Can't Turn You Loose; **Albert King**, Killing Floor/I'll Play The Blues For You/Angel Of Mercy; **The Soul Children**, I Don't Know What This World Is Coming To/Hearsay; **Isaac Hayes**, Ain't No Sunshine.

The soundtrack album from the film of the Wattstax concert, an enormous 100,000-capacity event held on August 20, 1972, organised by Stax to mark the seventh anniversary of the Watts riots – astonishingly it was only a dollar a ticket. Although this CD set goes a long way to capture the flavour of the excellent film, it's only half the story: on import-only vinyl, twenty-one years ago, there was *Wattstax Part II*. This had the rest of the music from the movie – among others The Dramatics, Mel & Tim, David Porter, William Bell and more Isaac Hayes – but the highlight was half a dozen hilarious inserts of vintage Richard Pryor. For the movie these were filmed while he was having his hair cut, in a particularly funky barbershop, then spliced into the concert footage, but on record they come over like short sharp stand-up routines.

Stax Funk – Get Up And Get Down; Stax CDSX020; 1990

Isaac Hayes, The Theme From Shaft/Theme From The Men; **Dynamic Soul Machine**, Moving On; **Fat Larry's Band**, Castle Of Joy/FLB; **Sho Nuff**, Funkasize You/You Choose Me; **Sons Of Slum,** What Goes Around (Must Come Around); **The Bar-Kays**, Holy Ghost/Son Of Shaft; **The Dramatics**, Watcha See Is Whatcha Get/Get Up And Get Down; **Inez Foxx**, Circuits Overloaded; **Roy Lee Johnson & The Villagers**, The Dryer Part 1 & Part 2; **The Mar-Keys**, Black; **Jean Knight**, Mr Big Stuff; **Sir Mack Rice**, Dark Skin Woman Part 1 & Part 2; **Bernie Hayes**, Cool Strut Part 1.

Stax Gold; Stax CDSXD043; 1990

Booker T & The MGs, Soul Limbo/Time Is Tight; **William Bell & Judy Clay**, Private Number; **Johnnie Taylor**, Who's Making Love/Cheaper To Keep Her; **Eddie Floyd**, Bring It On Home To Me; **William Bell**, I Forgot To Be Your Lover; **Carla Thomas**, I Like What You're Doing (To Me); **Rufus Thomas**, (Do The) Push And Pull Part 1; **Jean Knight**, Mr Big Stuff; **The Dramatics**, Watcha See Is Whatcha Get/In The Rain; **The Staple Singers**, Respect Yourself/I'll Take You There; **Isaac Hayes**, The Theme From Shaft; **The Bar-Kays**, Son Of Shaft; **Frederick Knight**, I've Been Lonely For So Long; **Mel & Tim**, Starting All Over Again; **Shirley Brown,** Woman To Woman; **The Soul Children**, I'll Be The Other Woman; **The Emotions**, So I Can Love You; **Mavis Staples**, I Have Learned To Do Without You; **The Temprees**; Dedicated To the One I Love; **Veda Brown**, Short Stoppin'.

Son Of Stax Funk; Stax CDSXD075; 1991

Isaac Hayes, Theme From the Tough Guys/Type Thang; **Sho Nuff**, Mix Match Man/Steppin' Out/Watch Me Do It; **Sons Of Slum**, Right On/What Does It Take/The Man; **Black Nasty**, Talkin' To The People/Getting Funky Round Here/Nasty Soul; **Roy Lee Johnson**, Watch The Dog/Shack/Patch It Up; **Rufus Thomas**, Do The Funky Chicken/Funky Hot Grits; **The Forevers**, Soul Town; **Israel Tolbert**, Shake Your Big Hips; **Sir Mack Rice**, Bump Meat; **Jean Knight**, Carry On/Do Me; **The Bar-Kays**, Sang And Dance/In The Hole; **Hot Sauce**, I'd Kill A Brick For My Man; **The Dramatics**, The Devil Is Dope.

3

1980s

It was a very different soul music that emerged blinking into the daylight after the long dark *Saturday Night Fever* of disco. Now that John Travolta had shown white people that dancing like Mick Jagger wasn't compulsory, more than a few of them were looking for a slightly more challenging nightclub soundtrack. Enter soft funk, performed by the sort of bands who'd been playing hard funk a few years previously, who could give up a groove like a goat gives up stink, and who just needed to cut out anything too obnoxious and tickle up the top end a bit. KOOL, FATBACK, THE OHIO PLAYERS all, er, mellowed out and drew up a new set of guidelines for the genre.

Economics was playing a part too. The entire focus of the music changed as the rising costs and a shrinking economy hit the whole industry hard, and the soul end of things in particular – much like the rule of thumb that has it that when America in general catches a cold the black population get pneumonia. Big bands were, once again, no longer viable. Horn sections were the biggest single casualty, guitarists got short thrift and even rhythm sections, soul and funk's engine room, couldn't relax as synthesisers took over to reshape the sound totally with new drum patterns and rebalanced leads.

Another employment opportunity lost to the sprawling, showy soul band came with the demise of the live circuit – the recession began to hit ticket sales at the same time as rising costs made bands unable to charge less. So groups just didn't go out any more, which, in tandem with the disco industry's avaricious appetite for records, reshaped soul music. It was now all about the studio, with the producer rather than the players the most important person. And the difference between now and twenty years ago was that technology meant the producer needed fewer and fewer musicians.

Due largely to this re-emphasis of how it was made, and by whom, and for what situation, once past the watershed of disco, soul music was effectively cut off from its roots. What that strain went on to become (house and 'dance' music) had no connection whatsoever to, say, OTIS REDDING. At this point, soul reinvented itself as rap. An essentially dumb street style, created from scratch, intrinsically black and thriving within the ghetto economy. It's the same template as was used for blues, jazz, R&B, street funk . . .

To say rap changed everything, from a musical point of view, is to understate the case vastly, yet culturally all it did was what had been threatened since the beginning of the previous decade: it put black music, for the time being, firmly in the hands of black entrepreneurs. So let's look at it stylewise.

The real difference was the introduction of technology to such a degree. Making records became a cottage industry – anybody could do it and it seemed like most people did. Individuality was eroded as, at the bottom end of the spectrum, it allowed everybody to achieve much the same standard. Also, if one artist had a hit with a certain type of sample then there'd be a scramble as producers and deejays rushed for it. Or one very like it. James Brown's 'Funky Drummer' was a case in point, and at one time in the eighties it was possible to buy more than fifty different records that contained bits of it. Most importantly, though, it meant hip hop evolved at a frightening pace: for around three months a certain sound would carry the swing, then it would be totally superceded by another sound, everything would sound like that for three months and then it would change again. Listen to 'Rapper's Delight' next to RUN-DMC's 'King Of Rock' – there's only five years between them.

Hip hop totally repackaged itself twice during the decade. The first wave – THE SUGARHILL GANG, and those naive beat box sides – had established it as the current state of soul, but didn't know what to do with it. Enter the next generation in the mid-1980s. These seventeen-year-olds had been around rap since junior school and accepted it not as a fad with definite parameters but as something that just existed and could be messed about with to their hearts' content. The Def Jam posse – RUN-DMC, PUBLIC ENEMY, Whodini, LL COOL J, ERIC B & RAKIM – all put a new spin on it. Also rap as political tool came to the fore to a much greater degree, which was great until the end of the decade when Los Angeles started producing its own crews, who changed the beat and the message. 'Gangsta Gangsta' was a 1988 NWA track, the first time the word had been offered up for public consumption.

Of course there was a backlash. Towards the end of the decade, hip hop culture and attitude were very much a part of young black life, but the way the style was going was exclusive to so many. Girls in particular. Rap in the clubs had reshaped social practices and there was a lot of sexual interplay being missed out on. Within hip hop – i.e. conforming to rap values of sound and style – a new genre evolved. Swingbeat took old soul values of sex and singing and constructed tunes and vocal arrangements around beat boxey backing tracks.

It was an instant success, which neatly coincided with a general broadening of outlook of the black experience – respectable people were looking for a valid cultural expression that wasn't gangsta rap, but wasn't soft either. As the 1990s came around, there were all sorts of possibilities open . . .

Paula Abdul

(Born June 19, 1963, Los Angeles, California)
Paula Abdul came to recording through her choreography for such artists as JANET JACKSON, Duran Duran, The Rolling Stones, ZZ Top and Dolly Parton. Which is why the former LA Laker cheerleader's visuals were always pushed as being as important as the music. Fair enough, but is it soul? She may not be the embodiment of soul, and she probably won't cause ARETHA FRANKLIN too many sleepless nights, but she's certainly an aspect of it. In fact Paula Abdul and her dancing cat are as fine an example as you could expect of the pop soul of the late 1980s, and they fulfill exactly the same function as, say, THE SUPREMES did twenty-five years previously. It's all about taking as a base whatever street style rhythms are being kicked 'cross the tracks, sanding down the sharp corners and then masking it in something the mainstream has no trouble coming to grips with while

not submerging the original idea. Soul for people who think they might not like it, but at the same time just about tuff enough not to cause offence elsewhere. (Incidentally, just as the old Motown etiquette classes made sure none of the company's charges were likely to upset white people, the record company at first had great reservations about Paula Abdul's cartoon cat, who was brought to life by a black animator, because it was felt its movements and facial expressions were 'too black'.)

Forever Your Girl; Siren SRN19; 1988

The style this album built itself on was the tightly syncopated electro-synth lines of the day – music that had borrowed bits from hip hop and bits from euro-pop then applied it to disco theory – then it was lightened up into a kind of Jam & Lewis kick groove, but without the bass, and topped off with Paula Abdul's completely colourless vocals. It was pleasant enough. The sort of perky proposition you need to brush your teeth to in the morning. And it spawned some enormous hits: 'Opposites Attract', 'Straight Up', '(It's Just) The Way That You Love Me', 'Cold Hearted' and the title track. But is Paula Abdul soul? Is a Burger King Whopper (albeit with cheese) a meal? Sort of. At the very least it'll hold you until you can get to something that needs a knife and fork.

Adeva

(Born Patricia Daniels, 1960, Paterson, New Jersey)
Former psychology student and teacher of handicapped children, Adeva (it's a pun) began a secondary career as a club singer in the mid-1980s, signing a record deal in 1988. Solid gospel roots – she and her five siblings used to make a large contribution to the local church choir – meant a big voice, confident control, heartfelt expression and an approach to phrasing that was both soothing and startling. It was also one of the few voices of the day genuinely soulful enough to be able to take the rather brittle, deliberately vacuous house style and turn it into something warm and deeply funky. And with haughty good looks, a towering flat-top haircut and a penchant for interesting

leatherwear, Adeva wasn't the sort of faceless chanteuse usually associated with that style.

Adeva!; Cooltempo CCD1719; 1989

The pairing of this large-lunged songstress with producer Paul Simpson, whose skill with a driving house beat had no detrimental effect on his ear for a melody, was a perfect match. Tracks like 'I Thank You', 'Respect', 'Warning' and 'Beautiful Love' all had the urgency of the most frantic club hits, but were rooted far enough into traditional soul structuring to make sense away from the dance floor. It was like a very modern take on an old school method, and worked all the way through the LP – again untypical of the dance genre. She never quite managed such spectacular heights again though.

Atlantic Starr

(Wayne Lewis, vocals/keyboards; David Lewis, vocals/keyboards/guitar; Jonathan Lewis, keyboards/trombone; Joseph Phillips, percussion; Barbara Weathers, vocals)
Atlantic Starr were a wonderful example of what was happening to popular soul music during the late 1970s and into the 1980s. When they first launched in Los Angeles in 1978, there was ten of them, they had a full horn section and they bust a pretty heavyweight sound. Not that it got them very far, as majority soul taste seemed to be softening as post-disco or second-generation Philly-influenced acts began establishing themselves. Atlantic Starr got themselves a new producer, worked hard to get across that MAZE-y, bright soul groove and started having hits.

As we get into this decade, and the recession takes hold, suddenly there's only four of them and a singer. And everybody can play keyboards. But in 1985, they got it right by coming to terms with what was going on around them and, rather than sound like a small band trying to sound like a big band – electronic horn parts and so on – they let the keyboards come into their own. Silky, obviously synthesised soul: instant 1980s and hits until the end of the decade. Atlantic Starr now gig occasionally, Weathers has a solo deal and the brothers work as producers.

*The Very Best Of; A&M CD0000152; 1989

Goes right through the three phases of Atlantic Starr, taking in all the big ones – 'Silver Shadow', 'If Your Heart Isn't In It', 'Always', 'When Love Calls' and 'Circles'. And, unsurprisingly, it's the lusher oldies, rather than the more brittle recent stuff that have stood up better.

Anita Baker

(Born Detroit, Michigan, December 20, 1957)
In the summer of 1986 (a time much better for its weather than its music) the apparently unknown Anita Baker sold out two nights at Hammersmith Odeon with a minimum of fuss or promotion. Enough to make the mainstream media sit up and take notice. Or at least to go so far as checking it out, where they discovered what the old-time soul crowd had known for some time, that Anita Baker was possessed of the kind of mesmerising voice that made tough men want to weep, or at the very least buy a bunch of flowers. She could swoop through the register to give a word as straightforward as 'sweet' three syllables and twice as many octaves. Her control and light jazz approach to phrasing is close to Sarah Vaughan – which isn't nearly as duff as some might think. She would wrap herself round a song and not let go until she'd gently coaxed every last drop of emotion out of it.

'Rave' is not a strong enough word for the next day's reviews. But, even leaving aside her wonderous pipes, this was hardly surprising as what she represented was a much sought-after alternative to most of soul's 1980s. *Rapture* – the LP that had sold the show to us, then sold by the lorry load in the wake of it – was a sheltering port in a sea of all things hipping and hopping. It was a whole album, and meant to be played as such. It was dedicated to romance in a way that was so grown up and genuinely sexy that it could never sound like slush. And it sounded like it owed very little to computers, which is the only way Anita Baker would have it.

A gifted lyricist and composer, she wrote much of the set and was always quick to tell how she had no truck with modern methods, how the only way to create the warmth that brought out the best in her singing was with traditional instrumentation. Both record companies she'd had dealings with fell into line, as there was a good chance she would have turned her back on music. Again.

As a teenager she'd sung backgrounds for various Detroit groups, before being offered the front spot in another local band, Chapter 8. In 1979 the group cut an album, reviews of which singled her out as being their main problem – the concensus was, astonishingly, that Anita Baker couldn't sing. So she didn't try to any more, got a 'proper' job and for three years worked in an office. Indeed it was only after a good deal of persuasion by Chapter 8's guitarist Michael Powell that she stepped up to the mic again. Both agreed that Chapter 8's mild funk hadn't been right for her (the band had a couple of UK jazz/funk scene hits in the mid-1980s), and they should go the sophisticated jazzy route. He was still with the group but wanted to branch out into production, and figured he could make a splash with her voice, while all she wanted to do was get it right this time. In 1983 she put out *The Songstress*, all cool tones and jazzy soul vocals, pretty much a rehearsal for the subtly more polished *Rapture*.

At the time of writing, a new Anita Baker album is imminent. This, however, isn't the eagerly awaited event you might suppose. Wonderful as the *Rapture* groove was, it turned out the singer really only had the one furrow to plough: while the second album was a progression from the first, the third, *Giving You The Best That I've Got*, wasn't quite as honestly titled as it might have been. Nothing prosecutable under the Trades Descriptions Act, just that it was more of the same but not so sensuous. Then *Compositions*, in 1990, sounded like outtakes from the other three, not only was the style sounding overworked but the tunes didn't have it and Ms Baker herself seemed unable to lift them. Maybe with four years to get this one together, she'll have relit a few of *Rapture*'s flames.

Rapture; WEA 75599604445; 1986

One of the top five female soul albums ever made. After the 1960s, that is. By now Powell had completely come to grips with what he was doing in terms of creating a lush, log-fire type ambience that offered up the sort of sex that doesn't involve anything at all messy or sweaty, while the music stays direct, managing to take every little twist and turn and secondary melody it needs to be interesting. And the singing. Good as *The Songstress* was, it's but a throat-clearing exercise compared with this: 'Sweet Love', 'Caught Up In The Rapture', 'You Bring Me Joy', 'Been So Long' . . . Sorry, I've just remembered an urgent appointment at the florist's.

*The Songstress; WEA 7559611162; 1983

The relative failure of this album isn't in any way a reflection of its quality, quite simply it was originally recorded for a small record label and wasn't promoted beyond the specialist market – in the UK you really had to seek it out – and Anita Baker quit the label soon after in search of a better deal. Then when WEA acquired the LP it was really sold to people who already owned *Rapture*, and it sounds a little patchy in comparison. It's still a head and shoulders above the pack though, and makes a good companion to its follow up inasmuch as you can hear the ideas being developed. Also the sinewey 'No More Tears' and 'Will You Be Mine' are enough to make it worth the money.

ALSO RECOMMENDED:

*Giving You The Best That I've Got; Elektra 9608272; 1988

Really for completists only, as apart from the stand-out title track the whole experience is one of déjà vu.

SEE ALSO: Various Artists; *Classic Mellow Volume 3*; Mastercuts CUTSCD17; 1994

Afrika Bambaataa

(Born The Bronx, New York City, 1958)
An enormously influential figure in the development and growth of early hip hop, as more or less the prime mover in what came to be called 'electro'. As writer/producer/performer, often

in collaboration with Arthur Baker, he was responsible not only for such club classics as 'Jazzy Sensation' and 'Zulu Nation Throwdown', but the genre-shaking monster jams 'Planet Rock', 'Looking For The Perfect Beat' and 'Renegades Of Funk'. Tracks that not only turned the Tommy Boy label into the cutting-edge hip hop force it remains today, but advanced the music's cause considerably by shifting it from the strictly turntable mix productions and taking it into the studio. There, to keep the essential quick cut base, he established the sampler as a Hip Hop's Most Wanted, then stretched the technology to get the most from what he'd filched, created additional sounds and stirred in computer-driven instrumentation. He furthered this circuit board bent by using, instead of obvious soul samples, snatches from such unlikely electronic acts as Tangerine Dream and Kraftwerk. It was the direction the by then almost stagnant field had been looking for – the records were just layer upon layer of musical madness, sounds that had never been heard in that area before, held together with the HARDEST beats – and were an instant sensation. So much so that within a year of it coming out it became impossible to keep track of the number of electro singles that had appropriated its bassline.

The media loved it, and loved him too. It was a time when the rap scene was woefully devoid of personalities and musically not much more than tired beats and irksome self-publicising lyrics. Bambaataa provided a tailor-made focus. As an ex-gang member – for two years in the mid-1970s he'd been a big noise with Bronx street warriors The Black Spades – who claimed he'd turned to music and hip hop's impromptu mixing/dancing/rapping 'cutting' contests as a substitute for urban warfare. He'd formed a Music 'gang', The Zulu Nation, with a message of peace, love and racial harmony. And as the New York art set attempted to absorb hip hop culture – rapping, break dancing and graffiti – Bambaataa started moving in circles entirely removed from The South Bronx. It affected what he did too. By the middle of the decade he seems to be more about copy-friendly cod street philosophy than bone-crunching beats and his musical company now includes Johnny Rotten, Boy George, UB40 and Nona Hendryx.

At present none of the early, ground-breaking sides are available, but, in mid-1994, there was something of an electro revival gathering pace. So it may only be a matter of time.

Regina Belle

(Born, New Jersey, 1963)
Regina Belle used to take an almost perverse pleasure in watching people's faces when she announced she played the trombone. It's an instrument more associated with Bozo The Clown than with a small and delicately formed soul diva. She'd taken it up when she was eight, and only because she'd mastered the tuba and couldn't quite get the hang of the baritone sax. She played steel drums and the piano too. In fact she only took up singing, in her teens, because she'd worked out how similar the human voice is to the saxophone and that was the only instrument that she had failed at. Using the kind of lung power it takes to blow a tuba before your tenth birthday, she taught herself to sing: 'I'd study artists like Ella Fitzgerald on television watch where and how they were breathing, then play their records and try to copy it. Usually I'd be gasping for air in the middle of a line, but eventually I got the hang of it. If you can breath correctly you can sing, if you can't you can't.'

Regina Belle could certainly sing. She studied opera and jazz at The Manhattan School Of Music, where, in the height of the disco era, she won a talent contest by singing a version of John Coltrane's 'Alabama' with her own lyrics based on a Martin Luther King speech made following the bombing of a black church in the state. Many of the audience were reaching for their handkerchiefs, and she ended up with a four-year job singing with slushy balladeers The Manhattans. Until *All By Myself*. An absolutely stunning, damn near perfect debut album, that was never repeated: follow up sets veered towards some dreadfully soulless, slushy, heading-for-the-cabaret-circuit material.

*All By Myself; CBS 450998; 1987

The voice training and the trombone blowing are put to marvellous use, as this set (part-produced by Anita Baker's producer Michael Powell) takes a straight soul slant, with sparse, sharp – very mid-1980s – arrangements and embellishes them with all manner of tiny instrumental flourishes in the gaps. It's the sort of backing she needs to drive her voice to heights of tone and control that never fail to impress but don't ever think about getting flashy. It's just a good honest funky soul album, swinging across a range of material in which the seduction numbers 'Show Me The Way', 'So Many Tears' and 'Please Be Mine' are deeply sexy, but its her handling of the shimmering up-tempo numbers, 'You Got The Love' in particular, that set Regina Belle apart.

Bobby Brown

(Born, Roxbury, Massachusetts, February 5, 1969)

In June 1989, it seemed that hardly anybody in the UK other than the specialist music business or the young soul crowd had heard of Bobby Brown. Or, if they had, they were determined not to worry too much about him. As a result, his record signing in a London store caused serious safety problems when 4,000 fans turned up – the inadequate number of police were forced to curtail the event after shutting Oxford Street; demand for tickets to his two Wembley Arena shows was enough to have more than sold out the stadium (four extra concerts were added at the last minute); his own record company were so caught on the hop they didn't have any new products to put out while he was here; and although T-shirts and posters were selling out inside the Arena, there were no bootleg merchandisers outside the gigs as they hadn't thought it worth covering.

Bobby Brown's popularity had crept up on America too. He was a former member of pre-teen pop/soul stars NEW EDITION, and one of the terms of his going solo was that he came back to open for them on their tour. In 1988 he honoured the arrangement, but after half a dozen shows on the marathon US road trip, such was the crowd reaction to Brown that his ten-minute opening spot had been extended to three-quarters of an hour; significant numbers of fans were going home after he'd done his set, not staying for the headliners; and when Brown had to pull out of the New York shows through illness, the audience were offered their money back and a lot of them took it. When this tour was finished he played the same 20,000-seater arenas as a headliner and filled them all over again.

Bobby Brown was special because he was the mass-marketable face of swing beat, the previously underground black soul style that had grown out of a hybrid of traditional soul values and rap technology and culture. It took a hip hop soundtrack of the hard, slapping beats, added computerised riffs and basslines that formed a crisp, cut up melody (but still very definitely a tune), with the frontpersons singing over the top. While it was soft enough to appeal to those a little phased by, or just fed up with, rap's aggression, it retained all the edginess of the style it evolved from. But while performers were very likely to break out a rap, and postured with all the macho attitude they needed to appeal to the 'fellas in the house', it was the first new black style for ten years that allowed scope for a lurrrve man. It also reintroduced performance values. Both points bringing us back to what made Bobby Brown special.

Brown was already a heartthrob from his time in New Edition, a group who'd been schooled by their old-time black manager in every aspect of soul performance. Now that he'd reinvented himself as a grown up, Brown made no secret of his designs on the 'lay-deeez': the entire album was street smart B-Boy love songs or out-and-out smoove; he'd strip to his shorts on stage; and at one show in Georgia he was arrested for public lewdness after his flexi-hipped slow dance with a girl invited up from the audience. Then, as far as showmanship went, Brown's dancing was the stuff of soul legend. He'd taken the swing beat street dances (a lot of jumping about, leg kicking, arm waving and groin pumping (remember, these people are still young) and just slightly adapted them for the stage, so what he presented looked young, energetic and fresh – Bobby Brown's records sold on the strength of his videos, which presented little other than him singing and dancing with expertise and clear enjoyment. Watching the ease with which he took the world (his album *Don't Be Cruel* sold over 10 million copies and won a shelf full of awards) it made me wonder why so few soul acts exploit the pop video to this degree, none of them were particularly expensive productions.

Bobby Brown was also a classic example of how, by the end of the 1980s, the soul scene was turning over so fast that styles could be seen to be evolving on an almost weekly basis – and even artists of his calibre couldn't keep up. When Brown's 1988 album hit big he went on a world tour to maximise its potential revenue. With only a few weeks off, this tour (counting the leg with New Edition) lasted over two years, during which time he was writing a new album while, quite literally, still living the old one. And by the time an artist goes straight into the studio from the tour – because the record company's screaming for the new set – the genre has reinvented itself out of recognition. Brown's follow-up LP, *Bobby Brown*, in early 1992 was one of the most eagerly awaited of modern times. It was also an enormous disappointment. Too much of it sounded like *Don't Be Cruel* – i.e. embarrassingly dated. True, it shifted copies into the seven-figure bracket, but it didn't do anything to stop the man who for a time was the biggest soul star in the world being perceived as Mr Whitney Houston after he married the pop diva in a splashy ceremony two years ago.

Don't Be Cruel; MCA 42185; 1988

A milestone in pop soul. Or in soul in general, inasmuch as it heralded the arrival of a post-disco, ghetto-orientated musical style that was as exciting as it was creative. A kind of street funk for the new generation, sitting alongside rap to restore the breadth of creativity that had been missing for a few years. Even without the videos the upbeat tracks are slamming – 'Don't Be Cruel', 'Every Little Step', 'My Prerogative' and 'I'll Be Good To You' are swing beat classics of tuff, syncopated dance soul. And although a couple of the ballads tip over into sloppy tunes, the ones that don't, 'Roni' and 'Rock Witcha' especially, prove what Bobby Brown was capable of as a New Jack Lurrrve God. All round appeal, and showing producers LA & Babyface and Teddy Riley to be the best in the swing beat business. At that time.

ALSO RECOMMENDED:

Bobby Brown; MCA MCD30001; 1992

Played two years later, there's nothing actually wrong with it – it even shows a maturity as an artist with a broadening of the material – it just wasn't right at the time. However, if you've got *Don't Be Cruel*, you don't really need this.

SEE ALSO: Various Artists; *Classic New Jack Swing Volume 2*; Mastercuts CUTSCD9; 1992

James Brown

➻The 1980s were not a happy time for James Brown. In 1980 he had his radio station W-RDW sold by auction, after a court had levied punitve damages against him over a property case at the end of of the previous year. Then, after five years of watching rereleased or remixed old singles and retro compilation albums vastly outsell his contemporary stuff, he had his best-selling record for fifteen years in 1986, 'Living In America', and he started to win awards for both that and lifetime services to soul.

But in 1988 his problems really began. In April of that year his wife Adrienne filed assault charges against him and requested a legal separation. Shortly after she was arrested for allegedly being in possession of PCP and subsequently dropped the charges against her husband and withdrew her request for separation. In May she was charged with criminal damage of a hotel room, apparently she set fire to some clothes – and PCP was found at the scene. A week later James Brown was arrested following a car chase, and spent a night in jail on charges of assault, possession of PCP and firearms offences. Over the next month Adrienne was arrested a number of times and submitted to drug counselling. In June, James Brown was sentenced to two years' suspended on the drug and guns charges, but by the end of the year, following a series of incidents involving the police – the most spectacular of which was a lengthy car chase – he was sentenced to six years in prison.

James Brown was released in February 1991. It is a mark of how highly he is regarded that the man who for years publicly spoke about what drugs were doing to his people – he had long been a member of Ronald Reagan's President's Council Against Drugs – could survive such a scandal with his integrity intact. However, when it comes to making music, for years James Brown is much more revered for what he stands for and what he's done than what he's doing.

Apart from the single 'Living In America' (see *Star Time* box set, Polydor 8491042), his output over the last fifteen years has been spotty to say the least – he seems completely at odds with modern soul music and has a worryingly M.O.R. taste in producers. Only a couple of original albums from that period remain on catalogue, and even they stretch the maxim that any James Brown is better than none at all.

Hot On The One; Polydor 8478562; 1980

Recorded live in Japan and, compared with earlier live sessions, is distinctly lacklustre.

In The Jungle Groove; Polydor 8296242; 1986

Remixes of acknowledged classics.

Love Over Due; Polydor 5100792; 1991

Recorded immediately after he got out, and although it goes back to his roots and works hard to capture the old, gimmick-free 'Hardest Working Man In Show Business' James Brown, he's clearly got a way to go yet.

Peabo Bryson

(Born Greenville, South Carolina, April 13, 1951)

The 1980s were crammed with balladeers like Peabo Bryson, who you couldn't really complain about because they had, er, nuff respect for soul tradition, but their approach didn't seem to be adding anything to anything. And the whole nature of the twin watersheds of rap and disco wasn't doing their cause a lot of good either: nobody danced slow in clubs any more; and radio stations found this material difficult to programme amid more contemporary sounding material – at Bryson's time, early 1980s, the Quiet Storm radio format, itself a reaction to rap, hadn't really got going yet (Quiet Storm was Black A.O.R., which for obvious reasons didn't want to call itself B.A.O.R.). In the 1980s good looks, a few good tunes and a reasonable voice wasn't enough, you needed something extra, which in Peabo Bryson's case was somebody to help him out. His duets with ROBERTA FLACK, Natalie Cole, D'Atra Hicks and REGINA BELLE are light and breezy, without losing any soul feel as the line swapping creates credible romantic situations.

Unfortunately, the album recorded with Roberta Flack, *Born To Love*, is not available on CD.

All My Love; Capitol CDEST2097; 1889

Features the twosome with Hicks, 'Palm Of Your Hand' and his wonderfully buoyant version of 'Show And Tell'.

Straight From The Heart; Elektra 9603622; 1984

His best-selling album since the one with Flack, and best known for 'If You're Ever In My Arms', the title track and 'I Get Nervous'.

Keni Burke

(Born Chicago Illinois, 1950)
Just as the 1970s had songs like 'Pick Up The Pieces' and 'Who Is He And What Is He To You', so the 1980s had tracks like 'Risin' To The Top', by Keni Burke. Tracks so sublime, so absolutely-can't-ignore-got-to-grab-a-gal-and-dance-NOW, they become deejay legend and consequently the artist assumes far more importance than he perhaps ought. Like AWB and CREATIVE SOURCE, Keni Burke never made anything else anybody ever wanted to play, but he still deserves props for a bassline that loped in at an easy hustle-type pace and just hung there, with a bit of cymbal and drum, laying down a groove for an interminable amount of time. Then the keyboards stroked in an expansive, tinkling chord. Twice. With a big gap in between each, then it's back to that bassline, this time with a flute looming up gently behind it. The main tune doesn't kick into the groove for over a minute and by then he could take you anywhere he wanted. He doesn't though. All that stands between you and that bassline is a lead vocal and the minimum of piano and flute. It's a very special five minutes.

Away from this Keni Burke wasn't completely useless, though. As a bass player he worked with CURTIS MAYFIELD, THE FOUR TOPS, SLY STONE, SMOKEY ROBINSON and BILL WITHERS, while he wrote and produced for, among others, Withers, THE O'JAYS, THE WHISPERS and PEABO BRYSON. He was also once a protégé of George

Harrison, recording on the former Beatle's Dark Horse label, but nothing he did anywhere else could sit in the same room as 'Risin' To The Top'.

The Wonderful World Of Keni Burke; RCA PD90682; 1988

It's got 'Risin' To The Top' so I guess it is sort of wonderful.

SEE ALSO: Various Artists; *Classic Mellow Volume 1*; Mastercuts CUTSCD3; 1991

Cameo

(Larry Blackmon, drums/vocals; Nathan Leftenant, trumpet; Thomas Jenkins, vocals)

One of the most memorable sights of the mid-1980s was that of Larry Blackmon on *Top Of The Pops*: his flat-top haircut soared a good twelve inches above his scalp; his eyes were staring manically; and he was wearing a black body-stocking finished off with an optimistically large red cod piece (by Jean Paul Gaultier, no less). He was singing, or rather braying in his loud nasal tones, 'Word Up', the very pinnacle of the band's stripped down, razor-edged techno funk, and a UK top five hit.

At this point in time, Cameo were one of the few defenders of the notion of lunatic, uncool, un-1980s funk, which is hardly surprising, as the band themselves began life in the previous decade as virtual P-FUNK protégés. They were formed by Blackmon in 1976, while he was studying at the Julliard School Of Music – presumably he had a more orthodox wardrobe back in those days. In the beginning there were thirteen of them (with Blackmon, Leftenant and Jenkins at the core) and they called themselves The New York City Players, changing it to the more manageable and less-chauvinistic Cameo when they signed to Casablanca (Parliament's label) in 1977. Unsurprisingly, GEORGE CLINTON noticed them and took them on tour as support, and from then on Cameo were all about flamboyant stagewear, pumping, big band funk and a string of eight gold albums as they filled the gap left by P-FUNK's collapse at the turn of the decade.

Then suddenly it stopped. *Style*, in 1983, became their first LP not to go gold. Realising large line-up brass-based funk wasn't quite where it was at in the age of electro, Larry Blackmon reacted with the sort of speed and intelligence rarely seen from a declining-fortuned pop band. Cameo reemerged as first a four-piece and then a trio, and using all his 1970s sensibilities of how to set up, maintain and elaborate on a groove, he revamped their sound as the hard-surfaced, computer chip-originated, but comfortingly weird 'She's Strange'. It was a perfect fusion of old attitude and new technique, made even more clever by having a lot of conventional melody, so as not to appear too removed from the mainstream. Indeed, in a four-year string of hits, culminating in the *Word Up* album, Blackmon gradually removed the tunes as he sucked his growing audience in – compared with the brittle, almost unadorned slapping of, say, 'Back And Forth', that first album was a series of lullabies.

But as time moved on, Cameo didn't seem to have enough nous to continue to stay in front. By the end of the 1980s and into the next decade he carried on peddling much the same recipe, but curiously without the earlier slightly bonkers humour, to an ever diminishing audience: *Machismo* barely scraped the UK top hundred, while the one after that, *Real Men Wear Black*, didn't even do that well. Maybe that was where it went wrong, these Real Men should be wearing Red Cod Pieces.

Although the band had a strong funk following, very little by Cameo Mark I was ever released in the UK, as a result there are no CDs on domestic catalogues and only their 1980 effort *Cameosis* is available on the format in the USA.

*The Best Of; Phonogram 56149292; 1990

As the *She's Strange* and *Single Life* albums have been deleted too, this is the only way to establish any sort of later career overview. And, of course, to own some of the funkiest records ever made. Like 'She's Strange' or 'Word Up' or 'Candy' or 'Attack Me With Your Love'.

*Word Up!; Phonogram 8302652; 1986

By now the formula's been worked back to almost pure rhythm, but where these are far from being conventional melodies there's an intricacy of the hooks and a texturing of the beats that gives them a subliminally tuneful feel. A bit like an updating of the James Brown 'Sex Machine' technique. It gives the set a massive impact, as when worked like this the beats can be so much harder without you actually screaming for mercy. It goes all the way through the tracklisting too, so it's far from a case of 'Candy', 'Back And Forth', 'Word Up' and five fillers.

Cherelle

(Born Cheryl Norton, Los Angeles, California)
Cherelle is always going to be more significant for what she became part of rather than for what she actually did, as it is one of her LPs, *Affair*, that plays like a blueprint for what swingbeat was to become as it edged away from rap. While the BOBBY BROWN style is much rawer, more macho, this is the more melodious end of it. Indeed, push any late model New Jack producer to tell you his influences and the chances are he'll say Jam & Lewis, the producers Cherelle had been working with since 1983, but with little effect until her duet with ALEXANDER O'NEAL, 'Saturday Love' in 1985 – and crisp as that was, it was more about him than her. *Affair* was her third album, by then street styles were starting to influence what had become the Jam & Lewis sound – JANET JACKSON's *Control* being a good example – and with this album they took it back, hardened up the beats and left bigger gaps in between to fill with spectacular swooping riffs – the swing that joined the beats. Drawing considerably on the styles laid down by CAMEO and THE GAP BAND, it refused to draw distinction between what was carrying the rhythm and what was responsible for the melody, both did both and it rocked with rap's excitement, soul's flow and the obviously techno sound that was needed to get kids' attention at that time. Whether, for reasons that don't need explaining, they pushed their experiments further with Cherelle than they might've with Janet Jackson is open to debate. Or maybe you can just hear more of what's going on behind her because she's hardly the biggest presence in soul music. But this set is an important milestone along the road to a style that would dominate in years to come. As for Cherelle, the nearest she came to a hit after that

was a remix of 'Saturday Love' and *Affair* is her only album left on catalogue.

*Affair; Tabu 466790; 1988

Unlike the original vinyl, the CD now features her duet with Alexander O'Neal 'Saturday Love'.

George Clinton

➻As the whole P-Funk thing lurched to the end of the 1970s, George Clinton appeared to have spread himself so thin you could see through him. What he'd set up so slyly ten years earlier had become so unfocused it was doing nobody – nor funk in general – any good. So in many ways the cloud of the collapse had a silver lining, because when he signed a solo deal in 1981 instead of half a dozen manifestations of P-Funk there was just the one. Of course as far as musicians were concerned it was simply a case of round up the usual suspects, but it seemed to revitalise both them and Clinton's funky mind of old. Under this new arrangement they started turning out some vintage, multi-levelled funk.

They'd come to terms with modern technology, but in truly cussed P-Funk fashion were using it to sound old time. It was something of a masterstroke of subtlety, as the actual sounds themselves were up to the minute, but what was done with them in terms of tune structure, arrangement and balance was completely traditional – or about as traditional as the Funk Mob could be. So while the hip hop friendly youth would tune in, it wasn't going to put off any established custom. They had their own take on technology too: 'Loopzilla', the first hit from this new arrangement, was so named because the bassline is a tape loop (this was pre-sequencers). Because it was not a straightforward riff (it has a long repeat), it was a loop of such length the engineer had to run it out of the machine, around a pen across the room and around another pen he was holding for the purpose.

What they did, though, entirely sensibly, was to use the studio to take care of the basics thus allowing themselves more creative space. The computer-aligned grooves were just that bit deeper, so more could be ladled on top before it spilled over the sides. We ended up with a series of albums that, for the first time in P-Funk history, gave up the best aspects of both Parliament and Funkadelic. The pumping dancefloor grooves were present and very correct, but they were laced with horns and guitars. It flew. Big phat soul patrol funk, shot through with a soaring rock fluency. And as Reaganomics were making themselves felt by now, there was a degree of sideways social commentary – 'You Shouldn't Nuf Bit Fish' and 'Double Oh Oh'. Ten years in the making and this really was Pure Funk.

By the end of this decade and going into the next, George Clinton and P-Funk were probably the most listened to band in black music – on more chart hits than anybody else, yet by then they didn't have a record deal. Gangsta rap had discovered this music in a big way and there were P-Funk samples, lifts of whole tunes or guest appearances by Clinton on nearly every one of the genre's high-profile releases: DIGITAL UNDERGROUND, Snoop Doggy Dogg, ICE CUBE, ICE T, N.W.A., DR DRE and so on. He told me he was selling more records now than he ever did with Parliament/ Funkadelic, and thanks to new music business rules he should be getting paid more for it too. So while new funk itself may have gone quiet, we can be sure it's only a temporary interruption. 'Normal' service will be resumed as soon as possible.

Strangely, *Computer Games*, the first George Clinton solo album, featuring 'Loopzilla' and 'Atomic Dog', and *Some Of My Best Jokes Are Friends*, with a beautifully textured, wryly funny title track, aren't on UK-released CD. It's easy to find on US import though, and well worth looking for.

You Shouldn't Nuf Bit Fish; Capitol CDP 7963572; 1983

The nine-minute title track is a real old-school Funkadelic jam, à la *Maggotbrain*, dealing with the evils of the world and some serious guitar and synthesiser licks. With Junie Morrison, Mike Hampton, Eddie Hazel and Bernie Worrell on the same record, it couldn't be anything else. But it can rock too, with 'Quickie' and 'Last Dance'. If anything this is the most melodious album from P-Funk Mark II, building three-dimensional arrangements confident enough to play in and out of the grooves rather than as a separate entity.

ALSO RECOMMENDED:

Urban Dance Floor Guerillas; Uncle Jam/CBS Associated Records 39268; 1983

This adds SLY STONE to the Funk Mob, but other than the endlessly funky 'Hydraulic Pump', there's too little cohesion to this project. However, it shouldn't be forgotten for two rather unfortunate reasons: it is Phillipe Wynne's last recording (he died in 1984); and the LP is the only surviving example of Clinton's intended House of Funk record label, Uncle Jam Records.

R&B Skeletons In The Closet; Capitol CDP7962672; 1986

Hasn't got the depth of the others, and is not even redeemed by the presence of 'Do Fries Go With That Shake'.

D. Train

(James Williams)
There were a couple of glorious moments back in the very early 1980s when it looked like electro, disco-influenced dance styles and Soul Music As We Know It, were going to come together to make something that was at once light, modern and funky. D. Train was one such time, as vocalist-turned-multi-instrumentalist James Williams never forgot that his primary objective was to put over a good tune, one he could sing to with gutsy soul tones. Hence, however he built up the clipped, thumping bass riffs and sweepingly syncronised keyboard parts, they were there to *serve* his songs. It was electro funk that should have been built on, but was too loosely associated with the white disco scene for ghetto youth to consider it seriously. Thus D.Train, and a handful of other artists on the Prelude label, exist in isolation.

D.Train – Dancefloor Artists Volume 2; Sequel DGPCD666; 1994

It was never particularly varied, but if you were into this groove, like a lot of the UK soul scene was, then it won't let you down. 'You're The One For Me', 'Keep On', 'Walk On By',

'Don't You Wanna Ride (The D. Train)' are all suitably kicking situations for Williams's urgent vocals.

SEE ALSO: Various Artists; *Prelude Deep Grooves*; Sequel NEDCD263; 1992

De La Soul

(Posdinous; Mace; Truhgoy The Dove. The only names they'll admit to, all from Long Island, New York)
In early 1989, the idea of a rap group that borrowed wholesale from hippie culture was preposterous. Although Schooly D's mind-numbingly psychotic so-called Yo Boy rap seemed to have vanished, gangsta was by then finding its feet, and even if you weren't actually 'packing a gat', as they used to say, unless you were PUBLIC ENEMY you were expected to be a self-obsessed, none-too-bright, borderline psycho. So when De La Soul appeared wearing wooden jewellery and clothes that weren't made of primary-coloured leather, scrawled flowers and peace signs on their album artwork with day-glo markers, sampled Steely Dan and called their philosophy The Daisy Age, they were like some cruel conceptual joke.

The group were the sharp end of a growing movement among young black America to reclaim rap from the increasingly anti-social path it was cutting for itself. The look was 'afro centric' – oversized downmarket clothes, leather and wooden jewellery, dreadlocks in some artistic arrangement and prominent maps of Africa coloured red, black and green. The outlook was similarly culturally aware: like the old-time artists such as CURTIS MAYFIELD or JAMES BROWN or GIL SCOTT-HERON, they wanted to serve their people by advocating black self-help and self-respect. The whole mindset got enormous support from the community too – curiously not every black rap fan thought misogyny and violence particularly attractive. And De La Soul made their apparent nerdiness a major selling point. They used it to send up and subtly subvert rap's standard posturing which served to mask their sneaky aggression as they worked to advance black pride. They were as funny as hell too, which is why they outlasted so many of their gentler counterparts.

But they couldn't outlast the genre's accelerated aging process. In fact their fall from view was indirectly a result of their own cleverness and determination to expand hip hop's boundaries. After their first album, music business rules came into play that all samples had to be cleared *before* the record they were used on came out. The idea was to protect the owner of the tune that was sampled, by removing the situation where if they heard a snatch of their music in somebody else's song it was down to them to track down the sampler and sort out payment. For their second LP they had used so many samples it took ages to clear them all, delaying the release of the album to beyond its natural shelf life. 1991's *De La Soul Is Dead*, damn near lived up to its meant-in-irony title, as it sounded dated the day it was released.

Although not much has been heard from them since, the social legacy they left behind was enormous. The idea of afro-centricity as a fashion statement isn't as dodgy as it seems – it's impossible for no cultural awareness whatsoever to rub off on young brothers and sisters who make a point of wearing maps of Africa. They showed there was a gentle, funny alternative to the gangsta lifestyle, yet it doesn't involve any sort of compromise. And they broadened hip hop's permitted references to expand the perceptions of its listeners. Oh yes, and they made one kicking album too.

Three Feet High And Rising; Big Life DLSCD1; 1989

What made De La Soul's woozy, steam-of-consiousness raps so effective was, while they seemed to picking at random anything they fancied, they were careful not to step outside hip hop's structural guidelines. In other words they weren't rewriting the book of rap to look for a new audience, they were just adding another chapter for the kids that were already there. It was 'real' hip hop, just sprinkled with daisies – and they never lost sight of who their home crowd was, which is why the mainstream never managed to co-opt them. On the same point, how it all appeared too casual was because it wasn't. The twenty-two tracks are short because they know what the attention span is for normal rap records, let alone ones that advance the ideas they're putting forward. The sharp edges are only just taken off, so there's still some bite there, and melodies as now-you-hear-'em-now-you-don't as these don't happen by accident. Although the songs may sport such artfully bonkers titles as 'Potholes In My Lawn', 'Magic Number', 'Me Myself And I', 'Eye Know' and 'D.A.I.S.Y. Age', there's none of them loafing on the job.

Dennis Edwards

(Born Birmingham, Alabama, February 3, 1943)
Dennis Edwards' career has not been dull. Originally a gospel singer, he turned to jazz (Dennis Edwards & The Firebirds) before coming to Motown to lead The Contours. Shortly after that, he joined THE TEMPTATIONS not once but three times – he replaced David Ruffin in 1969 and was lead singer during the golden days with Norman Whitfield; he left in 1977, but returned two years later, only to have it away again in 1979. He was back agan in 1987, after his solo career once again didn't quite happen, but didn't stay long, opting instead to work with David Ruffin and Eddie Kendricks as some kind of alternative Temptations.

But the big Dennis Edwards mystery – apart from why the Temps kept letting him back in – was how somebody who could make a just-up-from-slow jam as completely seductively brilliant as 'Don't Look Any Further' not only be unable to launch a career, but also be unable to have a hit. Even with that song.

SEE: Various Artists; *Classic Mellow Volume 2*, Mastercuts CUTSCD8; 1992

Eric B & Rakim

(Born Eric Barrier & William Griffin, New York City)
Much was made of jazz rap during the first couple of years of the 1990s, but if any of that was traced backwards, before it hit 'Bird' and 'Dizz' and so on, it would have to get through Eric B & Rakim. Way up front in the second wave of rap – mid-1980s, post-Sugarhill, when hip hop figured out it had a lifespan and

began to explore ways to expand – deejay Eric B and rapper Rakim were pure jazz rap in the way they constructed their material. Among the most musical of their generation, they built up from smokey drum and basslines (many filched from James Brown so as to score points for strength and directness), then, once that was phat enough, threaded the riffs through. Some quite unexpected instrumentation would recede and come forward, sometimes take bizarre solos, often two lead lines would play off each other, and every so often the music would come together in weirdly beautiful crescendos. Beat box jazz? If not, then it's something very close.

And all the while, like Miles's horn, Rakim's deep brooding voice prowls the soundscape, narrating some ghetto tale of love or life, celebrating Eric B's dexterity or being menacing just for the sake of it. While they meant a great deal to their home crowd – as they had clearly worked hard to advance dark black music but still keep the line from the past intact – they were never too glamorous or overly accessible and thus tended to get passed over by the mainstream. News at the moment is that they've split up, which would be an enormous loss.

Don't Sweat The Technique; MCA MCD10594; 1992

The most recent album – oddly, the two in the middle are off catalogue – and by now they've matured enormously and are presenting one of hip hop's most grown up albums. That doesn't mean it's X-rated, just that the music and words make you think. The jazzy build ups are confident enough to put odd little melodic off-shoots in and to go even deeper into the mix to increase the density. This time actual jazz samples are blatantly spliced in with the funk, taking this brew to the limits – the title track is a vibrant showcase of what can be achieved. The range is big, too, from the cold terror of 'Pass The Hand Grenade' and 'The Punisher' to ghetto politics on 'What's Going On' and the light, almost fun, 'Keep The Beat'.

Paid In Full; 4th & Broadway IMCD9; 1987

Their first LP, and while the technique is far from fully formed, it's such a dangerously cool rap set that you know you will see these two again.

Aretha Franklin

➻When the 1980s opened with Aretha Franklin playing a waitress in *The Blues Brothers* (a low-down funky gospel belting waitress, naturally), and signing a new record deal, things looked on the up. Sure enough, she embarked on a release schedule that looked almost workaholic compared with the previous five years and the purists flung their hands in the air in horror. The Queen Of Soul was doing disco. Aretha Franklin was duetting with upstart pop stars. Somebody was making her shoot the kind of energetic videos women of her age and size shouldn't even think about.

What she was also doing was having a string of hits and winning more awards than you could shake a stick at. True, 'Freeway Of Love' was a long way removed from 'Respect' but this was the 1980s, not the 1960s. *Somebody* was going to sing that song, and what Aretha Franklin bought to it lifted an ordinary piece of post-disco soul into another world. It was no different from much of what she had been doing twenty years ago, when she elevated more than a few ordinary pieces of pre-funk soul to celestial heights – imagine most of her old hits sung by, say, Diana Ross or Natalie Cole. The album that 'Freeway' came from was her first million-seller too, and it seemed strange that people who called themselves fans should make such a fuss about the woman finally getting paid. And, although Aretha Franklin has made a few questionable career decisions in the past, it's been equally true that nobody's made her do anything she doesn't want to for too long.

For ten years she was seldom out of the charts, tearing up songs and showing artists half her age what time of day it was. Indeed, so successful was this Aretha Franklin rebirth that her gospel-tinged light funk almost became a soul sub-section by itself. Then to move into the next decade, and to commemorate the recent death of her father – he'd been in a coma since being shot during a civil rights campaign in 1985 – she cut the pure gospel album *One Lord, One Faith, One Baptism*. Almost predictably, it won the Best Gospel Performance category at that year's Grammy Awards. Aretha Franklin continues to confound her more orthodox fans as she goes on recording 'lightweight pop songs' entirely enjoyably and rather successfully.

*Who's Zooming Who?; Arista 259053; 1985

The album that marked her commercial return to form, but was thankfully removed from the lacklustre dance stuff she had been doing. Produced with considerable understanding – of both Aretha Franklin and the genre – by Michale Narada Walden, it contains 'Freeway', 'Another Night', 'Sisters Are Doin' It For Themselves' and the title track, while featuring contributions from Carlos Santana, Clarence Clemmons and Annie Lennox, had genuine pop appeal without making too many compromises.

*One Lord, One Faith, One Baptism; Arista 258715; 1987

The gospel album of the decade. Recorded live at her father's church and, unsurprisingly, she seems to be putting more into this than the chart-oriented material.

ALSO RECOMMENDED:

*Jump To It; Arista 259060; 1982

Produced by LUTHER VANDROSS, and as well as the title track it features the undeniably funky 'This Is For Real' and '(It's Just) Your Love'.

*What You See Is What You Sweat; Arista 261724; 1991

Worth it, just, for her cool slinky cover of SLY STONE's 'Everyday People'.

The Gap Band

(Ronald Wilson; Charlie Wilson; Robert Wilson – all multi-instrumentalists, born in Tulsa, Oklahoma)
There was a time, about twelve years ago, when if The Gap Band's 'Oops Upside Your Head' was played in your average suburban disco, Costa Del Sol night spot or office Christmas party, people would sit on the floor in long lines and pretend to be rowing, while they joined in the choruses. It was a fascinating, baffling sight and got The Gap Band a dreadful name among anybody who had the remotest bit of cool.

Which was a little unfair – they didn't know how drunken

Brits were going to react to what was an honest 1980s funk record. Which is what they'd been offering since they'd signed a record deal in 1979, having toured for six years. The band was named in honour of the three main streets in Tulsa: Greenwood, Archer and Pine.

The Gap Band were a kind of low-rent CAMEO, heavily P-FUNK influenced and bringing 1970s values to the technology of the next decade. Their funk was never as determinedly different as Cameo's, which put them right into the more populist end of things, which shouldn't be sniffed at as it kept solid values alive through the disco doldrums. Even though their subsequent reliance on the kind of uncomplicated rhythm patterns featured in 'Oops' got a little tiresome, they were capable of flashes of absolute genius. Or one flash, anyway, in 1983. It was down-tempo smoove, easy-rocking on a big kick drum beat and an impossibly slow, springily simple bassline, and was 'Outstanding' by name and by nature. We had it played as the first song at our wedding reception, which, given the choice, was quite a big deal. Why they didn't do more of this sort of thing is beyond me, but they saw out the decade still on that 'Oops Upside' beat but to progressively fewer takers.

The Best Of The Gap Band; Mercury 824343; 1987

With the exception of 'Humpin'', the gang's all here – 'Burn Rubber On Me', 'You Dropped A Bomb On Me', 'Outstanding', 'Party Lights', 'Early In The Morning' and, brace yourselves, 'Oops Upside Your Head'. No, you won't get me sitting on the floor.

SEE ALSO: Various Artists; *Classic Mellow Volume 1*; Mastercuts CUTSCD3; 1991

Marvin Gaye

➤➤It would have been nice if Marvin Gaye's 1980s had never happened. That way, at worst we could have remembered him for how and what he'd been in the 1960s and 1970s, or, at best, he'd still be alive. I saw him on stage in London in 1980, and in spite of a wonderful, aching performance he didn't look either well or happy. The next year he'd quit Motown, who, without his permission, put out the *In Our Life* album, a statement of monstrous, drug-addled paranoia. More or less destitute he decamped first to London and the twenty-four-hour party people, then Ostend where he was rehabilitated pretty much as an act of charity by a Belgian hotel owner, small-time concert promoter and long-time fan Freddy Cousaert.

Off drugs, healthy and thinking straight, Gaye was able to negotiate a new deal with CBS, and in 1982 recorded *Midnight Love* in a Belgian studio. It sold over a million in a matter of days, went top ten on both sides of the Atlantic, the singer returned to America – and the problems began again. By the end of 1983, within a year of the album's release and after a US tour that was neither a critical nor commercial success, Gaye was back into drugs, big time, and holed up in his parents' house in the Crenshaw district of Los Angeles. Still technically bankrupt, dangerously freebased most of the time, out of condition, a psychological basket case – relatives reported suicide threats, and not bothering to get dressed most days – he'd sit on the wall wearing his pyjamas and chatting to passers by. He was also constantly fighting with his father. On April 1, 1984, his father shot him dead. His funeral service, four days later, was attended by Berry Gordy, Harvey Fuqua, Quincy Jones, Norman Whitfield and the Holland brothers. SMOKEY ROBINSON read the 23rd Psalm and STEVIE WONDER sang 'Lighting Up The Candle'.

Midnight Love; Sony 461072; 1982

It was always supposed to be a continuation of the *Let's Get It On*, *I Want You* series of very adult sensuality. But while the themes were there – 'Sexual Healing', 'Savage In The Sack', 'Sanctified Lady', 'Masochistic Beauty' . . . you get the drift – and the musical ideas were coming together nicely, it sounds unfinished compared with the others. Maybe it's the technology pushed to the forefront as some sort of 1980s-ish statement, but the brittle nature of much of the album's sounds sits uncomfortably with its sentiments. Although the songs are up to par with anything on *I Want You*, too often you find yourself waiting for the big swell of music to sweep you off, and it doesn't come. I wonder had it been released under different circumstances – a new record company working hard to play up the return of the lurrrve man – and not become his last complete studio album, how seriously would we be taking it ten years later.

Johnny Gill

(Born Washington DC, 1965)

Johnny Gill, BOBBY BROWN's replacement in NEW EDITION, is now a minor league swingbeat star at Motown, and an embodiment of exactly how far things had changed at that company by 1989. New Edition were the group that Motown spent so long looking for – a quintet of pin-uppable, obviously street-smart adolecents – but they had had their success elsewhere. When the members outgrew the group's confines they split quickly and efficiently, with each faction virtually assured a following of fans that had got older as they had got older. At which point Motown signed Gill and brought in big-name guest producers LA & Babyface and Jam & Lewis to provide him with a hit album. This broke with Motown's tradition not only of nurturing their own acts rather than signing established names, but also of not buying in flavour-of-the-month production teams, as there used to be so little their staff weren't capable of. While the album was the success it deserved to be, that certainly wasn't down to anything special on behalf of Motown, who had functioned in the whole matter as just another record company.

Johnny Gill; Motown 530025; 1990

It's efficient, if comparatively not too inspired swing – by this time the style was being made by the people who'd been buying it a year ago and they were starting to bend all sorts of rules. The hit 'Rub You The Right Way' is something of a genre classic, though, and 'Wrap My Body Tight' and 'My My My' aren't too far behind.

SEE ALSO: Various Artists; *Classic New Jack Swing Volume 2*; Mastercuts CUTSCD9; 1992

Grandmaster Flash

(Born Joseph Sadler, The Bronx, New York City, January 1, 1958)
'Grandmaster, cut faster/Grandmaster, cut faster . . .' This was
something of an all-purpose catchphrase for a few months, the
most popular usage after a deft piece of driving, as encourage-
ment to those nippy Sunday-morning league wingers, or in
acknowledgement of a particularly audacious pass. To be taken
this way was recognition of a record's impact, and whatever we
may have thought of its musical merits up next to, say, The
O'Jays' 'I Love Music', Grandmaster Flash's 'Adventures On
The Wheels Of Steel' was one of the ten most important rap
records ever. Not that anybody realised that back then. Most
people simply thought the whole notion of wrecking other
records to make your own disjointed, stuttering, technically
illogical cut-fest was so gloriously pointless it restored a healthy
measure of funky-in-your-face stupidity.

Whether or not Flash was the first turntable deejay isn't the
point. What mattered was he was the first one anybody had
ever heard of, and when his single 'Freedom' hit big in New
York in 1980 it put hip hop's public image back on the track it
had been following underground for a few years. It might have
gone wrong at the end of the 1979, when THE SUGARHILL GANG
went international and toured 'Rappers Delight', kicking it on
stage *with a band*. While those in the know knew this had little to
do with true D.I.Y. spirit of rap, your more casual observer
assumed it was how hip hop was done – you got a group to play
your breaks. And why not? It's how other records were made.
It's even how all the early Sugarhill records were produced as
the label had a straight house band to play in the studio.

If Flash, who'd been developing his quick mix at parties and
clubs since about 1978, hadn't so eloquently stated the case for
the turntable as the street-corner synthesiser, the chances are that
this is the route rap would have taken. If for no other reason than
it would have made much better sense to mainstream record
company executives – what has kept rap more or less exclusive
for so long is, as with street funk, it takes a special mentality to
want to do something so apparently irrelevant to anything other
than itself. That said, though, it was also Grandmaster Flash who
first advanced the cause of rap as a political medium. In 1982, he

dropped the first high-profile rap lyric to feature subject matter other than cars, girls and 'hip hip hoppy to the beat y'all', when 'The Message' put over a social comment as stark as its scratched mixed soundscape. So, in theory, without Grandmaster Flash, there wouldn't have been a Terminator X and there might not have been a Chuck and Flav either.

SEE: Various Artists; *To The Beat Y'All – The Sugarhill Story Old School Rap*; Sequel NXTCD 217; 1992

Hammer

(Born Stanley Kirk Burrell, Oakland, California, March 30, 1962) As the 1980s became the 1990s, MC Hammer, as he was known then, became the epitome of rap's relationship with the mainstream. Of what either side wanted from each other: Hammer was looking for massive stardom and was prepared to do what it took to get it; the mainstream wanted to shake its butt with some rap, but didn't want the social or political posing that was around at this point. Following in BOBBY BROWN's footsteps he recognised the need for the clearly defined image, the value of a good video, for running a tight ship along standard music business lines – so executives could deal with you and trust you – and how the balance must be struck between presenting a taste of the ghetto and something unthreatening enough to get on MTV and into middle America's living rooms. And when he got all of this together on and around his second LP, *Please Hammer Don't Hurt 'Em*, it topped the US charts for nearly six months, he was sponsored by Pepsi and British Knight, Los Angeles declared December 7 'MC Hammer Day', he got his own TV cartoon series – *The Adventures Of Hammer Man* – while Taco Bell signed him up for TV commercials. On the other side of the account, the album sold over 8 million, and as the videos were on heavy rotation on TV, and the world tour had sold out arenas everywhere, kids of all colours could feel that little bit hipper as, with varying degrees of proficiency, they did the Running Man and the Hammer, his two trademark dances. And their little brothers and sisters played with their Mattel Toys Hammer dolls.

It's been said, frequently, that Hammer owes far more to per-spiration than inspiration. That his whole approach was cyni-cally conceived with records that relied on riffs from proven songs (RICK JAMES' 'Super Freak', Queen's 'Another One Bites The Dust', PARLIAMENT's 'Tear The Roof Off The Sucker', JAMES BROWN's 'Superbad' to name but four) and stage shows more about exploiting traditional showbiz flash than anything as remotely modern as hip hop. But all he wanted to do, he said, was entertain people. That he wasn't steeped in hip hop's ways was unsurprising, his background was very different. Originally a batboy (he looked after the players' kits) for pro baseball team the Oakland As – they gave him the nickname Little Hammer because he looked like one of their home run stars Henry 'Hammering Hank' Aaron – he dropped out of col-lege and abandoned hopes of becoming a professional baseball player to spend three years in the navy.

On getting out at twenty-six years old, almost pensionable in rap terms, he formed a religious rap duo The Holy Ghost Boys and marketed their only single himself, using his car as the sales and distribution facilities. In 1988, with an investment of $10,000 from two Oakland players, in return for 10 per cent of his earnings, he cuts an album as MC Hammer, *Feel My Power*. It's enough to get him signed to Capitol who have him add four more tracks to the record, rename it *Let's Get Started* and by the middle of 1989 it's in the US top forty and on its way to selling 1.5 million. Just like Hammer was on his way to next year's *Please Hammer Don't Hurt 'Em*.

Hammer's rise might have been fast, but his fall left it stand-ing. Suddenly, as if a memo had gone round, Hammer couldn't get arrested. While he must have kept a team of carpenters busy putting up shelves for the awards he was picking up during 1991, his single 'Here Comes The Hammer' didn't make the top fifty, then the follow up album, *Too Legit To Quit* flopped resoundingly the next year. And Hammer was still providing a textbook example of what can happen when a specialist style meets the mainstream.

Hammer had responded to his pop success by going pop. Dropping the 'MC' was a big mistake (one not unnoticed in the black community) as it was an obvious rap reference. He pre-sented himself in interviews as aiming to transcend rap culture or racial politics. His shows became more musical and the album that went wrong used no samples and had obvious aspirations towards straight soul. What he'd failed to understand was that kids, black and white, were buying him as a black rapper, not a colourless pop star – there were loads of them about – and when that was what he tried to become they lost interest. Also, as this snubbing of the hip hop world gained pace, rappers began slagging Hammer off at every opportunity, which served to speed up the exodus from the Hammer fan club, as nobody dipping a toe into anything wants to be constantly reminded, by that constituency, that what they've just spent money on is rubbish.

In short, Hammer forgot his place, in relation to his audience. Which is why Snoop Doggy Dogg sells a lot more records in the mainstream than he does. Maybe he didn't see it coming because he lacked the fundamental understanding of the genre he was in, and hit a situation he couldn't get out of by working harder.

*Please Hammer Don't Hurt 'Em; Capitol CDEST2120; 1990

The most immediate thing that hits you, when playing this record in 1994, is how could anybody have mistaken Hammer for a rapper? This set has more music and melody than Bobby Brown's did, yet the latter was hailed as the return of the soul man. That said, it's pretty good pop/soul with an attitude. 'U Can't Touch This', 'Yo! Sweetness', 'Black Is Black', 'Work This' are enough dumb fun to be able to ignore 'Have You Seen Her'. While buried deep within is 'On Your Face' (!) a kicking taste of swingbeat rap, complete with some wild bass doo-wops and a sweet-easy action beat. It was a style about to break big, had Hammer seen that coming and jumped on it he might still be kicking it today.

ALSO RECOMMENDED:

*Let's Get Started; Capitol CDP790924; 1988

A shrewder mix of music and beats than people have given it credit for, too unformed to work entirely, but featuring more fresh ideas than what came later.

Freddie Jackson

(Born Harlem, New York, October 2, 1956)
Another 1980s lurrrve man who seemed nothing particularly special, but could bring most people to their knees when he hit his stride. He'd been around for a while before he launched his own career, having been Mystic Merlin's lead vocalist and after that singing back up for Evelyn King and Melba Moore, not cutting a solo set until he was nearly thirty in 1985. It was worth waiting for though. *Rock Me Tonight* is one of the all-time champion smooch sets, and it earned this mild-mannered former bank clerk an enormous and loyal following, particularly in the UK. He never quite hit this height again, as while future albums showed flashes of what he could do if all the conditions were right, they never quite pulled it off. Good as he was, especially live, like so many of his peers at the time he couldn't turn duff material into anything special and he suffered badly when he got unsympathetic production.

Fred Fact: Freddie Jackson began singing in public in the same church where Nick ASHFORD met Valerie SIMPSON.

*Rock Me Tonight; Captiol CZ364; 1985

It seems remarkable that anybody who could turn this set out couldn't do it again. As well as the title track, he oozes his way round the lush orchestrations of 'You Are My Lady', 'He'll Never Love You Like I Do', 'Good Morning Heartache' and 'I Just Wanna Say I Love You', proving he was capable of it more than once. OK, so it's not AL GREEN, but you'd think he had enough going for him to keep himself out of the cabaret clubs he now makes his living in.

SEE ALSO: Various Artists; *Classic Mellow Volume 3*; Mastercuts CUTSCD17; 1994

Janet Jackson

(Born Gary, Indiana, May 16, 1966)
It can't be easy being a Jackson. And being the youngest Jackson is probably hardest of all – unless, of course, you're Jermaine –

but Janet's held up very well. It's hardly likely she's had any time to go off the rails. Since first stepping on stage with her brothers at the age of seven, she's had a career as a child TV star – for five years from 1977 she had regular roles in US TV series *Good Times*, *Diff'rent Strokes*, *Fame* and *A New Kind Of Family*; she's had a recording contract since she was sixteen, when she was set up as a kind of sepia Tiffany, chubby and toothsome and making promotional appearances in high schools; then, just turned eighteen, she eloped and got married, to youthful Motown recording artist El DeBarge, only to slink home a few months later and have the marriage annulled. But, most spectacularly, in 1986 her third album, *Control*, found her transformed from a well-nourished, squeaky teenager into a svelte (well, almost) young vamp with an album of slamming eighties funk tracks, a street dance presentation that bristled with 'attitude' and, if lyrics and video costumes are to be taken seriously, a casual interest in domination.

It seemed that somebody at her record company had remembered she was black and stopped trying to force her into a shiny pop bracket – previously she'd duetted with Cliff Richard and had an album produced by Giorgio Moroder. She'd been put with producers Jam & Lewis, who didn't seem intimidated by the fact she was a Jackson and made her do it their way. Which was The Minneapolis Sound, a kicking synthesised, 1980s funk that was the very earliest roots of New Jack Swing. It worked better than anyone could have intended it to, having an effect way beyond the phenomenal sales figures for and awards won by the album.

Although in the first videos it looked as if all that 'Nasty Girl' stuff was drawing deep on her experience as an actress, there's no doubt the whole experience was the making of Janet Jackson inasmuch as she grew up. It probably helped having to spend so much time in Minneapolis, away from the family, and as time went on it became clear that she was by far the most rational of the famous Jacksons, presenting herself to the world as a proper person as well as a mature artist. OK, so it looks like she's got herself a face out the same catalogue Michael subscribes to. So perhaps all that *Rhythm Nation 1814* stuff was a bit flakey. And maybe the next album passed off some frightful adolescent poetry as lyrics. But she was responsible for taking Jimmy Jam and Terry Lewis to see SOUNDS OF BLACKNESS and talked the producers into working with them. And she's not awful in that John Singleton film *Poetic Justice* – it's the story that's confused. Anyway, no matter what her acting ability is, she wouldn't even have been eligible for the film, let alone wanted to do it, if she was her brother – the role was that of a black person.

*Control; A&M CDMID178; 1986

Jam & Lewis's finest hour, as if they wanted to make sure they didn't get lost behind the Jackson name and stepped up their big swing 'n' slap productions to previously undreamed of levels. Just as well, the set was so high profile and now they were advertising themselves with all the stops pulled out. But it wasn't all down to them, while Jackson can convincingly act the snarling she-monster on video, there's times on the record when she sounds just vulnerable enough to give the whole thing a touch of intrigue. For both content and presentation – MTV-friendly PAULA ABDUL-choreographed videos – *Control* is a classic 1980s soul album.

ALSO RECOMMENDED:

*Control – The Remixes; A&M CDMID149; 1987

Another very 1980s trait, a remix LP. This one, though, is worth it as some of the reworked tracks assume frightening proportions.

*Janet; Virgin CDV2720; 1993

It has its crisper moments – 'That's The Way Love Goes', 'New Agenda' and 'You Want This' – but it shows Jam & Lewis's production ideas starting to get left behind.

Michael Jackson

➡Michael Jackson stopped being really interesting musically when *Thriller* took off on its stellar sales curve. He ceased to have a great deal of relevance to soul music the day he decided to turn himself white. We discussed *Off The Wall* in the last section, and with that and the good-looking young man who made it so exciting in mind, the only thing to say is 'it's a shame' and remind you of what he's put out over the last decade or so.

Thriller; Epic 859330; 1982

The remarkable thing about this album was how roundly critics panned it at the time of release. The reason being that it's a brilliant set of singles, but doesn't stand playing all the way through. I for one couldn't be doing with it when I first played it through, then loved every one of those killer pop/soul singles. (No, of course that doesn't include 'The Girl Is Mine'.) Even twelve years later it's difficult to find somebody who can play it all the way through.

Bad; Epic 4502902; 1987

A genuine attempt to create an album this time, but the songs aren't as strong, as they lose focus by attempting to please too many styles.

Dangerous; Epic 4658022; 1991

Shot itself in the foot by trying too hard to be hip – Teddy Riley produced a lot of it – but taking so long about it the grooves were out of date about eighteen months before it was released. And it should never have been a double album. Did quality control leave with Quincy Jones?

Howard Johnson

(Born Miami, Florida, 1957)
A singer and percussionist, this man always seemed more comfortable as somebody else's sidekick: his solo albums were usually remembered for those who produced them (Jam & Lewis, Kashif, The System); and he finished up the 1980s as first half of Howard Johnson & Donna Allen, then teamed up with Regis Branson as Johnson & Branson. However in 1982 came Johnson's 'So Fine', originally a B-side but such a hypnotically-hooked, slow hustle, modern-day R&B silk cut it became a dance floor classic as soon as deejays found it. An absolutely unavoidable

milestone of a tune, as, in the teeth of advancing rap and electro and at the fag end of street funk, it reintroduced such a novel concept as dancing with girls – you know, actually *touching* them. Although it was all Johnson ever did that anybody was in any way interested in, its success on both sides of the Atlantic seemed to precipitate an almost anachronistic return to earthy, old soul values that ran parallel to hip hop for a number of years.

SEE: **Various Artists;** *Classic '80s Groove Mastercuts Volume 1*; Mastercuts CUTS15; 1993.

Oran 'Juice' Jones

(Born 1962, Houston, Texas)
Brought up in Harlem and coming to the Def Jam label's attention in 1985, Jones was a another facet of Russell Simmon's Campaign For Real Soul Music (see TASHAN – who used to sing background vocals for Jones). The idea was to adhere almost entirely faithfully to old-school soul benchmarks of tune and song structures, but to put the tunes together in a very modern environment. It resulted in the soaring presentation of rhythm tracks enhanced to the almost surreal status of lead instrumentation among a full orchestra that was very obviously synthesised. Close to a 1980s interpretation of the classic BARRY WHITE style and all very hip hop. Necessarily so too, as at that time Jam & Lewis were ruling the black airwaves and your stuff wouldn't get on the radio unless your drums were LARGE. Jones's street appeal went still further with a belligerent approach to drugs, women and firearms that preceded gangsta by five years and lent a malevolent edge to his music and vocals that turned what should have been weepy love songs into hairy-chested sagas of confrontation.

*To Be Immortal; OBR4660042; 1989

As if to state his gangster of the groove case, Jones stares menacingly off the back cover, standing in what looks like a graveyard, wearing a very sharp suit. But it would be a brave man that would mess with the record's steamroller rhythms and swaggering hooklines, as Jones's genuinely startling vocal approach injects edginess and overbearing in roughly equal amounts. As he sweeps through his favourite subjects – his money, his women, his drugs, his self – with an aggression that makes ALEXANDER O'NEAL come over like Mavis Riley, it's a tribute to his consummate skill that this musical and verbal beating up stays buoyant enough to make it altogether pleasurable.

Kool & The Gang

➡By 1978 Kool & The Gang's spicy jazzed-up street funk had become an anachronism, totally eclipsed by disco: their own efforts in this area were so half-hearted that even their most devoted fans had difficulty getting behind them. Thus that year's lamentable LP *The Force* was their lowest seller in six years. A change of direction came about almost by chance, as Robert 'Kool' Bell met, in both cases by accident and in the space of a few months, first vocalist James 'J.T.' Taylor and then producer/keyboardist Eumir Deodato. For the first time with a singer, the group's whole sound balance changed from the complex horn leads to a far more straightforward and widely accessible style. There was frontman focal point, instead of a line of guys hiding behind their instruments. They even bought a few sets of matching pastel-coloured suits to celebrate this new beginning. Ballads became a possibility. And Deodato's production throttled back their funk from snarling to purring. Perfect, apparently, for a Travolta-inspired generation who liked the idea of soul music but weren't too keen on anything that might leave them behind.

The first fruits of this collaboration appeared in 1979. *Ladies Night* was the band's first ever platinum album; it yielded three hit singles – one of them the million-selling title track; and was the first showing of nine years uninterrupted pop chart success in the UK. It also marked the surrender of a set of once almost frighteningly impeccable funk credentials.

*Kool & The Gang Celebrate – The Best Of 1979–1987

The Taylor Years – the singer went solo at the start of 1988, not, as it turned out, a spectacularly successful move for either party. Although it is some of the albums from this period that are available in their entirety on CD, this is also the time they stopped making albums as a fifty-minute musical exercise, in favour of collections of singles. Thus the later LPs tend to be two or three hits plus a bunch of fillers, so the best way to approach the *avec-vocals* Kool & The Gang is in this form. All the usual suspects are present (if not completely correct): 'Ladies Night', 'Cherish', 'Ooh La La La (Let's Go Dancing)', 'Get Down On It', 'Celebration' (the official song played to welcome home the US hostages held in Iran), 'Steppin' Out', 'Joanna', etc, etc.

ALSO RECOMMENDED:

*Ladies Night; De-Lite 822537; 1979

Not just because it's got three hits on it instead of the regulation two you get on later LPs, but because it was their first recordings as their new selves and some of the old Kool is still shining through. Enough to make the set bearable.

L.L. Cool J.

(Born James Smith, Queens, New York, 1968)
During hip hop's second coming, the sharper operators knew the only way to survive was to have a personality. Although in the mid-1980s the outside world still liked to palm the music off as being 'all the same', it had grown so fast within the first half of the decade that it was now subject to all the same rules rock, pop or soul was – it's not enough just to be a rapper any more, you've got to have something going on top of that. L.L. Cool J. did, he had a personality and charm that subtly redrew a few of raps constraints, and an intelligence and understanding of the music that means he's still kicking it today ten years later.

Most of it was down to confidence. Not just the crotch-grabbing macho posturing that was by now part of rap, but a real cool that allowed him to open his shows by strolling on stage with an enormous ghetto blaster radio, set it down and stand with one foot up on it gazing out at the crowd. Then he'd undercut it by sniggering, for he knew exactly how ridiculous this was. He'd lace his rhymes with a self-deprecating humour and a keen sense of the ludicrous. He'd experiment with the backing tracks by mixing it up with rock and rock 'n' roll. He wrote and recorded the first rap ballad 'I Need Love', quite an admission for a bad young B-Boy to make. And in recognition of the hordes of teenage girl who flocked to his shows – he was rap's first pin up, with L.L. Cool J. standing for The Ladies Love Cool James – he dressed his stage set up as a school playground. This was at the time of Schooly D, ultra-violent Yo Boy rap and riots at gigs in America – Cool J. was determined to present a fun alternative so that regular kids would want to come to rap shows. He knew that unless it broadened its fan base and spread out stylistically it would die. That his raps were still hard, and he was successful at it, did a lot to open up rap's outlook.

He'd been instrumental in setting up rap's second stage too. From the age of ten he'd been recording 'scratch' mixed tapes on his grandmother's stereo, and rapping over the top of them. When he turned twelve he began sending them to radio stations and record companies. Four years later, Cool J. was still at school, but getting considerably more proficient on the mic – he sent a tape to Rick Rubin who together with Russell Simmons was setting up the new rap label Def Jam. That was in 1984, and his demo 'I Need A Beat' became the first twelve-inch single on the label that was to dominate East Coast hip hop for the rest of the decade. A year later, when Def Jam had secured a distribution deal with CBS (another first), his *Radio* album was the company's first LP. And as the label was determined to break rap beyond the ghetto by developing it musically as far as possible (see RUN-DMC) and presenting a media-friendly face L.L. Cool J., articulate, quick-witted, good looking and funny, was exactly right as a spokesman.

Still recording, and at twenty-six one of rap's elder statesmen, Cool J. is currently establishing himself as a screen actor, having shown a considerable talent for gentle comedy in *Toys* and *The Hard Way*.

Mama Said Knock You Out; Def Jam 4673152; 1990

One of the most devastatingly effective rap albums, as much for what it sets out to do – and achieves – than for mere power of beat. Nearly ten years ago Cool J. said he wanted to expand rap's horizons, this album does that in spades by crafting infectiously melodious tracks that don't slacken up in delivering the beats. The snatches of tunes have been cut to fit inside the beats, not the other way around – extra rhythm put on top of a tune – so there's no mistaking what is the most important. It gives rap ballads like 'Around The Way Girl' and '6 Minutes of Pleasure' a potent edge, while hard-core work-outs like the title track and 'The Booming System' don't become endurance tests. Then, within the album itself, it's possible to vary the pacing to a far greater degree by altering the mood of the tunes. Lyrically he deals with everything from God to rap culture – now he's got money it's his car stereo annoying the locals, in a very funny continuation of 'Radio' – to other rappers to the lay-deez and all with a panache and verbal dexterity. At the time this set was all the more welcome because people had been writing him off for years, yet it proved he'd not lost touch either with where he's from or where he hopes to be going.

The 12" Tape; Def Jam 4730432; 1993

As his debut album *Radio* is deleted, this mini-album compilation of twelve-inch mixes is the next best thing for a taste of early Cool J. 'Radio', 'Rock The Bells' and 'I Need Love' are there, all in glorious full length.

Light Of The World

Gee Bello, percussion, vocals; David 'Baps' Baptiste, saxes/flute; Kenny Wellington, trumpet; Nat Augustin, trombone; Bluey Maunick, guitar; Breeze McKreith, guitar; Everton McCalla, drums; Paul 'Tubbs' Williams, bass; Peter Hinds, keyboards)
At the time it was said this band took more than its name from KOOL & THE GANG (they named themselves after Kool's *Light Of Worlds* LP). The nine-piece, horn-loaded young London band took an approach entirely similar to the US band's early days as they fronted their arrangements with jazz-attack brass parts, fused it with cleverly interwoven guitar and keyboards then set it off to a solid funk rhythm section. While it was never going to be anything particularly ground-breaking, it was always

well-crafted, expertly played and in-your-face-funky as only a nine-piece horn-loaded band can be. It was also a very successful angle.

Light Of The World were about the first of an explosion of British jazz/funk acts of 1979–1981, who started making records aimed at the clubs they still went to as punters, thus quickly acquired a high profile in the specialist press and among deejays who knew them personally. They were making music that although derivative was specifically tailored for those clubs, so had an instant audience. They weren't afraid to work hard for their money, and always seemed on hand to play small hall and club tours, providing live music excitement without the attendant fuss and economies of scale that kept the big American bands out of these environments. They built up an enormous – and enormously loyal – south-eastern following, which translated beyond club classics into several top forty singles, sustaining them as the longest lasting act of that genre. It was more or less the rise of rap that left them behind as the 1980s rolled on, but by then they'd made a sufficient name for themselves to fragment into Beggar & Co (horns for hire, who worked with the likes of Wham! and Spandau Ballet) and Incognito, who are still active, and to be able to reform every so often and play one-off, sold-out London shows to audiences of surprisingly lively superannuated white socks wearers.

Best Of Light Of The World; Ensign; CHEN29; 1992

A thumb through their finest moments, which, when visited ten years later, is an uncomfortable reminder of how the band never quite captured their live impact on record. All the songs you want are here – 'London Town', 'Swinging', 'Pete's Crusade', 'Midnight Groovin'' and so on – and the combinations of dance floor sensibility and sophisticated jazz melody are as good as you remember, as are Gee Bello's silky vocals, but somehow the whole doesn't quite add up to the sum of its parts. Maybe it's something to do with overly earnest, drippily optimistic lyrics so many of their fine tunes were saddled with, as without the performance as a distraction it's too easy to concentrate on them. Still, this CD is a brilliant souvenir of a hopeful, standing-on-the-verge-of-greatness musical period, that overcame its never-quite-fulfilled-itselfness by the fact that Light Of The World made it all seem so personal, as if you were part of it, rather than just looking on.

SEE ALSO: Various Artists; *Brit Funk Volume One*; Ensign CDCHEN32; 1992

Linx

(David Grant, vocals; Peter 'Sketch' Martin, bass, both born London)
Linx were always one step removed from the London jazz/funk scene of the very late 1970s. Both in terms of their music – a very British-based pop funk that wasn't merely slavishly aping American styles – and a fiercely independent attitude that wanted to see them treated as any other British mainstream band, not hived off into a company's Disco Department low-budget backwater. They also had no truck with the three or four deejays who had the south-east's post-disco soul scene virtually stitched up, both in the clubs and as record label A&R men. So much so on this latter point that after the twosome hawked demos of their first single 'You're Lying' round record companies, to have it rejected by the middle-aged white men who ran black music departments (on the grounds they felt it wasn't funky enough), they put it out themselves on their own label. It became *the* track to own in the summer of 1980. Once it was in the top twenty, those same corporate representatives formed an orderly, cheque-book waving queue and Linx signed with Chrysalis Records largely because it had no black music division, thus no preconceptions of how a black group should behave.

But, even in spite of a string of chart hits, made and promoted on their own terms, it wasn't entirely plain sailing. The duo had only met a few months previously in the hi-fi shop where Sketch worked, and all they had in common was their co-written music – unfortunately it was obvious to anybody who spent any time with them that they didn't particularly like each other. Then, as David Grant started pushing more towards pop while Sketch wanted to delve into more experimental funk, the old chestnut 'musical differences' meant even that wasn't a bond any more.

Grant went on to pop hits (both solo and with Jaki Graham) and a spell as a TV presenter. Not much has been heard of Sketch for the last ten years.

The Best Of David Grant And Linx: Chrysalis
CDCHR6051; 1993

It might only be the shorter edit of 'You're Lying' on this disc, not the gloriously extended twelve-inch version, but the record is so special it's almost worth the price of admission by itself. Once Sketch's loopy opening bassline and David Grant's scat singing falsetto have chased each other round a hi hat and the drums have come in with a 'whap!' that almost makes your head hurt, this tune moves into a groove so sure of itself it sweeps all before it. It's entirely relaxed, light to the touch and deeply funky, summing up Linx and their sharp black pop aspirations perfectly. They pulled it off again with the Samba-ish 'Intuition'; the chugging 'Throw Away The Key'; the more urgent, involved 'Can't Help Myself'; and got smoove on 'So This Is Romance'. As deservedly self-celebratory Brit Soul goes, it doesn't come much better than this. Good enough, in fact, to put up with far from inspired David Grant solo singles, and his and Jaki Graham's cloying reading of 'Could It Be I'm Falling In Love'. A tune you have to work particularly hard on to mess up.

Mantronix

(Mantronik, born Curtis Kahleel, New York City; MC Tee)
This New York duo of, respectively, a producer and rapper, came to hip hop relatively late, but were at the forefront of a revolution – they assumed a far lighter touch than had been the case and thus started to change the way the style was both made and marketed. Essentially they brought rap far closer to the pop/soul mainstream and by ushering in elements of this new Chicago sound called House they set in place the foundation stones of 'modern' dance music. Theirs was an approach that was musical instead of essentially rhythmical, and rather than build what they did around performance – the standard stage set up of turntables and a rapper in front, recreated in the

studio using more or less unadulterated samples – they set it in the studio and used the equipment to the full. Although never afraid of a strong beat by itself, they stood apart as Mantronik created a library of recordings of the most unusual sounds – his baby niece crying, a piano being dropped from a window, breaking glass, car horns, splashes loud and small, and so on – mutilated through his studio's computers into sounds close enough to real instruments to be recognised, yet just sufficiently off-centre to make them interesting. Then he played music or sequenced snatches of music with them. It was this tuneful element that allowed the pop world to absorb it, as it fitted reasonably easily into mainstream radio playlists without any drastic toning down of its essential toughness, and Mantronik became in demand as a producer for a number of other artists, most notably Joyce Sims's first album *Come Into My Life*.

Music Madness; 10 Records DIXCD50; 1986

Mantonix's second LP was more settled than its predecessor, but still had a completely fresh bonkersness about it that proved the duo were still impressing themselves with what they were discovering they could do. Big looping basslines play off hyperactive beats, while melodies come and go with such frequency they often collide with each other to create something totally new. Varying from 'Who Is It?' that was struck from a straight house music template, to 'Big Band B-Boy' that appears to involve Art Blakey and Benny Goodman, and the dumb rap good-time groove of 'Scream', this is a vastly superior example of what used to be called 'electro'.

The Incredible Sound Machine; Capitol CDEST2139; 1991

Although, technically, a 1990s LP, its sensibilites are so deeply rooted in Mantronix's original musical games, it's pointless to separate it into a new chapter. (Also, 1991 is only *just* the 1990s.) That said, though, it's a remarkable progression of what went before, taking something raw and in parts rather naive, then buffing it to a sophisticated sheen without in any way dulling the spirit. Grown up B-Boys? It had to happen some time.

Street tuff rapper MC Tee is long departed, replaced by hip hop diva Jade Trini and laid back rap love man Bryce Luvah, both of whom sing from a rap perspective – rhythmic delivery as important as the melodies – as well as (occasionally) rapping with a light almost musical feel. The backing achieves the form the earlier albums were never too far away from – it is music, but because it's been constructed using the hip hop rule book you're never entirely sure. There are a host of 'real' musicians and 'real' instruments involved, but they're put into Mantronik's digital toy box to be pulled about, filtered, cut up, sequenced and stitched back together into something that never forgets it's supposed to be a tune but is also sure the reason you're down with it is the beat – melodies are perceived as series of beats as well as snatches of song and each phrase chops out its own rhythm to complete a cunningly layered tune. It's a thin line between vibrant and inventive music and a complete mess, but Mantronix walk it as successfully as they do boldly.

New Edition

(Bobby Brown, born February 5, 1969 – to be replaced by Johnny Gill; Ricky Bell, September 18, 1967; Michael Bivins, August 10, 1968; Ronald DeVoe, November 17, 1967; Ralph Trevesant, May 16, 1968. All born in Roxbury or Boston, Massachusetts)

Put together by producer/song-writer/entrepreneur Maurice Starr when the group were all aged between thirteen and fifteen, they were official teen sensations for about a year or so, but are far more important for what they all did afterwards. BOBBY BROWN became swingbeat's first international star. Michael Bivins, Ricky Bell and Ron DeVoe formed BELL BIV DEVOE, a rap 'n' swing act whose first album went platinum. Michael Bivins also formed his own management and production company, one of his acts being BOYZ II MEN. Ralph Trevesant and JOHNNY GILL both had platinum albums in the charts at the same time in 1991. And Maurice Starr, after he split with New Edition in 1984, decided that if he did exactly the same with five white kids – taught them to sing, dance and rap in a tarted-up street style – the returns would be enormous. Within a year he'd auditioned another quintet of young Bostonians, New Kids On The Block. All in all, the old New Edition camp was responsible for six major US acts.

Greatest Hits; MCA MCAD10434; 1989

For the record, this has got 'Candy Girl', 'Popcorn Love', 'Mr Telephone Man', 'If It Isn't Love' and 'Lost In Love'. And they haven't stood the test of time too well.

Alexander O'Neal

(Born Natchez, Mississippi, November 14, 1953)
In many ways Alexander O'Neal sums up the 1980s lurrrve man, with an almost Thatcherite approach to its job description: don't say you're sorry or admit to being wrong; select your paramours on some sort of survival of the fittest basis; assume free enterprise culture applies to affairs of the heart; and always pay more attention to yourself than to whoever it is you're supposed to be looking after (the lay-deez). O'Neal's notion of a rational discussion was 'Pack your bags'. His idea of subtlety was to wheel a brass bed on stage during his concerts then invite an audience member to lie on it, while he took off his tie and lay on top of her. He would bashfully lead the crowd in a chant of 'Alex, baby, Alex!', and he once called an album *All True Man*.

No New Man, that's for sure, but O'Neal appeal seemed to cut through the force fields of many a usually stridently right-on female. Especially in the UK (where, curiously, his popularity was proportionately much higher than in America) – women would scramble for tickets to his arena-sized shows, at which there'd be a forest of arms in the air when he requested a volunteer for the big brass bed.

But in nearly all ways it's hardly surprising Alex, baby, Alex far outlasted his similarly sharply suited lurrrve rivals. First of all, he was far more convincing a specimen of macho self-centredness than most of the others. O'Neal looked like he meant it. There was a pervasive meanness about his eyes and body language that implied a night with him genuinely would be a walk on the wild side – rumours abounded that he was a one-time pimp who had nearly killed a couple of his 'girls' by pushing them out of a moving vehicle; and that once, while on tour in London, he had so exhausted the employees of a high-class Mayfair cat house they'd had to bring the next shift on duty early to sate his continuing libido. All grossly untrue (I should imagine) but did his reputation no harm at all.

The backbone of his success, though, was down to his material. A head and shoulders above the pack, it was written and produced by Jimmy Jam & Terry Lewis, the hottest team of the day who, in the exposure they got through O'Neal and JANET JACKSON, had much to do with redefining soul music during this decade.

O'Neal's association with Jam & Lewis went back to his youth. Brought up in Minneapolis, O'Neal was a keen high school footballer and considered good enough to one day turn professional, until, as a teenager, he started singing in local clubs. Jimmy Harris (as Jam was still known) and Lewis invited him to join their band Flyte Time, which became the regular backing group for fellow Minneapolis funkateer Prince. However, after turning his back on sport, O'Neal wasn't keen just to sing doo-wops and left to go solo, concentrating on live work.

His first album, *Alexander O'Neal*, over five years later in 1984, was produced and written by Jam & Lewis together with another ex-Flyte Time member/former Prince cohort Monte Moir. The hits 'If You Were Here Tonight' and 'A Broken Heart Can Mend' kick-started O'Neal's career.

Straight into rehab as it turned out. A year later, O'Neal was hospitalised for cocaine and alcohol addiction, but Jam & Lewis pulled him through by promising him a follow up album as soon as he'd recovered and paying half of his medical bills. That LP was *Hearsay*, O'Neal at his badass peak and the last new material he would release for two years until, somewhat uncharacteristically, he put out an album of festive songs for Christmas 1988. O'Neal's last album of any significance was *All True Man* in 1991, and even then the 'Minneapolis Sound' he continued to use was becoming dated – it's noticeable that his regular, sold-out UK tours are becoming more an exercise in nostalgia than a happening proposition. However, they are proof that the pipes are still intact, so maybe it's just a case of finding another producer . . .

*Hearsay; Tabu 450936; 1987

Containing the hits '(What Can I Say) To Make You Love Me', 'Criticize', 'Fake', 'Never Knew Love Like This' and 'The

Lovers', this album, together with what Jam & Lewis did on Janet Jackson's *Control*, are living, almost organic, proof that computers can sound soulful. Here, they drape sweeping electronic strings and synth lines over an almost skeletal drum slap and a sternly disciplined bassline to create a feel that's as hard as the times yet soft enough to be attractive. Minimalist plush? But obviously designed, a very 1980s trait, that actually provided a perfect setting to show up O'Neal's voice. His sense of urgency went with the underlying tautness, but as it was always big enough to match the, at times towering, arrangements and give the impression it was still holding back, he was never overwhelmed. Always in control.

This Thing Called Love – The Greatest Hits Of; Tabu 4717142; 1992

An amalgamation of original hits and remixed versions (the entire *Hearsay* album was released as *Hearsay – All Mixed Up*) from across all three Tabu albums. Pros: it contains all the best bits from the third LP *All True Man*; it has the magnificent ballad 'A Broken Heart Can Mend' (Alex Baby Alex actually gets sensitive!); the soaring duet with CHERRELLE 'Never Knew Love Like This'. Cons: a couple of the remixes are unnecessarily abrasive – fine in a club (just), but not in your living room; they could've found room for 'Saturday Love'.

All True Man; Tabu 465882; 1991

Although the whole O'Neal wagon is starting to slow down at this point, if you like what went before there's enough here to make it worth a punt. Apart from some crashing (quite literally) bores that sound like outtakes from *Rhythm Nation 1814*, essentially it's more of before, but as that's actually what's wrong with it, it's the restrained numbers that work best – the title track, 'Sentimental' and 'What Is This Thing Called Love' – while of the up-tempo stuff the most interesting are other people's productions – 'Every Time I Get Up' and 'Midnight Run', by Prof T & Lance Alexander and Foster & McElroy respectively.

Public Enemy

(Chuck D, born Carlton Ridenhour, New York, 1960; Flavor Flav, born William Drayton; Terminator X, born Norman Rogers, deejay.)

Though Grandmaster Flash introduced the idea of rap as a social commentary during the first wave of hip hop, by the second half of the 1980s hip hop was getting flabby. Unusual for a resolutely black music style, but in keeping with youth in general in the 1980s, the musical genre was apolitical. Once again like the decade, rap and rappers weren't bothered about much other than themselves and what they'd got, but by now such self-obsession had progressed way beyond the engagingly dumb bragging of THE SUGARHILL GANG and The Furious Five. Fantasy microphone toughness – 'I got more cars/girls/rhymes/money than you' – was spilling over into real violence as hip hop and a very scarey ghetto gun culture began to influence each other – Schoolly D, rap's Original Gangsta, had his first hit in 1986 with 'PSK – What Does It Mean' (it meant Park Side Killers, his Philadelphia street gang). Also hip hop hopefuls saw stardom as an expression of machismo rather than artistry. As musical advances made by such acts as RUN-DMC and Whodini weren't being followed up to any lasting significance anywhere other than Def Jam, rap was musically stagnating, while as a reflection of black life it was in danger of living up to the world at large's worst fears. Public Enemy were – still are – hip hop's wake-up call.

Like the Black Panther Party of twenty years previously, their political stance was deliberately confrontational, taking self-defence to the point of aggression (a feature of the stage show was paramilitary-uniformed, fake Uzi-toting security men) and demanding change instead of merely cataloging injustice. Public Enemy were equally hard on the elements of oppression within the black community too: 'Pollywanacraka' (railed against aspiring to be white); 'Nighttrain' (drug dealers); '1 Million Bottle Bags' (drunkenness); 'She Watch Channel Zero' (apathy) and so on. Away from any verbal offensive they were a call to arms, pushing the positive by chivvying away at complacency with black pride anthems. Songs such as 'Give It

Up', 'Black Steel In The Hour Of Chaos', 'It Takes A Nation Of Millions To Hold Us Back' and 'Brothers Gonna Work It Out' were all about the power potential should we decide to get down with the cause.

Of course none of this would have meant anything if the music hadn't delivered. Public Enemy never let their mission get in the way of the productions, as right from the start they stepped hip hop up a gear to deliver beats, samples and cut ups with astonishing power. Put together by Hank Shocklee, aka The Bomb Squad, it was a noise so dense it sounded as if entire songs had been condensed into single riffs, that were steam-rollered over and over again in a full-frontal assault that supported all sorts of odd melodic hooks, and powered itself with short sharp drum patterns and basslines that could hold up buildings. The only way it could be endured was in brief bursts, thus it's usual for Public Enemy albums to contain more than twenty tracks, with not one of them over three minutes. Then on top of all this, Chuck D's 120 per cent committed delivery spat out some of the most inventive rhymes with a sheer force that was matched only by its perpetual state of hyped up rage. Chuck was able to maintain this perpetual state of anger by having proceedings lightened up by Flavor Flav's cartoon antics, his mercurial clowning (on stage and on record) counter-pointing Chuck's blustering rhetoric. However, to dismiss Flav as a fool is a mistake. He is every bit as politically astute as Chuck – his lyrics are as hard, but their less-confrontational delivery tends to overshadow that. And it's Flav who is respon-sible for the subliminal melodies that add an astonishing depth to P.E.'s buzzsaw sonic assaults – he is a skilled player of four-teen different musical instruments.

As disparate as their styles is their backgrounds: when the twosome met in 1985, Flav was working for Chuck's dad's haulage company while Chuck was at university in Long Island studying graphic design. Hank Shocklee was at college with Chuck, and it was in 1983 that the campus radio station DJ Bill Stepney gave the twosome a one-off, rap-only show. It was such a success they got a regular slot – The Super Spectrum Mix Show – enough to promote themselves within the local com-munity, to hire themselves out, and run Long Island's first hip hop club. By now Flav and Terminator X were a regular part of the posse and the group's aggressive musical style and carefully worked out presentation dynamics had begun to attract widespread attention. Among it Def Jam Records, and the Public Enemy album *Yo! Bum Rush The Show* was released in May 1987. Shocklee and his brother Keith became their regular producers, and Bill Stepney now manages the group.

As an educated, middle-class young man, Chuck D has never complied with the popular mainstream image of a rapper, and as a quick-witted spokesman and skilled media manipulator, he's never made it particularly easy for Public Enemy's critics – the combination of his self-assured stance and the band's uncompromisingly black attitude has often been taken as an affront. That said, there's been a few controversies they've bought on themselves, not least group member Professor Griff's apparently anti-Semitic remarks, Chuck's somewhat confused response when he left in summer 1988 (was he or wasn't he sacked?) and Flavor Flavs's crack habit and record of domestic violence.

But in terms of musical innovation and sense of purpose, for nearly eight years now Public Enemy have been the rap act others emulate, although none has yet surpassed. And, quite fittingly for someone of his intelligence and articulacy, Chuck D. is now a regular on the American college lecture circuit. It all seems world's removed from 'hip hip hoppy to the beat, y'all'.

Fear Of A Black Planet; Def Jam 4687512; 1990

From a sub-title that ran 'Counterattack on world supremacy', to the final track 'Fight The Power', this album is Public Enemy in full, glorious, effect. A sonic and verbal assault from which no hooks, beat or rhymes get out alive. A sledgehammer of hip hop funk power manifests itself in such deliberately provocative jams as 'Anti-nigger Machine', '911 Is A Joke', 'Who Stole The Soul?', 'Burn, Hollywood, Burn' and 'Welcome To The Terrordome'. While the overall effect of the music is that of being shut in a galvanised dustbin while half a dozen people bang on the lid for an hour or so, but you come out of it exhilarated and motivated. It was the third in a trilogy showing incredible progression as, contrary to rap's standard singles mentality, each Public Enemy album improved on the one before. Not only did this continue the upward musical curve – riffs getting denser, beats getting frantic to the point of panic – but it was recorded fresh from the Professor Griff business, so Chuck and Flav could bounce off the media furore to present themselves as not only martyred but rising up above it all. In every respect, the unsurpassed most brilliant, whole and complete rap album ever made.

Muse Sick-N-Hour Mess Age; Def Jam 523 362; 1994

Don't let the clever-clever title put you off. This, the first new Public Enemy album after a three-year gap, has them firmly back on course. Under the catchphrase 'If you don't stand up for something then you'll fall for everything', the lyrics answer media criticism ('I Ain't Mad At All', Flavor Flav's track); challenge complacency ('What Side You On' and 'Godd Complexx') and black self-destruction ('Stop In The Name . . .'); and celebrate black power ('What Kind Of Power We Got?' and 'Give It Up'). While the backing is P.E. at their most melodic. Not that this means any throttling down, if anything it's more intense, it's a mark of their continued artistic growth that they can incorporate increased melody somewhere inside the emotional, machine gun-paced cut up cuts.

ALSO RECOMMENDED:

All three remaining Public Enemy albums offer a great deal in terms of musical and lyrical content, and remain milestones in rap's development. The group's personal progression is evident in the first two (*Yo! Bum Rush The Show*; Def Jam 450482; 1987/*It Takes A Nation Of Millions To Hold Us Back*; Def Jam 462415; 1988), from raw ideas into the sophisticated political force that crescendoes so spectacularly on *Fear Of A Black Planet*. While the fourth LP, *Apocalypse '91 . . . The Empire Strikes Black*, would be brilliant if it had been done by anybody else, and remarkable by P.E. standards if it hadn't come so soon after the one before. *Yo! Bum Rush The Show* was, at the time of writing, off catalogue in the UK but widely available on US import.

Raw Silk

A studio 'group' – i.e. producer Ron Dean Miller's creation of computers and session singers – Raw Silk had an enormous club hit in late 1982, in the wake of HOWARD JOHNSON's 'So Fine', with the altogether as smoove 'Do It To The Music'. As an example of how disco studio technique could be used to construct a track with considerably more depth it's second to none and a tribute to the mixing/arrangement skills of Nick Martinelli. Although Raw Silk only had one more sniff of success with the following year's 'Just In Time', the guidelines drawn up by the first hit's stretched out rhythms and come-to-bed lead lines are clearly defined on so much of the cool synth soul to come out in the first half of this decade.

SEE: Various Artists; *Classic '80s Groove Mastercuts Volume 1*; Mastercuts CUTS15; 1993

Sharon Redd

(Born Norfolk, Virginia, 1955)
Alongside D. TRAIN at Prelude Records was big-voiced singer Sharon Redd, who, in the label's practice of following soul tradition through to electro ends, brought her operatic-training to bear on the house beat for some shinily enjoyable moments in synthesised soul. On Sharon Redd records the backing seemed to be kicking it just that bit harder, maybe because her voice dominated so much of the mix, to give the whole thing a sly Funk Lite appeal. But then it's fairly certain Sharon Redd would have had some funk in her somewhere: her brother is Gene Redd, KOOL & THE GANG's pre-vocalist producer, her father worked with JAMES BROWN at King Records and her sister, Penny Forde, had a passable post-disco career and is the female vocalist in SNAP!

*Sharon Redd – Essential Dancefloor Artists Volume 4;
Prelude DGPCD698; 1994

Has all the hits that are recently enjoying a sharp-end-of-the-club-scene revival, after a prolonged shelf life, thanks to the gay disco scene adopting Redd (she was once one of Bette Midler's Harlettes). 'Can You Handle It', 'Beat The Street', 'Never Give You Up' and 'Love Is Gonna Get Ya', however, are tuff enough to merit renewed overground recognition.

SEE ALSO: (1) Various Artists; *Prelude Deep Grooves*; Sequel NEDCD263; 1992; (2) Various Artists; *Essential Dancefloor Classics Volume 1*; Sequel NEDCD668; 1994

Lionel Ritchie

➸Summer 1983, and one of the biggest songs in less hip dance halls and on mainstream radio was Lionel Ritchie's 'All Night Long (All Night)', a sunny, laid-back piece of soft funk. What it did, very cleverly and with the aid of an artfully constructed street scene video, was bring the *idea* of hip hop to both the traditional soul/funk fan and the mainstream, yet leave all of that rather disturbing 'attitude' outside on the pavement. With a similarly engaging break dancey video, Chaka Khan's 'I Feel For You' pulled off the same stunt – presenting rap culture, which was all about participation, as a safe spectator sport. It wasn't just a lucky stab at it either – pop producers had been (and still are) tearing their hair out trying to come up with a pop hip hop, but always fail because they never attempt to understand the genre they're trying to bastardise. 'All Night Long (All Night)' took it seriously, got into the feel and then took it back to the bare bones, rebuilding the style with orchestration in place of churning sampled riffs. The song was the huge hit it deserved to be, but it also endowed its singer with the kind of totally unwarranted credibility that had people fooled for years to come. Really, Lionel Ritchie had as much soul music relevance in the 1980s as Kenny Rogers, the country artist whom Ritchie wrote for and produced.

Although he didn't announce his split with THE COMMODORES until the end of 1982, it had been obvious for about three years that was the way he was going – he was writing more or less all the group's successful material; and as he quite naturally composed around his own voice, the group was looking more and more like Lionel & The Others. Then, once unshackled, he was free to indulge his first love of overly sentimental, country-tinged MOR ballads to astonishing effect. And in a bizarre tribute to his smooth crossing of the great divide into the hearts and record collections of the mainstream, he won American Music Awards as Best Male Vocalist in both R&B and pop categories in 1987.

Into the 1990s, and Lionel Ritchie's most solid funk credentials are concerned with him losing his title as music's Mr Happily Married Man. Wed for twenty years to teenage sweetheart Brenda – their domestic bliss was the subject of many a cosy media profile – the marriage broke up very publicly when a tabloid newspaper exposed the wild and very extracurricular goings on at the singer's longstanding secret 'love nest'.

Can't Slow Down; Motown 530023; 1983

It sold over 10 million copies and contains, among the anodyne ballads, a full length version of 'All Night Long (All Night)'.

SEE ALSO: Motown Various Artist compilations

Run-DMC

(Run, born Joey Simmons, Hollis, New York, 1964; DMC born Darryl McDaniels, Hollis, New York, 1964; Jam Master Jay, born Jason Mizell, Hollis, New York, 1965)

By 1982, three years into its offical existence, street style hip hop was pretty much dead in the water. Not just as far as the mainstream was concerned (who for a while had seemed comfortable with the more rock format-friendly electro), the core audience too was getting a bit fed up, as so little had changed since 'Rapper's Delight'. Added to this, the genre's practitioners had moved on from their block party scuffling days and were noticeably cut off from their original sources of inspiration.

Then, in early 1983, Run-DMC roared out of Hollis with their soon-to-be-trademark Homburg hats, glasses, black clothes and scowls that could strip paint. And a single called 'It's Like That'. There was no time to warn the villagers. The beast was loose!

This was the moment the second stage of rap got up and started running. The rhythm had gone right back to the original storyline of scratching, quick cut mixing and a beat box, but it was *how* they'd done it that was important. Jam Master Jay's demonic turntable skills chopped and shredded with such precision that whatever things had started off as they ended up fractured, cascading beats – nothing as wussified as a melody here – that took a boost off the beat box and hit the listener head on. To compliment this, the vocals wanted to tear your head off, as Run and D swapped lines, traded scats and bounced off each other with a practically telepathic understanding, equalled only by their individual vocal dexterity. This was put over to mesmerisingly full effect on stage (showmanship was another area neglected by crews who thought it was enough just to turn up) and was the power and the glory that would pave the way for the immediate likes of PUBLIC ENEMY and LL COOL J, while reinventing rap for the middle of the decade.

Run-DMC were never going to be anything other than rappers, having grown up steeped in it from as far back as they can remember specific music. It's notable that the second wave of rap took off as soon as the generation who could remember nothing else hit recordable age. LL COOL J, Whodini, Run-DMC, The Fat Boys were all young enough to have been aware of it for so much of their lives that they accepted it as a bona fide music form rather some bastard off-shoot of street funk. And thus they approached it as something to be messed about with and improved on, not as something that existed by itself to be preserved in aspic. Of course it was handy that Run's older brother was Russell Simmons, a Queens hip hop entrepreneur and promoter, who helped Run and his friend D get local gigs from the age of twelve. At the same time, Jay was perfecting his turntable skills with the Hollis-based sound systems and club circuit.

As it turned out, Simmons was a major player in the New Wave Of Rap: his company Rush Productions managed Run-DMC, he later (with Rick Rubin) set up Def Jam Records and at one point just about every other influential New York rap crew was under the Rush umbrella – PUBLIC ENEMY, LL Cool J, ERIC B. & RAKIM, Whodini and The Beastie Boys. (It was an irony that his brother's group was never on his label as he'd signed them to a different company long before he founded Def Jam.) Simmons was also one of the reasons these acts put on such well-produced live shows, as he, ten years older and an original street funk fan, knew the value of performance and made sure his artists could do it live before they went into the studio.

Run-DMC's upward curve was swift. Their initial impact translated into sales to give their debut LP, *Run-DMC*, rap's first gold album (500,000 sold), figures which accelerated sharply as they blended their rap with heavy metal. Whether it was an obvious choice or not (hard rock is about the only music more obnoxious than their spiky hip hop, and the crew couldn't have forgotten the impression Eddie Van Halen's guesting on MICHAEL JACKSON's *Thriller* made), as the guitar samples increased so did the returns. Three albums in, Run-DMC's 1986 *Raising Hell* album won the genre's first platinum disc (1,000,000) on its way to doubling that figure, while the group themselves earned a lucrative sponsorship with the clothing firm Adidas – another first for rap. But, most importantly for those coming through after them, it was this inclusion of heavy metal – particularly their version of 'Walk This Way', featuring Aerosmith in a highly amusing video – that broke MTV's never-admitted-to embargo on rap.

It was the combination of a movie and a legal battle that did for Run-DMC in the end. They wrote and produced their own hip hop adventure film *Tougher Than Leather* – they play a rap crew on the trail of the drug dealer who murdered their road manager – with a suitably kicking soundtrack, but a legal battle with their record company held up the release of both for over a year. By the time they came out in 1988, the music had moved on way past that particular set of songs, and the film, quite simply, was hopeless. It set them back so far – as in hip hop credibility and topicality is everything – that even with two excellent albums since then, they've still got a way to go before they catch up.

*Raising Hell; Profile 828018; 1986

Run DMC's finest hour, and a fascinating look at their world where street-culture attitude collides with the dynamics of rock presentation. 'Walk This Way' is one of the funniest rap records ever made: Steve Tyler screams the rock song in reply to the duo's deft double-handed rhyming, while Jay's turntables take on Joe Perry's guitar. It all just makes the rap crew seem so cool compared to these two clapped out looking rockers, which is a pose they strike for the rest of the set. There is a lot of live instrumentation on this, but it's been phased and cut up so deftly that it adds weight to the core rather than confuses any issues. Which is a good thing, as the lyrics themselves are a vibrant, throwaway take on the urban black culture of the day: 'You Be Illin''; 'My Adidas'; 'Dumb Girl'; 'Proud To Be Black'; and 'Peter Piper'.

ALSO RECOMMENDED:

King Of Rock; Profile FILECD 205; 1985

Their second album and the one where they started to get wild with the guitar samples.

Down With The King; Profile FILECD440; 1993

Seen as another step along the way to a comeback, and a step in the right direction, as without losing the old-school skills its music is starting to sound interestingly modern.

Snap

(Turbo B, born Durron Butler, rapper; Penny Ford, singer)
Snap's first album won't change either the world or soul music as we know it, but as one of the few light rap albums to actually work, it was a lot of fun while it lasted. It also remains a rare example of something with genuine soul power coming out of (a) house music and (b) a continental recording studio. It all began when two Frankfurt-based record producers (Michael Munzing and Luca Anzilotti) toughened up some basic house tracks by dropping in proper basslines, melodic riffs and drum patterns with a bit of menace. They topped it off with Penny Ford's swooping vocals on some tracks and big, blustering raps from Turbo B all over the place. It had an airiness that kept it right for radio and repeated playing, but at the same time was deep enough to stick in the mind and make most funk fans drop some foot. They never did it again though, curiously opting to try to come over as a German-sounding rock band (i.e. not very good) for most of the follow up.

World Power; Arista 260682; 1990

'The Power', 'Ooops Up', 'Mary Had A Little Boy', 'Witness The Strength' and 'Cult Of Snap', each one deeply unfashionable, but so what?

Soul II Soul

(Jazzie B, born Beresford Romeo, London, January 26, 1963; Nellee Hooper; Philip 'Daddae' Harvey)
As much a state of mind as formal band – a floating pool of dee-jays, producers, singers and musicians assembled around the core crew of three – Soul II Soul became brand leaders in blurring the boundaries between the new post-house music club-land and the more traditional concert circuit. The collective – as they liked to refer to themselves – evolved out of an entrepreneurial spirit born in Jazzie's schooldays when he began buying watches from a local jeweller to sell on at a mark up, progressing, as he and Harvey became the Arthur Daleys of the North London sound system scene, to hiring out their equipment when they weren't using it. They then even began supplying deejays to clubs almost on an agency footing. Bristol-based Hooper, formerly of MASSIVE ATTACK, joined the firm after hiring a PA and almost coming to blows with Jazzie B over who was actually going to deejay the function it was intended for. Once part of the Soul II Soul organisation, Hooper's musical skills and production abilities allowed the team to *create* records rather than simply play them. The sound system gained an enormous following courtesy of totally unique 'slates' – one-off singles – and tapes, regular club work (they were by now promoting their own events) and Jazzie's London radio show. Also, ever aware of a marketing opportunity, there was the Soul II Soul logo'd clothing and accessories which were, by now, selling so well at gigs they opened two dedicated shops.

Of course, from there it was just a tiny step to releasing records for home listening pleasure. Once secure in a contract, having recruited vocalist Caron Wheeler and come up with the corporate philosophy 'A happy face, a thumping bass for a loving race', the team blended house, hip hop, reggae and pop into an entirely radio-friendly restrained, deceptively melodic groove. America loved it too. Within a year of the first LP, the bashfully titled *Club Classics Volume 1*, which topped the charts on both sides of the Atlantic – Soul II Soul added to their collection of four British DMC Dance Music Awards, three American Music Awards, two Grammies and three Soul Train Awards, and were voted Best New Foreign Band Of The Year in *Rolling Stone*'s Critics' Poll.

And the 'collective' expanded in all directions: producing and arranging for artists including Sinead O'Connor ('Nothing Compares 2 U'), JAMES BROWN, The Fine Young Cannibals and Neneh Cherry; setting up a clothing company; discussing proposals to set up a record label and Soul II Soul Visions, a film & TV production company and a talent agency; and negotiating a deal made with Motown to run jointly a black UK record company. But somewhere along the way the music seemed got neglected and following albums appeared not only derivative but subject to diminishing returns. It's unlikely that the world has heard the last of Soul II Soul, and even if it has, at the time of writing Jazzie B's crew remain Britain's most successful black band ever.

Club Classics Volume 1; 10 Records DIX82; 1989

The record that, very deservedly, brought Soul II Soul to world attention, but also an album Jazzie B never really managed to get out of his system, as so much else sounded like this sublime set's outtakes. Using vocalists Caron Wheeler, Do'reen and Rose Windross, supplementing the superbly relaxed basslines with woodwind and a string section – London's Reggae Philharmonic Orchestra – and using subtle dub mix techniques to stir up an ethereal sense of excitement, there had been no soul sound like this. Classy, cool and still uncompromising, if you didn't have this on your car stereo in summer of 1989, you had to leave your windows wound right up. It was the law.

Volume IV; The Classic Singles 88–93; Virgin CDV2724; 1993

'Back To Life', 'Jazzie's Groove' and 'Keep On Movin'' from *Volume 1*, plus the best bits from the following two – 'Get A

Life', 'Joy', 'A Dream's A Dream'. There's also the bonus of the first single, the none-too-successful 1988 release 'Fairplay'. While this handy Soul II Soul primer cuts out the dross of later years and even provides a couple of entertaining remixes, it also shows how little artistic development there was over the course of five years.

The Sugarhill Gang

(Master Gee, born George O'Brien; Big Bank Hank, born Henry Jackson; Wonder Mike, born Michael Wright)
Seldom, in any music style, has a group had so much effect yet remained almost totally insignificant themselves. The Sugarhill Gang's 'Rapper's Delight' was the first contact most people had with the style that was to become the soul music expression of the 1980s and 1990s, yet after a tour that wasn't much more than an extended jam of that one record and a couple more very minor hits, they disappeared. Apparently Hank is a New Jersey dustman now, while Mike and Gee both run small businesses, neither of which has anything to do with music.

Maybe they didn't last because they were a manufactured group – they were put together by Sylvia Robinson, former R&B singer, nightclub owner and now, with her husband Joe, owner of Sugarhill Records (Sugar Hill was the upmarket part of Harlem in the 1930s). Although they'd been in the record business before, when they founded a label called All Platinum, Sugarhill was a new venture, set up to deal specifically with rap – Sylvia, the creative side of the partnership, was aware of the phenomenon through her teenage children, in whose culture home-made hip hop cassettes or recordings of club deejays rapping over existing records were changing hands for up to $50. She also realised that disco was over – the new generation of teens simply weren't interested – and as a small independent company hers could quickly react to changing fashion. The trio were assembled from three guys she knew or knew about who could rap – facts are fuzzy in this area, but a consensus has it that Hank was a nightclub bouncer and Gee was still at school. 'Good Times' was selected as not only had it been a big hit, but as a disco record it had been tough enough to get people thinking funky again. Plus, that Chic bassline was already familiar to radio programmers, so they'd have no problem slotting 'Rapper's Delight' into whatever pop or soul playlist they were operating..

The record sold over a million, launched the label, the style and the notion that making hip hop records is a licence to steal – Sugarhill were eventually forced to give CHIC joint writing credits and royalties. Interesting fact: the backing band on that session – and on many early Sugarhill releases – is Positive Force, who later put out the totally brilliant and now unbelievably unobtainable single 'We've Got The Funk'.

SEE: Various Artists; *To The Beat Y'All – The Sugarhill Story Old School Rap*; Sequel NXTCD 217; 1992

Tashan

(Born Thomas Pearce, New Jersey, 1963)
Although young enough to have been part of his hometown's hip hop revolution of the 1980s, Tashan was at the sharp end of Def Jam's corporate policy to make sure that, while the label turned rap into a dominant market force, 'proper' soul values didn't get lost in the mix. A kind of cultural counterbalance to the likes of LL COOL J and PUBLIC ENEMY, that allowed co-owner Russell Simmons to put out the music he liked best.

A locally established songwriter/producer in his late teens, Tashan came to the company in 1985 as a producer for the label's rap 'n' soul act Whodini and it was noted that he too could carry a tune. Working as a songwriter and singer while absorbing rap influences, Tashan was among the first to develop the notion of the B-Boy ballad – bedroom soul crooned over a beat box backing track – and although he is still very much active, his work tends to look dated against New Jack Swing's in-yer-face handling of hip hop's hormones.

Chasin' A Dream; Def Jam DEF4501582; 1986

Tashan's first and finest LP, the one that explores the post-synthesizer modern electronic studio to the extent of its rhythmic, computer-programmed, sequenced excitement, but never forgets that the real object of the exercise is to knock out some decent tunes. The most decent of which are 'Got The Right Attitude', 'Strung Out On You', 'Thank You Father' and the title track. It's a remarkable cocktail of sex, social conscience and religion, hung together with B-Boy spikiness and a certain dangerous smoulder that, when delivered in Tashan's multi-tracked honey-dripping falsetto, brings to mind a scratch-mixed MARVIN GAYE.

Tone Loc

(Born Anthony Lock, Los Angeles, California, 1962)
Living proof that hip hop success and a sense of humour need not be mutually exclusive. Tone Loc's first album, 1988's *Loced After Dark*, was powered by sludgy beats, juddering riffs and his smokey, vaguely menacing voice talking some of the wryest, wildest rap routines ever heard. Routines is the right word here, as many of the songs told stories of ghetto life and rap culture more in the manner of a hip stand-up comedian. The star turn was 'Wild Thing', a wry slant on sexual boasting and a huge hit, helped on its way by a video that mercilessly ripped off that Robert Palmer clip with the mini-skirted girl group.

Loced After Dark became the first black rap album to go to the top of the US pop charts, and turned Tone Loc into a star. Problem was, by the time he got round to releasing his second set three years later, the axis of LA rap had shifted so far over to gangsta that his warm humorous tales came across as a bit limp by comparison. Loc is now making a steady career as an actor.

*Cool Hand Loc; Delicious Vinyl 510609; 1991

Whether it sold as well or not, this is actually a far superior album to the first inasmuch as the music has a real roundness to it. As these edges aren't as unfinished, they allow Loc's voice to flow out of the beats rather than battle with them, which gives the set a far spookier feel than its predecessor. Which only goes to make the sharply observed street life tales that much more telling. Stand-out tracks are the self-explanatory 'Pimp Without

A Caddy', the sex rhyme send up 'Freaky Behaviour' and the genuine, Barry White-style rap ballad 'All Through The Night'.

ALSO RECOMMENDED:

Loced After Dark; 4th & Broadway IMCD125; 1988

Worth it for 'Wild Thing' and the, er, dope dope rap 'Cheeba Cheeba'.

Trouble Funk

(Robert Reed, drums/vocals; Tony Fisher, bass; James Avery, guitar; Timothy Davis, percussion; Taylor Reed, keyboards/trumpet/vocals)
This Washington DC group were the cutting edge of go-go music, a style that grew up in that city and, for a brief moment in the late 1980s, threatened to make a huge impact on the transatlantic soul scene. It was a live sound, played with 'real' instruments and built round a thumpingly solid bass 'n' drum groove that supplemented itself with all manner of percussion, building up different rhythms within. It was apparently open-ended too, allowing the brass, guitars and keyboards to drop in and out, play a solo here a few lines there, while the vocals were mostly chanted or called in response to the audience. In that respect, it shared a lot of its values with the previous decade's street funk, and reintroduced live music to clubs, as bands would keep a groove going all evening, with only varying changes of tempo as different players took to the stage.

According to Trouble Funk bass player Tony Fisher, the style grew out of Washington DC's strong tradition of high school marching bands where most members had something percussive to play and the beat was necessarily as rigid as a metronome. As that city apparently never developed much of a rap scene, yet had always been a strong funk centre, live music wasn't such an alien idea. The UK music media leapt on it. It was announced as a proper music alternative to hip hop's technology (it took the mainstream press years to come to terms with rap) and for a while was high fashion. Indeed Trouble Funk played some wildly entertaining UK shows. But that was something you wouldn't want to go to three times, and playing the albums at home, no matter how much 'atmosphere' they'd captured at the sessions (many go-go recordings were live jams) it still got boringly repetitive after about ten minutes. Which kind of limited their long-term chances.

Drop The Bomb; Sequel NEBCD 663; 1993

'Drop the bomb' was T. Funk slang for bringing the tune to one of many crescendoes. Being wound up waiting for the band to drop the bomb was an integral part of being in a Trouble Funk audience and could be a lot of fun. Fun they do capture here, as the album is just eight extended killer grooves with the wiggy bits popping in and out, and of course the requisite number of explosive devices ready to be lowered.

SEE ALSO: Various Artists; *To The Beat Y'All – The Sugarhill Story Old School Rap*; Sequel NXTCD 217; 1992

Luther Vandross

(Born New York City, April 20, 1951)
I don't know if anybody reading this has got a copy of Gary Glitter's 1975 *GG* album. Probably not, but if you have, check down the credits and you'll see Luther Vandross was one of the backing singers. It hardly seems fair that the man who was to become Mr Lurrrve of the 1980s had to play second fiddle to the manic, Baco-foiled, former Gang leader, but it wasn't the only indignity he suffered. At one time or another, Luther Vandross has sung doo-wops for Bette Midler, Barbra Streisand, Sister Sledge and David Bowie, and provided the voices for, among others, Kentucky Fried Chicken, Miller Beer, Kodak and Burger King commercials. But it was all part of the plan to raise money to record his own songs *his way*, and to use these superior demos to convince record companies he could make his own creative decisions – after years of doing what he was told at other people's sessions, when he launched his own career he wanted control.

He got it too. In 1980 he signed a deal with Epic Records that allowed him the creative freedom to choose his own producer and his own material. It's a pity he didn't make more of it too, but Luther Vandross suffered from that problem all too often associated with .background singers stepped forward – they don't quite have the charisma to carry it off by themselves, if they had they'd have been stars years ago. He came over as too much technique and not enough feeling, and because his technique was so much better than his rivals he went further. Thus he was ultimately of greater disappointment.

Sure, Luther Vandross's songs are wonderful and they're sung expertly too. They're very pleasant to have on in the background, but when it comes to the kind of all-conquering, emotional lurrrve fest you and the lucky partner of your choice hope to lose yourselves in, too many of them don't make the grade. They stop short at the point at which he might lose control – the point at which BARRY WHITE, MARVIN GAYE or AL GREEN seemed to start at. This would come over vividly in his live performances, curiously more so as his career progressed, as there were far too many occasions when it seemed we were expected to be dazzled by what he's actually doing rather than swept along in the moment. It's as if he was so frightened of what might happen if he stepped outside his rehearsed phrasings that he holds back. And really, what good is a lurrrve man who won't go all the way?

*The Best Of Luther Vandross – The Best Of Love; Epic 465801; 1989

This twin-CD set is easy to recommend, in spite of the above comments, simply because it is the best of what he had to offer. The high points of eight albums, (the Vandross emotion factor therefore doesn't appear too stretched) so what you have is a collection of the very highest quality pop/soul. The sort of thing that nobody could find offensive – which, presumably, is why it's sold so well – but most people will have trouble recalling it ten minutes after it has finished playing. Among the hits that include 'Give The Reason', 'Since I Lost My Baby', 'Never Too Much', 'I Really Didn't Mean It' and 'Any Love', this set goes back as far as the two hits he had as lead singer of the disco group Change in 1980, 'Searching' and 'The Glow Of Love'.

Stevie Wonder

➻➻Stevie Wonder's 1980s started off brilliantly. The legions of less-adventurous Wonderfans felt he'd got back on the right track with *Hotter Than July*, a comparatively lightweight LP, but undeniably more conventional than its predecessor, *Journey Through The Secret Life of Plants*. They were so relieved, his string of hits continued well into 1981. With the single 'Happy Birthday' he launched his campaign to have Martin Luther King's birthday (January 15) recognised as a national holiday – six years later, after two marches on Washington, his wish was granted, although the most redneck states officially refuse to honour it. In 1983, he co-wrote and guested on Gary Byrd's huge black pride hit 'The Crown'. That year he seemed so relaxed he even participated in a *Saturday Night Live* TV sketch that had him playing tennis.

Then suddenly it all went wrong and for nearly five years he didn't record a note that was in any shape or form soulful: 'I Just Called To Say I Love You'; 'That's What Friends Are For'; 'Moments Aren't Moments'; 'Part Time Lover'; 'Stranger On The Shore Of Love' . . . Somebody should have seen the signs in 1982 when he joined up with Paul McCartney for that dreadfully mawkish 'Ebony And Ivory'. Let him have some time off, after all what he did in the previous decade must've worn him out.

This period through the middle 1980s wasn't so much lame as paraplegic. And even when he did pull himself out of it, it was with *Characters*, funky only as relative to what had been done before. Likewise the 1991 soundtrack for Spike Lee's film *Jungle Fever* was seized on as a return to form, yet save for a chunky little workout called 'Fun Day' – which isn't really anything you haven't heard before – there's nothing on the set that would have got shelf-room fifteen years before.

At the time of writing the world is well into the second decade of the wait for a genuinely innovative new album from Stevie Wonder. Hell, if this goes on much longer just plain 'interesting' will do.

Hotter Than July; Motown 530044; 1980

It's not vintage Stevie Wonder, but with 'Masterblaster

(Jammin')' , 'I Ain't Gonna Stand For It' and 'Happy Birthday' it more than passes muster.

Original Musiquarium; Motown 530029; 530034; 1982

This is a double-CD greatest hits, which, at the time of release, contained four new songs. One of them was 'Do I Do', which became a deejay favourite as a last record of the session for the entirely valid reason it sent everybody home happy. Which is one reason you should choose this set if you're shopping for a Best Of Stevie Wonder.

SEE ALSO: Motown Various Artist compilations

Characters and *Music From The Movie Jungle Fever* are both off catalogue.

VARIOUS ARTIST COMPILATIONS

Classic '80s Groove Mastercuts Volume 1; Mastercuts CUTS15; 1993

Raw Silk, Do It To The Music; **Howard Johnson**, So Fine; **Krystol**, After The Dance Is Through; **Royalle Delite**, I'll Be A Freak For You; **Shot**, Main Thing; **Thelma Houston**, You Used To Hold Me So Tight; **Meli'sa Morgan**, Fool's Paradise; **Loose Ends**, Hangin' On A String; **Change**, Change Of Heart; **Lilo Thomas**, Settle Down; **Cheryl Lynn**, Encore.

To The Beat Y'All – The Sugarhill Story Old School Rap; Sequel NXTCD 217; 1992

DISC ONE: **The Sugarhill Gang**, Rapper's Delight/Radio Comercial; **Funky Four Plus One**, That's The Joint; **Grandmaster Flash**, Adventures Of Grandmaster Flash On The Wheels Of Steel/8th Wonder/Birthday Party/Monster Jam/Good Times/Another One Bites The Dust/Rapture;

Grandmaster Flash & Melle Mel, White Lines (Don't Do It); **Trouble Funk**, Pump Me Up; **The Sequence**, Funk You Up; **Grandmaster Flash & The Furious Five**, Freedom; **Spoonie Gee**, Spoonin' Rap; **The Sequence**, And You Know That.

DISC TWO: **Lady B**, To The Beat Y'All; **Super-Wolf**, Super-Wolf Can Do It; **Grandmaster Flash & The Furious Five**, The Message; **The Sugarhill Gang**, 8th Wonder; **Spoonie Gee & The Sequence**, Monster Jam; **The Treacherous Three**, Yes We Can-Can; **West Street Mob**, Break Dancin' Electric Boogie; **Grandmaster Flash**, Flash To The Beat; **Busy Bee**, Busy Bee's Groove; **Grandmaster & Melle Mel**, Jesse; **Melle Mel & Duke Bootee**, Message II (Survival); **Crash Crew**, We Are Known As Emcees (We Turn The Party Out).

DISC THREE: **Trouble Funk**, Drop The Bomb; **Wayne & Charlie (The Rapping Dummy)**, Check It Out; **Grandmaster Flash & The Furious Five**, It's Nasty (Genius Of Love); **Kevie Kev (Waterbed Kev)**, All Night Long (Waterbed); **Trouble Funk**, Hey Fellas; **Busy Bee**, Making Cash Money; **Reggie Griffin**, Mirda Rock; **Grandmaster Flash & The Furious Five**, Scorpio; **Crash Crew**, Scratching; **Funky Four**, King Heroin; **Melle Mel**, The Mayor.

Probably more first-generation rap than anybody could possibly want, but this is the definitive statement on a pivotal period in US black music. But the best thing about it is these are still kicking nearly fifteen years later. Plus there's a bit of go-go thrown in too – these Trouble Funk tracks are one of the very few examples of the music available at the moment.

*Essential Dancefloor Classics Volume 1; Sequel DGPCD 668; 1994

Jocelyn Brown, Somebody Else's Guy; **Gayle Adams**, Love Fever; **Indeep**, Last Night A Deejay Saved My Life; **Sharon Redd**, Can You Handle It; **The Whispers**, And The Beat Goes On; **Shalamar**, Take That To The Bank; **Phil Hurt**, Giving It Back; **Wish**, Nice And Soft; **Collage**, Romeo Where's Juliet; **Young And Company**, I Like (What You're Doing To Me); **Crown Heights Affair**, Dancin'; **Bohannon**, Let's Start The Dance.

An excellent selection of very late 1970s and 1980s records, that in many cases meant far more than the people who made them. If this is the only chance there is to get Jocelyn Brown's enduring club classic 'Somebody Else's Guy', it should be grabbed. With both hands.

Prelude Deep Grooves; Sequel NEDCD263; 1993

Saturday Night Dance Band, Come On Dance, Dance; **Mustique**, In The Bush (remix); **Sine**, Just Let Me Do My Thing; **Bobby Thurston**, Check Out The Groove; **Sharon Redd**, Can You Handle It; **Hi-Gloss**, You'll Never Know; **D. Train**, You're The One For Me; **The Strikers**, Body Music; **Sharon Redd**, Never Give You Up; **Unique**, What I Got Is What You Need; **Sharon Redd**, Love How You Feel; **D. Train**, Music.

A comprehensive sampler of the label that managed to salvage something as disco went through soul music like a rat up a drain. Whether it would have continued to develop this melodic sound is another matter though, so maybe it's best that it ended about where this snapshot puts it.

Brit Funk Volume 1; Ensign CDCHEN32; 1992

Beggar & Co, Somebody Help Me Out; **Beggar & Co**, Feel The Real (Again); **Incognito**, Parisienne Girl; **Light Of The World**, Time; **Danny Williams**, I Hate Hate; **Black Slate**, Amigo; **Light Of The World**, London '85; **Warriors**, Destination; **Galaxy**, Head Over Heels; **Ray Carless**, Tarantula Walk.

A representative cross-section of black British music from the 1980s, running from reggae through funk to more or less straight jazz.

4

1990s

Into the 1990s and swingbeat singing was sweetening itself still further into some very intricate harmony styles. It seemed that crisp black pop was on the up again, and as a result other rules started relaxing. Bands were forming, kids were realising it was all right to do just about anything and soul music opened itself up to embrace rap, rock, jazz, doo-wop, gospel, poetry and even traditional soul. Indeed, the only common denominator seemed to be a widespread return to high-profile consciousness, as black rage built up as a backlash to the 1980s' uncompromising economic and social policies – Los Angeles rappers had been grimly predicting some sort of civic disturbance long before the Rodney King verdict. How this anger could be so freely expressed was through a proliferation of tiny independent record companies as, at the end of the previous decade, the major labels were reluctant to promote obviously street-based styles. Much the same had happened to hard funk in the early 1970s. Of course, such de-regulation also gave rise to Gangsta Rap, soul's supreme irresponsibility.

The real downside of soul so far in the 1990s, though, was an accelerated aging process. There were so many records being made, and styles were turning over so quickly that immediacy became very much part of the package – an act could get an idea from the street to the shops in weeks instead of months and being new was more important than building to last. Acts' careers could be over in less than a year and their records off catalogue for ever. It was significant while researching this that there is much more old soul than modern soul available.

As a result, the last section of this book has a much wider spread and less acts as you just can't buy the records any more. Whether this is a good thing or not remains to be seen.

Arrested Development

(Speech, born Todd Thomas, Milwaukee, Wisconsin, 1969, lead vocals/turntable instruments; Ajile, dancer/choreographer/ vocals; Headliner, percussion/vocals/turntable instrumentalist; Nadirah Shakoor, lead vocals/percussion; Montsho Eshe, dancer/vocals; Rasa Don, drums/percussion; Kweisi Asuo, DJ/vocals; Aerie Taree, vocals/poems; Bab OJE, spiritual advisor/percussion/vocals)

If you've just ploughed through the line-up, then by now you'll have got the idea that Arrested Development might be just a tad contrived. Two years ago, they burst on to the rap scene with a desire to be different. While stressing the need to return to good honest folksy values, they presented themselves as what had always been looked on as a contradiction in terms, rural rappers. (Incidentally, it coincided with a noticeable US trend for black people to move south, starting to populate areas outside of big cities, so it wasn't that far removed from reality.) They kitted themselves out in old timey-looking work clothes and a lot of ethnic garb, had a stage set that looked like a farmyard, and served up some gentle, rather touching songs. Very welcome indeed.

Then came the philosophy. Speech would, rather pompously, describe their music as 'cultural, southern hip hop folk ethnic funk' and you knew you were in trouble. Music shouldn't need this much explaining by its creator, and this is where the whole experience starts to unravel – it's far more about the *theory* of Arrested Development than their music. Which is why the mainstream took to them in such a big way – if the truth be told when you put the first album (*3 Years . . .*) on it becomes hard work pretty quickly. Which is a shame. Because most people wholeheartedly support them in what they're about, and the couple of singles they had hits with show they can make music as a form of entertainment rather than a particularly dull sociology lecture.

*3 Years, 5 Months and 2 days In The Life Of . . .; Cooltempo
CCD1929; 1992

In spite of the general patchiness and self-righteousness on
overload, there's enough on it to make it worthwhile. 'People
Everyday' (their take on SLY's 'Everyday People'), 'Give A Man
A Fish', 'Mr Wendal' and 'Fishin' For Religion' are all as relaxing and clever as you'd like them to be, the combination of
unusual (in hip hop) sounds and tempos a refreshing cool
breeze. It's one more step along the road to a more laid-back,
older marketplace rap, but whether it deserved the column
inches it received is another matter.

By the time they made the second LP, *Zingalamadni* (Chrysalis
29274; 1994), they'd changed the line-up, and while the theories
are just as up front, this one hasn't even got the tunes.

Bell, Biv, Devoe

(Ronald DeVoe; Michael Bivins; Ricky Bell)
The other three from NEW EDITION, who re-emerged very grown
up: scowls; street fashion; overly healthy libidos; and late model
swingbeat that pushed its arrangements nearer rap than was
the norm. It could have been an interesting development, as,
stylistically, they seemed to be about to break through to a
balanced hybrid of rap 'n' swing – perhaps meeting SALT 'N' PEPA
coming at it from the other side – but that was four years ago,
and since then they haven't made another new record.

*Poison; MCA MCD06094; 1990

Although they've still got one eye on the teen appeal and the
themes and presentations are designed to keep the hormones
a-fluttering (remember, their original New Edition fans would
be seventeen or so by now), but it's tough enough not to irritate
the grown ups either.

Mary J. Blige

(Born The Bronx, New York)

Like QUEEN LATIFAH, Mary J. Blige is moving hip hop, both the music and the culture, towards a, er, less intense marketplace. Although nowhere near as laid back as Latifah, Blige's instincts are similar as she sings straight R&B over the sort of grooves most people would be rapping across. Her gospel/soul-based voice is big enough not to get swamped, but the grooves are as tough as they need to be, so although she opens up the style it leaves the underlying attitude intact. At which point she's shrewd enough to use it as a strong platform to display other influences.

It would seem that in the cases of the very young hip hop practitioners, even more so than the second wave, they hold nothing sacred. To them, theories and basics are there to have something done with them, so why not sing? Judging by Blige's album sales, the difference between now and when Russell Simmons tried that ten years before is that today the public is ready for it.

What's The 411?; MCD10681; 1992

Traditionally soulful hip hop, a rare beast indeed, as Blige stretches out among a pretty hardcore backing track to take us on a stroll through her range. We visit cool jazzy tones, straight balladeering, the up-tempo party-time tip and even get as far as a couple of funk numbers that see her flirt with hard core and get away with it.

Boyz II Men

(Nate Morris, born 1973; Michael McCary, 1973; Shawn Stockman, 1974; Wayna Morris, 1975. All Philadelphia, Pennsylvania)

It would be virtually impossible to have remained unaware of this group's 1992 monster 'End Of The Road' – thirteen weeks at the US number 1 to set a new record – and their Christmas hit of the same year 'It's So Hard To Say Goodbye To Yesterday'. But such balladeering was only ever half of the Boyz II Men story. They really excelled when they kicked up high and harmonised over some thumping hip hop backing tracks, in exactly the way you'd expect a group managed and founded by Bell Biv DeVoe's Michael Bivins. It isn't just their versatility across a spectrum of styles that sets the group apart, though. What's given them lasting success is that within each style they appear to have a far greater flexibility. Each voice fulfills a set purpose, giving their arrangements a greater breadth, and a far more sumptuous sense of harmony – it appears to go all the way back, making others seem a bit shallow by comparison – plus tight structures which allow far more showing off when individuals step out front.

This is the result of their church origins and a solid grounding in Philly soul vocal tradition (the story is that Bivins heard them harmonising in a playground and approached them on the spot) lending a real discipline and sense of purpose to their work. Also it's quite obvious that at some point they've had formal training. Put together with the best arrangements and increasingly subtle backing there is no reason why this act shouldn't carry the style beyond this current trend and establish themselves in true Soul Classic style.

Cooleyhighharmony; Motown 5300892; 1992

An entirely accurate summing up of the teenage, new-to-recording Boyz II Men. It's raw, it's vibrant and – in spite of the polished tracks doing so well, plus half the set being slow jams with the others up-tempo – it is an exact recreation of street attitude in a studio situation, getting by on enthusiasm almost as much as expertise.

II; Motown 530 4312; 1994

Michael Bivins is no londer in charge, Jam & Lewis share production credits with the group, the vocal arrangements are far superior to its predecessor, the music is much more subtly crafted and it kicks with the very best in modern-day street funk. The division between lively and downbeat is far less clearly defined and the essential cleverness here is a featherlight, totally swinging backing, with a very easy-action vocal oozing through the gaps in the sharp rhythms to blend into a kind of mid-tempo hustle for the 1990s, achingly hip and remaining accessible to anybody who wants to think about it. Set apart from all this, though, is an album highlight – an a cappella reading of 'Yesterday' that seems to be there for no reason other than to prove how good they are. Which it does to such a degree it even manages to raise the song above its built-in mawkishness.

Digital Underground

(Shock G; Humpty Hump; Money B; Kenny K; Schmoovy-Schmoov; Piano Man; all from the Bay Area – San Francisco, Oakland and Berkeley)

Determined not just to use P-FUNK samples, Digital Underground opted to continue that group's satirical cartoon experience. They employed Overton Loyd, whose felt-tips were responsible for much of Parliament's artwork, to draw their early record sleeves, involved GEORGE CLINTON on their second album and wrote songs that created a whole world of character-acting and story-telling. P-Funk impressionists attempting to relaunch the Mothership was not an uncommon late 1980s scenario, but it worked so well for the Underground because they appeared to *understand* the theories – as opposed to just ripping off the practice – and they have used this knowledge to build an updated, less flashily cosmic notion of P-Funk. With a wonderful balance, they've blended a strong sense of black pride, deliberately exclusive social commentary and daft ghetto tales, then wrapped them up with a lunatic, surreal humour and a biting sense of irony. They know there's more to their mission than being 'whacky', that the whole point about being funny is to have something serious to be funny about. Which is why Loyd and Clinton were so quick to endorse the act, and it ought to serve as reminder for rap crews everywhere that f.u.n. is a big part of funk.

Sex Packets; BCM BCM377; 1990

The mainstay of this album is a wild, five-part concept piece about the sex packet – a black market, chemically produced hallucinogenic that provides vivid dream sequences about the girls or guys on that particular packet's cover. So real, it seems, that participants are warned to take their clothes off first. It's a marvellously cracked idea, and the narrative conclusion makes it obvious that they've put some thought into it – another genuine P-Funk connection, these guys take their stupidity very seriously. The album's backed by varied and deeply funky music too, which is Digital Underground's other great strength, mixing a lot of instrumentation in with their beats and melodic samples to cross as broad a spectrum of moods as possible. Which was why tracks like 'The Humpty Dance', 'Doowutchalike' and 'Freaks Of The Industry' made such an impact among old-school funk fans who appreciate a few surprises.

Sons Of The P; Big Life BLRCD12; 1992

The title is a mark of respect to George Clinton and the funk mob and, as a sign of the group's funky progress, the messages are pushed further to the fore: 'No Nose Job' is a statement about MICHAEL JACKSON; 'Heartbeat Props' tells listeners that wearing a Malcolm X hat isn't quite enough, they should turn out for *living* black leaders; and 'The DFLO Shuttle' concerns itself with a mythical train that will take us to a land where black people can live properly. Musically, *Sons Of The P* is far more sophisticated, without de-emphasising any hip hop excitement – it features guitars, piano, keyboards and percussion among the computers, and their robust sense of humour has been in no way blunted as 'Good Thing We're Rappin'' testifies – a lengthy, acted out centrepiece track detailing the band's apparent previous life as pimps.

Dr Dre

(Born Andre Young, South Central Los Angeles, California)
If you're looking for controversy in that highly strung world of gangsta rap, you won't have to look too far. And when you find it, there's a very high chance the name Dr Dre will be mentioned. A former Nigga With Attitude, now turned producer, solo artist, record company executive and all-round gangsta entrepreneur, Dre was at the grass roots of gangsta before it

even had a name. Back in 1985, while Schooly D. was holding the audience when it came to mindless violence and misogyny, Dre and the other NWAs – one of whom was ICE CUBE – were making singles and selling them out of their cars, sometimes reaching the five-figure sales bracket. Enough to finance the first NWA album and such thought-provoking tracks as 'A Bitch Iz A Bitch' or 'Dope Man', co-written and co-produced by Dre.

The breakthrough came the following year with *Straight Outta Compton*, a Dre-produced LP of quite staggering belligerency. And it's worth remembering that while it gained instant media notoriety for an FBI-enraging track called 'Fuck Tha Police', it wouldn't have lasted five minutes on the car sound systems if the beats hadn't been right. It became the first high-profile example of that hard-surfaced yet curiously melodic LA technique (Dre is an accomplished musician). The third track was 'Gangsta Gangsta', now the style had not just a name but a customised one at that.

The album went on to sell nearly 3 million and marked the start of Dre's platinum touch. He produced a Texan rapper called D.O.C., who sold over a million of his first album. Michel'le's eponymous Dre-produced rap album went platinum. As did NWA's follow up, *100 Miles And Runnin'*, while in 1991 the one after that, *Efil4zaggin*, sold even more and got to number 1 on the US pop charts. This event proved what had been suspected for a long time – that a large proportion of gangsta rap's fan base was thrill-seeking white kids, who want a walk on the wild side but will go no further than their Walkman. Not that this matters, by then gangsta rap was such big business, having more or less subverted the genre, that a few complaints from irate middle-class parents weren't about to stop anything. Not even Dre's next project (the one *after* his own platinum-selling solo album *The Chronic*) *Doggy Style*, which he produced for Snoop Doggy Dogg. Musically and stylistically unremarkable, the album sold over 4 million in three months and by now is probably the genre's best-selling record. Unfortunately, at the time of its release the artist is on $1 million bail for his alleged part in a drive-by shooting that left one man dead. It's difficult to imagine what gangsta rap's going to do next.

The following are all Dr Dre productions. Such is the nature of the beast that his role as producer will be the most important presence.

NWA; Straight Outta Compton; 4th & Broadway BRCD534; 1988

Curiously, it's Dre's essential understanding of melodies that get these foul-mouthed litanies of life and crime in South Central off the ground. As this is California the pace is far lazier than, say, PUBLIC ENEMY, thus there's a lot of space in between the beats to slot different 1970s funk samples – these will become a gangsta rap trademark – to build up guitar riffs and basslines to an almost tuneful degree. But just because it's light doesn't mean it's soft. The beats needed to hold such fancy fretwork down are necessarily oppressive. Cuts on this album like 'Express Yourself' (practically a cover of CHARLES WRIGHT's original), 'Gangsta Gangsta' and the title track became the style's blueprint.

DR DRE; The Chronic; EastWest 7567922332; 1992

Dre on the solo trip, and wisely he saved the best for himself. Having been through the samples cupboard and come up with snatches of ISAAC HAYES, P-FUNK and DONNY HATHAWAY, Dre adds a lot of instrumentation in his own studio, from keyboards and bass guitars to flutes and drum kits. It's all stitched round his smokey delivery to construct an album of hazy, slightly edgy funk.

SNOOP DOGGY DOGG; Doggy Style; Death Row 6544 92279; 1993

Very much *The Chronic Part II* – in some cases, the only thing that has changed is the voice. If not the same samples, then the same sort – CURTIS MAYFIELD, Willie Hutch, etc – but Snoop's soft, high-pitched, vaguely Southern voice is quite a revelation. Always riding the rhythms with such a light touch it adds a particular menace to his tales of sex and violence. Stand-out track is the one where The Dramatics line-up behind him crooning, 'It's a doggy dogg world.'

ALSO RECOMMENDED:

*NWA; Efil4zaggin; 4th & Broadway BRCD 562; 1990

Astonishingly unpleasant of lyric, but what did people expect 'The Secret Seven Go To South Central'? What it shows, though, is Dre's production at its pre-instrumentation peak.

En Vogue

(Dawn Robinson; Terry Ellis; Cindy Heron; Maxine Jones)
When En Vogue played Hammersmith Odeon in London, it was difficult for a non-believer to see how they could sell out one show, let alone the three they were booked for. Sure, we all ogle them on the videos – we all watch *Baywatch* too – but not seriously enough to leave our houses and spend money on them. But it was standing room only. Each night. And seeing En Vogue fans in the flesh – a large proportion of older teenage black girls – the group becomes a lot easier to understand: En Vogue are THE SUPREMES for the 1990s. A group of stunning looking, spectacularly fashionable girls, harmonising around the style of the day and with the sort of adapted-from-street-dance moves that are careful not to distance them from their audience, but at the same time look like they have been choreographed. Another important similarity is having a writing/production team to take care of the more tiresome end of being a star – in this case, New Jack graduates Thomas McElroy and Denzil Foster, writing the kind of hard edged swingbeats that show the group off in their mini dresses to their best advantage. And finally, again like The Supremes, the girls in the audience want to be them while the guys want to be with them.

*Born To Sing; Atlantic 7567820842; 1990
*Funky Divas; EastWest 756791212; 1992

It would be wrong to attribute all this quartet's success to their legs and a good choice of material from Foster & McElroy – if En Vogue weren't capable of singing the songs, they wouldn't have lasted to a second album. But they did, and both sets stick pretty much to the game-plan and give the girls plenty of scope to show off group and individual talents that can weave jazz elements and gospel sensibilities into their skin-tight harmonies. The backing tracks are largely a smoothed out swingbeat, subtly rebalanced as the drums are made very big with the melody aspect slightly simplified, but it's all strong enough to handle the flavours of rock and reggae occasionally woven around this core. Then, just to raise the temperature a wee bit, there's a breathy ballad or two and now and then the girls get into a bit of quite heavy-duty hip hop. Both LPs enjoy a degree of consistency – with each other as well as within – and while the first one features 'Hold On', the second one's got 'My Lovin' (You're Never Gonna Get It)'.

Reg E. Gaines

New to recording this year (1994), Gaines describes himself as 'poet/lecturer/director/producer', but what he means to say is 'funky as hell'. He's a poet perhaps in a truer than usual sense of the word, as his raps are written with no apparent notion of music and delivered in a weird fractured meter that dances to its own beat as he urgently stresses and de-stresses what at first seem the wrong words and syllables. It doesn't let you relax until you've played it again, and again, and again. Until it makes perfect sense. But even then, it won't let you relax because it is set to music: ghostly blues, distorted jazz, smokey funk or an over-the-edge rock, each one slightly out of whack with the words, itself and life in general. This is funk poetry of the highest order. Disturbing to the point of pleasure.

Please Don't Take My Air Jordans; Mercury 314514; 1994

If you kick off your debut album with a cut that reclaims Jimi Hendrix from the rock fraternity, in such a direct way that nobody dares argue with you, then it's pretty certain you've got something going on. Gaines goes even further than that with 'Just Another Misunderstood Brother'. His tack is to pay no attention to where Jimi went – the white rock world is totally unimportant to him – but he rounds on the black community for refusing to recognise this genius and keep him as its own. He lays in with such a strangely paced, calculated venom you end up apologising out loud. And over the LP he keeps this temperature up for three-quarters of an hour, with subject matter that runs to racist police, naked consumerism, watching sport in a bar, riding the subway . . . life in general.

Gangstarr

(The Guru, born Keith Elam, Boston, Massachusetts, rapper; DJ Premier, born Christopher Martin, Brooklyn, New York)
If the fourth phase of rap is to involve a broadening of influences, a more relaxed musical presentation and greater spread of intelligence, then Gangstarr will be near the front. Following on from ERIC B & RAKIM's lead – that you can use what you like to make what you like, and in that respect jazz is your natural conclusion – this duo have put together some astonishingly grown-up hip hop. While jazz samples will be positioned near enough the top of the mix to be audible, which is what got them the reputation as the first jazz rap crew – it's the beats Premier creates that sets them apart. He'll approach a track in one of two ways, either by mangling up samples into dense, muddy rhythms then enlivening them only by drums or turntable scratching, or he'll take an odd snatch of melody, cut it to length – doesn't matter if it doesn't fit the sample's original time pattern – then turn over and over to form the rhythm for the cut he's about to build. Either method can then take melody lines and snatches of leads but both will end up as a sultry, loping backing that never forgets it'll have a lot of listeners laid back in their favourite armchair – i.e. like the best jazzers it's as concerned with creating an ambience as with the specifics of each piece.

On top of that is The Guru's rapping. Relaxed, with a gruff amiability, but right to the point – he's got a lot to say but isn't going to waste his time shouting. You'd probably switch it off if he did. Also, in between the black pride sentiments are tales of ghetto life that refuse to moralise clichedly. They don't glamorise either, what they do is talk about stuff from the point of view of why it goes on, and attempt to engage in a dialogue of understanding. It's a combination of excitement, sharp ideas and a challenging entertainment factor that should go a long way to seeing rap into middle age.

Step In The Arena; Cooltempo CCD1798; 1991
Daily Operation; Cooltempo CCD1910; 1992
Hard To Earn; Chrysalis 284352; 1994

The only worrying thing about Gangstarr is there's been very little progression within the unit over three albums. True, their technique has gone a long way to refining itself, but it's not considering any new ideas. With that in mind, the first album is raw, the second has some almost celestial high spots – 'The Solioquy Of Chaos' and 'Take It Personal' – while the third is of the most consistently high standard. Stand-out moments being 'Tonz O' Guns' and 'No Shame In My Game', as they seem to have turned up the heat on those within the community who are doing so much to wreck it.

Jazzmatazz; Chrysalis 21998; 1993

The Guru's personal project, billing itself as 'An experimental fusion of hip-hop and jazz'. It brings in such jazzers as DONALD BYRD, Roy Ayers, Ronny Jordan, Courtney Pine and N'Dea Davenport, to have them contribute to his woozy hip hop backing tracks. It works so perfectly as the hip hop groove is a modern-day recreation of that smokey, post-bop jazz groove that chugs along waiting for the lead players to drop in and do their bit. Which is what they do, easing into the vibe like they'd never been anywhere else.

Guy

(Teddy Riley; Damion Hall; Aaron Hall; all born New York City) Although there's three of them, Guy was really Teddy Riley, former child prodigy turned prodigous producer – he played drums and keyboards proficiently at the age of five, was performing professionally by the time he was twelve, then went on to produce for MICHAEL JACKSON, KEITH SWEAT, Kool Moe Dee and so on. Riley is also the man credited with inventing New Jack Swing, the hip hop influenced R&B with testosterone that combines a tough beat box rhythm with sequenced melodies that can come up fractured or flowing depending on the mood. The Hall brothers were childhood friends of Riley's who had proved their vocal abilities by soloing in their church from a very early age, and were recruited to give voice to his musical vision.

It worked too. The style took off immediately in a world that had for too long been starved of music or traditional soul values presented in a way the post-rap generation could come to terms with. Drawing elements from rap and old soul to shape a style that was flexible enough to be either, or both, without compromising itself, New Jack Swing was tough enough for the brothers on the block to flex to and sufficiently soft for romance. With or without Riley at the helm, swingbeat singers and groups blossomed until it became *the* young black expression of the 1990s, providing a credible, more universally supported alternative to gangsta rap. Guy broke up two years ago – Riley's outside production commitments being the major factor – and more recently the producer has put together another vocal group, Blackstreet, to further swingbeat's cause.

The Future; MCA MCD06119; 1990

Although this sounds a little dated today, there's such sheer enjoyment and exuberance in the grooves that it remains a valuable lesson in what 1990s soul music was capable of. Riley and his crew are street-style ruff, in as much as the beats are hard and sharp but the keyboards are so airily light they flow above the rhythm with a detachment that counterpoints the drums to a much greater impact. Then the vocals are apt to flip the script and break into rap at any time. It's almost as if the music has pushed the temperature up so high that these three B-Boys can't be constricted to singing and are bursting through with rap and rhyme as a funky celebration. Blending street and studio to create something with this much youthful spirit has been the essence of the best soul music for the last forty years. It's little wonder Teddy Riley's New Jack Swing has inspired a generation.

SEE ALSO: *Classic New Jack Swing Volumes 1 and 2*; Mastercuts CUTSCD9/CUTSCD5; 1992/1992

BLACKSTREET; Blackstreet; Interscope 6544-92351; 1994

Blackstreet are Teddy Riley with Chauncey Hannibal, Dave Hollister and Levi Little, and they are to gangsta what Guy were to rap. This whole concept is much tuffer, much more street-based and incorporates far more dangerous-sounding, rumbling raps along with the sweet harmonies – even if the lyrics don't stretch as far as hos, bitches and gats, the tone is sufficiently smokey to put across a real menace. Curiously, in complete contrast to this delivery and the uncompromising black messages, the grooves themselves are far more musically complete. The backing is much richer, being built around basslines rather than drum beats, and uses more recognisable melody samples to emphasize the idea of a tune. In many ways, *Blackstreet* seems to be steering the JODECI, BOYZ II MEN type thang back to rap – from where Riley hijacked the original style in the first place. It could shape up to be an interesting development.

Ice Cube

(Born O'Shea Jackson, Los Angeles, California, June 15, 1969)
When Ice Cube quit NWA in 1989, it was the beginning of the end for that group. Sure, DR DRE's innovative backing tracks kept them going for at least one album longer than they had any right, but the real damage was done by the departure of their most intelligent lyricist. Without Cube they had nothing to say, but Compton's loss was the world at large's profit. Without the constrictions of a group obliged to live up to the name Niggers With Attitude, he's been able to develop beyond gangsta's immediate concerns and present a lifestyle alternative to fast sex and faster death. With a perpetual scowl and a tonsorial approach that in the last three years has involved a dripping perm, an afro and shaving it clean, Ice Cube has advanced the notions of gangsta as social revolution. It was a shrewd play that seems to accept the idea that LA's gang culture isn't going to go away, so the best thing to do would be to try to channel it in some way. Thus, while his albums are littered with pumping machismo and gunplay, there's an increasing leaning towards the idea that this energy should be used to take control of the situation.

{sound system and deejay operation. Often playing to crowds of up to two thousand in parks or the local skating rink, Dre supplied the beats while Cube rhymed, largely freestyle, about his environment.

'Even back then,' he maintains, 'I wanted to focus on reality, to stir things up by talking of things that went on in the neighbourhood that weren't getting exposed elsewhere. I wanted the kids to be aware of what life was about, then they stood more chance of being able to do something about it.' One of the reasons Cube left NWA was because they appeared to be deviating from this path.

These early experiences also gave Cube the grounding to become one of rap's most dynamic performers, bringing a rare (in modern-day hip hop) sense of showbusiness to his concerts, acting out his ghetto dramas with the aid of another rapper, dancers, smoke, a lightshow complete with searchlights scanning the crowd, and all manner of sound effects. He brings his words to life so vividly it's hardly surprising that after two acclaimed co-starring roles (*Boyz 'N The Hood* and *Trespass*), Ice Cube has heavy Hollywood options to weigh up.

Lethal Injection; 4th & Broadway BRCD609; 1993

Everything that Ice Cube is about came together in this set – the hardest beats, the most intriguing attitude and the unexpected lyrics. It's not nearly as 'conceptualised' as *Death Certificate*, or as fierce as *The Predator*, which was made in the wake of the LA riots, but he continues his exploration of the gangsta groove for more than just a litany of 'hos 'n' gats'. Very smoothly, it manages to be life-affirming, without being preachy, simply by injecting a note of pride and an enormous element of fun into what's happening, all to the accompaniment of mesmerising beats that take the current trend for tunefulness and ever so slightly fracture it. It's an attitude that serves Cube's lighter-than-most delivery to the full, as his words bounce along the grooves to the sly 'You Know How We Do It'; the ironic 'Ghetto Bird'; and the springy, bottom-kicking funk of 'Bop Gun', built round a large section of 'One Nation' and featuring vocals by GEORGE CLINTON. This album is the basis of his surprisingly spritely stage set, but that doesn't mean Ice Cube's gone soft – 'What Can I Do', 'Lil Ass Gee' and 'Enemy' are suitably chilling.

Kill At Will; 4th & Broadway BRECD572; 1991

Sludgy, depth-charge-type beats, gangsta politics and lifestyle delivered in an almost growl, a guest appearance by Chuck D and an overall vibe of calculated desperation, this was a murderously powerful statement of intent from the not yet fully formed Cube.

Ice-T

(Born Tracey Morrow, New Jersey, 1959)
Is Ice-T a ledge-living, gun-toting, drive-by doing, all-round terrifying Original Gangsta, or is he a fraud? It's a debate that's been going on for years and probably won't be decided in my lifetime. But the real answer is, it doesn't really matter. So much of rap – pop music in general – is a pose, an act to let the fans buy a piece of escapism, and as long as it's convincing while you're watching the show or playing the record then there's not really much more to worry about. And Ice-T gets paid to look convincing. Remember, this man was an actor before he was a rapper (his film career is still moving on an upward curve) and he used to have a nifty sideline teaching Hollywood squares how to rap – or, to be more precise, how to act like rappers. But where it really counts – through your stereo – he can deliver.

OG Original Gangster; Sire 7599 26492; 1991

Up there with *Fear Of A Black Planet*, as one of the top three rap albums ever. Although the beats are fresh funky cut up, Ice's delivery transcends them to take on a life of its own. Whether he's taking us out gangbanging ('Midnight'), hanging with the dope dealers ('New Jack Hustler'), in prison ('The Tower') or helping us to keep up with him on tour ('Lifestyles Of The Rich And Infamous'), every story is told with a gift for drama and narrative that brings things vividly to life. It's like being an extra in a particularly manic thriller for an hour and a quarter, and it's a mark of his skill that never once on this journey around his own personal hell do you start looking at your watch.

BODY COUNT; Cop Killer; 7599268782; 1992

Ice-T's thrash metal band – there's one thrash track on *OG* – is the epitome of what happens to funk if you leave it on its own for too long. Their speedmetal is as good as anybody else's yet with Ice-T writing the lyrics and out front, you end up with such wry cultural cross-over observations as 'There Goes The Neighbourhood', such blunt political statements as 'KKK Bitch' and, of course, the one that all the fuss was about, 'Cop Killer'.

Jodeci

(JoJo, born Charlotte, North Carolina, 1973; K-Ci, born Charlotte, North Carolina, 1971; Mr Dalvin, born Hampton, Virginia, 1973; Devante Swing, born Hampton, Virginia, 1971) Jodeci sing like angels, yet pose gangsta-style for their album sleeves, giving it plenty with big boots, bare chests, tattoos and scowls that could peel paint. The group prefer to be known only by street names, which is unsurprising for Jodeci are the person-ification of 1990s ghetto soul music as the demarcation lines between song and rap grow increasingly blurred. (It's ironic that while the world at large has never considered rap to be a bona-fide soul music, this decade's trend for very soulful and entirely mainstream-acceptable harmony singing borrowed as much from hip hop as it did from doo-wop.) As with previous swing-beat practitioners, they marry gospel style harmonising – the foursome are graduates of two church choirs – to beat box back-ing, but while their words of lurrrve are sweet, their beats are tougher and their presentation less compromising: New Jack Swing moving into New Jack Attitude, as gangsta (the music and the lifestyle) became an integral part of young black life.

What sets Jodeci apart from the pack, though, implying they might have a future beyond any trends, is their methods for constructing what they do. Rather than put words to music, they start with the lyrics, turn it into a song by demoing it a capella, then add the backing. This means they can take the street sounds and attitudes as far as they will go within a pre-scribed setting – so while the finished product will always sound hard, there'll be no danger of the music swamping the singing. In other words Jodeci are totally aware of what it is that makes them special and are playing it up to the max.

*Diary Of A Mad Band; MCA MCD11019; 1993

Their second album. By now the almost unqualified success of the first, *Forever My Lady*, among older teenage girls had left the group as the undisputed champions of sweaty street-style smoove. They were lurrrve men for the nineties, and, totally aware of what it was they were supposed to do, Jodeci mined this seam for all it was worth. While they still sing like choir-boys, they've learned the value of holding back, and the vocal arrangements are now full of aching pauses; like the lurrrve gods of old, they've worked in those bits where the singing kind of tails off into noises; they've managed to up the tempo without slackening off on the temperature; and are confident enough to share a couple of tracks by bringing their girl backing singers up front. The music works much harder (has more money to spend?) too, creating instrumentation that is lush enough to support their notions of seduction, but has all the necessary B-Boy hard edge lurking just below the surface. It's a wonderfully accomplished album that brings one of soul's central themes bang up to date.

Forever My Lady; MCA MCD10534; 1991

It's a rather unformed version of *Dairy*, showcasing the group's raw talent to be such that even the thin arrangements and hesitant seduction can't quite cover it up.

Kam

(Born Craig Miller, Watts, California, 1971)
'You can only kill so many muh'fukas and slap so many bitches.' Kam's epitaph for gangsta rap may be worryingly pragmatic, but this former G, now a dedicated follower of Allah, is in fact offering a far more attractive alternative. As one of the first signings to ICE CUBE's Street Knowledge label, Kam takes his mentor's notions of socially responsible gangstadom one stage further, to start at 1992's gang truce and work forward to direct black rage against the common enemy – in this case not only white people but less than righteous black people too. *And* to instigate the kind of nine-millimetre street justice that effectively rules out reoffending. If not a representation of gangsta's future, then this must surely be a logical parallel. Most remarkably, it's an attitude that proves the LA gang scene to have come full circle: twenty-

five or so years ago, when The Crips first surfaced, they fashioned themselves after the Black Panther Party as a (necessarily) heavily armed neighbourhood self-defence organisation.

*Neva Again; EastWest 7567 92208; 1993

Using considerably more imagination than most, this stirs the 'O.G.' regulation P-FUNK samples into a dark stew of muddy, malevolent-sounding rhythms, pierced by sharp riffs and lead lines (there's a lot of strikingly effective guitar overlay involved here). All of which serves to cushion brooding verbals that rhyme in an almost threateningly laid back manner. Subject matter runs to the LA riots, what can be achieved by the gang truce (unfortunately, eighteen months later, that's now reading like 'should've been achieved'), life 'n the hood and, in the particularly inventive 'Hang 'Um High', he all but justifies lynch mob tactics in the cause of black social advancement. Never less than powerful.

R. Kelly

(Born Robert Kelly, Chicago, Illinois, 1970)
One of swingbeat's original stars, Kelly made his mark with (a) exciting performance skills that he'd been honing since a childhood spent busking with a keyboard; (b) a multi-instrumentalist talent – he'd taught himself to play by ear; and (c) a way with a rude lyric and a suggestive gesture that would make a docker blush. It was renegades like Kelly who did much to move the music on from the original LA/Babyface and Teddy Riley phase, as they took it back to the street and stirred in whatever influences or attitude (in Kelly's case lewdness) they thought it needed.

*Born Into The '90s; Jive CHIP 123; 1991

Classic swingbeat, because it manages to slip some intriguing melodic snatches in between the beats, to give the production another level. At this point he's more suggestive than openly licentious, so it's easy to understand how he got his reputation as Mr Lurrrve for the early 1990s.

SEE ALSO: Classic New Jack Swing Various Artist compilations

Nu Colours

(Lawrence Johnson; Fay Simpson; Carol Riley; Lain Gray; Pat Scott Knight)

When the multi-part singing boom occurred in the very early 1990s, it seemed an ideal access point for a UK black soul scene somewhat eclipsed by rap, yet this young London quintet were one of the very few that got as far as making an album. Which, assuming others would have been up to this calibre, is a great shame. Each member is a church choir graduate and a fan of the Gamble and Huff vocal method (cascading, layered arrangements that rely on timing as much as harmonising) as applied to modern soul music. Originally put together by Johnson from other gospellers he knew or knew about, the aim was to function as a self-contained backing unit and they worked with acts as varied as Paul McCartney, STEVIE WONDER, Primal Scream, Maxi Priest and SOUL II SOUL before fronting their own album. Where they proved of genuine value was in their blatant anglicisation of what they did, instead of slavishly looking to utilise hip hop or swingbeat-style rhythm tracks and doing their best to come over as American. They stirred in a housey sounding backing and by exclusively singing, rather than trying to rap as well, avoided the Derek B syndrome. You know, sounding sort of stupid by trying to say 'Yo!' with a London accent.

*Unlimited; Wildcard 511160; 1992

Far more a statement of intent than a fully formed showpiece, *Unlimited* proves the group have got the vocal arrangements right, as with varying lead voices and backing vocals weaving in and out of each other they create a soaring cathedral of sound. They're also cleverly ambiguous about whether they're singing about God or lurrrve, but while about half of the set rocks with a true conviction, the writing lets them down elsewhere – too often the underlying song is weak enough to put the group across as being all style and no substance. It's something that can be rectified, though, and on the half dozen times they get it right – 'Greater Love', 'What In The World', 'Love Unlimited' in particular – they hit a soulful groove you imagine impossible within the traditionally cold world of 1990s house beats. It makes supporting domestic talent particularly painless.

Omar

(Born Omar Hammer, Canterbury, Great Britain, 1969)
Omar's 1990 hit 'There's Nothing Like This' is a perfect example of the Emperor's New Clothes syndrome, frequently applied to UK soul music by the domestic press. The song and singer were held up as the future of British soul, yet the piece was never anything more than an average three minutes of smoove and the high spot of a dismally uninspired album. Such situations where the average is hailed as the messaniac usually have more to do with an act being perceived as a 'knows their place' alternative to rap than any artistic value. And all too often the artist concerned never recovers as they try to cater for what they believe is their bright new future, thus curtailing their natural development – see Seal or Neneh Cherry or Terence Trent D'Arby or Pauline Henry.

Omar, however, managed to survive being the 'Future Of Soul Music As We (Would Like To) Know It' to come back four years later with soul credibility and credentials intact, displaying the sort of musical progression he might well have followed had he been left alone. Maybe his impressive musical pedigree gave him an advantage: he played drums, piano, trumpet, tuba and guitar before his voice broke; he performed in his secondary school's brass band and a Kent Youth Orchestra; spent two years at Manchester's Chetham School Of Music, then a further two at the Guildhall studying jazz method and composition. Or perhaps it was his business acumen – before his first album was picked up by a major label, he had shifted 35,000 copies through the record company his dad owns and he co-runs. But it was probably his single-minded determination to make progressive black soul music primarily for his home crowd. 'The most gratifying thing is to be impressing my peer group, 'cos I know they're buying it for the music and not because it's part of some big hype. Too much soul music now seems to be record companies telling new acts to rip off the same beat that somebody else has just had a hit with. But the core crowd aren't falling for that. I'm not either.'

For Pleasure; RCA 74321208532; 1994

Away from pressure to produce, Omar seems to have sought refuge in the unhurried, breezy likes of MAZE, EWF, STEVIE WONDER in the 1970s, Roy Ayers's Ubiquity and the Cedar Walton/ Norman Connors end of things to come up with a jazz/funk set of great intrigue and subtlety. The style has been a lost art of late, but was always such a valued expression it should've survived into future generations. While Omar's set is more a revisiting than a forwards thrust, such is its delicacy of tone and touch and flashes of genuine excitement – particularly during such multi-tracked vocal adventures as 'Saturday' and 'Need You Bad' – it should serve as inspiration for a genuine 1990s form of jazz/funk.

Portrait

(Michael Saulsberry, keyboards/drum programming/background vocals; Eric Kirkland, lead vocals/drum programming; Irving Washington III, lead vocals; Phillip Johnson, lead vocals. All members born between 1969 and 1972, in South Central Los Angeles, except Johnson who is from Tulsa, Oklahoma)

'We're totally self-contained. We write, produce and arrange for ourselves and we deliver finished tapes to the record companies. It's not like the old days when singing groups had almost no say in what they did, and very often didn't get paid.' Portrait's Michael Saulsberry knows what he's talking about – his dad was one of the doo-wop group The Penguins, who had an enormous hit with 'Earth Angel' in the 1950s and got paid very little for their trouble. Portrait seem to have the nous and the business knowledge to avoid that happening again. Also, they have a feel for harmonising that goes so deep – or should that be soul deep – as to allow them to experiment with the music they're framing it in. Their debut album has sold a million, for very good reason, and it seems relaxed enough for them to go forward from there.

Portrait; Capitol 793496; 1993

They haven't wasted a moment of their creative freedom. The album they've come up with is an astonishingly varied and marvellously assured debut, swerving from kicking B-Boy attitude funk 'Here We Go Again!', 'Problems' and 'Down Wit Dat' to the devastatingly smoove 'Day By Day' and 'Heartache'. Remarkably, they manage to push every button you expect them to, yet they never once sound cliched.

Queen Latifah

(Born Dana Owens, East Orange, New Jersey, 1970)
Women have been having a pretty rough time in the third wave of hip hop, but it's difficult to imagine anybody – even the most whacked-out gangsta – referring to Queen Latifah as a 'bitch' or a 'ho'. And it's not just a matter of 'packing a gat' either, you'd have to be deaf and blind to imagine for a minute that she fits into either of those categories. Queen Latifah is exactly what's been missing for so long in hip hop – glamour. Sure, there's a lot of sexiness knocking about in rap, but as it too often involves an entirely cliched presentation of yourself or a toughness that, in all but a very few, tends to come off as defensive, glamour is a bit thin on the ground. Queen Latifah has the self-assurance to rise up above this, though, and as a result has relaxed and allowed herself to become glamorous.

Such ease with herself is evident in the music too. It never seems to be trying too hard, and a result of this laid-backness is freedom to explore all sorts of avenues within hip hop, rapping and singing and brushing up against reggae, balladeering, swingbeat, hustle, all areas of contemporary black music while putting her own stamp on each one. It's a very sophisticated (in the nicest possible way) approach, which is doing a great deal to cater for the generation of aging B-Boys and fly girls who no longer have the energy for a steady diet of PUBLIC ENEMY and can't play Snoop Doggy Dogg in front of their kids anyway.

Even without her own hip hop career Queen Latifah would have a future though. Running alongside it is her management company and record label, The Flavour Unit, with Naughty By Nature and Black Sheep on the books. Then there's the acting: parts in *Juice*, *House Party 2* and *Jungle Fever* on the big screen, while on television a role in *The Fresh Prince Of Bel Air* led to her starring in the sitcom *Living Single*.

Black Reign; Motown 530272; 1994

The full range of Queen Latifah's music power. From street style slang rapping on a crisp cut up beat, to the smoove approach, to the mildly ragga, all the while singing her own back ups to add a melodious flow to a production that already has a breezy, summery warmth to it. Subjects discussed include sexual irresponsibility ('Coochie Bang'), hanging out doing nothing ('Just Another Day'), disrespect of women ('U.N.I.T.Y.') and she's no slough at dumb party sucker MC stuff either. It's a marvellously rounded rap album that, with an aging rap fan generation, might well point the way for a more easy-going style to emerge as the fourth generation of hip hop.

ALSO RECOMMENDED:

All Hail The Queen; Gee Street GEECD5; 1989

The same flowing, intelligent, varied-in-influence rap package, it's just not quite so mature as the above. With no hit singles, it still managed to sell a million.

Salt 'n' Pepa

(Salt, Cheryl James; Pepa, Sandy Denton; Spinderalla, Dee Dee Roper, deejay)
One of rap's most important contributors, this spunky trio re-defined the role of women within the genre by setting themselves up as some kind of New Jack feminists. At a time when women in hip hop seldom lasted beyond a couple of noveltyish singles, they cut out a career by presenting themselves as never less than in charge when it came to sexual or relationship politics. This had been tried before, but what made their stance so

attractive was that it was openly sexy: of course they fancied men and wanted to have as much fun as anybody else – this was played up on stage and on video – they just didn't want to be messed around. They came to epitomise the term 'sassy', and their UK shows would be packed with young teenage girls (who would never dream of going to any other rap show) and a few nervous-looking lads that got dragged along. Curiously, not many blokes came to ogle, because as attractive as Salt 'n' Pepa are, their aggressive sexual persona can be a bit intimidating. More so on stage than off, it must be said.

Their beginnings in music were far more faithful to soul tradition, though. Their first record was in that wonderful old R&B fashion of a reply to a song by a man – 'Showstoppa', in 1987, an answer to Doug E. Fresh's 'The Show'. And, further to the tradition, they'd been plucked from behind a shop counter – they both worked at Sears-Robuck in New York, where fellow worker Hurby Azor asked them to do some vocals for his night class project in audio production. That tape became their first record, and Azor still produces them, though they are beginning to do more and more for themselves. Recently, they've been increasing the melody in their numbers, and starting to sing more. They'd begun sampling from well-known soul songs, but have now moved on to writing original material, pushing them into the realms of fully fledged pop stars. Which is a mark of how good at rap and how good *for* rap they've become: they're taking it into the pop charts their way – their beats are still true to their street rap roots – and have the nous and ability not to stagnate.

The Greatest Hits; ffrr 82891; 1991

An ideal taster of what S 'n' P are all about, going from the brassy (in more ways than one) rapped up covers of 'Tramp' and 'I Gotcha', to their contraception anthem 'Let's Talk About Sex', through to the blatantly sexy 'Push It', 'My Mic Sounds Nice' and 'I Like It Like That'.

Blacks Magic; ffrr 8281642; 1991

At their most melodious, this pulls off some deft experiments in balancing hip hop and melody, and does it so that both ends sound even tougher. Anyway, who could resist an LP with a track called 'Negro With An Ego'.

Of the other two albums, *A Salt With A Deadly Pepa* (ffrr 828102; 1988) has much more going for it than that title – they're younger, rawer and sassier – while *Very Necessary* (ffrr 828454; 1994) has much tougher beats yet still kicks a mature round sound, featuring the recent hits 'Whatta Man' and 'Shoop'.

Gil Scott-Heron

➠It would be an understatement to say that one of the more pleasant surprises of recent funk times came in 1994 with the announcement that Gil Scott-Heron was back behind the mic for his first new studio recording in twelve years. Better than that, he was back with Brian Jackson and producer Henry Cecil and bumping some cool jazz/funk with lyrics to live up to anything from the old days.

It was like an old friend coming home. As long as there'd been funk and soul and getting down with some beat, there'd been Gil Scott-Heron, flipping the script and making us laugh while giving us something to think about. Then suddenly there had been nothing. All you heard about Gil Scott-Heron during the 1980s was how he was not turning up for shows, missing deadlines and generally being difficult. The news in the middle of the decade that he'd been deported from the UK for possession of a tiny amount of cocaine was alarming, given his public anti-drug stance, but somehow oddly inevitable. The general opinion was that that was one brother we could ill afford to lose.

But it now seems as if normal service has been resumed, and whatever demons were driving him are off his back. During the past five years, Gil Scott-Heron may have been without a record deal, but he's been touring almost constantly in the USA and Europe, has become a big draw on the college lecture circuit and is finishing his fifth book. Oh yes, and there's the album.

*Spirits; TVT 4310; 1994

The most remarkable thing about this set is how deeply personal it appears: a blistering guitar-driven version of 'Home Is

Where The Hatred Is' comes over as some sort of white powder exorcism; 'Don't Give Up' is devoted to how hard some people have worked to bring him down; and 'Give Her A Call' hinges around the line 'When I get back to my life I'm gonna have to give her a call'. However downbeat this might seem, though, it's actually an album of enormous optimism, opening with a life-affirming stance over gangsta rap – or 'all you nine-millimetre brothers'. Making the very valid point that it was his generation out there getting shot at in the 1960s, but not by each other, his sentiment is simple: 'I ain't coming at you with no disrespect/All I'm saying is you better damn well be correct/If you're gonna speak for a whole generation'. All this is put down with music that's perfectly balanced jazz with a hint of funk, dense and smokey enough to put him in a kind of sonic half light, prowling about and letting off words and rhymes to loom out of the haze. At times it's quite beautiful and very probably worth a twelve-year wait.

7669

(El Boog E, born El-Melek A. Moore, Brooklyn, New York, 1968; Big Ange, Angela Hunte, New York City, 1971; Thicknezz, Mallore Irvine, Los Angeles, California, 1974; Shorti, Marcy Roberts, Southbend, Indiana, 1971)
Another example of Motown's commitment to the present day, but one that went a bit astray in the marketing department. While this all-girl quartet could be correctly perceived as a natural reaction to gangstadom – they sing and rap to a hard-core backing and deal with such subjects as sex and violence – putting them on their album sleeve topless, astride Harleys, in a marijuana field did nobody any favours. It became the selling point and (a) made them look like they were trying too hard; (b) detracted from an album that had a lot to say musically and lyrically; and (c) just put some people off because it was tacky. This last point, however, couldn't have been further from the truth. 7669 may have been brought together by a management team rather than organically formed, but they gelled into an articulate, witty, sexy four-pronged rap 'n' swing

attack. Their main thrusts are a feminism-for-the-nineties that pragmatically approaches matters regarding *how* they are treated – it's the 'hos and bitches' backlash – rather than theorising on the way it's supposed to be; the destruction of the black community by violence and irresponsibility; and the plain fact that they can't get enough good, er, loving these days. It's a natural continuation from the party line taken by SALT 'N' PEPA for the last few years, that black women have to regain control and deserves better than the implications of that dreadful inner city-type burlesque cover.

*7669 East From A Bad Block; Motown 530284; 1994

Of course none of their good intentions would be worth anything at all if they didn't have the beats to back it up. Mostly written by the group and produced largely by Full Force, the tunes wind their way through a hip hop spectrum that ranges from beat box ballad, to hard-core rap, to high-stepping swing beat, but all with a wonderfully smokey restraint that adds an extra sensuality to the drop-dead sexy voices. It's in this way they ooze through harmony singing and rapping with such power you wonder why there isn't more of this sort of stuff.

The Sounds of Blackness

(Forty-piece gospel choir, St Paul, Minnesota)
It's not really so strange that an act like Sounds Of Blackness should exist – a thirty-strong choir with a ten-piece band and a penchant for almost swingbeat arrangements to their songs of praise – what's surprising is that there aren't more like them. Think about it, nearly everybody that comes into US soul music quotes the church as their starting point, so why hasn't somebody attempted to do something like this elsewhere?

Probably because they didn't have JANET JACKSON nagging them. According to Terry Lewis, while she was staying in St Paul to record *Rhythm Nation 1814*, Jackson (a big gospel fan) heard about the choir, who were locally famous but mostly still amateur. She checked them out, was duly impressed, and dragged Jam & Lewis to the next night's show, already suggesting the twosome should consider recording them. They went in sceptical, but by the end of the show were trying to work out how they could get all forty into their Flyte Tyme studio.

It has become one of the most fortunate associations in soul. Jam & Lewis – who co-write and co-produce the Sounds' material with their M.D. Gary Hines – enjoy writing and arranging for a unit that size, while the choir have embraced stardom as if born to it. Every time they come back to play London, their choreography has got a bit fancier. On the sartorial side, during their first visit in 1991, their idea of costume was everybody wearing black and matching baseball hats. Then it was a type of paramilitary dress uniform with one fringed epaulette each. And last time they came looking very crisp, with all forty kitted out in black and vibrant orange African-type print fabric, that could be worn in any style and combination. The overall effect of this number, so stylishly dressed and giving it plenty on stage as they moved in unison and sang some enormous harmonies, is a sight most people won't forget. While the records are little short of brilliant, they really come into their own when they function as souvenirs of the show.

Africa To America – The Journey Of The Drum; A&M 549009; 1994
The Evolution Of Gospel; A&M 395361; 1991

In both cases, Jam & Lewis produce most of the long accompanied songs, while Gary Hines concentrates more on the a capellas – one notable exception, on *The Evolution of Gospel*, is Hines' soaring production of SLY's 'Stand', a song you've not really heard unless you've heard it sung by thirty people. The obvious differences between the sets are that Jam & Lewis seem to have got the hang of it more by *Africa To America*, as the choir are fitting around them and not the other way around. Not that that's a complaint. The second album is a lot smoother, more like a contemporary pop/soul record, thus it loses a little of its predecessor's charm, but the vocal arrangements seem to gain in complexity.

Al B. Sure!

(Born New York City, 1969)
Although young enough to be part of the rap generation and one of the prominent voices of early New Jack Swing back at the very end of the 1980s, Sure!'s (the only name he'll admit to) approach is based firmly in traditional soul. Indeed he was so unphased by the state of soul music in the 1980s that he made no attempt to get into the music business during his formative years, restricting any involvement to teaming up with a cousin and writing old-style soul ballads for their own amusement. In 1987, friends persuaded them to enter a tape in a national song-writing contest, and they won, thanks to a vote from judging panel chairman Quincy Jones. Since then, although Sure! first came to fame as one of the original swingbeat balladeers – he did much to wrench the developing style away from rap, by slowing the tempo slightly and fusing still-kicking backing with sweet soul singing – he's increasingly veered towards straight soul, to become one of the few youngsters to follow such a route.

*In Effect Mode; Warner Bros 925662; 1988

Very much like the smoother end of BOBBY BROWN, this album introduced the singer with the slamming 'Off On Your Own', 'Rescue Me' and 'Nite And Day'. But while it set the still teenage Sure! up as modern young buck, out to update the whole notion of lurrrve with something a bit more lively, he also strayed into unadulterated mawk with a version of 'Killing Me Softly' that was just plain undecided – it wasn't strong enough to stand with the others or straight enough to be considered as such.

*Private Times . . . And The Whole 9; Warner Bros
759926005; 1990

Two years later and Sure! has sufficiently grown in confidence to adjust his priorities – now the ballads definitely come first. Whereas before he couldn't quite decide whether to play it hip hop or trad and did neither, this time he achieves both as he structures an obviously sequenced music around his singing, so creating a very up-to-date straight soul song – indeed, it carries a tradition on so smoothly that even Diana Ross joins him for one track and doesn't sound out of place. The kicking swingbeat end of things isn't forgotten, though, and while the rhythms are pumped right up he's kept them in with the album's main aim by sanding down the edges with more attention to flowing melodies. Such is Sure!'s success at creating a well-rounded contemporary soft soul album, you might even find yourself appreciating a worryingly wet version of 'Hotel California'.

Keith Sweat

(Born Keith Crier, Harlem, New York City, 1960)
When Keith Sweat's debut album *Make It Last Forever* came out, he was holding down his day job in a Wall Street brokerage firm. As the sales graph climbed steeply, he still refused to quit, and only after it had passed the million mark (on it's way to selling six times that) did he go full time. Maybe this reluctance was because he'd spent the early part of the 1980s in groups that never quite followed through on their initial promise – The GQ Band and Jamilah, or maybe he wasn't keen on the embryonic New Jack Swing that co-producer Teddy Riley brought to the project. Perhaps he thought it would never catch on. If he believed the last point he couldn't have been more wrong – as soon as that album's sales figures earned him the clout to start producing himself, Sweat virtually abandoned the style in favour of a lush, romantic croon, that went down well as long as he was the only one doing it. Once the all-engulfing wave of swingbeat harmony singing hit in the beginning of the nineties, Keith Sweat found himself eclipsed by far more exciting lurrrve men. It's another mark of how fast soul styles change that, within five years, the man who was practically the blueprint for swingbeat as we know it was completely left behind.

*Make It Last Forever; Elektra 9607632; 1988

Although this set – Sweat's only real contribution – is a 1980s release, it belongs in the following decade because it was far more important for what it led to than what it was. Through the club hit tracks 'I Want Her', 'Something Just Ain't Right' and 'Don't Stop Your Love', the album was more or less a testing ground for the swingbeat style that Teddy Riley consolidated on GUY's self-titled debut album. All the skipping slap-beat drive is there, but the melodic ideas are yet to be formed and rely on Sweat's naturally smoove voice to take care of the tunes. An important milestone along soul's highway.

SWV

(Sisters With Voices: Coko, born Cheryl Gamble, 1974; Leelee, Leanne Lyons, 1975; Taj, Tamara Johnson, 1974. All born in New York City)
SWV's beginnings read like a modern version of one of Berry Gordy's signings: three friends all with gospel backgrounds – i.e. they sing in church – start practising secular harmonies in the school yard. Their idea is to kick it in exactly the same style as the guys by sweetening up the street style of the day with their freshly squeezed harmonising. The only difference between then and now is that instead of auditioning live, SWV mailed out demo tapes. The results were more or less the same too – half-a-million-selling single and an album that has crossed into the pop world with utter integrity as it presents an honest, easily accessible aspect of black soul.

It's About Time; RCA 7863 660742; 1983

More than just a bunch of chicks singing swingbeat – although that's pretty rare in itself. While the Sisters blend rap attitude and R&B harmonising, they've vertically explored what they're doing too, to construct layers in both the music and how their voices work with each other to provide some quite startling twists on three-part arrangements. An album with depth as well as a necessary instant sassiness.

Tony! Toni! Tone!

(Raphael Wiggins, bass/synth bass/keyboard/drum programs/ vocals; Dwayne Wiggins, guitar/bass/drum program/vocals; Timothy Christian, drum kit/keyboards/drum programs/ synth horns/vocals. All born Oakland, California)

From a city with a strong left-field funk tradition – SLY STONE, Larry Graham, DIGITAL UNDERGROUND – these two brothers and a cousin made their name by harmony singing. Their tunes evoked the 1970s and the trio's funk heroes, but never actually copied anything. They never actually *did* anything either: although sales were reasonable there was a lack of direction about them that seemed to stem from the Foster & McElroy productions – a bit of a struggle going on against the apparent swingbeat expectations. Then they took off on their own and blossomed into one of the most innovative, enjoyable left-field funk bands performing at the moment.

*Sons Of Soul; Polydor 514933; 1993

An apt title for their first as a self-contained unit, as it's a very modern approach to old soul values. Songs, singing, tunes and a sense of humour – one number has the chorus line 'my ex-girlfriend is a wh-o-o-o-ore', so I hope they've got a sense of humour. At the same time, the underpinning by computerised instruments keeps everything in line, to the degree they sound slightly mechanical, which is what is expected these days. The best tracks are 'Anniversary', nine minutes of unashamed smoove; the pumping 'Leavin" and 'My Ex-Girlfriend', that would be a hustle if that sort of thing existed any more. The entire set is a textbook example of traditional soul given a sympathetic 1990s treatment.

*The Revival; Polydor 841-902; 1990

Sons Of Soul's predecessor and not nearly so well-rounded, but worth almost any price for the sublime summer track 'Oakland Stroke'.

Wreckx-N-Effect

(Markell Riley; Aqull Davidson; both born Harlem, New York City)
Originally a trio – third member Brandon Mitchell was shot and killed in 1990 – Wreckx were developed by swingbeat guru Teddy Riley (Markell's older brother) as the raucous, wilder

side of the music – it was this group that first made public the term New Jack Swing with their 1989 single of that name. But while the style developed into (a) a lurrrve thang or (b) a gangsta pose, they seemed determined to have fun. The kind of pointless, sometimes saucy, but never less than self-celebratory fun that is the basis for the best in funk and has been missing from too much modern soul music. Look no further than the gloriously daft chart hit 'Rumpshaker'.

Hard Or Smooth; MCA MCD10566; 1992

Produced by Teddy Riley, by this stage the group were confident enough and the style sufficiently developed not to worry about how it would be categorised. It takes the best from rap and traditional soul to serve it up with a vibrancy that goes beyond both: 'Rumpshaker', 'Wreckx Shop' and 'New Jack Swing II' are state-of-the-art hip hop fooling about; 'Straight Out Of The Projects' features a rap from BOBBY BROWN; while 'Tell Me How You Feel' and 'My Cutie' are B-Boy lurrrve songs, with all the hormone bustin' energy being young and randy ought to involve.

SEE ALSO: *Classic New Jack Swing Volume 1*, Mastercuts CUTSCD5; 1992

Zhane

(Renee Neufville, born Brooklyn, New York, 1970; Jean Noris, Moorestown, New Jersey, 1970)
Living proof that Motown Records has entered the real world and their A&R department is looking beyond 'the next Jackson 5'. Zhane are a low-key, jazzy-flavoured singing duo, both formally trained, as un-hip hop as possible in appearance and outlook, yet they undercut their silky compositions with a firm but fair scratch 'n' beat-box track.

Pronounced Jah-Nay; Motown 530283; 1994

The emphasis here is on the songs. These delicate ballads and mid-tempo swingers all tell stories, and while the rhythm track pushes them along, it never intrudes on the melodies that evoke a very 1990s slant on light jazz/funk. That they wrote and co-produced most of the set makes it all the more remarkable.

VARIOUS ARTIST COMPILATIONS

Sweet Soul Harmonies 1; Virgin VTCD20; 1994

En Vogue, My Lovin' (radio edit); **Eternal**, Stay; **Color Me Badd**, I Wanna Sex You Up; **SWV**, Right Here (Human Nature radio mix); **Boyz II Men**, Motownphilly; **Pasedenas**, I'm Doing Fine Now; **O'Jays**, Love Train; **The Temptations**, My Girl; **Harold Melvin & The Blue Notes**, If You Don't Know Me By Now; **Gladys Knight & The Pips**, Best Thing That Ever Happened To Me; **Soul II Soul**, Back To life (A Capella); **The Young Disciples**, Apparently Nothin' (edit); **The Family Stand**, Ghetto Heaven (remix); **Marvin Gaye**, (Sexual) Healing; **Earth, Wind & Fire**, After The Love Has Gone; **Omar**, There's Nothing Like This; **Detroit Spinners**, Ghetto Child; **Levert**, Casanova; **Jade**, Don't Walk Away; **Sister Sledge**, Thinking Of You (Ramp Radio Remix).

An interesting mix of old-school and new-wave harmonisers, made by the inclusion of 'Motownphilly' and 'Casanova'. Also, if you've got to own a copy of that Color Me Badd single then it might as well be as part of a collection as classy as this.

Sweet Soul Harmonies 2; Virgin VTCD31; 1994

The Detroit Spinners, Could It Be I'm Falling In Love; **The Isley Brothers**, Summer Breeze; **The O'Jays**, I Love Music; **Eternal**, Save Our Love; **Seal**, Crazy; **Fat Larry's Band**, Zoom; **SWV**, Downtown (1994); **Charles & Eddie**, Would I Lie To You; **Marvin Gaye**, What's Going On; **M. People**, Don't Look Any Further; **En Vogue**, Hold On; **Pointer Sisters**, Slow Hand; **Soul II Soul**, Keep On Moving; **Sister Sledge**, We Are Family (original version); **The Supremes**, You Can't Hurry Love; **The**

Pasedenas, Tribute; **Bill Withers,** Ain't No Sunshine; **Paul Young,** Everything Must Change; **Jamiroquai**, Too Young To Die; **Al Green**, Let's Stay Together.

Although not quite up to the ridiculously high standard of *Volume One*, any compilation with enough nous to put 'Would I Lie To You', 'Keep Moving' and 'Could It Be I'm Falling In Love' on the same record has to be worth the entry fee. Pity you've got to put up with Jamiroquai, Seal and the truly awful M. People, though.

Classic New Jack Swing Volume 1; Mastercuts CUTSCD5; 1992

Johnny Gill, Rub You The Right Way; **Guy**, Her; **Today**, I Got The Feeling; **Wrecks-N-Effect**, New Jack Swing; **R.Kelly & The Public Announcement**, She's Got That Vibe; **Guy**, Do Me Right; **Ralph Trevesant**, Sensitivity; **Samuelle**, So You Like What You See; **Bell, Biv, DeVoe**, Poison; **Father MC**, Treat Them Like They Want To Be Treated; **Jasmine Guy**, Another Like My Lover; **Keisha Jackson**, Mama Told Me.

Classic New Jack Swing Volume 2; Mastercuts CUTSCD9; 1992

Tammy Lucas & Teddy Riley, Is It Good To You; **Aaron Hall**, Don't Be Afraid; **Ready For The World**, Yo That's A Lot Of Body; **Bubba**, I Like Your Style; **Basic Black**, Whatever It Takes; **Groove B. Chill**, Swingin' Single; **Johnny Kemp**, Just Got Paid; **Guy**, My Fantasy; **Today**, Why You Get Funky On Me; **The Nation Funktasia**, Cool-Aid Express Card; **LaRue**, Serious; **Bobby Brown**, My Prerogative.

Above The Rim – Music From And Inspired By The Motion Picture; Death Row Records 6544-92359; 1994

SWV, Anything; **Sweet Sable**, Old Time's Sake; **H-Town**, Part Time Lover; **Tha Dogg Pound Gangstas**, Big Pimping; **2nd II None**, Didn't Mean To Turn You On; **D.J. Rogers**, Doggie Style; **Nate Dogg & Warren G.**, Regulate; **Thug Life**, Pour A Little

Liquor Out; **Jewell & Aaron Hall**, Gonna Give It To Ya; **The Lady Of Rage**, Afro Puffs; **CPO-Boss Hog**, Jus So Ya No; **Paradise**, Hoochies Need Love Too; **Al B. Sure!**, I'm Still In Love With You; **O.F.T.B.**, Crack 'Em; **Rhythm & Knowledge**, You Bring Da Dog Out; **B Rezzell**, Blowed Away; **Jewell**, It's Not Deep Enough; **Tha Dogg Pound Gangstas**; Dogg Pound 4 Life.

Supervised by DR DRE, this is as good a cross-section of current (1993/1994) gangsta sounds as you're likely to get. No, it doesn't matter if you've never heard of half of these people before, you probably never will again either.